Alexander Graham, Henry Spencer Ashbee

Travels in Tunisia

With a Glossary, a Map, a Bibliography, and Fifty Illustrations

Alexander Graham, Henry Spencer Ashbee

Travels in Tunisia
With a Glossary, a Map, a Bibliography, and Fifty Illustrations

ISBN/EAN: 9783337209247

Printed in Europe, USA, Canada, Australia, Japan

Cover: Foto ©Andreas Hilbeck / pixelio.de

More available books at **www.hansebooks.com**

Travels in Tunisia

With a Glossary, a Map, a Bibliography,
and Fifty Illustrations.

BY

ALEXANDER GRAHAM,
F.R.I.B.A.

AND

H. S. ASHBEE,
F.S.A., F.R.G.S.

LONDON:
DULAU & CO., 37 SOHO SQUARE, W.
1887.

[All Rights reserved.]

INDEX.

ACCOMMODATION, 2, 89, 96
Agbia, 168, 170
Ahmed Bey, 37
Ain-Draham, 182, 184, 186
Ain-el-Caïd, 176
Ain-Hedjah, 168, 169, 170
Amphitheatre of El-Djem. See El-Djem.
Amusements, 3, 65, 110
Animals, cruelty to, 6, 131
Aphrodisium, 57, 59
Aqueducts, 37
Arabs, their character, 5
  ,,   courteous and hospitable, 6, 68, 80, 158
  ,,   cruel, 6, 131
  ,,   results of their occupation of Tunisia, 7
  ,,   their jealousy, 63, 196
  ,,   dress of the women, 64
  ,,   music, 65, 110
  ,,   treatment of women, 77
  ,,   mode of living, 100
  ,,   equipment of animals, 6, 151
  ,,   a tent described, 154
  ,,   a house visited, 198
Archæology, Tunisia a good field for, 1
Artesian well, 97
Ass stolen, 41
Assuras, 163
Attar of roses, 23

Bagla, river, 110
Bagradas, river, 11
Bagradas river and Regulus, 45
Bahira, lake, 14, 34
Barbers' shops, 24
Bardo, palace, 29
Bazaars. See Souks.
Bedouin women, 199

Bedouins, 42, 77, 200
Beggars, absence of, ii.
Béja, 11 (note)
Beni-Mazeu, 188
'Bernous of the Prophet,' 14
Bernous, garments, 23
Birds, 137, 149 (note), 158
Bir-el-Arbain, 54
Bir-el-Bouita, 54, 55
Bir-el-Bey, 53
Bled-es-Sers, plain, 164, 165
Bône, a pleasant town, 9
  ,,   described, 10
Bordj-Messaoudi, 166, 169
Borghaz, lake, 14
Bou-Chater, ruins of, described, 48
Bou-Kohil, mountain, 166
Bouquets, 69
Bridges, 2, 7
British influence, decline of, 203
British Museum, inscription removed to, 172, 174
Bruce, J., on Temple at Dougga, 172 (note)
  ,,   quoted on Tabarca, 183 (note)
Bulla Regia, 188

Cæsar, Julius, quoted on Utica, 48
  ,,   mentioned, 48 (note)
Cairwan. See Kairouan.
Calle, La, 181
Cambon, V., on population of Kairouan, 128 (note)
Carbonaro, MM., 41, 205
Caroline, Queen, her visit to Tunis, 31
Carthage, site of, 14, 33
  ,,   modes of conveyance, 33
  ,,   chapel of St. Louis, 33
  ,,   the cisterns, 34
  ,,   literature, 34, 35

290   INDEX.

Catada, river, 38
Cato, 48 (note)
Cats, 169
Chachia caps, 23, 40
Chambi, mountains, 146
Charles V., 90, 183
Chemtou, 193, 194
Chenneni, 98
Chotts, 97
Cisterns, 114
Coffee-houses, 24, 65, 80
Col de Babouch, 186
Collin, M., 39 (note)
Colonia Scillitana, 146
    „   Simittu, 194
    „   Sufetanæ, 157
Compagnie Transatlantique, ii., 2
Coral fishing, 181 (note)
Cork oak, gigantic, 187
Couscousou, national dish described, 90, 159, 201 (note)
Cret, Captain, 113
Crosha, river, 57
Cuscusu. See Couscousu.

Dancing, 111
Dar-el-Bey, town, 57, 59
    „ palace, 30
Date-gathering, 99
Decauville road, 107, 108
Defla, river, 54
Desfontaine on Tabarca, 183 (note)
Diligence, journey in a, 11
Djard, 98
Djedeida, 11 (note)
Djerba coats, 23
Djiljie, mountain, 158
Djilma. See Oued-Gilma.
Djiriba, marsh, 57, 59
Doctoring the natives, 150
Dogs, 81, 100, 165
    „ flesh of, eaten, 201 (note)
Domestic life, 196
Donkey. See Ass.
Dougga, situation, 171
    „ ruins, 172
    „ the sheik, 174
Dress of women, 64

Duruy, V., quoted on amphitheatre at El-Djem, 85 (note)

El-Bahira, lake, 14, 34, 202
El-Bekri, quoted on the marble of Carthage, 35 (note)
    „   „ the aqueduct of Carthage, 38
    „   „ Kairouan, 119, 120, 121
El-Darb, river, 146
El-Djem, first view of the amphitheatre, 78
    „ surrounding plain described, 78, 85, 86
    „ the fondouk, 79
    „ the café, 80
    „ the amphitheatre, its present filthy condition, 82
    „   „ its size, 82, 83
    „   „ by whom built, 83
    „   „ described, 83
    „   „ never finished, 84
    „ inscription found at, 91
El-Edrisi, quoted on Sufetula, 140 (note)
    „   „ coral fishing, 181 (note)
El-Hout, lake, 182
El-Kebir, river, 184
El-Kef, 189, 190
El-Kerib, plain, 167
El-Mahdi, 90
El-Nefzaoui, Sheik, 205
Embroidery of Tunis esteemed, 23
    „ done by men, 23
Enfida estate, 52
Englishmen, rare, 16, 104
Esparto grass, 93, 97, 145
Es-Sahel, 87

Falhar, river, 176
Fatima, hand of, 24, 26
Female dress, 64, 197
Fernana, 187
Fez caps, 23, 40
Flavius Secundus, mausoleum erected by, 147
Fleas, 81

INDEX.

Flies, 63
Fondouks, 3, 55, 79, 81, 110, 164, 168
Forests, destruction of, 7
Fortresses, 170
François, our servant, 104

Gabès, the town, 96
„ the river, 97
„ the inland sea, 97
„ an artesian well, 97
„ the gardens, 99
„ the scenery, 101
Galea, Mr., 93, 96, 102, 103
Game, 149 (note)
Gatte, Mr., 104
Gayangos, P. de, iv.
Gerges, 140 (note)
Ghardimaou, 11, 13
Gilma. See Oued-Gilma.
Gnats, 60 (note)
Gorat-el-Kerib, plain, 167
Gordian, the elder, 83
„ the younger, 84
Gouletta, 14, 202
Gourbi, one described, 154
Government, good, ii.
Greeting, mode of, 156, 159
Gregory, 140 (note)
Groumbelia, 53
Guerra-el-Hout, 182
Guide-books, 4
Guérin, V., quoted on Utica, 47 (note)
„ „ Bir-el-Bouita, 54 „
„ „ Sebkha-Djiriba, 60 „
„ „ population of Kairouan, 128 (note)
„ „ El-Djem, 85 (note)
„ „ Sufes, 157
„ „ Teboursouk, 175 (note)
„ „ Sicca Veneria, 190 „

Hadjeb-el-Aïoun, 131, 133, 149, 152
Hadrian, Emperor, 37
Hadrumetum, 61
Halfa. See Esparto.
Halk-el-Menzel, lake, 58
Hammam-el-Lif, 51, 52
Hand of Fatima, 24, 26

Harbours, 2
Harem life, 196, 198
Harness, 6, 23
Hassan, mosque rebuilt by, 119, 121
Hatob, river, 152, 153
Herglah, 58
Hélouis, Captain, 61, 107
Herrech, mountain, 194
Hesse-Wartegg, quoted on Bedouins, 43 (note)
„ „ quoted on population of Kairouan, 128 (note)
„ „ quoted on fattening of women, 201 (note)
'Home, sweet home,' 205
Horrea Cœlia, 58
Horse-livers, eaten, 201 (note)
Horses, mode of picketing, 155
Hotels, 2, 96, 110
„ See also Fondouks.
Houses, an Arab one described, 94

Information, difficult to obtain, 3, 153
Inland sea, 97
Inscription, an, 167 (note)
„ removed to British Museum, 172, 174

Jasmine, oil of, 23
Jews, not jealous, 65 (note), 201
„ hospitable, 201
„ at Kairouan, 110, 128
Jewesses, dress of, 64
„ immorality, 65 (note)
„ artificial obesity, 200
„ their dress, 200
„ their beauty, 201
„ of Gabès, 101
Jouaouda, mountain, 167

Kabika, mountain, 176
Kairouan, the hotel, 110
„ music and dancing, 110
„ various spellings of name, 112 (note)
„ its holiness, 112, 127
„ its influence lost, 113

INDEX.

Kairouan, the kasba, 113
" the reservoirs, 114
" its foundation, 115, 117
" walls and gates, 116
" houses, 117
" mosques, 117, 118
" streets, 118
" bazaars, 118
" industries, 23, 118
" surrounding country, 128
" devoid of wells, 128
" population, 128
" inhabitants corrupt, 129
" their courtesy, 129
Kairwân. See Kairouan.
Kasr-el-Menara, 56
Kasserine, the river, 146
" the ruins, 146
Kazezin, spring, 110
Kelbia, lake, 108
Kenatir, river, 56, 58
Kerkenah, islands, 92, 93
Kerma, river, 184
Kerouan. See Kairouan.
Kerwan. See Kairouan.
Keys of their Spanish homes kept by the Moors of Tunis, 24
Khallad, river, 176
Kheir-ed-din, 52
Khoumair, country described, 180
" people " 184
Ksiba, 71, 76
Ksour, 158, 161, 162
Ksour-es-Sef, 86, 88
Kusskussu. See Couscousou.

La Calle, 181
La Goulette, 14, 202
Languages, ancient, 172 (note)
Lapine, M., 149, 150
Largeau, M., quoted on destruction of forests, 7 (note)
Law-courts, 203
Lemarchand, M., 203
Literature, iii.
" neglect of, 204
Logerot, General, 99
Louis, Saint, chapel of, 33

Lubomirski, Prince J., on domestic life, 198 (note)
Lumbroso, A., 90, 91

Macgill, Thos., quoted on character of the Arabs, 5 (note)
" " quoted on fattening of women, 200 (note)
Magaran, 39
Mahedia, difficulty of obtaining food, 89
" a couscousou, 90
" its position, 90
" its history, 90
" the roadstead, 91
Mahia, mountain, 176
Maltzan, Freiher von, at Kairouan, 113 (note)
Manouba, 11 (note), 15
Marble, 172 (note), 193
Marcius, brothers, 172
Marsa, palace, 30
Marseillaise, 68
Mascula, 52
Medjerda, river, described, 11, 12, 13, 45, 177, 193
Medjez-el-Bab, 11 (note)
Melian river, 51
Mellegue, river, 189, 193
Menzel, 77, 98
Merilah, mountain, 152
Merkey, mountain, 15
Mirage, 60 (note)
Mohammedia, palace, 29, 37
Monastir, 106
Montagu, Lady Mary Wortley, her visit to the harem, 199 (note)
Moors, their character described, 5 (note)
" keep the keys of their Spanish homes, 24
" women, 197
Moureddine, 108
Msaken, 70
Music, 65, 110
Mustafa-ben-Azooz, 141
Musti, 167

Nebour, 189

INDEX.

Noah's ark, 204
Nostrils of asses, slit, 6
Novaïri, on Kairouan, 117
Novak, N., 91, 105
Nouba, mountains, 146

Oasis of Gabès, 99
Obeid-Allah, 90
Okbah founds Kairouan, 115, 117, 118
Olive-crushing, 77
Ornaments, female, 199
Oudena, ruins of, described, 43
Oued-Gilma, 134, 135, 149
Oued-Meliz, 11 (note), 193, 195
Outfit, 179, 181

Palaces, ruined, 29
" abandoned, 37
Pariente, S. R., 202, 205
Payne, John Howard, 205
Pellissier, E., quoted on population of Kairouan, 128 (note)
" " Kasserine, 147 (note)
Perfumers of Tunis, 23
Perronell, Capt., 133, 149
Phœnician tombs, 105
Playfair, Sir R. L., iv., 44
" quoted on archæology in Tunisia, 1 (note)
" " aqueduct of Carthage, 39 (note)
" " esparto grass, 93 (note)
" " artesian wells, 98
" " population of Kairouan, 128 (note)
" " river Sbeitla, 139 (note)
" " couscousou, 160 (note)
" " temple at Dougga, 172 (note)
" " Tabarca, 183 (note)
" " Fernana, 187 (note)
Ploughing, 87
Poiret, Abbé, quoted on wheat, 161 (note)
Polygamy, 196, 200
Population, sparse, 161
Presents, 161

Prison, one described, 42
Prostitution, 201

Qairouân. See Kairouan
Qirwan. See Kairouan

Radès, 14
Railways, 2
Ras-el-Wad, 99
Ras-er-Rajel, 185
Rats, 81
Reade, Sir Thos., 172, 173
Reclus, E., quoted on character of the Tunisians, 5 (note)
" " Msaken, 70 (note)
" " the people of Sfax, 95 (note)
" " inhabitants of Kairouan, 129 (note)
Regulus and the Serpent, 45
Renan, M., on Phœnician tombs, 106
Reservoirs, 114
Retrospect, 178, 206
Reukaha, mountain, 158
Rivers, neglect of, 7, 57, 137, 177, 178, 193
Roads, 2, 7
Romans, their power, 85 (note), 86
Roses, attar of, 23
Roudaire, Commandant, 97

Sahab, companion of the Prophet, 124
" his tomb, 127
Sallecta, 85
Salutation, mode of, 156, 159
Sandwith, T. B., 205
Sardine-salting, 181 (note)
Sbeitla, first glimpse of the ruins, 137
" no accommodation, 137
" the river, 139, 143
" ruins described, 141
" our "Grand Hotel," 148
" our mode of living, 148
Sbiba, 151, 152, 153, 158
" the caïd, 156
" the river, 157
" the ruins, 157

INDEX.

Scenery, 3
Scillitana Colonia, 146
Scillium, 146
Scipio, 47 (note), 48
Sea, inland. See Inland Sea
Sebbala, 45
Sedjoumi, marsh, 14
Selloum, mountain, 146
Septimius Severus, 37
Serpent-worship, 27
Servant engaged, 104
Sewing done by men, 23
Sfåkès. See Sfax
Sfåksika. See Sfax
Sfax, soap made at, 23
   „ the roadstead, 92
   „ built upon the sand, 92
   „ its commerce, 93
   „ the sponge market, 93
   „ the gates, 93
   „ characteristic doorways, 94
   „ character of the inhabitants, 95
Sgiff, river, 158
Shaksperian reading, 205
Shaw, Rev. Dr. Thos., quoted on the amphitheatre at El-Djem, 83
Shops. See Souks
Sicca Veneria, 190 (note), 191, 194
Sidi-Abdallah-ech-Cheid, mountain, 167
Sidi-Abd-er-Reubbou, 167
Sidi-Ahmed-Zei, koubba, 158
Sidi-bou-Rouis, 166
Sidi-bou-Said, 14
Sidi-el-Hani, lake, 77, 108
Sidi-Hani, river, 165
Sidi-Khalifa, town, 57, 59
Sidi-Mehrani, koubba, 158
Sidi-Monella, koubba, 158
Simittu Colonia, 194
Slippers, 23
Soap, 23
Sobeitala. See Sufetula
Soliman, 53
Souk-Arras, 11
Souk-el-Arbäa, 11 (note), 189, 193
Souk-el-Tleta, 164, 169
Souks, 20, 63, 94, 118

Soussa, 50, 61, 71, 76, 106, 107
Sponges, 93
Stays, a punishment, 199
Steamers, 2
Story-telling, 69
Street-naming, 104
Sufes, 157
Sufetanæ Colonia, 157
Sufetula, its situation, &c., 139
   „ its destruction, 140 (note)
Sunset, magnificent, 164
Superstitions, 26, 27
Syllectum, 85, 87

Tabarca, island, 182
Tacape, 96
Talismans, 26, 27
Taphrura, 92
Tarboosh, caps, 23, 40
Tarja, 11 (note)
Tebourba, 11 (note)
Tebournok, river, 53
Teboursouk, 175, 176
Temperature, 178
Thabarca, 183
Thacia, 166
Theatres, 3
Thibursicum, 175
Threshing, 158
Thugga, 171
Thysdrus, 75, 85, 86
Tissot, Charles, 97
Tombs, Phœnician, 105
Tourki, 53
Towns, sameness of, 4
   „ one described, 5
Tramway, 107, 108
Tressa, river, 166
Trisha, mountain, 165
Trozza, mountain, 132
Tunis, rapidity of journey to, 9
   „ stations between Tunis and Bône, 11 (note)
   „ the 'Burnous of the Prophet,' 14
   „ description of, 15, 26
   „ its population, 16, 17
   „ the streets, 17

INDEX.

Tunis, the kasba, 17
 „ the mosques, 18
 „ Moorish work, 18
 „ the souks, 20
 „ commercial rather than manufacturing, 23
 „ its manufactures, 23
 „ perfumery shops, 23
 „ barbers' shops, 24
 „ coffee-houses, 24
 „ gateways, 25
 „ the hand of Fatima, 26
 „ windowless house, 28
 „ a house described, 28
 „ ruined palaces, 29
 „ the Dar-el-Bey, 30
 „ lake El-Bahira, 34
 „ fine view of, 36
 „ women of, 197
 „ a house visited, 198
 „ women artificially fattened, 200
 „ French court of law, 203
 „ court of the cadi, 203
Tunisia, a good field for the study of archæology, &c., 1
 „ difficulties of travelling in, 1
 „ reliable information impossible, 3
 „ sameness of the towns, 4
 „ description of one, 5
 „ results of Arab occupation, 7
 „ women classified, 197
 „ neglect of literature, 204
Tunisians, their character described, 5 (note)

Tunisians, life in the south, 21
 „ the perfumers, 23

Uthina, 43
Utica, 47

Vandalism, modern, 38, 173
Voisins, Mme. de, on mirage, 60 (note)
 „   „   quoted on dress of women, 64 (note)
 „   „   „ Msaken, 70 (note)

Washing, 108
Wedding ceremony, 41
Wheat, 161 (note)
Whitewash, 15
Women, in the harem, 196
 „ different classes, 197, 199
 „ their dress, 64, 197
 „ stays, a punishment, 199
 „ artificially fattened, 200
Wortley Montague, Lady Mary, her visit to the harem, 199 (note)

Zaghouan, mountain, 15, 76, 106, 176
 „ to Tunis, 36
 „ town of, 39
 „ skull caps dyed there, 23, 40
 „ the spring and temple, 41
Zanfour, 162, 163, 169
Zaouias. See Mosques
Zaouiet, 76
Zeroud, river, 109
Zouida, 88
Zramedine, 77

LONDON:
Printed by STRANGEWAYS & SONS, Tower Street, Cambridge Circus.

TRAVELS IN TUNISIA.

CHAPTER I.

GENERAL REMARKS.

<small>TUNISIA A GOOD FIELD FOR STUDY—DIFFICULTIES OF TRAVELLING—THE 'COMPAGNIE TRANSATLANTIQUE'—INCONVENIENCE OF PORTS—BAD ROADS—WANT OF ACCOMMODATION—NO FOOD—NO AMUSEMENTS—SCENERY—INFORMATION DIFFICULT TO OBTAIN—A TUNISIAN TOWN DESCRIBED—CHARACTER OF THE ARABS—CRUELTY TO ANIMALS—RESULTS OF ARAB RULE IN NORTH AFRICA.</small>

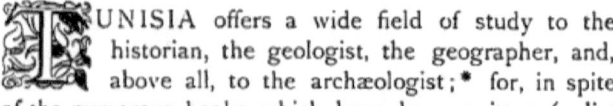UNISIA offers a wide field of study to the historian, the geologist, the geographer, and, above all, to the archæologist;* for, in spite of the numerous books which have been written (a list of the principal works will be found at the end of this volume), much still remains in every branch to reward the explorer. The traveller must, however, have ample time at his disposal, and be prepared to face difficulties, hardships, and privations. To the ordinary tourist—to him who travels for his pleasure only—Tunisia cannot be recommended.

<small>* Lieut.-Col. Sir R. L. Playfair remarks: 'In archæology immense strides have been made. Tunis was one of the few places in the world where an almost unexplored field remained for the archæologist. It may be said to be one vast museum—certainly a perfect library of epigraphical treasure. Even the ancient names of places have hardly changed, the modern nomenclature being simply a corruption of the Latin words.

'Great Roman roads radiated from Carthage, and even an immense</small>

GENERAL REMARKS.

The communications are slow, defective, frequently impossible. The 'Compagnie Transatlantique,' whose magnificent fleet of British-built steamers, well manned and well appointed, sweep the coasts of North Africa from Oran to Algiers, Algiers to Tunis, Tunis to Djerba, are favoured with so little traffic that they are forced to combine the postal, passenger, and goods services. This necessitates remaining several hours (sometimes a whole day) before the same port. The harbours of Tunisia are too shallow to admit vessels of heavy tonnage, so that large steamers are obliged to anchor from two to four miles from the shore, making it necessary to land in small boats—at all times inconvenient, and in bad weather impossible. The only railways in the country are the one connecting Tunis with the Algerian ports of Bône and Philippeville, a small local line between Tunis and its port Gouletta, and another between Tunis and Hammamet, a watering-place a few miles south. In the interior there are neither roads nor bridges; vehicles are consequently not everywhere practicable, and travelling, even on horseback, is difficult and dangerous after heavy rains. Accommodation is even less satisfactory. Excepting the two chief towns (Tunis and Soussa), which are provided with hotels of an European character, there is in reality no accommo-

---

series of secondary ones can still in many instances be traced by military columns, testifying to the ancient prosperity of the country and to the genius of its occupants, whether Punic or Roman. Every town on the course of these roads had its temples, basilica, palaces, forum, and thermæ, its theatre and amphitheatre. Triumphal arches and city gates are still found in all their classic grandeur, and at every step the traveller meets Roman farms of almost monumental character. Near the cities are extensive cemeteries and magnificent mausolea, and even sepulchres of the so-called Megalithic type.'—*Consular Reports*, No. 3 (1886), p. 29.

GENERAL REMARKS.

dation properly so called. In towns which appear on maps in large type, it is difficult to obtain food or lodging, and the *fondouks*, or country inns, which are occasionally met with in the interior, are the most miserable establishments imaginable — dirty and full of vermin; on a par with the rest-houses of North China, but in no way comparable with the *dâk-banglas* of India. As food of any kind is seldom to be obtained, and water is nearly always undrinkable, the traveller should carry with him provisions, bedding, and, in doubtful weather, a tent.

In so incommodious a country amusements can scarcely be expected. In Tunis, it is true, the Italian theatre of a very ordinary description is usually open during the winter, and a French company of moderate pretensions gives occasional performances; but visitors hailing from the capitals of Europe or America are not likely to find in them either pleasure or recreation. The Arabs have no theatre of their own, and since the French occupation performances in the native 'cafés'— singing or dancing—have almost ceased.

The north and west of Tunisia are mountainous, but scenery of the interior is, as a rule, unlovely, consisting of vast plains—treeless, waterless, uncultivated—without even a habitation to relieve the monotony of the landscape. The hills which intersect these enormous plateaus are usually rugged, bare, unwooded; but some of the passes, especially those towards the northern frontier, are well timbered and equal at times, though they never surpass in sublimity, the celebrated Châbet of Algeria, between Bougie and Setif.

A source of constant vexation is the difficulty, or rather impossibility, of obtaining reliable information, not concerning ruins, curiosities, out-of-the-way things, but about every-day concerns. This, too, in a country for which no special guide-book exists, and which is without a series of reliable maps, is exceedingly trying to the traveller's patience. There is a French guide-book, entitled *L'Itinéraire de Piesse*, published in 1878. Not unfrequently had we to undergo such unsatisfactory conversation as the following:—

Q. How far is it to X——?

A. A long way.

Q. Shall we be able to reach it before sundown?

A. There is no moon to-night.

Q. This is immaterial if we arrive before sunset.

A. If you had started very early in the morning you would have been there in good time. Your horses travel slowly.

Q. Well, we left B—— at eight o'clock this morning, and we have just arrived here; so you can judge the pace at which we travel.

A. The roads are bad.

Q. Please to tell us the exact distance to X——.

A. It is a long way.

Q. How many 'kilomètres' are there from here to X——?

A pause. The Arab under examination looks graver than usual, and our interpreter puts an end to the conversation by informing us that Arabs know nothing about kilomètres.

Most of the towns of Tunisia (apart from the picturesqueness which the colouring of every Oriental town invariably imparts) offer little attraction, either on account of their general plan, the arrangement of their streets, or the architecture of their buildings, whether public or private. A certain sameness prevails everywhere. A village resembles a city, except that it is less well built and maintained; or rather, a city is nothing more than an overgrown village. An Arab town of these parts may be described in few words :—low, brick-built, whitewashed houses, consisting generally of one storey, with arched doorways more or less pretentious, and barred windows, planned externally without any attempt at symmetry—turning their backs, as it were, on narrow, tortuous, ill-paved streets, in which all kinds of ordure and objectionable matter are deposited. In the midst is a mosque of one uniform pattern, differing only in size and extent from that of some other town. On higher ground stands the Military Governor's residence, the *Kasba*, or Citadel. The whole is enclosed with a whitewashed rubble wall, crenelated, pierced for musketry, and buttressed at intervals, pretty at a distance, much less so in close proximity, and quite useless for purposes of defence. Such is the ordinary Tunisian town, almost devoid of architectural pretensions, if we except the Roman shafts of marble or stone that are conspicuous at corners of the streets, the support and mainstay of ill-constructed buildings. Nor are the inhabitants more interesting or less uniform than their dwelling-places. Their character has been differently summed up by various writers.*

---

* To cite but two authorities :—

Thomas Macgill (*Account of Tunis*, 1816, p. 37) says : 'They are proud, ignorant, cunning, full of deceit, avaricious, and ungrateful.' To this stricture, severe as it is, indolence, apathy and cruelty, must yet be added.

'The Tunisians, or Moors, are for the most part religious, but without any fanaticism ; their natural disposition is grave, dignified, affable, and corrupted as they may be by the usages of trade, they are generally more honest than their Israelitish and Christian rivals. Few of them, except perhaps among the merchant class, avail themselves of the example of Mahomet, to have more than one wife at a time. By their industry, their taste, their commercial intelligence, in short, by

As far as our own experience goes, the Arab in the interior of the country is courteous in the extreme, hospitable, and obliging—good qualities, nevertheless, which do not preclude his readiness to cut the 'dog's' throat, were he not restrained by the severe penalties of the law. Cruel he undoubtedly is, and callous to the sufferings of his animals. From this one may not unjustly infer that obnoxious human beings might meet with little commiseration at his hands. The originator of that poetical myth of the Arab and his horse, which has done duty so often in the picture-books of our youth, must have been endowed with a vivid imagination, or, more probably, could have had but little acquaintance with the people themselves. Rare is it to meet with an animal that does not bear marks of mutilation or ill-treatment—an ass with slit nostrils,* a mule with dilapidated ears, a cow whose tail has been broken by twisting, a dog or a cat with ears and tail docked, or a horse whose skin indicates by its scars punishment more severe than could be inflicted by a stick. The beasts are almost always overloaded, and the trappings and harness—bits, saddles, or breechings—are simply instruments of torture. On remonstrating once with an Arab upon this cruel treatment, he replied, with a stoicism not to be surpassed, 'We have suffered, why should not they?'

---

their comparative instruction and their literary culture, but not by their morality, the Tunisians are considered superior to all other Moors.'—*Nouvelle Géographie Universelle*, Reclus, XI. 196.

* It is the rule, not the exception, for donkeys to have their nostrils slit. Frequently did we inquire the reason of this mutilation, without ever obtaining a satisfactory explanation. One said it was to prevent their braying, which it certainly does not do; another, that it enabled them to breathe more freely, and consequently to travel faster. Probably custom, the origin of which has long been forgotten, is the sole reason of this absurd and barbarous practice.

GENERAL REMARKS.

Little as we may sympathise in the occupation of Tunisia by the French, whose half-century of rule in Algeria is a doubtful success, no pity can be felt for the Arabs, ruler or subject, who have now to submit to a foreign yoke. For more than a thousand years have they possessed one of the richest and most beautiful lands of the world, under a climate little short of perfection. In the course of centuries they have slaughtered and driven out more people than at present inhabit the entire country; they have neglected the rivers and watercourses, choked up and befouled the cisterns and wells, cut down the forests without replanting,* allowed roads to disappear and bridges to decay, mutilated the monuments, degrading and misusing the fragments; permitted the soil to go out of cultivation—in short, they have converted a land of plenty into a desert, a fertile garden into a wilderness. Moreover, those who have held for long centuries

---

* The following remarks of M. Largeau concerning the Desert of Sahara are equally applicable to Tunisia:—'The decline of this country,' he writes, 'is due to the disappearance of those waters which used formerly to fertilise it. But what has caused these waters to disappear? How is it that these immense rivers, fountains of moisture, reservoirs of freshness, sources of vegetation, have dried up? I attribute this drought to the destruction of the forests (*déboisement*), and I find the principal cause of this destruction in the sanguinary struggles of the nomad shepherds of different tribes, who, coming from the north and north-east, invaded the Sahara desert, destroying and driving before them their predecessors. . . . . All these transmigrations, all these substitutions of races, were not made without resistance, bloody combats, and cruel massacres; and in a country where rain was probably a rare occurrence, where, perhaps, the earth was not made productive except by irrigation, massacre or departure of the agricultural population would naturally carry with it the complete ruin of the soil. Admitting that these wars did not entirely destroy the forests of the country, the shepherds completed the work. Flocks are the wealth of wandering tribes; but for flocks it is necessary to have prairies, and not woods, which have, in addition, the inconvenience

the destiny of the country in their hands, have neglected their people, squandered their treasure; and finally, with impending bankruptcy, sold the land of their forefathers to the detested infidel. For all this weight of desecration, destruction, and fanaticism, there is no counterpoise. Not a single work of literature worth recording, no new development of science or industry, nor any great monument of art or utility, will be handed down to future generations as evidence of a nation possessing either culture or progress.

---

of sheltering wild beasts. It is a remarkable fact that the countries overrun at the present time by shepherds, particularly by Arab shepherds, present the same aspect of aridity and desolation. And, nevertheless, it is proved that the greater part of those districts were at one time marvellously fertile. The Sahara, then, having had its trees cut down, the rains have become still rarer, and the surface soil, swept by the winds, has left bare a sedimentary carapace, through which the waters of the springs and the rain filter, in order to form subterranean rivers, which the well-sinkers of Oued-Rirh bring back to the surface for the irrigation of their oasis. It is not necessary to go to Africa to study this phenomenon, it is found in a lesser degree in several parts of France, where it is also due to the devastation of the mountain forests, and in a great many parts boring has proved the existence of veritable subterranean rivers. By thoroughly examining the shores one would possibly find the spot where these rivers join the sea.'—*Voyage au Sahara algérien.*

CHAPTER II.

LONDON TO TUNIS.

October 28th to 31st.

THE START—MARSEILLES—ON BOARD THE 'VILLE DE ROME'—THE PLEASANT CITY OF BÔNE—IN THE RAILWAY CAR—VINEYARDS—A JOURNEY IN A DILIGENCE — THE SERPENTINE MEDJERDAH — TUNIS REACHED.

LEAVING London by the mail train on the morning of Wednesday, October 28th, we reached Paris in time for the *Rapide* of the same evening, arriving at Marseilles on the following morning. A *Bouillabaisse* at the *Réserve*, a pleasant walk along the *Corniche*, and a saunter down the *Cannebière*, agreeably occupied our time until, at 5 p.m. precisely, the steamer, *Ville de Rome* (of the 'Compagnie Transatlantique') left her moorings direct for Bône. We had selected this route rather than proceed to Tunis direct, in order to revisit scenes that, on a former journey, we had passed under less favourable circumstances, the time occupied being about eight hours longer than by the direct route.

At 2 a.m., October 31st, we entered the harbour, and were pleased to find on rising that we could step from the vessel on to the quay.

Bône is one of the most pleasant towns in Algeria. Second only to Algiers in extent and population, it is in some respects even more desirable as a place of residence. The harbour, as already noticed, is very convenient, the largest vessels being able to enter at all hours and seasons. The town is purely French—in the arrangement of the streets, the construction of the houses, and the contents of the shops. Were it not for the tropical vegetation and the native costumes, one might suppose oneself still on the other side of the Mediterranean. The wide, handsome street, which runs from the harbour through the centre of the town, reminding one somewhat of the *Cannebière* at Marseilles, is arcaded on one side and lined with fine stone-built houses of good design. Here are the principal shops and 'cafés,' and at the upper end is a charming garden, in which are palms and other tropical trees. Beyond this, on rising ground, stands the modern Roman Catholic Church (quasi-Byzantine), a structure grotesque in outline, and presenting the appearance of a badly restored ruin.

Outside the town, in the same direction, the road is crossed by the stately arches of a Roman aqueduct, partially restored, although no longer in use. A short distance beyond is the public garden, remarkable for its avenues of ancient palms, and a collection of carved and inscribed stones of Roman origin.

The population of Bône is almost entirely French; there are few Arabs, and fewer Europeans of other nationalities.

Our acquaintance with Bône was begun on a former, and renewed on a subsequent occasion; the present visit was but a passing one. Our destination was Tunis, to which city there is but one direct train daily from Bône, leaving at 5 a.m. The speed at which the train travels is not rapid,—the journey, a distance of 355 'kilomètres' (224 miles), occupying fifteen hours.[*] The scenery throughout is picturesque. As far as Souk-Ahras, the last town on the Algerian frontier, the line runs through vineyards and cork forests, then winds among majestic hills clothed with oaks and occasional clumps of eucalyptus, with plateaus of grass not unlike our own common lands. On reaching a lower level, vines, in greater luxuriance, cover the hillsides. The growers' houses are square, white-washed buildings, with flat roofs, some of the more important being fortified and loopholed. This is true of many railway stations. Excepting the houses in the vineyards, there are neither homesteads nor villages. From Souk-Ahras to Ghardimaou the scenery is of a different character, less majestic, entirely uncultivated, but more picturesque. The line follows the course of the *Oued* Medjerdah, the ancient Bagradas, and winding round the hills, now boldly crosses it, now tunnels through a hill only to meet the constantly winding stream at another of its bends. The hills are by no means barren, but generally green with arbutus, olives, corks, or dwarf-oaks. Looking down upon the river and the now almost disused road, well did we remember the unpleasantness of a previous journey in the diligence through the same district. It was on the 28th November, 1883, just before the completion of the railway connecting

---

[*] The following are the names of the stations on the Tunisian Railway between Bône and Tunis, the distances being from Bône:—

Kilomètres.			Kilomètres.		
107	...	Souk-Ahras.	289	... ...	Medjez-el-Bab.
116	...	Tarja.	321	... ...	Tebourba.
165	...	Ghardimaou (breakfast).	330	... ...	Djedeida.
176	...	Oued-Meliz.	345	... ...	Manouba.
199	...	Souk-el-Arba.	355	... ...	Tunis.
248	...	Béja (town 15 kilomètres distant).			

the Algerian and Tunisian lines. A more disagreeable day's travelling it is not easy to imagine. Rain had been falling for a couple of days previously, rendering both road and river difficult, converting the sandy track of the one into a mass of mud, and the dry bed of the other into a swelling torrent. Although warned against undertaking so hazardous a journey (one of the last made by the diligence), we nevertheless started at daylight. The track used by vehicles follows the valley along the banks of the Medjerdah, winding through the pass at different levels and crossing the river at short intervals.

Twenty-seven times in the course of the day did the five horses harnessed to our rough cart, that served as a diligence, dash down the ravines, and, plunging into the stream, carry us over by sheer force. Bridges there were none. The fords were visible as a confused mass of huge stones, and as the vehicle jolted over them, one felt that body and limbs were about to part company. We were going with the stream, and consequently every passage of the river became more hazardous. Never shall we forget the last crossing. It was pitch dark; but the driver (a Maltese,—as usual in these parts) fortunately knew the track well enough. Standing up and placing his little lantern in his cap, he gave a whoop and a crack of the whip and, lashing the tired animals into fury, he swept us into the water, which rose above the body of the cart, and—thank goodness!—in a moment we were over. This was not all our trouble. Four times we had to alight, and, standing in mud more than ankle deep, had to lift the cart out of the slush; and once with pickaxe and shovel (which the driver had with him), and some branches of trees, we found ourselves under the necessity of excavating the horses and digging out the carriage. It was pleasant after such a journey to reach our night's quarters at Ghardimaou, although it was only a rough shanty on the slopes of a mud hill.

Eastward of Ghardimaou the scenery again changes entirely, and the railway crosses a vast plain, through which the Medjerdah, almost lost to view, continues to meander between deep yellow banks. Native homesteads there are none; houses of an European character are few; but here and there the landscape is dotted with white *koubbas*, or tombs of saints, and relieved by the black *gourbies*, or tents of Arab encampments. Nevertheless flocks of sheep and goats intermixed are grazing among the stunted bushes, while strings of camels wend their way silently over the great plain.

Daylight had departed before we approached Tunis, and the objects of interest through which the line passes —the Bardo Palace, the gardens of Manouba, the aqueducts, the city walls—were but dimly seen. At 8 p.m. the train drew up at the terminus of Tunis.

CHAPTER III.

TUNIS.

*November 29th to December 4th, 1884.   October 31st to November 8th,
and December 1st to December 5th, 1885.*

THE 'BURNOUS OF THE PROPHET'—VIEW OF THE CITY—WHITEWASH
—MIXED POPULATION—THE STREETS—THE KASBA—THE MOSQUES.

OF all the white cities of Tunisia no one is whiter than Tunis, whence its appellation of *The Burnous of the Prophet*, a title as appropriate as it is poetic. To gaze upon this bewildering mass of snow-white habitations from the Kasba walls or the terraced roof of the Dar-el-Bey, when the stillness of the air is broken by the voices of *muezzins* calling to evening prayer, awakens feelings of solemnity that words would fail to express. From the city, spread out like a sheet, the eye wanders seawards over the shallow lake Borghaz, or el-Bahira, 'the little sea,' as the Arabs call it, on one bank of which Tunis is built. Immediately in front is the modern port Gouletta, with its busy quays and shipping; to the right, the village of Radès, pleasantly situated on an olive-clad hill; to the left, the rising ground that marks the site of ancient Carthage, backed by the headland and whitened houses of Sidi-bou-said. Turning inland, the saltmarsh of Sedjoumi skirts the southern walls of Tunis, and framing the horizon is one long succession of mountains and hills, vying with each other in beauty of outline and culminating in the rugged peak of Zaghouan. Nearer the city walls, to the right, are the Bardo Palace and the Gardens of Manouba, and beyond is the graceful outline of *Djebel* Merkey. All this, when viewed through the lucid atmosphere and touched with the gorgeous colouring of this favoured clime, combines to make a fairy picture difficult to rival, never to be forgotten.

The whiteness of Tunis, as of every city in the Beylik (for all are white), beautiful at a distance and picturesque as an object in the landscape, loses its charm on closer inspection. If economical in most things, in whitewash the Arab is extravagant. He applies it without discrimination — from the mosque to the koubba, from the palace to the hovel. Bricks or mud, marble or stone, iron or lead, all pass under the same brush; inscriptions are choked up, tracery is hidden, and carved capitals of beautiful design are thus made to look like stucco imitations.

Quitting our eminence, and passing rapidly through the bazaars, to which we shall have frequent opportunity of returning, we saunter for a while about the Place de la Bourse, a small square at the bottom of the town and close to the walls, where stands the British Consulate. This is the central spot of Tunis, to which every street converges. Passing out of Bab-el-Bahar, the principal gate of the city, we have before us the wide Boulevard de la Marine, laid out with a view to extension as far as the lake Bahira. On this boulevard are the Post Office, Hotel, Bank, State Tobacco Factory, Roman Catholic Church, and European Cafés. It is the lounge of French officers and better-class Europeans generally. To the left is the quarter occupied by Maltese and Italians; beyond is that assigned to the Jews—as dirty as it is interesting, and not separated by any wall or boundary, as in many Eastern towns. The natives—

Moors or Arabs—dwell, for the most part, in the upper part of the town, where the Dar-el-Bey is situate, the bazaars being round about it. They have also formed suburbs about the many gates of the city, the principal resort of natives from the interior, and consequently very curious, animated, and interesting.

Few cities of the East (not even Cairo, Constantinople, or Bombay) surpass Tunis in varieties of type or costume :—the sleek, fair-skinned Tunisian of Moorish descent, well dressed, in coloured slippers trodden down at the heels, white stockings or socks, and *djebba*, or coat of some bright and delicate hue; in Fez cap, around which is wound a turban, either white or coloured—red indicating that the wearer has performed the Mecca pilgrimage, and is henceforth entitled to be called *Hadji;* green denoting a *Scherif*, or descendant of the Prophet, either in the male or female line ; the Mameluke of Greek or Syrian origin, scarcely to be distinguished from the native of Tunis ; the negro and half-caste remnants of slavery ; the native soldier, miserably clad in semi-European regimentals, with red Fez cap ornamented with a gilt star; the Jew, distinguishable only by a dark blue or black turban and by his manly bearing ; the Algerine, more martial and stalwart than the Tunisian ; the Maltese, the Sicilian, and the Spaniard, whose nationality is nearly extinct; to these must be added the French soldiery, now an important item in the population of Tunis. Then there are the civilian French, such as 'coiffeurs,' café-keepers, or owners of 'Magasins de Nouveautés.' The one nation not represented is England; the Englishman proper, to be met with everywhere else in the East, being here conspicuous by his absence.

Such is briefly the outward appearance of the population of Tunis, numbering at present about 130,000 souls. Considering its former importance, its remarkable history, its existence even prior to Carthage, one might expect to find in the capital of Tunisia more monuments of interest to the general traveller as well as to the antiquary. Apart from the streets themselves, with their picturesque population and gay surroundings, few of the buildings, public or private, offer in their exterior any striking architectural beauties. The streets, however, the best of which are in the vicinity of the Kasba and the Dar-el-Bey, inhabited mostly by Mamelukes, high functionaries and wealthy Moors, are a never-failing source of interest and delight—irregular, constructed apparently without any fixed plans, with Roman shafts of marble or stone built into, or protruding from, the rough walls, with abrupt twists and unexpected bends, leading up and down hill, now into a blind alley, now into a quaint little square, and anon offering a vista under arches, the curves of which intersect each other until the eye becomes dazed by the intricacies of the perspective —without names, without numbers—a labyrinth, in fact, in which the wanderer constantly misses his way, but to which he never tires of returning. Such are the streets of Tunis. Of the *Souks*, or passages in which the shops are situated, mention will be made in another chapter.

The culmination of this maze is the Kasba, or fortress and prison combined, once an important stronghold, now little more than a mass of ruins, in course of part-reconstruction by the French. It is entered on the side of the town through a square, the most extensive open place of which Tunis can boast, and delightful by reason of its trees and colonnades. One side of the square forms the façade of the Dar-el-Bey. The entrance to the palace, through which the reader will accompany us later on, is from a street in the town.

Admission to the Mosques of Tunis being denied to all but Mohammedans, one must be satisfied with such glimpses as can occasionally be obtained through an open door. The very steps are forbidden to the tread of an unbeliever. Any attempt, therefore, at description of their interiors would be a departure from the rule which we have imposed upon ourselves. The most important, called Djamäa Zeitouna, or Mosque of the Olive-tree, situated at the point where the two streets leading from the Place de la Bourse to the souks terminate, is the most frequented. The court and prayer-chamber are supported by a number of shafts with marble capitals, mostly of Roman origin, and the main entrance, under an arcaded loggia, is reached by an imposing flight of steps. Smaller, but far more picturesque in outline, is the Bishia Mosque, whose graceful octagonal minaret rises close to the Dar-el-Bey. On the other side of the town a little mosque, mostly frequented by women, conspicuous for the ornamentation of the entrance, and by an orange-tree growing in the centre of the tiled *patio*, deserves passing mention.

Whatever interest these and a few other buildings possess may be traced to particular periods of the Arab occupation. The overthrow of the Moors in Sicily, in the thirteenth century, and their expulsion from Spain, two centuries later, brought to the towns of North Africa a people renowned in art, and possessing a culture far in advance of other nations on the shores of the Mediterranean. The arts of Tunis originated with these Moors of Sicily and Spain, but never, apparently, took hold on the native population; and the beautiful plaster vaulting and arabesque tracery, the carved-wood ceilings and

ENTRANCE TO WOMEN'S MOSQUE, TUNIS.

gilded decorations, that attained such perfection at Seville and Granada, received but little encouragement, either in Tunis itself or in any part of the country. The few monumental works that remain will be referred to in succeeding chapters.

CHAPTER IV.

TUNIS.

THE SOUKS — THEIR IMPORTANCE — KEPT BY MOORS AND JEWS — DESCRIPTION OF THE SOUKS — GOODS SOLD IN THEM — THE SOUKS OF THE TAILORS AND PERFUMERS — FIRST IMPRESSIONS — BARBERS' SHOPS — COFFEE-HOUSES — COFFEE MAKING — THE GATEWAYS — THE FOUNTAINS — THE DOORS — TALISMANS — THE HAND OF FATIMA — BLACK KEYSTONES — SERPENT WORSHIP — THE HOUSES.

SO much has been said and written about the Souks of Tunis that one hesitates to describe them for fear of repetition. They form, however, so large a part of the city, are of such importance socially as well as commercially, and excite so much curiosity, that it would be a grave omission to pass them over in silence.

To one who has visited the great cities of the East — Constantinople or Cairo, for instance — the bazaars of Tunis, extensive though they are, are not very striking. Neither in the quality of the wares, the sizes of the shops, nor the richness of the fabrics, will the souks bear comparison with those of the former cities. Display, indeed, there is none, and more goods might probably be found in such an establishment as the *Bon Marché* of Paris, or a co-operative store in London, than in fifty Tunis shops united. Nevertheless the souks are so attractive that the traveller returns to them again and again without satiety. The reason of this is not far to seek. The people more than the shops, the buyers and sellers rather than the merchandise displayed, are a never-ending source of delight. In an European shop all interest is concentrated in the wares exposed for sale; in the souks it is the motley multitude that attracts the eye wherever one turns. The souks, in fact, are the life of Tunis. It is here that the stranger gathers all that is possible to learn of the daily life and habits of the people, debarred as he is from what is termed social intercourse. For the native the bazaar is all-important; it is to him not only a place of business, but one of recreation and information. He visits no friend, receives no one at his own house; he has no club, no newspapers, no theatres, no amusements. In the bazaar he meets his acquaintances, hears the news, pursues his avocation, gains his living. His shop closed, he retires to his dwelling, partakes of his evening meal, and spends the rest of his time in his harem. The shopkeepers are principally Moors, with a large proportion of Jews, who carry on their avocations unmolested, as in all other Oriental towns at the present day. The chief souks occupy the space between the grand Mosque and the Dar-el-Bey, although others, almost equally interesting, are to be found in various parts of the town, notably in the vicinity of the different gates. For the present we shall confine our remarks to the former.

Starting from the Boulevard de la Marine, where the traveller will probably reside, passing under the Bab-el-Bahar and across the square to which it gives access, two narrow, irregular streets, lined with common-place European shops, lead to a small open space, flanked by the grand Mosque. This is the heart of Tunis, and at this point the souks proper commence, or rather cluster around it. The souks differ from the streets by being narrower and covered in. The roofs consist either of rough brick vaulting, plastered and whitewashed, and pierced at intervals with unglazed holes which admit the necessary light, or of wooden planks loosely laid across, between which the sun's rays abundantly penetrate. The industries are never mixed, but each trade has a souk or street of shops to itself. The shops themselves are mere holes in the wall without doors or windows, and utterly devoid of any architectural design. The floor of the shop is somewhat raised above the level of the street, and on it the merchant sits crosslegged, his goods arranged around him on the floor or on shelves, but within his reach, without the necessity of displacing himself. The customer remains outside, standing, or seated on one of the two small benches which are usually provided in front of the shop, one on either side. There is little or no display of goods, but as the whole street is devoted exclusively to one industry, the intending purchaser knows at once what article or articles are to be obtained in that particular street. As all the shops are open, each trader can see what his neighbour is doing; trade secrets do not exist, and competition is practically unknown. As soon as a stranger enters a bazaar, the eyes of each successive shopkeeper are upon him as he passes. Should he stop before any particular shop and begin to bargain, the conversation is overheard by traders on either side, and not unfrequently men from more distant shops will come and listen to what is going on. His requirements and the prices in debate are consequently soon known throughout the entire bazaar. Should the merchant with whom he is treating not possess the article required, a neighbour will bring it from his stock, and it is no breach of commercial etiquette for the customer to purchase it, as the two vendors will afterwards adjust the division of profit.

Tunis is a commercial rather than a manufacturing town, and the bulk of the goods sold in the souks are foreign, or made in other places in the Regency. The red skull caps, here called *chachias*,* in Egypt *tarboosh*, and in Turkey *fez*, worn by every man in the beylik, are made and finished at Tunis, although the dyeing is done principally at Zaghouan. Attar of roses and oil of jasmine—the latter a specialty of the Regency—are made in Tunis. Soap is manufactured largely at Sfax. Harness and leather slippers are made in Tunis, although those of Kairouan are more esteemed, partly on account of their bright colour. Djerba produces the *bernous*, and the loose coat known as a *djerba;* but both are also made in Tunis and in other towns. Finally, the embroidery of Tunis is the best in the Regency. The souks in which the stranger will prefer to linger are those of the tailors and the perfumers. As sewing and embroidery are done exclusively by men, the garments of both sexes are sold in the same bazaar; consequently more women are to be seen among the customers (never among the vendors) of the former bazaar than in any other, which adds much to the diversity and interest of the scene.

The perfumers of Tunis are altogether a superior class; they are richer, better educated (they may frequently be found reading), more richly dressed than their compeers; and their shops, if smaller, are better appointed, and arranged with more care, taste, and luxury. Each perfumery shop is a picture in itself. The merchant squats in the centre of his small aperture, framed, as it were, by his wares; his bottles and packets to right and

---

* A description of the way in which the chachia caps are manufactured will be found in Chapter XX. of Macgill's *Account of Tunis.*

left, festoons of coloured candles assuming the shape of a Fatima hand above his head, and bowls of henna and native spices on each side of his little counter. This is known as the Souk-el-Attarin, and is perhaps more picturesque than the others, owing partly to the cross perspective of a line of arches with painted shafts of red, and green, and white, and to the scenic effect produced by the accidental position of a series of small apertures in the roughly constructed roof. Many of the shopkeepers in this bazaar can trace their descent from the great Moorish families of Seville and Granada. It is a pretty legend that the keys of their Spanish homes are still preserved, and are handed down from father to son, in the hope that the dwellings of their great ancestors may one day be restored to them.

The first impression on entering any of these souks is one of bewilderment and perplexity—their intricacy and labyrinthian formation; the motley crowd surging to and fro, pressing and jostling, and heedless of strangers; loaded camels and donkeys forcing their way through streets scarcely wide enough to allow two human beings to pass without touching; the noise of hundreds of voices crying, touting, bargaining—all this fairly overwhelms the traveller, until a few visits shall have accustomed him to the strange scene and to the unfamiliar sounds.

Not the least curious of Tunisian houses are the barbers' shop. They do not form a souk of themselves, although they are frequently found in clusters, and, unlike other shops, they are closed by a fancifully painted or neatly carved door, or a net suspended across the entrance.

Coffee-houses are to be found everywhere, and are much frequented in Tunis, as in Paris. They are generally large, square chambers, whitewashed and undecorated, around which are constructed rough stone or earthen benches, covered with matting; on these the customers sit, or lie, sipping their coffee and lemonade, and playing cards or dominoes. In one corner is a small stove, where the coffee is made, and its preparation is in this wise: The attendant takes several small tin pots with long handles, and puts into each pot a portion of sugar and fresh-roasted coffee, upon which he pours water almost boiling. Then, pushing the pots into live wood embers in an earthen bowl, and holding them there till the contents are on the point of boiling, he removes them simultaneously with his right hand. Then, without putting any of them down, and with a turn of the hand, he pours the coffee into as many cups, which he holds in his left hand, and without spilling a single drop. The cups are without handles, and are served inside other cups to prevent burning the fingers. The dexterity with which the pouring out is performed is worthy of note. The coffee, delicious in flavour and retaining the full aroma of the berry, is apt to be thick. One has to wait until it is almost cold before it can be drunk. The natives are not particular: they swallow the grouts, for it is both meat and drink to them. This luxury is only one halfpenny a cup.

The Gateways of Tunis, apart from their Oriental look, have no special features of interest. As the gates are closed at night, stone fountains, often of a monumental character, are to be found outside the walls for the convenience of caravans and wayfarers arriving after sunset. Behind the fountain (synonymous with washing-place or trough in Eastern countries) is a loggia, or arcade, consisting of two or more horse-shoe arches, forming the front of a deep porch. Along the back wall runs a stone bench. Delicate shafts with capitals of Arab design support the arches, but everything in the way of building materials is so covered with whitewash in this country that the beauty of the decorative features is frequently concealed.

All Oriental cities have a charm and a colouring of their own, differing essentially from what is commonly termed 'the picturesque' when speaking of European towns. In spite of a dearth of architectural monuments, Tunis, with its labyrinth of streets, its flying arches from house to house across the narrow thoroughfares, its arched doorways with their delicate carvings in stone or marble, its wilderness of shops, their wooden columns painted with spiral bands in gaudy colours of blue, and red, and green, has much to charm the eye, and colouring enough to balance the wearying monotony of whitewash. Very curious, too, and characteristic, are the wooden doors of ordinary Moorish houses, with their quaint devices formed with countless round-headed nails: crescents and crosses, graceful curves, and crude imitations of symbols of deities of long-forgotten Phœnician origin, are mixed together in endless variety. Like the horse-shoe nailed on the cottage wall in our own country, these nails, a remnant of a still older superstition, are regarded as a protection to the abode and a charm to keep off the evil eye.

A still more universal charm against this dreaded influence is the uplifted Hand of Fatima. There is scarcely a house-wall, Moorish, Arab, or Jewish, on which this emblem is not to be seen in some form or other. It is most frequently met with as a simple red daub, as if produced by a natural hand dipped in blood or other red colouring matter, and with outstretched fingers impressed simply upon the door or wall. Sometimes it is neatly painted in the Prophet's favourite colour — green; at others it may be found worked out in nails on the door, or in carved stone on the lintels or jambs. Its correct form is that of an open hand, the fingers extended and the palm turned towards the spectator; but, like other religious symbols, it has now assumed a conventional shape. Not unfrequently it may be seen painted on the skins of horses and mules. It is also a favourite device for articles of jewelry worked in silver, and worn as a locket or brooch.

Another talisman, equally curious, is that employed to guard animals from the effect of the evil eye. It consists of two small triangular cushions, made of velvet or stuff, embroidered with metal, and connected with cords, finished off with knobs or tassels in gay colours, and is hung round the neck of the animal. Intimately connected with these and many other superstitions is the employment of black stone or marble, and, failing these materials, black paint, in the voussoirs of arch construction. They tell you that the black stone, especially when it occurs as the keystone of an arch, the one black spot where all else is dazzling whiteness, is symbolical of sin. No human work is perfect. To attempt perfection would be an act of defiance to the spirit of evil, whose powers of destruction are illimitable. The black stone, emblem of imperfection, becomes a homage or sign of concession to this power, and thus secures the protection of all the other stones of the fabric—the white stones without spot or blemish. Passing from this pretty legend, there is yet another form of superstition, unmistakably Oriental in its origin, that prevailed till recent times, and is not yet quite extinct. It is the reverence for serpents. 'Blessed is the habitation,' say they, 'where the serpent dwells.' Neither hunger nor thirst is ever known to this member of a family. His food is prepared and his presence expected before the commencement of the daily meals. No one eats till the serpent has finished and has crept back satisfied to his hole. If he is not the ruler of the house, he possesses an importance the owner himself does not even attempt to share.

The absence of windows in the labyrinth of houses constituting the Arab town is the more remarkable, as many of the houses are two or more storeys in height. Here and there, at some distance from the ground, is an opening grilled or shuttered; sometimes projecting beyond the face of the wall, sometimes perched high up athwart the thoroughfare, with close-guarded windows looking both ways: this indicates the women's apartments. A glance or a salute directed at any of these shuttered openings might result in a smile of recognition from some veiled favourite in her forced confinement, but would certainly not meet with any response. Dwelling-houses, whether Moorish or Arab, are all based on the same model, as much so as our ordinary houses in Bloomsbury or Bayswater. A small vestibule within the doorway opens into a court or *patio*, varying in dimensions according to the wealth of the proprietor. Around it are a number of small rooms, forming the men's apartments, the kitchen and other offices. In houses two or more storeys high an upper floor is appropriated to the women, and a small well-hole is so constructed in the centre of the house that water and other necessaries can be drawn up, the gallery above being so concealed by woodwork that women are invisible to those in the court below.

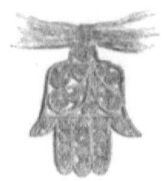

CHAPTER V.

TUNIS.

THE PALACES—THE MOHAMMEDIA—THE BARDO—THE DAR-EL-BEY.

AS each Bey, on accession to power, has been accustomed to discard the palace occupied by his predecessor, and to build a new one for himself, the royal residences around Tunis are numerous enough. The materials, however, of which they are built are so indifferent, and their construction is so faulty, that, without constant repairs, they would of themselves soon fall to decay. Not only are the deserted palaces uncared for, but their materials and fittings are carried off in order to erect new edifices, frequently worse designed and worse built than those sacrificed. In this way has the public money, sorely needed for roads, bridges, and other works of utility, been diverted and squandered.

The most extensive and striking of these royal ruins is the Mohammedia, about ten kilomètres south of Tunis, noticed in Chap. VII.—a standing testimony of the folly and incompetence of the later rulers of the country

The Bardo, two kilomètres from the Bab-es-Sadoun, and west of Tunis, is as pretentious as the Mohammedia, although covering a smaller site, and is remarkable, setting aside its historical interest, for prevailing bad taste and incongruity of design; and although it has not been dismantled, its construction is so weak, and otherwise defective, that some few years hence it will be unsafe to occupy. In its turn it has been set aside in favour of the Marsa, where the present Bey now resides. Descriptions of the Bardo are so numerous that we shall not attempt any detailed account of it, nor are we induced to do so in consequence of any architectural features it possesses externally. Surrounded by a moat, and furnished with a crenelated wall and bastions, it has the appearance of an Arab barrack or fortification rather than a palace. For purposes of defence it would be perfectly useless, on account of the flimsiness of its construction. Internally it consists of a series of passages and courtyards, leading to a vast number of buildings, put together unskilfully, and without any apparent design, with the exception of the principal staircase and some private rooms for the special use of the Bey. In these latter are some domed ceilings of beautiful plaster-work. There are no features of interest, in spite of many precious objects which it contains. Shafts and slabs from Carthage, mosaics and marble carvings from Italy, tiles of native manufacture, furniture from France, tawdry hangings, pictures and engravings, glass and gilding, are all brought together from every country in Europe—an unseemly collection of things good and bad, but mostly bad.

A far more satisfactory edifice, and in many respects the most noticeable building in Tunis, is the Dar-el-Bey, or town palace, where His Highness, the present Bey, holds weekly receptions. The main façade, arched and supported by graceful shafts, forms one side of the Kasba Square. Although erected so recently as the beginning of the present century by Hamouda, one of the most intellectual of the Beys, it is an excellent specimen of

COURT IN THE DAR EL-BEY

Moorish work, and the carved ceilings, the plaster arabesques, the gilded decorations and gorgeous colouring of some of the apartments, will compare favourably with similar work at Seville or Granada. The room set apart for the Wuzeer, and the great dining-room of the palace, are gems of art, scarcely surpassed by anything in the Alhambra. The walls are covered for the most part with old tiles, for which Tunis was once famous, showing great fertility of design and wondrous harmony of colour. Here, as at the Bardo, the effect is marred by the introduction of French furniture, trumpery artificial flowers under glass cases, and common lithographs. The disposition of the private apartments, especially those of the women, is interesting. The harem consists of a large square room, or patio, at one end of which, opposite the entrance, is a spacious recess, forming the sleeping-chamber of the Bey. Ten doors, five on each side, give access to as many small chambers. These melancholy rooms, whitewashed, ill-appointed, and devoid of decoration, are lighted from above, or by means of small windows placed high above the level of the eye, and inaccessible. They are more like prison-cells than the dwelling-rooms of innocent women. One side of the Dar-el-Bey looks on to the Souk-el-Barka, or Souk-el-Bey, and through one of the windows, arranged for the purpose, the ruler can find amusement, during his sojourn in the city at the feast of the Ramadan, by watching the sale of jewels and other objects of native art in the bazaar below. At other times of the year the Dar-el-Bey is empty, or is occupied by foreigners of distinction, whom the Bey may wish to honour during their sojourn in his capital. Queen Caroline resided there for a short time. There is some talk of converting this palace into a museum, for which there is much need in Tunis. No building could be better adapted to the purpose. It is well constructed (the principal court being of white and black marble), is of beautiful architecture, and is spacious and well lighted; many of the apartments are of Moorish work, and when the tawdry modern furniture and fittings are removed the great excellence of the native work will be more apparent. It is lamentable that such elegant ornamentation should be associated under the same roof with other decorative work in the worst possible taste. Annexed to this palace is a series of state-rooms of more recent date, decorated after the manner of a French café, presenting a striking contrast with the beauty and refinement that characterises the older work.

COURT OF THE BARDO, TUNIS.

CHAPTER VI.

TUNIS TO CARTHAGE.

BY RAIL OR ROAD?—SITE OF CARTHAGE NOT STRIKING—CHAPEL OF ST. LOUIS—EL-BAHIRA—CARTHAGINIAN LITERATURE—THE CISTERNS —UTTER RUIN—AUTHORITIES SUGGESTED.

TO take the railway to Carthage, or rather to the Malga station at the foot of Carthage hill, seems a prosaic mode of conveyance to a site that is linked in association with so many poetic memories. The journey by road is preferable, occupying about the same time, and enabling the excursionist to reach the principal points of interest without alighting. There is nothing in the aspect of the spot to charm the eye, nor is there anything in its surroundings to excite the imagination or to kindle enthusiasm. Cape Carthage, the headland of the northern shore of the Gulf of Tunis, is an ordinary eminence of red sandstone; and the other adjacent hills on which the great city was built are but undulations of the surface, nowhere precipitous and not marked by any striking contours. Were it not for a modern chapel erected on the highest ground, in commemoration of St. Louis and his ill-starred expedition against the Saracens, and forming a conspicuous landmark, the site of Carthage might be passed by unnoticed. Approached from the land side, the sandy plain, some ten miles long, to be traversed after leaving Tunis, is devoid of interest. On the left a few whitened houses, surrounded by olive plantations, are dotted on the surface, with here and there a solitary palm-tree or a line of cactus hedge; on the right lies the stagnant El-Bahira, the lake of Tunis, some seven miles across, its banks clothed with reeds, its shallow waters haunted by pelicans and flamingoes, and its bed a deposit of mud and sewage that has been poured into it from the city of Tunis for a period of more than 3500 years.

Of Carthage itself and its remains it would almost seem presumptuous to say anything. The store of literature up to the present year, relating either to its history or archæology, is as abundant as it is generally meritorious. A glance at the annexed bibliography shows how great have been the attractions of this subject to authors of many nationalities, and how each successive exploration has been followed by a fresh contribution to Carthaginian literature, including romance, poetry, and drama.

It seems strange that the only standing memorials of both Punic and Roman Carthage should relate to the water supply. The ruined reservoirs, which El-Bekri calls 'the cisterns of the demons,' may still be seen on the southern slopes. At the present day they are nearly filled up with earth and the accumulated deposit of many centuries. A settlement of Arabs is located within them. This work may be assigned to Carthaginian times, although partly reconstructed at a later period, and used in connection with the aqueduct that brought the waters of Zaghouan and Djougar to Carthage and Tunis. And below the citadel hill is another range of great reservoirs, called, for the sake of distinction, the smaller cisterns, still used by the peasantry. This is a work of the Romans, built for the storage of rain-water.

For any indications of monumental grandeur one

may look in vain. The wealth of marble * and porphyry —the glory of the earlier as well as of the later Carthage —has long since disappeared, crumbled to dust, removed to enrich the palaces and mosques of North Africa, or transported across the Mediterranean to embellish the edifices of Spain and Italy.

The piteous interest attached to this old-world metropolis is increased rather than diminished by a study of the patient investigations of numerous explorers during the present century. The subject is perhaps one for the consideration of the antiquary and the historian rather than for the general traveller, but we may note with gratitude the diligent and successful researches of Beulé and Davis, and the investigations, amongst many others, of Falbe and Sainte-Marie. To the pages of these authors we commend inquiring readers for information relating to the topography and antiquities of Carthage; and for a history of the great Punic city, its rise and development, Mr. R. Bosworth Smith's *Carthage and the Carthaginians* should be read by every one contemplating an excursion to this old-world site.

---

* 'Marble at Carthage is so abundant,' says El-Bekri, the Arab writer of the eleventh century, 'that if all the inhabitants of Africa were to assemble to carry away the blocks they could not accomplish the task.'

CHAPTER VII.

TUNIS TO ZAGHOUAN AND OUDENA.

November 2nd and 3rd, 1885.

VIEW OF TUNIS—THE BAB-EL-ALOUA—SALT MARSH—THE MOHAMMEDIA
—THE AQUEDUCT—RECENT DESTRUCTION—THE TOWN OF ZAGHOUAN
—THE TRIUMPHAL ARCH—THE SPRING—THE TEMPLE—A WEDDING
CEREMONY—A DONKEY STOLEN—BEDOUINS—THE RUINS OF UTHINA
—FINE POSITION—RETURN TO TUNIS.

THE distance from Tunis to Zaghouan is said to be forty English miles. It is probably not more than thirty-two miles, or fifty kilomètres, for the four horses that drew our landau in the morning of November 2nd accomplished the distance in a little over four hours. Passing the Bab-el-Aloua, the outlet of one of the most interesting and characteristic Arab quarters of the city, the route traverses some olive plantations which abound on this side. Looking from the higher ground, which we reached by a gentle ascent, a magnificent view of Tunis and its background of mountains is obtained, while the near distance is made picturesque by the pleasing outline of the Bab-el-Falla, out of which shoots up erect a stately palm-tree. The track now enters an extensive salt marsh, formerly a lake, and which an enterprising speculator endeavoured some years ago to fill up and reclaim. But the salt water always rises, more or less according to the time of year, and the scheme was given up as impracticable. Three kilomètres further brought us to the vast ruined palace (mentioned in a previous chapter) erected some thirty-five years ago by Ahmed Bey at a cost of about half a million sterling, and called after him the Mohammedia. It is a curious custom that forbids one ruler to occupy the house of his predecessor, a custom that by its extravagance has contributed as much as anything else to the downfall of the Regency. The palace with its outbuildings, covering many acres, has been dismantled and abandoned. The gardens, planted with groves of orange and fig-trees, and once gay with the bright colouring of tropical vegetation, is now a wilderness—the home of the jackal, or a rough shelter for a few Bedouin families. The country beyond this is a dreary waste, once a region of extraordinary fertility, but now desolate and uninhabited. Through the centre of it marches in stately grandeur the long line of piers and arches that in Roman times brought the abundant waters of Zaghouan and Djougar to the cities of Carthage and Tunis, fertilising in its course, by a proper system of irrigation, a tract of country embracing several hundred square miles.

Perhaps there is no monument ever erected by these old Romans that is stamped in a higher degree with the impress of Imperial will, or that exemplifies so strongly the force of the Roman character, as this so-called aqueduct of Carthage. We know it was a work of necessity, that it was conceived by the Emperor Hadrian on the occasion of his first visit to Africa, A.D. 123, and there is reason to believe that it was not finally completed till the reign of Septimius Severus, seventy years later. Through the greater part of its course it was subterranean, but where it passed over this plain of the Oued Melian, as well as the adjoining plain of the Oued Medjerda and other depressed surfaces, it was carried on a series of arches, varying in height with the fall of the ground. 'The waters flow to Carthage,' says El-Bekri, 'on ranges of arches, placed one above the other, reaching even to the clouds.' The statement seems exaggerated when speaking of that portion of the aqueduct we are now following, which does not exceed seventy feet in height; but a little further on, where it crossed the Oued Melian, the ancient Catada, there was a series of magnificent piers and arches, rising more than 120 feet above the river. These were standing a few years ago in all their grandeur, useless, it is true, for the purpose of carrying water, but a fitting monument of a great people and a dignified memorial of a beneficent work. As an apology for its wanton destruction by a French engineer attached to the Government of the Bey, we are told that a new bridge was required at this spot, that the ancient work obstructed the flow of the river, and its materials were of use for the purposes of reconstruction. Not only here, but in the Medjerda valley also, which is traversed by the Tunisian railway, there is the same thoughtlessness and disregard for this ancient monument. In the latter case a long line of piers and arches has been broken near the centre to allow the passage of the line of rails. A slight deviation in both cases would have prevented these acts of Vandalism. The construction of the aqueduct varies in different parts of its course. In the plain of the Melian, where quarries were not far distant, it is beautifully constructed with magnificent blocks of limestone, each being two feet in height; but in the Medjerda valley, far removed from any stone quarries, the soil of the plain mixed with lime forms the material with which the piers and the superstructure are built. The method employed here was that of building in sections, after the manner of modern

THE AQUEDUCT OF CARTHAGE

concrete construction, known to the Romans, who learnt this system from their predecessors, the Carthaginians. In the view of the aqueduct here given these sections, three feet eight inches high, are clearly shown, as well as the thick layer of mortar between each section, and the ends of the slight framework of olive-wood for stiffening the fabric at intervals. The channel or duct that conveyed the water was three feet wide and about six feet high, vaulted over, and with openings at intervals for ventilation and for the purpose of cleaning.

Shortly after passing the Oued Melian we reached Magaran, a post-house on the line of the aqueduct. Here the ducts from the course at Zaghouan, as well as from that at Djougar, some twenty miles distant, meet, the two waters flowing thence to Tunis in one conduit. The extension of the modern aqueduct follows the line of the original work, iron pipes underground being substituted for the original channels.*

We now approached the little town of Zaghouan, situated on the northern slopes of the mountain of that name. It is a pleasant spot, embosomed in gardens of orange and fig-trees, a wilderness of cactus, myrtle, rose,

---

* 'The total length of the aqueduct was sixty-one Roman miles, and it was estimated to have conveyed upwards of 7,000,000 gallons of water a-day, or eighty-one gallons per second, for the supply of Carthage and the intermediate country. M. Collin, a French engineer, planned and executed the modern water supply at Tunis. The portions of this original aqueduct that ran underground were comparatively unimpaired by time, and served, with a little repair, for the modern work. Where the old aqueduct passed high over the surface of the country iron pipes and syphons have been substituted. The contract price was 7,800,000 fr., but the work certainly cost the late Bey nearly 13,000,000 fr., and, useful as it certainly is, there is no doubt that it was the commencement of his financial difficulties.'—Sir R. L. PLAYFAIR, *Footsteps of Bruce.*

laurel, and arbutus, while here and there, standing erect in this luxuriant undergrowth, a tall palm lifts its head into the clear sky. The air is sweet with wild thyme and violet lilies. Hawks disport themselves in mid air, the eagles soar aloft, lizards lie basking in the sun, and crested larks innumerable flitter across the track. The town itself has no attractions—narrow, irregular streets, unpaved and ill cleansed, and houses that betoken an impoverished community. And yet the trade carried on here must be considerable, for it is the only place in the Regency where the knitted *chachias*, the national head-gear, are dyed. The properties of the water here appear to be particularly adapted for the purposes of dyeing.

A triumphal arch, of no special merit, still forms the principal entry to the town. Whatever public monuments may have existed in the time of the Romans have long since disappeared, and the stones reused in the building of the more modern Arab town.

We had a letter of introduction to the Chief Inspector of the waterworks at Zaghouan; but knowing him to be absent, and his house being at some distance, we sought accommodation in a half-ruined dwelling belonging to a Frenchman, who combined the business of inn-keeping in a very moderate way with that of baking bread for the few soldiers quartered in the town. The place had some pretensions, having originally formed the harem, or women's apartment, of a large Arab house. The walls of the principal chamber were covered with Moorish tile-work and the ceiling trabeated. With this exception all else was dilapidated. The cooking, such as it was, had to be done in the open courtyard. A shed answered for the bakery, and a small loft, scarcely weathertight, with ill-fitting door and window, served as a sleeping apart-

RUINED TEMPLE ZAGHOUAN

ment for ourselves and M. Carbonaro, junior, of the British Consulate at Tunis, who accompanied us on this excursion.

The afternoon of our arrival at Zaghouan was spent in an excursion, two and a half kilomètres distant, to the famous spring which, issuing from the mountain of that name, supplied water to Carthage, as it still does to Tunis. Here are the ornate remains of a temple in the centre of the arc of a semicircular colonnade. The area in front, ninety-four feet wide and eighty-six feet long, was paved with large flat stones. The spring flowed under this area, passing into a basin shaped like a double horseshoe, to which there was access by a flight of steps at either end. Here commenced the conduits in connection with the great aqueduct and the branch channels for the supply of the adjacent town and the irrigation of the land.

A wedding ceremony enlivened the evening of our sojourn in this dreary village. A procession of some dozen women bearing torches and accompanied by a posse of children, mostly relatives of the bride, were proceeding to the residence of the bridegroom to congratulate (or condole with) him on his approaching marriage. As they passed through the streets they uttered the most plaintive wailings, which did not cease on their entering the door. We were told that their lamentations (or expressions of joy) would be continued throughout the night—a statement the truth of which our curiosity was not sufficiently eager to verify.

Strolling out early the following morning we found some little excitement had been created by the arrest of an Arab on the charge of stealing a neighbour's donkey. Incidents of this kind become a source of amusement to these usually quiescent people, shouting, screaming, gesticulating, and doing everything that could be done to make matters worse, if not for the reputed owner, at least for the unfortunate ass, whose bridle was jerked first one way and then the other. All this was going on in a steep street almost too narrow to turn round in. A few old men of the place were giving gratuitous advice, and perhaps would have continued to give it to the present time if the town policeman had not arrived, and led the thief away to the common prison. And what a prison! A closed cell or stall in the stable where our horses were sheltered! A rough padlock secured the door, and a square hole in the panel enabled passers-by to exchange greetings or maledictions with the unfortunate occupant.

From Zaghouan there is a carriage-road southward to Kairouan by way of Djougar. The preferable mode of reaching Kairouan is by way of Sousa. (See Chap. XVII.)

At 8 a.m. we started for the ruins of Oudena, a distance of about twenty-four kilomètres in a northerly direction. This is a pleasant drive through a beautiful undulating country, covered with olive-groves, and presenting charming views of mountain scenery. The population of this region is purely nomadic. There are no indications of any settlements. We met a body of these nomads, consisting of two men and twenty-four women of various ages, all on foot, and the usual accompaniment of baggage-camels and donkeys. The women, especially the younger ones, were well dressed, with a profusion of silver jewelry and 'charms' round their necks or on their arms. Their faces, as customary with Bedouins, were uncovered, and after a little parleying

through our friendly interpreter, M. Carbonaro, they came close to the carriage that we might examine their gaudy decorations.*

At 11 a.m. we neared the upland on which the ruins of Oudena, the ancient Uthina, were clearly visible; and in the absence of either tree or shrub to afford shelter from the sun's rays, we improvised our breakfast-table under the shadow of the carriage. Then ascending the hill on foot for about a mile, the remains of this great town, covering several hills, were spread before us. Here can be traced the walls of temples, basilicas, and other public buildings. The ruined theatre, the stone seats of the amphitheatre lying in the hollow between two hills, the broken aqueduct, huge cisterns covering more than an acre of ground, long lines of walls and towering masses of rubble, give some faint idea of the extent and importance of the city of Uthina in the days of the Romans. All has been neglected and long since overthrown. The jackal glides stealthily amongst the fallen masonry, and some half-dozen Bedouin families find shelter in the cisterns and the overthrown theatre. There is no finer position for a city in all Tunisia.

Regaining the carriage, which we had sent on to the ruined bridge over the Oued Melian that skirted the ancient city, we soon reached the Mohammedia we had passed the previous day, and in less than two hours arrived in Tunis.

---

* Although classed as nomads, these Bedouins have certain settlements called 'Douars,' which are nothing more than 'a number of tents, whose inhabitants are generally subject to the oldest and richest Bedouins. Several " Douars," sometimes many miles distant from each other, form a Ferka (section), which is governed by a Sheik. Every Bedouin tribe, of which there are a great many, has, according to its size, several Ferkas, which together are subject to a common head—the Caïd.'—HESSE WARTEGG, *Tunis*, p. 245.

CHAPTER VIII.

TUNIS TO BOU-CHATER.

November 6th, 1885.

OUR JOURNEY CURTAILED BY BAD WEATHER—SEBBALA—THE WAYWARD MEDJERDA—REGULUS AND THE SERPENT—UNCERTAINTY OF AGRICULTURAL PURSUITS—THE LONE LAND—LOST IN THE MARSH—UTICA THE ELDER SISTER OF CARTHAGE—THE CISTERNS—THE FARM—A KIND RECEPTION—UTICA PAST AND PRESENT—FINE WEATHER AGAIN—RETURN TO TUNIS.

INCESSANT rain the previous night augured ill for an excursion to Bou-Chater; and when the carriage, with six small horses, was at the door of the hotel at 7 a.m., another downpour caused us to hesitate about undertaking the journey. We had intended, after visiting the site of Utica, to proceed to Porto Farina, on the north-east coast, where Sir R. L. Playfair (who was making a consular tour in that district) had kindly undertaken to convey us in the gunboat placed at his disposal as far as Bizerta. After making a circuit of the remarkable lake there, we proposed to return to Tunis by way of the Arab town of Mater. Notwithstanding the bad weather and the terrible state of the roads we started soon after 8 a.m., and skirting the walls of the Bardo outside the town, soon entered an extensive olive wood several miles in length. At 10 a.m. we passed on the left a small stone-built fountain, embellished with shafts and capitals from some Roman edifice, and with a rest-house attached to it, as is

SEBALA

usual in the Regency. Leaving the olive plantations we entered upon a tract of open country, and at 11 a.m. halted at a charming spot known as Sebbala (the Fountain). This is an Arab construction in the form of a loggia with four arches, the shafts and capitals being of white marble. A great drinking-trough stands in front of it, and behind, at either end, is a small café and a shop. Clusters of cypresses, hedges of prickly pear and arbutus, and a tangle of luxurious evergreen, give a colouring to this pretty spot that, on our return in the bright sunshine the following day, was a welcome change from the marshy and scrub-covered plains of the country beyond. A gathering of some twenty Arabs, drinking coffee or playing cards, prevented by the rain from continuing their outdoor employment, enlivened the scene; while camels and donkeys were wending their way here, either for shelter or refreshment. In another hour and a half, after traversing a broad marsh, we approached the banks of the Oued Medjerda, spanned at this point by a modern bridge of seven arches, and at the foot of which is a small rest-house.

This stream, the most important of the rivers of Tunisia, is associated with numerous remarkable events in the early history of this country, and is linked with many of the myths and fables that have been interwoven in the traditions of the primitive inhabitants. The story of Regulus and his affrighted soldiers, striving in vain against the monstrous serpent that haunted the banks of this river Bagradas, is an old-world legend not difficult of explanation by the modern traveller. Stretching serpent-like along the plain that extends from the Numidian mountains to the eastern coast of Tunisia, never visible till you reach the verge of its steep banks, winding and twisting in a way that can only be explained by a study of the friable nature of the soil, no wonder that this stream, one day a dry bed, the next a rushing torrent of water, rendered yellow by sandy mud, became the seat of a superstition, till at last it assumed a living form. Scarcely 300 miles in its entire length, and not more than 100 yards wide at the point where we were now crossing, it is of no value for purposes of navigation. It has many tributaries, but, with few exceptions, they are mountain streams dried up in the summer months. The eccentricities of this river have been a puzzle to geographers. At the commencement of the Christian era it emptied itself into the sea some few miles north of Carthage. Four times since that period it has shifted its outlet, and now at the present day it debouches sluggishly close to Porto Farina, many miles northward.*

The uncertainty attending agricultural pursuits in the vicinity of this wayward river can be illustrated by what happened recently to a merchant of Tunis, who had purchased the olive crop near a small town lying on the eastern slopes of the Medjerda valley. On the occasion of his visit, previous to gathering the fruit, the rainy season had set in; the waters rose and gradually submerged the trees, while the unfortunate owner, looking on, was unable to stir for a whole fortnight on account of the impassable condition of the country.

The flat region we now traversed was formerly covered by the sea. So marked are the confines of the Mediterranean here, that there is no difficulty in recognising the ancient coast line. The forlorn aspect of any low-lying land, once covered by water, is here intensified

---

* For full information respecting the geography of the Medjerda valley the reader should consult the work entitled *Exploration scientifique de la Tunisie, par Charles Tissot. Tome I. Géographie.* Paris, 1884. 4to.

by the absence of trees or shrubs of any kind, as far as the eye can compass. It might well be called the Lone Land. It happened that on the previous day the wife of the farm-bailiff we were about to visit a few miles further on was journeying over this marsh from Tunis, with her little children and an Arab guide. She had come direct from the South of France, and had, probably, associated her new home in North Africa with tropical vegetation and welcome shade. The track was obscured, mud and slimy grass clogged the horses' feet, and the little party was unable to proceed. Night came on, and the anxious husband, accompanied by his labourers, scoured the damp marsh, lantern in hand; and, before the morning broke, succeeded in finding his family, worn out with hunger and fatigue.

At 2.30 we crossed a tributary of the Medjerda, spanned by a modern bridge. So accustomed are the natives here to fording the streams that our driver took no notice of the bridge, but dashed through the river, in which, fortunately, there was but little water. A gradual ascent of about five kilomètres brought us to a group of farm buildings clustered round some Roman cisterns, and in the vicinity of several low hills. This is Bou-Chater, the site of Utica, one of the oldest-known cities of the world, and commonly called the elder sister of Carthage of the Phœnicians.*

Through the kindness of the resident-bailiff at this

---

* 'Founded twelve centuries before the Christian era, Utica may claim to be one of the oldest colonies that the Phœnicians from Tyre established on the African coast. It preserved its independence during the rise of Carthage. After the first Punic war it suffered at the hands of Carthage, in consequence of having taken part in an insurrection against its younger sister. The territory was ravaged at a later period, and the city besieged by Scipio during the second Punic war by land and sea. It submitted to Rome at the commencement of the third

farm (which consists of many thousands of acres leased to a wealthy and enterprising French capitalist), we obtained a comfortable lodging for the night, and, having brought a good stock of provisions, we were better off than the misty atmosphere and terrible state of the roads led us to hope. The rain ceased at sunset, and the prospects of fair weather on the morrow were encouraging. Any attempt to continue the journey to Porto Farina was out of the question, as the track beyond Bou-Chater was quite impassable. An early visit to the great cisterns—two of which have been repaired and converted into magnificent farm stables, each 120 feet long and 19 feet wide—and a survey of the site of the ancient city from the higher ground formerly occupied by the citadel, occupied three or four hours of the following morning. The city was built on a promontory, and was enclosed with a wall of great strength and solidity. It contained a large harbour for war vessels, with a palace for the Admiral or Governor in the centre, a citadel, an amphitheatre, numerous temples, and an immense arsenal. 'The adjacent country,' says Cæsar, in his *Commentaries*, 'is of great fertility. The trees supply plenty of timber. The fields are covered with corn, and there is water in abundance.' What a mighty change! No longer a promontory, for the sea has receded some six or seven miles. No wall of defence that took Scipio and his gallant soldiers four whole years before they succeeded in scaling it, but long lines of

---

Punic war, and after the destruction of Carthage became the metropolis of Africa and the residence of the Roman proconsul. Cato resisted Julius Cæsar here, and, fortune favouring his great rival, put an end to his own life within the walls. On the rebuilding of Carthage Utica lost its position. It afterwards became a great centre of Christianity, but was finally destroyed by the Arabs in the seventh century.'—V. GUÉRIN, *Voyage*, tom. ii. 11.

RUINS OF UTICA

earthen mounds and half-buried masonry. No war harbour, but tufts of reeds with masses of walling peeping out here and there to mark the quays, that once were above the water line. No palatial edifice on an island in the centre, but a confused heap of rubble, two pillars alone standing up erect in defiance of wind and weather and the ravages of time. No citadel, but two whitened koubbas of saintly Mohammedans to mark the highest ground. No amphitheatre, but a great hollow of shapely form between two hills, with an arena of green turf and banks of seats clothed with herbage. No temples or public monuments, but fragments of marble, *frusta* of shafts, and great blocks of hewn stone. The plough passes ruthlessly over these green hills and marshy lands, literally turning up marble—the marble of the palaces and temples of Roman Utica. The older city of the Phœnicians, awaiting the spade of the explorer, lies below.*

We left Bou-Chater at midday in bright sunshine, with pleasant thoughts of an agreeable visit and of much kindness shown us by the manager of the farm. Notwithstanding the wretched condition of the track after heavy rain, we were back again in Tunis, after six hours' quick locomotion.

---

* The principal works relating to Utica and the river Medjerda will be found under the heads of Daux, d'Hérisson, and Tissot, in *The Bibliography*.

CHAPTER IX.

TUNIS TO SOUSSA.

November 8th and 9th.

OUR START — OUR CONVEYANCE — STATE OF THE 'ROADS' — HAMMAM-EL-LIF — SOLIMAN IN THE DISTANCE — GROUMBELIA — TOURKI — BIR-EL-BOUITA — A TUNISIAN FONDOUK — KASR-EL-MENARA — SEBKHA-DJIRIBA — HERGLAH — SEBKHA-HALK-EL-MENZEL — TRAVELLING WITH A LANTERN — APHRODISIUM — MIRAGES.

THE journey from Tunis to Soussa is usually performed by sea, the steamer leaving the former place on the afternoon of one day, and reaching its destination the following morning. The journey by land, which we accomplished in two days, affords an opportunity of seeing a considerable stretch of country, and charming views of the whole coast line. Leaving our luggage at the hotel, and taking handbags, wrappers, waterproof sheeting, and provisions, we started early on the morning of November the 8th in a carriage drawn by four small horses. The hackney-carriages of Tunisia are not remarkable for elegance or comfort. A kind of low glass case, furnished with two small windows, is placed on the top of a rough, double-seated vehicle, thus forming a closed conveyance, which cannot be converted into an open one without entirely removing the superposed glass box. Nor, when both windows are shut, is it possible to alight except with assistance from without, as the windows and doors, being in separate pieces, do not open together; and the former, whether open or closed, are fastened from the outside.

The rain, which had fallen heavily on the previous night, had rendered the roads in some parts barely passable. We use the word *road*, and must continue to do so for want of a more appropriate term. In point of fact there are not, throughout the whole of Tunisia, any roads at all as we in Europe understand them, but simply tracks, such as have been used by the natives from time immemorial with their droves of camels, mules, and cattle; following in most instances the more permanent roads that were formed by the Romans during their occupation of the country. From Tunis to Hammam-el-Lif a road is in course of construction, but was not in a sufficiently advanced state to be serviceable, so that it was necessary to take the open fields on either side, making progress somewhat tedious.

In a bracing air, tempered by the bright rays of the morning sun, we drove through the Bab-el-Djezirah, and, leaving the modern racecourse on our left, passed, after an hour's drive, a well-designed fountain with two marble shafts, and forming a loggia in front of a rest-house. For about three miles the track continued over an olive-covered plain, our little horses dragging their load wearily at foot pace through the mud and slush that reached almost up to the boxes of the wheels; the range of hills, on a spur of which Hammam-el-Lif is situated, towering up in front of us, and appearing to bar our passage.

Crossing the Oued Melian over a recently constructed bridge, we entered a track of country in better cultivation, dotted with plantations of olive and cactus, and an occasional palm-tree with wells at frequent intervals. On rounding the hill close to the seashore we found ourselves suddenly in the main street of Hammam-el-Lif, the ancient Mascula. As its name indicates, this is a bathing-place, with warm springs issuing from the hills, and is a favourite summer resort both for health and pleasure. It can scarcely be called a village, for it consists of a royal palace and a few bath-houses, almost deserted during the winter months. Both palace and houses are built of rubble, whitewashed, and are altogether unattractive and devoid of any architectural pretensions. The situation, however, in the centre of the Bay of Tunis, is very beautiful, commanding an uninterrupted view of the entire sweep of the seashore—Radès, Gouletta, the hill of Carthage, and the bold headland of Sidi-Bou-Saïd. Pushing on at once, we soon entered a vast marsh, covering the space intervening between the hills and the sea; here commences the celebrated Enfida estate, the disputed ownership of which may be said to have brought about the French Protectorate. It is bounded by the towns of Hammamet, Zaghouan, Kairouan, and Soussa, having an area of about 250,000 acres, and a population of not less than 7000 inhabitants. The entire property was sold to the *Société Franco-Africaine* in 1879, by Kheir-ed-din, Prime Minister of Tunis, and is still in their possession. The marsh was in parts parcelled out with stakes and wire fencings, as if for enclosure, but no trace of a road or track was anywhere discernible to the eye of the uninitiated. Over this swamp we toiled for a full hour, and after passing, on the right, a large, square drinking-fountain, with running water brought down from the hills, and further on to the left, a dome-shaped well, we at last reached firmer ground, and were once more within sight of olive-groves and other signs of cultivation. Soon, on our left, gleaming in the bright sunlight, stood out the whitened walls of the Arab town of Soliman, its minarets and snow-white cupolas outlined sharp and clear, and framed in the deep blue of the receding hills. A short distance further brought us to a small dilapidated well on the left, with a ruined building behind it. At a quarter-past 12 o'clock we reached the most noted fountain of these parts, the Bir-el-Bey, near which are some Roman ruins of no great importance, and gardens in fair cultivation; altogether a pretty spot. At half-past 1 p.m. a magnificent olive-grove was traversed, and the road, becoming drier and firmer, we hoped that our difficulties of locomotion were at an end; but, alas! they were soon to begin again, more unpleasantly than before. Shortly before 2 p.m. we entered the village of Groumbelia, and here we supposed our jaded beasts would be allowed to enjoy the rest they sorely needed; but the driver appeared to know better, for after an interval of a few minutes off we started again. Groumbelia is a collection of straggling, unattractive huts, and is altogether a poor place. In twenty minutes we reached Tourki, a miserable village, with a dilapidated well and gardens hedged in with prickly pears, and surrounded by olive-groves. We now observed, scattered over the fields to right and left of the track, some thirty or more large blocks of cut stone, remains of some Roman buildings; but on examination we failed to discover any inscriptions, or a clue to the name of the place. At 3.15 p.m. we crossed the river Tebournok, now dry and bridgeless, and a few minutes later observed, to our right, at about a mile from the road and on rising ground, the ruins of a fortress, apparently of Byzantine construction, with a koubba in the middle of an olive-garden. Here the pasture seemed rich, and flocks were abundant. Shortly before 4 o'clock we passed over the dry bed of the Oued Defla, close to a picturesque well with a cluster of palm-trees, and immediately afterwards, to our right, the remains of a Roman town on the banks of another dry watercourse. In another half hour we reached the Bir-el-Arbaïn, or 'Well of the Forty,' and, as the sun was nearing the horizon, entered a vast forest of arbutus, juniper, dwarf pines, furze, and other shrubs. This is a wild and romantic district. A good ten miles had still to be accomplished before reaching our night's quarters, and, as our horses were quite tired out, the prospect of being benighted in this wilderness was not agreeable. However, our coachman urged on without intermission his sturdy little animals, and at half-past 6 o'clock, as darkness was closing round us, we drove into the fondouk of Bir-el-Bouïta.*

The scenery between Tunis and Bir-el-Bouïta is nowhere grand, but it is diversified—at times picturesque, at others exceedingly wild; the route was animated by strings of camels, Arabs on mules and donkeys, carts loaded with merchandise, and an occasional carriage like our own; the air was clear and

---

* V. Guérin, who, in February 1860, followed the same route, and to whose admirable and erudite work we would refer our readers for a more detailed description of the district, was much struck with this wild and lonely spot. He writes:—' From the roof of the caravansary I gaze for a long time on the surrounding scene, illumined by a magnificent moon. On one side, the little town of Hammamet, with its gardens and its gulf; on the other, a vast wood in all its solitude, lie unrolled before me. The silence of the night is broken only by the plaintive cries of the jackals, answered by the barking of dogs from a neighbouring douar. As long as I was in Tunis, in the European quarter, I had not, so to say, entirely left Europe; here I am, indeed, in the heart of Africa.'— *Voyage*, i. 81.

genial, and a good road was alone wanting to render the journey enjoyable. Considering the importance of the traffic between Tunis and Soussa, the chief commercial towns in the beylik, it seems incredible that no proper road should exist.

The fondouk at Bir-el-Bouïta, which, in comparison with other similar establishments in this country, is of a luxurious description, struck us, notwithstanding, as by no means a comfortable lodging. The Tunisian caravansary closely resembles the rest-house of North China, consisting simply of a large square court-yard, surrounded by a number of small apartments or cells, all opening into it; the former destined for quadrupeds, the latter for their owners. No furniture of any kind is to be found in these wretched hovels, nor is any accommodation procurable. In the fondouk of Bir-el-Bouïta, on the other hand, the human habitations, some six or eight in number, are on an upper floor, and open on to a flat roof; they are consequently well away from the animals. Further, they are furnished with a bed-settle and rough mattress, a rickety table, and a chair or two. The Arab who had charge of this establishment was profuse in his attentions, and desirous of giving satisfaction to the utmost extent of his very limited means. He brought us some live charcoal in an earthen pot, an amphora filled with very doubtful water, and a couple of empty bottles to serve as candlesticks. This done, he left us with a satisfied look, as if he would have said: What more can the noble travellers possibly require? We cooked our modest supper from the provisions we had brought with us, regaled ourselves with a cup of tea, and, rolling ourselves up in our rugs, soon fell asleep.

The next morning a brilliant sun awoke us to the

pleasant consciousness of another glorious day, and, getting the horses out at sunrise, we were on our way again before seven—the air chilly, but clear and invigorating. Our route ran but a short distance from the seashore, vestiges of Roman buildings being everywhere visible landward. In half an hour we reached a Roman mausoleum, now called by the Arabs, Kasr-el-Menara, or 'The Lighthouse.' Its situation on the gentle slope of a hill, and in close proximity to the sea, suggested to them, no doubt, the idea that in former days it might have been used as a beacon; but of this there is no evidence. It is of circular form, about 48 feet in diameter, and stands on a square base: the present height may be estimated at 34 feet. Altogether, this monument bears a strong resemblance, though on a smaller scale, to the tomb of Cecillia Metella, near Rome. Shaw, the traveller, speaks of three inscriptions, or votive tablets, to be seen on the face-work; but these have entirely disappeared, as well as nearly every block of facing-stone that the Arabs could remove with the aid of their miserable implements.

From the numerous Roman remains in the vicinity of this monument, it would appear that the whole district was once thickly populated. Here we observed several bushes covered with shreds of rag, which we had not before noticed in Tunisia, although the custom is common in Algeria.* At a quarter-past 8 o'clock we crossed the Oued-el-Kenatir, over a modern bridge of two arches, by the side of which are the ruins of one of Roman construction of twelve arches, showing how much more important the river must have been formerly, and how

---

* Consult *Mœurs, Coutumes et Institutions des Indigènes de l'Algérie*, par le Capitaine Villot. Constantine, 1871.

entirely the face of the country has changed since the time of the Roman occupation. Indeed, not only here, but along the whole coast of Tunisia, alterations of surface during many centuries, changes in the shore-line and the formation of marshlands, owing to long neglect of the courses of rivers and of mountain streams, have altered the aspect of the country, and rendered the identification of ancient towns a matter of considerable difficulty. Another modern bridge of three arches spanning the Oued Crosha was crossed at 9 a.m. At this point the road branches off; that to the right in the direction of Sidi-Khalifa, the ancient Aphrodisium, the Arab town of Dar-el-Bey; that to the left, over a flat marsh lying between the sea and the shallow lagoon, in that of Sebkha-Djiriba; both uniting again at Herglah. We had instructed our driver to take the former track, because it followed the old Roman road, and, although a longer route, was preferable to a journey over the marsh. In this country one cannot travel without reliable maps. What is more important still, you must rely upon yourself and not trust to the natives, even for ordinary information; if you do, you will probably discover the error when it is too late to rectify it. For more than five hours did we plod wearily over this terrible marsh; our courageous little horses moving at a walking pace, and frequently coming to a standstill through sheer inability, without the aid of the driver and his companion, to extricate the wheels, half-spoke deep, from the tenacious mud. As for ourselves, we preferred to lighten the vehicle, and, for nearly two-thirds of the distance, proceeded on foot, dragging one leg after the other wearily enough, and then resting for a few seconds to brush off the clinging mud against the rough scrub that dotted the marsh at short intervals. Along this portion of the route, frequently below the sea level, there is nothing whatever of interest. About midway there is a French military post (a rest-house, we suppose, for benighted travellers), and further on we passed a cheering object to break the monotony of the journey—a dead donkey, while troops of flamingos were disporting themselves on the banks of the lake. At 3 p.m. we halted before a fountain at the foot of the rising ground on which the small Arab town of Herglah stands. For eight long hours had our poor horses been plodding along without a moment's rest, a drop of water, or a mouthful of food. The indomitable courage and endurance of these wiry little animals are marvellous. Here, at the well, women were drawing water, while others were going to and fro with large amphoras gracefully poised on their heads or shoulders.

A miserable village is Herglah, altogether unattractive; and yet to one emerging from the desolation of the marsh over which we had just passed it presented itself almost as an oasis. Although the soil consists of nothing but sand, the village is surrounded by olive-gardens, groups of cactus remarkable for their venerable appearance, and numerous low green bushes, bearing a small yellow fruit, in appearance not unlike diminutive lemons. This is the Horrea Cœlia of the Romans, and was once a busy sea-port. Here we remained an hour to rest our horses.

Leaving Herglah at 4 o'clock we soon reached, over a stony road, the banks of Sebkah-Halk-el-Menzel, another shallow lake; and at Oued-Kenatir, further on, we crossed a bridge approached on both sides by a long paved causeway. It was now 5 o'clock, and the sun was already sinking below the horizon; we were fortunately on firmer ground, but still at a considerable distance from our destination. In these latitudes twilight is unknown, and darkness sets in almost immediately after sundown. Our driver seemed doubtful about the road, or was perhaps anxious as to our safety, for he caused his attendant to alight and go forward with a lantern. In this manner, and with horses thoroughly tired out, we moved at a walking pace, thankful to arrive at the gates of Soussa at 8 p.m.

We had accomplished a long day's journey (thirteen hours), as wearisome and tedious as it was long. After leaving the Kasr-el-Menara we had encountered absolutely nothing of interest, and had to bear the disappointment of seeing on the opposite side of the marshy lake the site and some of the ruins of the ancient town of Aphrodisium. The town, of which there are numerous remains, extended for nearly a mile. Beautifully situated on several low hills, and surrounded by olive-woods and gardens in high cultivation, it attracted the attention of the Vandal kings, and remained a royal residence till the armies of Belisarius cleared the land of this scourge of North Africa. Aphrodisium is now a confused mass of stone and rubble. The palace is marked by an enclosure constructed with huge blocks of stone; its triumphal arches, with the exception of one which has no special features, are overthrown; the temple, supposed to have been dedicated to Aphrodite, is scarcely traceable; weeds choke the stream that once ran pleasantly through the town; the surrounding woods and gardens have disappeared, and miles of swamp and reeds hide the line of the seashore.

Possibly in the summer, when the soil is dry, travelling over the Djiriba marsh may be attended with less difficulty and inconvenience; but as no water is procurable, and as it is without shade or any habitation except the military station already noted, it must be an unpleasant track to traverse at all seasons *—in winter, or after heavy rains, it is absolutely dangerous. The traveller by road should always take the other track before mentioned.

---

* V. Guérin, who, following the same route as we had done, but early in the month of February, was inconvenienced by heat and gnats. Mme. de Voisins speaks of the wonderful mirages which are frequently to be observed on the marsh. She affirms that on one occasion, while passing over it, she, her servant, and her horse, were repeated *ad infinitum*, the three alone forming, as it were, an interminable caravan, while on the horizon there appeared a grove of palms and a city. We ourselves can bear testimony to this last illusion. A great white city, on the banks of a distant lake, was clearly outlined on the horizon.

ENTRANCE TO THE KASBA, SUSA.

CHAPTER X.

SOUSSA, THE ANCIENT HADRUMETUM.
November 10th and 11th.

A SORRY PLACE — AN AGREEABLE RECEPTION — ROMAN SHAFTS — KOUBBAS—DOORWAYS—ARAB JEALOUSY OF RELIGIOUS BUILDINGS—SOUKS — FLIES — DRESSES OF THE WOMEN — ARAB MUSIC — THE MARABOUT CAFÉ—THE 'MARSEILLAISE'—ARAB POLITENESS—STORY-TELLING—A BOUQUET.

IN spite of its commercial importance and proportionate wealth, Soussa, the second town in the Regency, is a disappointing place, offering neither resource nor attractions for the traveller. From the sea, as we had afterwards the opportunity of observing, its aspect is remarkable, rising like a whitened pyramid from above the water's edge, and culminating as usual in the walls of the Kasba and the elevated watch-tower of the citadel. Once within its gates all the charm is dispelled. It is enclosed with a crenelated wall common to all Tunisian cities, and entered through several gates, some of which, especially that giving access to the quays, are curious and characteristic. Its streets, narrow, tortuous, and ill kept, lead from an open space in close proximity to the harbour, where the European hotel is situated, past a mosque in no respect remarkable, up to the Kasba, the chief feature of which is a painted gateway more curious than beautiful. The view from the Kasba is very extensive, and embraces an illimitable sweep of land and water.

Our first visit was to Captain Hélouis of the staff,

for whom we had letters of introduction, and who received us with that urbanity which we experienced at the hands of every French officer with whom we came in contact throughout Tunisia, furnishing us with maps and much valuable information for our journey into the interior. The reception was the more agreeable as the captain is a perfect master of the English language. Having determined upon our future operations, as far as anything could be determined beforehand in a country in which travelling forms more or less a chapter of accidents, we found no difficulty in filling up the two spare days at our disposal.

Here, as in Tunis and other towns of the Regency, the angles of buildings are frequently formed with shafts from some Roman temple or other monumental work. We know that the Romans had an architecture of their own, and adopted a style by which their presence has been identified at some period or other in various parts of the then known world. It is equally certain that the Arabs, who have possessed this country for more than twelve centuries, have not only for a long period evinced little knowledge of building construction, but have shown an utter disregard for beauty of form, and even for fitness, in all their later edifices, whether public or private. Not unfrequently one meets with Roman shafts reversed, the richly carved capital, whether of stone or marble, forming a base for some other piece of purloined material, or for a superstructure of stone and earth, put together at random, the ill-constructed mass being coated over with the never-failing whitewash.

There is no single building in Soussa, public or private, of modern times, to arrest the traveller's attention. Even the Grand Mosque may be passed by without the stranger knowing that it is a mosque. One or two

A KOUBBA, SOUSSA.

koubbas are curious, and the doorways of the larger houses have frequently some merit of design. None of these can be classed as modern works. The doorways of Soussa are, as a rule, different in design from those either at Tunis or Sfax, leading one to suppose that during a certain period of Arab history, many centuries ago, a traditional treatment was observed. In the example we have given the quaint form of the upper lintel, with its rich carvings and the arched recesses over it, produces an effect that is far from disagreeable. The door of olive-wood is painted red and green, the colours of the Prophet. The other devices, including the crescent, the star, and the sword of Mahomet, being painted white, on either a red or green ground.

The jealousy with which the Arabs guard their sacred buildings from the profane touch, or even look, of the unbeliever, may be illustrated by what happened to us when making a drawing of this doorway. It is that of a mausoleum of some marabout, or holy man; and through the small grated windows on either side of the door can be seen the saint's sarcophagus surrounded by banners and other paraphernalia. While this sketch was in progress, the shutters with which the windows are provided were suddenly closed from within, so that our view of the interior was cut off.

The souks, with less display than those of Tunis, are equally busy and characteristic. The costumes and types which one meets with, however, are less diversified, and the shops seem to be chiefly in the hands of Arabs.

The great pest of Soussa is the flies; even at this cool season they were very troublesome; what they must be in summer it is painful to contemplate. They are only kept under by constant whitewashing, which goes on here even more diligently than in the capital. This also has its drawback on account of the glare, undoubtedly the cause of much of the ophthalmia and blindness so prevalent here and in other seaport towns.

The Arab women of Soussa envelop themselves in a black *bérnous* of thin woollen material, which entirely covers their heads as well as their bodies, and gives them the appearance of nuns; their faces are, of course, hidden, although they are able to see through the open texture of their head-gear. The Jewesses, on the other hand, indulge in gayer apparel here than elsewhere, and display the beauty of both face and form with great freedom. Their costume is, in fact, so remarkable, that it will not fail to strike with astonishment every traveller who sees it for the first time.*

---

* Rather than attempt a more minute description of the female costumes seen in Tunisia, we prefer to offer our readers the details furnished by a lady, whose knowledge of such matters must of necessity be superior to our own. Mme. de Voisins writes: 'The women have not, like those of Algeria, the wide Turkish trousers, reaching to the ankles, but tights (*un maillot*). They do not wear the white *kaik*, or *k'ssa*, under which the Moors in Algeria have something mysterious and attractive, but a frightful black veil, *adjar*, enveloping their head, the upper part of the body, and which they hold stretched out by extending their arms horizontally on a level with the waist, in order to enable them to see where they are walking, a fashion as ungraceful as it is inconvenient. Thus attired, in the streets they have the appearance of veritable bundles.

'The countrywomen (*femmes des tentes*) are clothed, like the Bedouins of the province of Constantine, in a wide gown (*sazou*) of wool or cotton, reaching down to the knees, attached at the waist by a girdle, a bit of cord, a leather strap, or, unheard-of luxury! by a silk handkerchief rolled up. This gown serves them, at one and the same time, as a shift, a petticoat, and a robe; they have neither stockings nor shoes. Their headdress consists of a rag of stuff, which they wear in the Creole fashion. One can see nothing more primitive than this costume, under which these women with a copper-coloured skin, black

JEWISH GIRLS, TUNIS

In Soussa we had the opportunity of hearing Arab music, an enjoyment we had not experienced since we left Algeria. The most important native café of the place is in the centre of the souks, and consists of a large circular chamber with a high vaulted roof. It must have been originally a koubba. It is entirely without decoration, and with no other furniture than a continuous low wooden platform around the walls, one or two benches in the middle of the room, a stand with a large amphora, and a small stove for preparing the coffee. The walls are blackened by smoke, and the whole place bears the appearance of never having been swept or cleaned since it was built, very many centuries

---

eyes, white teeth, find means, nearly all of them, to look pretty, and to display forms worthy of antique statuary.

'The Israelitish women dress in a manner as little decent as it is uninviting. If I did not fear to seem puritanical, I might add that their way of dressing is emblematic of their morals, of which the laxity surpasses anything one sees in Europe; but the men, not more austere themselves, profess on this score an indulgence and a *laisser-aller* more extensive than the courtiers of the *Œil-de-Bœuf* under Louis XV. The Jewesses wear, then, in the town of Soussa, a gauze shift, light and transparent, with wide sleeves, tight round the body, and of which the lower part, very short, is hidden under a pantaloon of rich silk, or of simple calico for the women of the lower classes, fitting as closely as tights, and very richly embroidered from the part which forms the garter above the knee to the ankle, where it terminates. Over this clothing is thrown a partially closed jacket, unlined, with braces instead of sleeves to hold it at the arms, very sloping on the breast, and sufficiently open so as not to debar an indiscreet observer from distinguishing under the gauze shift those charms which it in no way conceals. The lightest silks, the brightest colours—green, pink, yellow, sky blue, cherry red—are employed for this elegant tunic. The headdress consists of a silk handkerchief worked with gold, worn in the Egyptian manner, on the top of the head, above false hair, for the Mosaic law prohibits married women from making a display of their own hair. Whatever may be their shortcomings in the practice of other ordinances, the Israelite ladies respect this precept, and procure from Paris or Marseilles

ago. On our entrance some thirty men were reclining on the benches, and the establishment might be considered fairly full; but room was at once made for us with that politeness and almost stately decorum which one cannot fail to admire among the Arabs. Three musicians occupied one of the benches, sitting in a row, cross-legged, tailor-wise. Their instruments were a mandoline, a violin, and a tambourine. He of the tambourine commenced an old Arab ditty about love and sentiment, in which, as our interpreter explained, the moon and the stars were frequently invoked. His voice was a high tenor, and he frequently broke into a

---

chignons and frontlets, which enable them to elude the severity of this prohibition. For foot-gear they have elegant high-heeled slippers (*mules*) of morocco, or of velvet embroidered with gold, adorned sometimes with precious stones.

'Such a costume surpasses all the extravagances and disguises of fairy art. At Soussa one is so accustomed to it that no one regards it with any attention. Whence does it originate? Who invented it? An Adamite without doubt, or some beautiful girl troubled by the heat of the climate, and so formed that she need not fear the most exacting scrutiny. Observers may find at Soussa ample matter to satisfy their eyes: one does not see a disproportioned body (*taille*), or a badly shaped limb. All is as it should be, according to the respective ages, and criticism is impossible. Stays, dresses fitting too tightly, and other exigencies of European fashion, have not deformed or distorted anything, the shapes are as Nature made them—admirable. The Venus of Milo is no myth at Soussa; and when I saw passing before my door women so simple, so ingenuously natural in their quasi-nudity, I asked myself which was the less indecent, their costume or that of our Parisian women, who exaggerate at one time certain parts of their body, and at another wear tightly-fitting garments, more unchaste than the nude itself.'—*Excursions dans la Régence de Tunis*, p. 146.

The above description, detailed as it is, is not altogether complete. The Jewish women frequently wear on their heads a pointed or conical-shaped silk cap, of some bright colour, embroidered with gold and stiffened with cardboard: this they keep in position by means of an embroidered silk handkerchief bound tightly round it.

falsetto. His prolongation of the notes was extraordinary, playing with them as it were, and sustaining them with a continuous *tremolo*. His own instrument was laid aside during the solo, but he was assisted by the mandoline. The accompaniment was of longer duration than the song; *i.e.*, after the voice had ceased at the end of each couplet, or verse, the instrument took up and continued the melody, playing with it as the voice had done, and varying it in a style to which we have no equivalent in Europe. The effect of a treatment so strange and novel was not in the beginning altogether pleasant; but the first shock of surprise over, and our ears somewhat accustomed to sounds so foreign to them, we listened with delight, unable to determine whether the voice or the instrument afforded the greater satisfaction. The song was classical, poetical, and thoroughly moral in sentiment. Scarcely had the solo ceased than the three musicians burst forth together in a modern, popular song, each one playing his own instrument at the same time. It differed entirely from what had just been sung, and was of a jovial, not to say boisterous, character. During the whole performance the audience displayed no emotion, no sign of approbation, or the reverse; they sat listening calmly, without moving a muscle, without a smile, without an attempt at applause. To convey to an European an exact idea of this music is most difficult, if not impossible, as it does not follow in any way the rules or methods recognised in our schools. It has, however, a rhythm and sequence which are soon understood and appreciated; the notes are slurred and blended together, and the motive appears to terminate abruptly on the leading note. The only kind of European music with which it might be compared is that of the gipsies of Hungary;

as with them no notes are used, no time is beaten, and the performance seems to be entirely by ear; it is not, however, martial, but plaintive and sentimental. With less reserve than the native portion of the audience we had more than once applauded the entertainment. This the performers seemed to appreciate, and in their turn wished to pay us a compliment. Evidently taking us for Frenchmen, they struck up the *Marseillaise;* but this we really could not suffer, and at once begged our interpreter to explain that we were English, and that the air which they were playing belonged in no way to us. They immediately changed their tune to something of a nondescript character. It could scarcely have been Arab, and it certainly was not British.

We now begged our entertainers to accept some refreshment at our expense; this they at first refused, but eventually each partook of a glass of lemonade, and, retiring with a deferential salute, departed to continue their performance at some neighbouring establishment.

There is a decorum, a self-restraint in the Arab very pleasing to contemplate. No pushing, no prying, no intrusion, no molestation of any kind. They did not seem to be disturbed by our presence, nor did any one disturb us. After a few minutes we felt as much at home as we should have done in any English place of entertainment. And yet we were probably as strange to them as a couple of Chinamen would be in a London music-hall; whether they would fare as well as we did is doubtful.

On our way home we paused for a short time before another café, where an entertainment of a different kind was being held. Through the open door we could see over the length and breadth of the room. It was quite full, or, as we should say, crammed, for squatting

Arabs, unencumbered by clothes, occupy but little space. One old Arab, with stick in hand and seated on a chair raised somewhat above the other guests, was telling a story. The same immovability of feature and apparent stoical indifference were observable on the countenances of his hearers, as we had already remarked in the café we had just quitted. As we stood before the door with that awkward stiffness which every Englishman must feel in the presence of Arabs, but of which he is unable to divest himself, the master of the establishment motioned to us to enter; this we declined, being loth to disturb the attentive listeners, and not understanding what the story-teller was narrating. Behind his right ear was a small bouquet. Offering each of us a similar posy, he saluted us with a polite bow. This custom of wearing flowers, prevalent throughout the whole of Tunisia, is as peculiar as it is charming. It is practised by the men, never by the women. The flowers used vary according to the season, rosebuds or small yellow flowers being preferred. The form of the bouquet itself never varies: it is in three stages—the top one consisting of a single flower or bud, the second of three or four, and the lower one of several. The flowers in the same bouquet are all alike. The bouquet is worn on the right side of the head, stuck under the turban, and above the ear.

CHAPTER XI.

MSAKEN.

DOUBTFUL INFORMATION—A GOOD COACHMAN—ANOTHER BOUQUET— KSIBA — A LOVELY VIEW — A CONSCIENTIOUS GUIDE — THE WALK ROUND MSAKEN—OUR DISAPPOINTMENT—THE MOSQUE—NOTHING TO SEE IN MSAKEN.

THERE is not much in Soussa to detain the traveller. Our main occupation was to acquire information as to our future movements. This accomplished, as far as its accomplishment was possible in a land of uncertainties, we found ourselves (November 11th) with a spare afternoon and a blue sky over head. Having read glowing descriptions of the town of Msaken,* an hour and a quarter's drive from Soussa, we decided to pay it a visit. These eulogies not having been confirmed by the few people in Soussa whom we had questioned, we attributed their doubtful or even negative replies to want of knowledge; and our curiosity being aroused, we determined to see for ourselves what

---

* Msaken is described by M. Reclus as a town (*bourg*), eleven kilomètres south-west of Soussa, surrounded by a thick forest of olives; it was formerly a holy place, of which the entrance was forbidden to Jews and Christians.—*Nouvelle Géographique Universelle*, xi. 228.

Madame de Voisins, who seems to pride herself more on the smartness of her style than upon the correctness of her general information, calls Msaken a '*centre de population*,' a '*lieu saint*,' and the Seville, the Padua, the Oxford, the Cologne of Tunisia. But then she had not visited the place, as she herself owns—a proof how imprudent and misleading it is to write about anything one has not seen.

Msaken was really like. We started immediately after lunch; the four horses, which were harnessed abreast to the carriage we occupied, fairly squeezed themselves through the narrow gateway of the town, and dashed past the grain-market and Arab cemetery just without the walls. They were fresh, and our coachman was evidently bent on making a good impression, and showing how well they could do their work. The balmy air and the aromatic odour of the herbs on the plain, as we emerged from the olive-groves with which Soussa is surrounded, were most enjoyable after the stuffy and not very sweet-smelling streets of the town. Our Jehu was a first-rate whip, and the skill and dexterity with which he piloted us over the roadless plain, across grips, between trees, and along the edges of precipitous banks, without overturning the vehicle, were truly marvellous. His horses understood him better than we did, for the gift of tongues had not been vouchsafed him; he was, however, possessed of the usual politeness, and as we stepped into his carriage at starting he presented us with a bouquet similar to those given us by the host of the café on the previous evening.

The first object which struck us on the road was a Roman cistern, of no great size but still in use. The French barracks at Soussa are outside the walls, adjoining the Kasbah, and consist of some twenty small brick-built houses. Passing these, after a slight ascent, we crossed an open space, from which the olives have been cleared. This is the spot where the French encamped when they took Soussa, and the marks of their tents are still traceable. One miserable village, Ksiba, is passed about half-way between Soussa and Msaken; it has two koubbas and boundless filth; one or two olive-mills attest its sole industry.

As one traverses the higher ground in this direction the view over the immense sweep of plains, partially cultivated, but for the most part covered with olive-plantations, is very striking, and eminently African.

We had not penetrated far into the town of Msaken before our driver halted in front of a small house open to the street, and not unlike a shop in the souks. Here some four or five well-dressed men were seated. Permission, it seemed, had to be obtained in order to visit the town. This was soon granted, and a one-eyed Arab of solemn demeanour was appointed to escort us. No word was spoken; like lambs we followed our stately guide through street after street under a broiling sun, or, better said, alley after alley, each one differing from the other solely in the greater or less quantity of mud and filth with which it was encumbered. Few people were astir at this hour, between 1 and 2 o'clock, when none but dogs and Christians are supposed to walk abroad. A few children, however, watched us with curiosity; and a woman or two, enveloped in coarse brown garments, passed us by on the opposite side of the street. The occasional creaking of a door drew our attention to the fact of its being ajar, and of our being gazed at by mysterious, inquisitive inmates, but of which sex it was impossible to determine. For a good half-hour had we silently, patiently, resignedly, followed our one-eyed guide, evidently a conscientious man, bent on thoroughly doing his duty—on taking us strictly and literally *round* the town. Nothing, absolutely nothing had we seen but blank walls—not a single building approaching even to mediocrity. The sun's rays were disagreeably powerful, and the mud did not always admit of our taking the shady side of the way, even when the walls were sufficiently high—not always the case—to afford any shade.

We began to make signs to our implacable conductor that we had had enough of bare walls and glare. He could not, or would not, understand our pantomime, and kept us steadily on the march, until, fortunately, as we turned a corner, we perceived our carriage at the other end of the street, and unhesitatingly made for it, leaving our *cicerone* to follow or not as he thought fit. By means of many words and more dumb show we made the solemn old gentleman, who had accorded us permission to visit the town, understand that we had in fact seen nothing—that it was the inside of the Mosque which we wished to visit, not the outside of the houses. A smile, a malicious one it appeared to us, passed over his countenance, as if he relished our discomfiture. Nevertheless, he waved his hand in the direction of the Mosque, and spoke words conveying doubtless an order that our request should be granted. In spite of this our guide seemed very loth to let us even approach the sacred edifice. Without more ado, however, we passed under the portal and across the outer court which led to the door of the prayer-chamber, whence we were able to obtain a good view of the interior. This mosque differs in no respect from others in Tunisia; the interior is supported by sixteen Roman shafts of different diameters, and of various descriptions of stone, surmounted by capitals of various designs and quality of carving; the mihrab is a simple recess; no traces of Arab work of any description are visible. A few devout men were worshipping; we thought it better not to disturb them, but preferred to remain at the doorway, especially as it commanded the whole interior of the mosque, covering a square of about fifty feet each way.

Instead of finding in Msaken, as we were led to expect, a university or a seat of learning, we found the place scarcely a town at all, but rather an overgrown agricultural village, in which olive-pressing and corn-grinding alone occupy the inhabitants. Its extent is, however, great, for it covers perhaps as much ground as Soussa itself. The only noticeable peculiarity was the construction of the entrances to private houses; they consist of a large covered porch, forming an open outer gateway, and furnished with brick benches on either side. Apart from this, the houses externally have the same mean appearance common throughout Tunisia. Many of them seemed to be unoccupied and falling into ruin. Altogether there is a sadness and a forlorn aspect about Msaken which are quite depressing. Interest, if there can be any in such a place, is centered in the fact that it is still unsophisticated and quite untouched by European civilisation.

Our afternoon was by no means wasted; we had enjoyed a pleasant drive, had satisfied our curiosity, and had been able to note for ourselves (experience which the traveller has frequently to acquire) one place in Tunisia not worth a visit.

CHAPTER XII.

EL-DJEM, THE ANCIENT THYSDRUS.
November 12th and 13th.

DEPARTURE FROM SOUSSA—A LOVELY MORNING—ROUGH TRAVELLING—
ROMAN RUINS—A BEAUTIFUL VIEW—MENZEL—LAKE SIDI-EL-HANI—
ZRAMEDINE—OLIVE-CRUSHING—PLOUGHING—FIRST GLIMPSE OF THE
AMPHITHEATRE—THE GREAT PLAIN—BIRDS—THE FONDOUK—THE
CAFÉ — ARAB POLITENESS — RATS — THE VILLAGE OF EL-DJEM—
DESCRIPTION OF THE AMPHITHEATRE—REFLECTIONS—ES SAHEL—
MAHEDIA.

WE had decided to start for El-Djem at 6 a.m., and our carriage was before the door to the minute. It was not so easy, however, to get away from the Hôtel de Paris at so early an hour. No one was about on our emerging from our bedrooms; and it was not until we had lit the kitchen lamp, and made some commotion in the house, that the waiter came out of the hole in the wall which served as his sleeping apartment. By half-past six, however, we were on the road.

It was one of those lovely mornings common enough in this country, but not to be experienced in Europe, or, at any rate, in England. The sun had not yet risen, and the stars were still bright. The air, chilly at so early an hour in the month of November, was clear and lucid. The dew was thick on the ground, and there was every indication of the continuance of fine weather. As we skirted the Arab cemetery close to the city walls, we observed a group of women clustered round a grave, where they had probably spent the night. The village of Zaouiet, through which we had driven the previous afternoon, was passed at 7 o'clock; and then turning to the left, we took the direct road to El-Djem. At half-past seven we passed, to the left, the extensive remains of a Byzantine fortress; but the dilapidated state of its rubble walls furnished no clue to its origin or extent. To the right vestiges of numerous houses were discernible.

For several miles we continued among the olives which surround Soussa on the land side—a fact of which we had unpleasant reminders in the constant jolting over the grips and ridges formed to retain every drop of rain-fall. A quarter of an hour more brought us to the remains of another fortress on the right, but of no importance. At 8 a.m. we alighted to examine, at a short distance to the left of the track, a Roman cistern, about forty paces long and in four compartments, no longer in use. It is on high ground, from which the olives have been cleared. Turning round at this point, and facing the direction whence we came, a view of unparalleled extent and magnificence unfolded itself. The sun had now risen in great splendour, and the whole landscape was lit up and tinged with gorgeous colouring. The Mediterranean, a sheet of azure, lay to our right; and although some eight or nine miles distant, yet the ships riding before Soussa were clearly defined. Soussa, with its snow-white walls, surmounted by the watch-tower of the Kasbah, appeared like a pyramid of marble; and on the plain, embowered in groves of olive and cactus, lay the white villages of Zaouiet and Ksiba—the whole picture framed by a long range of receding hills, centering in the noble peak of Djebel Zaghouan.

Having partaken of nothing but a cup of black coffee before starting, hunger began to remind us that ruins and fine scenery were far from being necessaries of existence; so we unpacked our provision-basket and ate our frugal lunch under the shade of a spreading olive-tree. In a quarter of an hour we were again on the move.

Menzel, a poor village, closely surrounded by hedges of cactus, was skirted to our right at 10.15. An Arab and two women, almost the only people we had met since we left Soussa, were carrying wood; or, rather, in fact, the women were laden with the wood, while their lord and master walked empty-handed in front of them. This is invariably the case. By 10.30 we had quitted the olive-groves, and found ourselves on an almost uncultivated plain of vast extent. At 11.15 Sebkha-Sidi-el-Hani, some four miles off the route, opened out to our right. The banks of this great lagoon are flat and unpicturesque; herons were flying overhead, and the far-distant hills were clearly visible.

Another hour's jolting over the melancholy plain, devoid of any kind of shelter, brought us to Zramedine, a small oasis of olives, palms, and cactus. The latter, which usually serve merely as hedges or enclosures, here form large compact groves. The trees are very luxuriant and of great age. Women with long cleft sticks were busy gathering the fruit, and stole furtive glances at us as we passed. We halted for a few minutes to refresh our horses at the village-well, where women were as usual loitering, gossiping, and drawing water. Close by, two Bedouin girls, dark-skinned and bright-eyed, but lightly clad, were grinding at a mill, or, rather, crushing olives between two large stones. We approached to examine their movements, propitiating them

with a few sous, which they eagerly accepted. They
were not at all shy, and did not run away or desist from
their labour; on the contrary, they were pleased at being
noticed, and proud of their primitive occupation. It
should be observed that the Bedouin women do not cover
their faces. The women of the better class are usually
richly clad, and bedecked with a great variety of silver
bracelets and other ornaments. Ploughing was being
industriously pursued all round Zramedine; and all kinds
of animals—asses, cows, camels, yoked together indiscriminately—were employed at the work. The Biblical
injunction, 'not to muzzle the ox that treadeth out the
corn,' is little heeded by the Arabs. Any four-legged
beast is equal to the light labour of scratching the surface
with the rude implement that does duty for a plough.
It is not unusual to see a camel and a donkey yoked
together; when seen *en silhouette* on the horizon the
donkey appears to be walking under the camel.

We now began to strain our eyes in the direction of
El-Djem, which, from the distance indicated on our
maps, ought to have been visible; but it was not till
after another hour's drive that the great Amphitheatre
was observed standing up on the plain like an excres-
cence on the horizon. Distances are so illusive in this
wondrously clear atmosphere, that it is better, as experience taught us on many occasions, to trust to a map
rather than to the eye in calculating the lengths of any
section of a journey. Although this monument was
clearly outlined, yet it took us fully two hours to arrive
at the village which has sprung up at the foot of the
great ruin.

The plain we had passed to reach El Djem is in
many ways remarkable, and offers an interesting study
to the geographer. At this season it is without water,

and clothed only with sparse and stunted scrub; no
vegetation, no trees, no habitations—nothing, in fact, to
relieve the sad monotony of the landscape. The friable
soil is rent in all directions by enormous fissures, now
quite dry, but probably full of water after heavy rains.
In width and extent these fissures vary considerably,
but the average depth is about 10 or 12 feet, having
almost vertical sides like a railway cutting. Around
these yawning gaps, spread serpent-like over the plain,
locomotion is somewhat difficult, impossible by night,
and after heavy rains attended with considerable risk.
In addition to the crested larks, which are so numerous
in these parts, we had noticed during our day's journey
herons, eagles, hawks, owls, linnets, and coveys of
partridges.

In comparison with the fondouk which we were
now to occupy, that at Bir-el-Bouïta was a palace.
This wretched place consists of a series of chambers
or stables around a court-yard on a level with the
ground, and are used for man or beast indiscriminately.
The one we occupied was nothing more than a long
vaulted room, the unpaved and unboarded floor covered
with the dung of animals and the refuse of former
travellers; there were no windows, and the rickety
double door, which was full of holes, could not be shut.
There was no furniture whatever, but, when we were
known to be English, an unsteady table, covered with
dirt and tallow, and a wooden settle, such as the Arabs
use in front of their houses, converted the vault into
an *appartement meublé*. A couple of lengths of old
matting were spread on the earthen floor, a solitary
candle was stuck in an empty wine-bottle, a brown jar
filled with water was put in a corner, and the resources
of the establishment were exhausted. The jar, or

amphora, be it remarked, had a rounded bottom like a soda-water bottle, and could not possibly be made to stand without support. The water which it contained was so brown and thick that we thought a mistake had been made, and, emptying it out in the open court-yard, desired that the jar might be refilled. This was done, but with no better result: the water was really not fit for washing purposes. The modest cold collation which we extracted from our provision-basket was soon despatched, and we sallied forth in quest of coffee. The meanest village in Tunisia boasts its café, nor is that institution, so dear to the Arab, wanting in El-Djem. It is, in fact, a very noteworthy and even picturesque little nook, occupying one of the lower arcades of the Amphitheatre, and forming part of this stupendous ruin. Some ten or twelve Arabs immediately made room for us as we entered. One young man, quite a scholar, for he spoke a little broken French, addressed us. 'Were we French?' 'No, Englishmen; friends of all Mohammedans.' A gleam of satisfaction was visible on the countenances of the company, one of whom was a green-turbaned Hadji, as our interlocutor communicated to them our reply. Coffee was brought us by a dark-skinned man in a coarse brown gaberdeen, handing the cups with a grace and dignity peculiar to his race. He, nevertheless, pocketed with equal graciousness and no less dignity the silver piece which we proffered without offering any change, thus allowing us to pay five times as much as the coffee was worth. At the further end of the café, exactly under the vaulted arch of the Amphitheatre, sat an old man sifting coffee. He was clothed in a few rags only, and appeared to be the butt of the village, for jokes were passing evidently at his expense. Undisturbed either by the raillery or by our presence,

AMPHITHEATRE AT EL DJEM

the veteran continued his occupation until, the portion duly sifted, he handed it solemnly to the proprietor. We pitied the old man, and offered him a cup of coffee. Without a word of thanks or the least expression of surprise he accepted, and, cup in hand, sat down, gazing at us silently and attentively. Soon after we took our departure.

We had loitered among the ruins until it was quite dark, and had to pass through the village in order to regain the fondouk. In the first narrow street we entered, a dog, one of the nuisances of the country, came out of a doorway, snarling and barking at us. We insensibly grasped our sticks and prepared for defence. To our surprise, our old friend of the café, who had been waiting for us, stood at our side. He walked before us, quieted the dog, and accompanied us to our lodging, at the door of which he saluted us, and, placing his right hand on his breast, departed with a grandeur of deportment worthy of a prince.

We had been warned against fleas in the caravansera of El-Djem, but were fortunate enough not to be thus molested; possibly the time of year not being propitious to these little tormentors. Vermin, however, of an equally pertinacious and more obtrusive kind, did not fail to worry us—rats. Should any of our readers have the misfortune to pass a night where we did, we would advise them, before retiring to rest, to leave out, at some spot as remote as possible from where they are lying, provisions sufficient to occupy these rapacious animals until the morning. Nor must they stint the measure, for their number is legion. They emerge from holes in the wall high up out of reach, and the agility with which they clamber up the rough stones is marvellous. Nor are they at all shy, but, confident of their ability to elude pursuit, they do not hesitate to pay their visits in broad daylight. Several times did we shoot at them with our revolvers, but without picking any of them off. The braying of asses, the barking of dogs, the scrambling of rats, were the sounds which enlivened our night's rest, and made slumber cheerful, to say the least of it.

Our inspection of the Amphitheatre during the previous afternoon had been incomplete, and we were among the ruins at sunrise. At every step we had to pick our way, for the edifice is now converted into the stable and *cloaca* of the village—a fact which does not prevent the streets, almost the doorsteps of the houses, from being similarly befouled. In the middle of the village is a well, only a few feet deep, from which the inhabitants draw their water; its brink is slightly below the level of the streets and unprotected, so that with every rain-fall all the filth of the place must flow into it.

But enough, more than enough, about the village and fondouk of El-Djem. Let us now return to the Amphitheatre of ancient Thysdrus, upon which the miserable modern dwellings are literally grafted, the lower arcades on one side, which is in a fairly perfect condition, being used by the Arabs as shops and stables.

Few remains of ancient civilisation are more calculated to rouse the imagination and awaken in the beholder's mind serious meditation than this stupendous Amphitheatre of Thysdrus—not even the Coliseum at Rome, with which it has the most affinity, and to which it stands second in size, in grandeur, and in architectural pretensions. If the associations of the latter are more numerous and of greater historical importance, the monument of Thysdrus is enshrouded with mystery infinitely more calculated to call forth suggestive reflections.

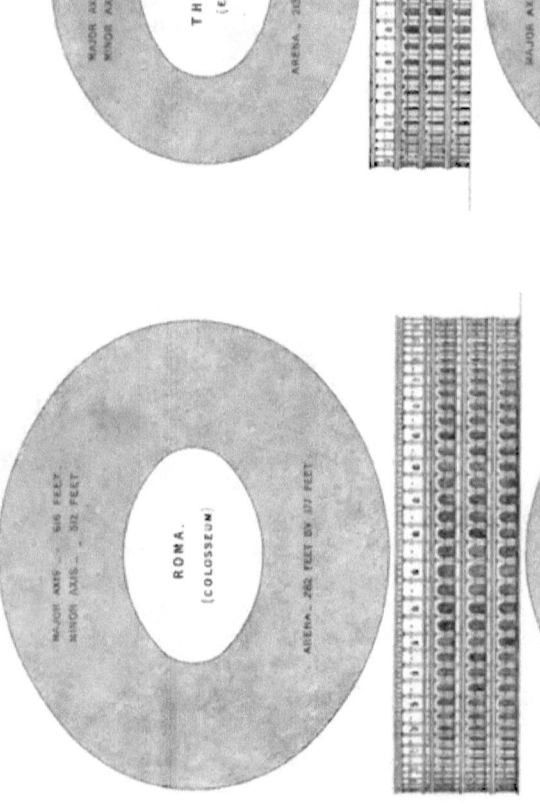

When, and by whom was it built? Was it ever finished? Did the combats for which it was destined ever take place within its walls? Has its partial destruction been wholly effected by the hand of man or by natural causes? What was the extent of the city of Thysdrus, and of what materials were its houses constructed? How was it supplied with water? These considerations suggested themselves as we wandered among the arcades; and when, having succeeded in reaching the upper storey (climbing on hands and knees over the dilapidated vaulting which once supported the steps), the immensity of the structure, rearing its colossal form on the edge of a treeless, waterless, inhospitable plain, became apparent.

Like other great amphitheatres of the Roman Empire, the divisions and arrangements of the one at Thysdrus possess no distinctive features. Externally there are three tiers of open arcades, of varying dimensions, surmounted by an attic, similar to the better known example in Rome. There were two principal entrances, one of which is entirely destroyed. The ranges of seats in the interior have long since disappeared, and the arena is choked with earth and a confused mass of stone and rubble. The extreme major axis may be estimated at 489 feet, and the minor axis at 403 feet. Assuming that the attic was intended to be of the same proportionate height as its prototype in Rome, the total height of the external wall, measured from the ground, would have been 124 feet 6 inches.

Guérin shares the opinion of Shaw, who remarks:—

'It seems to have been built about the time of the Antonines, agreeing exactly in proportion and workmanship with the buildings of that age. And as the elder Gordian was proclaimed Emperor at this city, it is not improbable that, in gratitude to the place where he received the purple, he might have been the founder of it.* Upon one of the medals of the younger Gordian we have an amphitheatre, not hitherto accounted for by the medalists; but it may be too peremptory perhaps to fix it here at Tisdra.'†

There are many indications in the structure itself that it was never finished; and it may be stated, without controversy, that the attic or top storey was only begun. The amphitheatre may have been sufficiently advanced to admit of performances being held, and wooden benches may have been temporarily provided for the spectators. The key-stones of the lower tier of arches, which were intended to carry carvings in relief, are left in a rough, unornamented state, with the exception of two on the north side, upon which are represented the bust of a female and the head of a lion. Its present ruinous condition appears to be rather the work of man than the result of natural causes, each successive generation having pillaged the edifice for the sake of building materials.

On more than one occasion it has served as a place of defence, and nearly two centuries ago the tribes of the

---

* The supposition seems to rest on very slender evidence. The well-known love of the elder Gordian for gladiatorial displays, and his munificence in this matter at Rome (Gibbon's *Decline and Fall*, vol. i. chap. vii.) may have originated the idea of attributing the Amphitheatre of Thysdrus to him. That he projected the work in order to show his gratitude to the city where he had been raised to the purple is within the range of probability. He was proclaimed emperor against his will at the advanced age of eighty, a time of life when honours fraught with danger are not usually sought. The dignity was accepted because his refusal would probably have cost him his life. As it was, he enjoyed the distinction for the short period of six weeks. We may assume, then, that the archæologists who have fathered the Thysdrus amphitheatre on the elder Gordian have done so without close investigation. Till further evidence be forthcoming, we must be content to leave the whole question unsolved.

† *Travels or Observations relating to Barbary*, chap. v.

district having taken refuge here after refusing payment of the annual tribute to the Bey, artillery was brought to bear against its massive walls, and a breach equal to one fourth of the perimeter prevented its ever being used again for a similar purpose. The town of Thysdrus was neither extensive nor opulent; and although history is almost silent on the subject of its rise and progress, yet we learn from the writings of Hirtius, a contemporary of Julius Cæsar, that, after the battle of Thapsus, the Emperor mitigated the fine imposed upon Thysdrus on account of the wretched condition of its inhabitants. There can be little doubt that the whole plain encircling the town was highly cultivated and covered with thriving farms during the Roman occupation.* That the houses of Thysdrus have disappeared may be accounted for by their having been built of rammed earth and not of stone. There are no quarries in the immediate vicinity, the stone used in the construction of the amphitheatre having been transported from Sallecta, the ancient Syllectum, about twenty miles distant. Nevertheless, from the fragments of marble and carved stone still to be met with, and from the treasures which have from time to time been discovered, we may assume that Thysdrus was once embellished with public buildings of a monumental character.† A thorough and system-

---

* 'The Coliseum of Thysdrus calls to mind that of Vespasian, and equals in grandeur, with more elegance perhaps, the amphitheatre of Verona. Formerly a numerous and wealthy people filled it. What must have been the power of a municipality that could raise such colossal edifices on the borders of the Desert!'—V. DURUY, *Histoire des Romains*, v. 466, where will be found, as well as at vi. 319, views of the amphitheatre.

† Guérin mentions the finding of a statue, '*d'un goût très-pur*,' about the year 1847. At nearly the same time a box of gold coins was discovered, of which we were able to secure forty-one during our stay in Tunis.

atic exploration of the site would not fail to be attended with fair success. That Thysdrus was plentifully supplied with water is beyond doubt. Guérin discovered an inscription proving the fact. Further, the network of fissures, already mentioned, which cut up the surrounding plain, indicate the former existence of watercourses for the supply of the town and for irrigating the adjacent country. One word more: a word of admiration for a people who could, in a simple colonial town, at a vast distance from their own metropolis, conceive and execute so stupendous a monument! Lamentable, indeed, is the decline since their day — desolation, ruin, drought, sterility, where once reigned industry and abundance. It could hardly be expected that the Beys of Tunis or their immediate predecessors would respect the monuments of this once great colony of the Roman Empire. Their rule is now, happily, over. Let us hope that the French, whose *Société des Monuments Historiques* have done such good service in their own country, will extend a protecting hand to the monuments of North Africa, and prevent further spoliation of such noble remains as the Amphitheatre at El-Djem.

Instead of returning to Soussa, we had arranged to proceed to Mahedia and there join the steamer, which would touch at that port the same evening on its way south. Thus we should avoid passing the same route twice, save several miles, and gain time. We directed our coachman to take the road *via* Ksour-es-Sef, which would have enabled us to visit the ruins of Syllectum, and some Phœnician tombs to the south of Mahedia. But as we passed Aphrodisium on a former occasion without being able to reach it, so were we here doomed to miss Sallecta. Our driver was the dullest and most stubborn of louts; and in spite of reiterated explanations impressed upon him by an Italian gentleman who happened to be at the caravansera, and who was good enough to serve as interpreter, he persisted in taking a somewhat shorter road straight across the plain. One of the horses, as we perceived after starting, had fallen lame, which was another inducement for him to shorten the distance as much as possible. This accident also diminished the speed, and consequently we took five hours to perform a journey which, with good horses, might easily have been done in half that time. The district through which we were about to pass — the southern extremity of Es-Sahel—is, if possible, even more monotonous and depressing than that which we had traversed on our way to El-Djem.

In a quarter of an hour we had left behind us the olive-groves on the east of El-Djem, and found ourselves once more upon an extensive plain covered with scrub, where there was some attempt at cultivation. Here and there an Arab, alone or aided by his wives and children, might be seen ploughing or sowing. With a donkey, or camel, or a cow, harnessed with cords to an implement resembling a crooked stick rather than a plough, he scratches up the soil between the scrub and tufts of weeds, and then scatters over it a few handfuls of seed. Any attempt to clear the ground or to uproot the tufts of rough herbage does not occur to him, and would possibly be regarded as unnecessary labour. Allah will provide! A profound sentiment, but at the same time the curse of the country.

By 2 o'clock we had quitted the plain, and rejoiced to find ourselves once more among the olive-groves. In this district the olives may be seen in great perfection; young trees had been planted to replace the unfruitful ones, and evidence of capital and industry is abundant. The white buildings of Ksour-el-Sef, that we should have passed but for the stupidity of our driver, were gleaming in the sunshine some four miles distant; but access was impossible, as there is no cross-track. Passing some strips of barren sand that separate the coast towns here from the interior, we drove through the village and past the pleasant gardens of Zouida, laden with golden fruit. After watering the horses at a well sunk in the sand we entered the town of Mahedia at 3 p.m.

CHAPTER XIII.

MAHEDIA.

November 13th.

A HUNT FOR DINNER—'KUSS KUSSU'—DISPOSITION OF MAHEDIA—ORIGIN OF THE NAME—HOSPITALITY—TAKING SOUNDINGS—ON BOARD AGAIN.

THERE is no hotel at Mahedia, and no restaurant or other establishment where food can be procured. Our scanty supply of provisions having been consumed, the first thought after depositing our luggage at the office of the *Compagnie Transatlantique*, and settling with our coachman, was to obtain what the Americans would call a good square meal—some dinner. We hastened to pay our respects to the British Consular Agent, cherishing the hope of an invitation. The inhabitants of Mahedia dine at mid-day and sup in the evening. The steamer was due at 8 p.m., an hour when food on board would be difficult to obtain; besides, we were really too hungry to wait five hours. The Agent received us with great politeness, offering every assistance, but when we broached the subject of food, evidently a most unusual request, he seemed quite at a loss. After a little pressing he called one of his servants and gave him some instructions. What they were our ignorance of the language prevented us from comprehending, but we hoped that our friend was sending a message to his own cook. The emissary departed, and in about a quarter of an hour returned with a Maltese, who, after some further conversation, thought he might be able to get us something cooked. He was, however, so dirty, and his aspect so forbidding, that, famished as we were, we had serious misgivings whether it would be possible to relish anything that his kitchen might produce. We thanked the kind Consular Agent and his Maltese acquaintance, and returned to the steamboat office. While our tickets were being prepared we again hinted, in as delicate a manner as possible, at our present needs. One of the Company's staff, M. Adolfo Lumbroso, was good enough to take compassion on us, and, conducting us to his home, appeased our hunger with an excellent *kuss kussu* (a national dish of which we shall have occasion again to speak later on), and extended his hospitality by an introduction to his family, in whose company we spent a pleasant hour.

The position and arrangement of Mahedia are peculiar. It occupies a small narrow peninsula jutting out directly into the sea, and consists of a single street, at one end of which, that adjoining the main land, stands the Kasba, while the other is terminated by a fortress overlooking the sea, formerly of importance but now dismantled. In spite of the twelve pages devoted to it by Guérin,[*] Mahedia offers no resource and little attraction to the traveller. Of Arab origin, having been founded A.D. 912, or 300 of the Hégira, by Obeid-Allah, otherwise El-Mahdi, whence its name, it possesses no antiquities owing to its bombardment by order of the Emperor Charles V. Consequently almost all traces of its former strength have disappeared. If we except a fine mosque, a restoration evidently of the original

---

[*] *Voyage*, i. 100.

edifice, the interior of which is supported by shafts and capitals from some Roman edifice, there is no building worthy of special notice. Mahedia, we were told, is exceedingly healthy; a fact easily accounted for by its exceptional position. We inspected in the house of M. N. Novak, the Austrian Consular Agent and manager here of the *Compagnie Transatlantique*, an interesting Roman inscription brought from El-Djem, which has been reproduced by V. Guérin.

We would here express our gratitude to M. N. Novak for much kindness and attention during our two short visits to Mahedia. With some regret we bid adieu to the pleasant family of M. Lumbroso and, gladly accepting seats in the Company's boat in correspondence with the steamers, were soon skimming the waters with our good friend M. Novak. The roadstead of Mahedia is so shallow and uncertain that steamers arriving in the night are not able to approach the land within a couple of miles, even in fine weather, until soundings are taken. This is done by a rowing-boat, which puts off some time before the steamer is due. A safe anchorage found and the vessel sighted, Roman candles are ignited in the boat in order to indicate her whereabouts. For more than an hour we were tossing about on the water before the *Ville de Bône* was declared to be in sight. The night was dark but tranquil, and the sea being fairly calm, the time passed quickly away in pleasant company. At length we perceived a huge black mass in the offing, which gradually approached us, and in ten minutes we were on the deck of the *Ville de Bône*.

CHAPTER XIV.

SFAX.

November 14th.

A TOWN BUILT ON THE SAND—THE SPONGE MARKET—COMMERCIAL ACTIVITY—AN ARAB HOUSE—HADCHIS—JEWISH WOMEN.

AT midnight the *Ville de Bône* got under way, and at 11 o'clock on the following morning, November 14th, anchored off Sfax, within sight of the low shores of the Kerkenah Islands, where refractory prostitutes and women guilty of adultery are banished. The roadstead before Sfax is so shallow that the steamer could not anchor within at least two miles of the shore; but a pleasant breeze enabled us to reach the land in about twenty minutes in one of the little boats lying in waiting. To rejoin the steamer at sundown when the wind had fallen took considerably more than an hour.

It has been suggested that Sfax occupies the site of ancient Taphrura, but this seems doubtful. The modern town is literally built upon the sand, a wide belt of sand separating it from luxuriant gardens on the land side. The Romans were not likely to have chosen such a site for a town of any importance, although vestiges of Roman constructions may be traced without the present walls. Only recently some excavations near the shore, in connexion with an extension of the quay, brought to light a circular niche lined and paved with mosaic, forming part of a large edifice, most probably a bathing establishment. The character of the work indicates a late period of the Empire. Situated as it is, Sfax has but a poor appearance from the sea, in spite of its Kasba and white crenelated walls flanked with bastions. In commercial activity it scarcely yields to Soussa. Esparto grass* (better known by its Arab name of Halfa), dates and grain, are exported largely. The land in the vicinity of Sfax is very productive, yielding two crops yearly. The olive is exceedingly fruitful, and trees of two years' growth bear fruit. The date-palm flourishes, although the fruit is not of the best. The chief source of wealth, however, is the sponge fishery; the shallow bay of Sfax, as well as the coasts of the Kerkenah Islands, yielding this zoophyte in large quantities, although not perhaps of the finest quality. In the office of Mr. Galea, our Consular Agent, whose acquaintance we had the good fortune to make here, we saw a sponge well shaped and of the following dimensions : 1 foot 10 inches by 1 foot 8 inches by 1 foot 6 inches—possibly the largest sponge known. The sponge market is on the quay, or rather on the shore, for a quay can scarcely be said to exist in close proximity to the landing-place. It is a scene of great activity. The sponges are exposed for sale in circular groups on the open ground.

Sfax is entered by two gates only. Before reaching

---

* 'The trade in esparto grass ought to be the most important on the coast, but it is being rapidly annihilated, owing to the unwise restrictions placed upon it by the Tunisian Government. This valuable fibre is found in Algeria, Tunis, and Tripoli. It was first brought into use by Mr. Lloyd, owner of the *Daily Chronicle*, who had an establishment at Oran, and up to the present time the trade has remained almost entirely in the hands of the English.'—PLAYFAIR'S *Consular Report on Tunis*, Commercial. No. 3 (1886), Part I., p. 33.

that facing the sea one has to traverse the European quarter, peopled chiefly by Maltese and Jews. It is as busy as it is dirty. Hundreds of camels and asses may be seen grouped without the walls, and merchandise of all kinds, as well as bales of esparto grass, encumber the open spaces. Within the gate one finds oneself involved in the usual narrow, tortuous, ill-kept streets, with a mosque enriched with Roman shafts. The souks are well furnished, and quite as characteristic as those of Soussa. Were a proof needed of the prosperity of Sfax, we might point to the handsome private houses, the stone doorways of which are frequently embellished with intricate and varied designs, delicately carved. While admiring one of the doorways belonging to a house in the Rue de la Poste, now occupied by the French as their *Trésor*, an officer politely invited us to inspect the arrangements of the interior. It is a fairly representative Arab house. From the street one enters through a vestibule into a patio, or open courtyard, furnished with a well. Several apartments open into the patio, in each of which is fitted a richly painted wooden screen, with a Moorish arched opening in the centre. Behind this screen the bed, or sleeping couch, was placed. The ceilings are of wood painted like the screens. A steep and very narrow stone staircase leads to the first floor, consisting of several small rooms destined for the occupation of the women. The windows are small and grated, and an open balcony, overlooking the patio, on to which the upper chambers open, is furnished with a kind of wide projecting ledge, effectually preventing those in the courtyard from seeing any one passing along the balcony. Immediately above the well there is an opening, through which the women were able to draw water without going down to the lower floor.

A DOORWAY IN SFAX

The men of Sfax appeared more active and busy than in other towns of the Regency, and the life of the people seemed more energetic.* One meets the usual number of blind and one-eyed; but that which will not fail to strike the traveller is the unusual number of green turbans met with at every turn. Nor are these descendants of the Prophet confined to the wealthy class; the humblest servant, if he can prove his lineage, has an equal right with a Cadi to encircle his brows with Mohammed's favourite colour, and to call himself Hadchi.

As we turned the corner of one of the narrow streets on our way to the shore to regain the steamer, we found ourselves suddenly among a bevy of young Jewish women, of whom two were of superlative beauty. They were twelve or fourteen in all, and were returning from the bath, where they had accompanied the maiden who walked at their head, and who was to be married on the morrow. The bride was more richly attired than her companions, and wore gaiters embroidered with gold, and a profusion of jewelry. She was stout, under twenty years of age, and very comely.

---

* 'The people of Sfakès, or Sfâksika, are distinguishable from their co-religionists of Tunisia. One recognises them by a certain difference of costume, for they do not like to be mistaken for other Tunisians. It is in their force of character, above all, that they differ from other citizens: they have more initiative, more industry, more ingenuity; in everything they are more active and more earnest than their neighbours. They are said to be zealous Mussulmans: the children even frequent the mosques, and the women do not neglect their prayers.'—*Nouvelle Géographie Universelle*, Reclus, xi. 216.

CHAPTER XV.

GABÈS.

November 15th and 16th.

A TOWN OF SHANTIES—NATIVE VILLAGES—RAS-EL-WAD—THE OASIS—DATE GATHERING—DOGS—TENT DWELLERS—OUED GABÈS—DRESS OF THE JEWESSES—CHARACTERISTIC SCENERY—A DIP IN THE SEA.

E dropped anchor off Gabès at 5 o'clock in the morning of November 15th, and were on shore by half-past seven.

We had intended to continue our voyage as far as Djerba, a distance of 60 kilos; but on learning that the *Ville de Bône* would reach that island in the evening and leave early next morning, that it took two hours to land and at least an hour to embark, we resolved to remain at Gabès until the steamer should return and carry us north again.

In the numerous shanties which compose the port of Gabès—one of them designated as Grand Hôtel!!—there is no sleeping accommodation for European travellers, so we gladly accepted the hospitality of our Vice-Consul, Mr. Galea.

A very few words will suffice for Gabès, which is not a city, nor even a town, but one of those heterogeneous places where civilisation is in its infancy, or rather where a new civilisation is being engrafted upon an old one. Whether Gabès occupies the actual site of the Roman Tacape is a matter of doubt. The stretch of

OUTSIDE THE WALLS OF GABÈS

sand on which the modern port is built did not probably exist at that period, having been formed by the action of the tide during many centuries. Gabès is called after a river of that name, which here flows into the sea ; and the port consists of the Club-house of the French officers, a respectable stone building, and some hundred wooden huts, such as one sees in the far west of the United States. They are used as go-downs, general stores, cafés, barbers' shops, and other similar establishments of a most primitive description, and are kept by French and Maltese. Here, too, are the compounds and factories where the esparto grass, the chief product of the district, is received, packed, and shipped ; and strings of camels and asses, laden with this valuable commodity, may be seen at early morning slowly wending their way towards the merchants' quarter.

The town of Gabès has been made familiar to us of late years by a daring proposal of the late Commandant Roudaire to create an inland sea by the submersion of a large tract of the Sahara, some hundreds of miles in length, taking advantage of an immense natural depression which stretches from near Gabès westward. A glance at any map of North Africa, in which the great Chotts in this district are clearly defined, will enable any one to form a fair idea of the proposed scheme. The whole subject, however, from a geographer's point of view, has been so exhaustively treated by the late M. Charles Tissot in his *Géographie comparée de la Province Romaine d'Afrique*, that we must refer the reader to this work for much valuable information on the subject. As a matter of public interest, an experimental Artesian well has been recently sunk at a point on the coast, 18 kilomètres north of Gabès, with very satisfactory results. A column of water is thrown up sufficient to irrigate 60,000 palm-trees; and there is reason to believe that, by the sinking of further Artesian wells, the supply will be so abundant that an enormous tract of country, now dried up and desolate, will be converted into a garden of plenty. To use the words of Consul-General Sir R. L. Playfair, 'This seems to me the true solution of the problem of an inland sea.'

About a mile and a half inland, and separated from the port by a sandy waste, are the native villages of Menzel, Djard, and Chenneni. Their interest for the traveller consists in their truly Arab character, unaffected as yet by European civilisation, rather than in the remains of any monuments of antiquity. Both streets and houses are very curious—the former narrow, tortuous, and often covered entirely over with beams of palm, rendering them almost obscure; the latter very low, never rising above one story, and with doors and rafters of roughly-hewn palm wood. Numerous koubbas are seen in all directions. The most important of this group of villages is Menzel, which boasts of the residence of the Kaïd, as well as a large open market-place surrounded by shops, where extensive business is transacted in European manufactures as well as in native produce. Around these villages, and particularly between them and Gabès, the plain is dotted by numerous gourbies, or Arab encampments.

It seems probable that the ground upon which the modern port now stands was formerly covered by the sea, and that it has in course of time been raised by the soil brought down by the river, and partly, as before observed, by the constant action of the tide, which at this part of the Mediterranean rises to the height of about seven feet.

When the French first occupied the district, General

Logerot fixed his camp at Ras-el-Wad, meaning 'Head of the River,' some six miles inland, where it still remains. This inhospitable spot, a veritable desert, without any kind of shelter, is accessible by a road formed with much difficulty and expense across a sandy plain, broken up in all directions by hillocks and deep ravines. Even at this cool season of the year we were almost stifled by the heat and blinded with dust, which rose in such clouds that the view was at times entirely obscured. A more ill-chosen station it is difficult to conceive.

The real charm of Gabès, however, is in its gardens, covering an area of some forty-eight square kilomètres, and extending along the winding banks of the river, whose waters irrigate and fertilize in a marvellous degree this strikingly beautiful oasis. Under the shade of lofty and graceful date-palms entwined by clinging vines, one wanders among orange, citron, almond, fig, and pomegranate trees, or madder and hennah bushes, springing out of a soil producing cereals and vegetables of every kind, and in boundless profusion. The whole oasis is divided into gardens by hedges of impenetrable cactus, or by small artificial water-ways, over which one has frequently to leap in order to pass from one garden to another. The date season being now at its height, we watched with interest the men climbing the palms and cutting down the golden clusters, while women and children below gathered the fruit as it fell, and spread it on mats to dry in the sun. Others filled the panniers of the attendant camels, who were allowed to enjoy a share of the abundant crop. The dexterity with which the Arabs ascend the spiral, branchless trees is marvellous. This feat they perform by means of a rope encircling the trunk and their own body. The rope is of sufficient length to enable them to plant their feet on the rough bark, and by shifting the rope with their hands, while their feet firmly grasp the tree, they literally walk up the perpendicular stem with astonishing ease and certainty. As we were watching their proceedings, they bade us partake of the dates at our pleasure—an offer of which we gladly availed ourselves.

One great inconvenience of moving among the villagers or tent-occupiers throughout Tunisia is the constant attacks of the dogs, which rush out in numbers from every hovel or gourbi, barking and snarling in the most savage manner. Whether the bark is ever followed by the bite we had happily no occasion of judging; but our good friend Mr. Galea prudently sent with us on this occasion an Arab boy armed with a stout stick in order to protect us from too formidable attacks.

The tent-dwelling Arabs, numerous around Gabès, lead poor lives. The men labour in the fields or in their own gardens, when they are prosperous enough to possess or rent one; the women cook, spin wool and camels' hair, and weave the cloth of which their tents are made; the children tend the animals and poultry, sweep out the tent, and assist in cooking. We saw two little girls skinning a sheep's head and feet and roasting them on wood embers ignited in the open field, while other children were cutting up the intestines of the animal and hanging them on lines to dry in the sun, preparatory to future degustation. These nomads have dark skins, and are not unfrequently quite black; the children are dirty in the extreme, and their entire clothing consists of a piece of cotton, generally in rags, but thrown round them with a grace to which an European child is an entire stranger; the women, scarcely less dirty than their offspring, wear their hair in matted locks, like the curls on an ill-kept poodle dog, do not cover their faces, and are

THE OASIS OF GABES

not shy, but, on the contrary, seem pleased at being noticed.

One of the most pleasing sights here is to watch the Jewish women and girls fetching water in the early morning, or at sunset, from the Oued Gabès, or washing themselves or their garments in the running stream. They dress quite differently from Jewesses in other parts of Tunisia, and do not wear, or at any rate do not display, the tightly-fitting trousers, but envelop themselves in loosely-flowing robes, or more generally in a simple length of cotton stuff, which they fold gracefully around them. They delight in gay colours, chiefly orange and red, which harmonise agreeably with their slightly bronzed complexions. They wear a profusion of silver trinkets—chains, bracelets, anklets, &c., which they do not put off even while washing. The attire of the Arab women is more sober in colour, being almost invariably dark blue. The men dress generally in white.

The scenery of Gabès is purely African—the sandy desert, surrounding an oasis out of which sylph-like palms rear their lofty crests, the numerous koubbas which here serve as landmarks, the countless gourbies dotting the arid plain in all directions, the strings of camels in constant motion, laden with the produce of the interior—all combine to form a picture unmistakably Oriental.

The weather was so beautiful during our sojourn at Gabès that we were tempted, in spite of the sharks and dog-fish which occasionally approach the coast, to take a plunge in the sea. The Arab lad who accompanied us shuddered as he saw us leap into the water from the end of the wooden jetty. At first we thought his concern for our safety was the cause of his sudden change of countenance, but it was in reality nothing more than the shock occasioned to his feelings by our immersing ourselves in cold water at this time of the year.

'That boy,' we said afterwards to Mr. Galea, 'no doubt thinks us mad for bathing in the sea in the month of November.'

'Of course he does,' was our friend's laconic reply.

CHAPTER XVI.

GABÈS TO SOUSSA BY SEA.

November 17th and 18th.

DEPARTURE FROM GABÈS—DECLINE OF BRITISH INFLUENCE—STREET NAMING—RETURN TO SFAX—SERVANT ENGAGED—MAHEDIA—PHŒNICIAN TOMBS—MONASTIR—SOUSSA.

THANKS to the kindness of Mr. Galea, we had spent two most agreeable days in this beautiful oasis of Gabès, and had obtained much interesting information on many subjects connected with the commerce of the country and the prospects of an extension of trade under the present occupiers of the Regency.

Every Englishman must be struck with dismay at the decline of British influence in a country where, not many years ago, we were respected and our counsels were followed. In spite of what may be said to the contrary by those who may be prompted possibly by jealousy, it cannot be denied that British influence is salutary. The most superficial observation of those parts of the world where the English dominate will suffice to demonstrate this. Although the natives of North Africa are pleased when they learn that the traveller is an Englishman, they have little or no faith in our ability to serve them, or of our weight in the councils of nations. Englishmen are nowhere to be met with; very few English commercial houses have factories or branches in the country; there is no market for British manufactures; and even the esparto grass, which is shipped almost exclusively to Great Britain, is hampered with a vexatious export duty. Consular reports give ample evidence on this subject.

As in France, so in Tunisia, the French continue their mania for rechristening streets. Here they change the Arab names for those of the officers who may have been engaged in capturing the towns in question, so that the native may be reminded at every turn in his path of the nation he loves the least. Here we see Boulevard Boulanger, there Rue Général this or Colonel that.

At one o'clock in the morning the steamer left for Sfax, reaching that port in five hours. Hitherto we had managed fairly well without an interpreter; but as we now contemplated a journey right across Tunisia, we were prudently advised to take one. Such an individual we obtained at Sfax, through the kind assistance of Mr. Gatte. François, so he called himself, our future interpreter, cook, and servant-of-all-work, was a Maltese, who spoke no English, and only a very little bad French. He might have been taken for a bandit, a sea-captain, a horse-keeper; for anything, in fact, but what he really was—a cook. He wore a small felt hat, a loosely-fitting coloured shirt without any necktie, a looser jacket, no vest, and trousers, over which he drew a pair of high jack-boots. His appearance was altogether free and easy, and he looked as if he could turn his hand to anything. His capabilities were, however, as experience subsequently proved, very limited.

The arrangements necessary for the engagement of François, and another ramble through the streets of Sfax, occupied our time until 6 p.m., when we steamed off again, anchoring the following morning before Mahedia. The sea had been perfectly calm during the night, and the loveliness of the weather remained unchanged.

Before taking leave of M. Novak on the previous occasion, he requested us, should we desire to make an excursion to some Phœnician tombs recently discovered in the vicinity of Mahedia, and the weather permit our landing, to telegraph to him before leaving Sfax. Of this we gratefully availed ourselves, and on landing found at our disposal a private carriage, well equipped with three stout mules. Nor was this all, for a friend of M. Novak was good enough to accompany us, in order to insure our seeing all that could be seen during the short time the steamer lay at anchor. Not an instant was lost; the coachman gave the word of departure to his sturdy animals, who started off at a good round pace and, following closely the sea-shore, we found ourselves in less than an hour at our destination.

The tombs lie within half a mile of the sea, about four miles south of Mahedia, and as nearly as possible equidistant between that town and Sallecta. They are cut in a spur of the rock, from which was quarried the stone of which the Thysdrus amphitheatre was built, and which here rises about twelve or fourteen feet above the general level of the shore. About a dozen tombs, out of many hundreds which no doubt may be found here, were explored a few years ago by M. Melon, and have been fully described in a paper entitled *La Nécropole Phénicienne*, and published in the *Revue Archéologique*, 1884. This necropolis, which extends along the shore for about three or four miles, has been ransacked by Arabs at different periods, and consequently few objects of interest or of value were met with during the recent exploration. The tombs are very similar in plan and arrangement, but with varying dimensions, and the entrances are all on the east side. A sharp descent by a flight of steps cut on the left or south side of a square trench conducts to a stone door, averaging three feet square, forming the entrance to the sepulchral chamber, the floor of which is some two or three steps lower down. On either side is a bed of stone, on which the bodies were placed, and at the end is a small niche for a funereal lamp. The walls of these chambers are not quite vertical, but incline inwards towards the top. The late M. Renan, to whom M. Melon's drawings of these tombs were submitted, was of opinion that they belonged to a class of sepulchres rarely met with, the formation being different from those discovered at Tyre, as well as other Phœnician settlements on the coast of Africa.

After an examination of as many tombs as our limited time would permit, we hastened back to the steamer, and at a quarter-past one p.m. were off Monastir. Some fifty casks of oil were here waiting for shipment, so that we had ample leisure to enjoy the lovely panorama along this part of the coast. Little of the town of Monastir is visible from the sea; but the coast, clothed with olives apparently down to the water's edge, presents a striking appearance. On rounding the cape, with its islands and forts, Monastir becomes more prominent, and presents an enchanting picture with its white crenelated walls, its towering Kasba, and its numerous white koubbas, encircled by olives and palms, the peak of Zaghouan rising boldly in the distance. Crossing the bay, we anchored off Soussa at 8 p.m.

CHAPTER XVII.

SOUSSA TO KAIROUAN.

November 19th.

AN UNINTERESTING ROAD — MOUREDDINE — MEN WASHING — ROMAN CISTERNS — A FRENCH TRAMWAY — FIELD FIRES — LAKES KELBIA AND SIDI-EL-HANI — WELLS — HILLOCKS — AIN-KAZEZIN — FIRST SIGHT OF KAIROUAN BY MOONLIGHT — FONDOUKS — OUR INN — JEWISH MUSIC AND DANCING — FANATICISM CHECKED.

THERE was no inducement to remain in Soussa longer than the time needed to complete our arrangements, and to procure provisions for our journey into the interior. These matters of detail were concluded on the morning of November 19th, and at midday we took our departure.

Although Captain Hélouis had kindly offered to convey us to Kairouan by the tramway which has been just laid by the French between the two towns for military purposes, we preferred to hire at Soussa a carriage in which we could continue our journey beyond Kairouan, and that might be available as a sleeping-place in case of emergency. It was the usual rough kind of landau, drawn by four small horses and driven by a man of colour, exceptionally energetic and obliging.

If one sets aside the absolutely African aspect of the scenery, a few ruined Roman reservoirs, and such glimpses of Arab life as can be caught by the way, the route from Soussa to Kairouan is devoid of either interest or beauty. The entire distance is 52 kilomètres. After passing the olive-groves which surround Soussa, and the villages of Messaadine and Moureddine, the road traverses vast plains, flat or slightly undulating, waterless, treeless, and almost devoid of cultivation.

Immediately after quitting Soussa by the Bab-el-Gharbi we passed between the Arab and European cemeteries, and for three hours jolted over a track, winding among the olive plantations, and broken up by the ridges and grips cut across it to secure the rainfall.

At two o'clock we passed through Moureddine, already mentioned, where olive-pressing is an important and successful industry, scarcely to be credited to so filthy and, as far as appearances go, so miserable a place. Here we observed men at a tank washing—an operation which they performed by stamping on the garments and pressing out the impurities with their feet. Shortly after leaving Moureddine the olives cease altogether, and the plains become entirely desolate and shelterless.

At three o'clock we alighted to examine a disused and partially ruined Roman cistern, of no great importance, which we perceived immediately to the left of the road.

The Decauville road, as the military tramway is called, and the carriage track do not follow parallel lines, but intersect each other at an acute angle about half way; the former we struck at a quarter to four o'clock, when we crossed and recrossed it several times. At this spot numerous fires, kindled by the labourers who were clearing away the weeds and scrub previous to ploughing, lit up the plain for a great distance all around, and imparted a weird aspect to the desolate and melancholy scene.

The two lakes of Kelbia and Sidi-el-Hani, which we

had skirted on our way to El-Djem, were visible on either hand at four o'clock, although at some distance from the route.

Another Roman cistern to the left of the road attracted our attention at a quarter-past four o'clock, and in another quarter of an hour we observed several koubbas in the same direction.

At a quarter to five o'clock we entered a flat grassy tract of land, forming a slight depression in the plain and pierced by numerous wells. Here groups of Arabs were drawing water in rude pitchers, and camels and asses, cows and horses in great numbers, were eagerly slaking their thirst. The scene was gay and animated, recalling some one or other of those old-world narratives familiar to us in chapters of Bible history. The Oued Zeroud, which rises in the Djebel Touila and loses itself in the marshy tract to the south of Kairouan, is probably the source of supply to these wells. The plain is here dotted for several miles around by small hillocks, thorns and stunted shrubs springing out of them. These are the sites of former encampments, each little mound marking the spot covered by a tent or gourbi, the refuse and ordure left by the occupiers having imparted fertility to the spots. Such a district, where water is abundant, would naturally be a favourite halting-place for caravans and pilgrims passing to and from the holy city.

Another hour brought us to a small lake hemmed in by very marshy ground, where the road was so bad that we had to leave the carriage and proceed some distance on foot. We had intended to enter Kairouan by daylight, but the sun was sinking below the horizon and the city walls were not yet in sight. Our coachman, who had declined to stop at the wells already noticed, where the Arabs were watering their cattle, now pulled up at Ain-Kazezin, and while resting and refreshing his horses we again walked on.

It was now seven o'clock. The city was in view some four miles distant, and the moon so bright that the minarets and whitened walls stood out as sharp and clear as in broad daylight, while the shadows were distinctly marked in soft outlines. We had some little difficulty in crossing the Oued Bagla, where a bridge was in course of construction, and at half-past seven o'clock we halted before the door of the inn, immediately without the walls of Kairouan.

The native fondouks are of necessity important establishments in a town where not a day passes without the arrival or departure of a caravan, either religious or commercial; but since the French occupation they are not frequented by Europeans, although all restrictions concerning unbelievers have been abolished. The miserable barrack where we were to be lodged, kept by an Italian, and notable for its uncleanness, detestable cooking, and lack of decent furniture, is at present the only inn for Europeans.

After hastily despatching a meal, the remnants of the dinner prepared for some French sub-officers whom we found at table when we entered, we sallied forth into the city, and sauntering through some of the principal streets, now almost deserted, entered an establishment to which we were attracted by a lamp over the door, and by strains of music from within. It was a low-pitched, white-washed room, without any attempt at decoration, and furnished with a few rough tables and benches, at which some twenty Arabs were sitting. The performers consisted of three men and two women, Algerian Jews, seated cross-legged on a low platform at one end of the apartment. Before them were placed several candles, stuck into empty bottles, by way of foot-lights. Their music was, as usual, of a plaintive character. Then one of the women—robust, middle-aged, and uncomely—slipped down from the platform and began to dance among the audience. Her movements were simple and unvaried, even to monotony; not altogether devoid of grace, they were marked with that tincture of sensuality peculiar to all Oriental dancing, or rather posturing. Putting the corners of two handkerchiefs in her mouth, so that the ends hung down behind the shoulders, and extending her arms, she jumped up and down, or moved backwards or forwards, and then, suddenly advancing towards one of the audience whom she had singled out as the probable possessor of a few pieces of money, she took up her position close to him, gazed at him steadily and amorously, and wriggled her body in a lascivious manner. Nor did she desist until the object of her attack had rewarded her pertinacity with a coin, however small. The transfer was effected by the donor wetting the piece with his spittle and sticking it on her forehead.

We had, of course, not escaped the stout Jewess's importunities, and our contribution had evidently given satisfaction, for the musicians, taking us, as usual, for Frenchmen, now struck up in our honour the Marseillaise, which we stopped at once, as on a previous occasion.

Having already witnessed this kind of performance in Algeria, we were not a little surprised at finding the inhabitants of Kairouan, hitherto held to be such uncompromising and exclusive fanatics, tolerating and even finding pleasure in the performances of the universally detested Jews. It is a proof, were one needed, how thoroughly the French have shattered the prejudices of the natives; or rather, how completely they have stifled them, at any rate for a time.

CHAPTER XVIII.

KAIROUAN.

November 19th, 20th, and 21st.

BAD WEATHER—DECLINE OF RELIGIOUS ENTHUSIASM—THE KASBA—THE GREAT CISTERNS—THE CITY WALLS—ITS ORIGIN—THE SOUKS—DJAMÂA-EL-KEBIR—THE SACRED WELL—MOSQUE OF THE THREE GATES—MOSQUE-TOMBS—THE SUBURBS—TOMB OF THE COMPANION—EDUCATION—ASPECT OF THE COUNTRY—POPULATION DEGENERATING—COURTESY OF THE INHABITANTS—A THUNDER-STORM.

FAIR weather is of paramount importance to the traveller in Tunisia. An African town loses all its charms under a leaden sky and a downpour of rain. The spell is broken. The glistening walls and wondrous effects of light and shade are exchanged for one dreary monotony of whitewash; and streets and alleys, innocent of paving, become one long series of muddy pools. Such was the aspect of Kairouan* on the evening of the first day after our arrival, dulling the long-awakened curiosity to tread the ground of a once forbidden city, and to penetrate every nook and corner of its holy places.†

Our first care was to deliver a letter of introduction

---

* The name is variously written by different European authors, as Cairwan, Kairwân, Kerouan, Kerwan, Qaïrouân, Qirwan, &c. We have followed the spelling adopted by the French in their most recent official publications.

† An Arab proverb says that seven journeys to Kairouan are equivalent to one pilgrimage to Mecca.

to Captain Cret, the French commandant, and to procure an official order to enter the various mosques of the city. Without this permit they would have been closed to us,* like those of all other towns in Tunisia. It certainly seems anomalous that Kairouan, the hot-bed of Arab fanaticism, should be the one place in the Regency where the mosques are not forbidden to unbelievers. But this may be easily accounted for. Kairouan the holy has long ceased to exercise paramount influence over devout followers of the Prophet; and the spirit that once animated the enthusiastic disciples of the new creed, and led them on from victory to victory, till they were stopped at last at the walls of Tours, has little in common with the sentimental fanaticism and hopeless degeneracy of an effete race. So that when the first French soldiers arrived the other day under the walls of the city, the gates were thrown open without a murmur or a struggle; and the sanctity of the city, and of all that had been closed against the infidel, whether Christian or Jew, for twelve hundred years, with its precious mementoes of hundreds of saintly men, vanished, never to be revived.

While the document was being prepared by the interpreter of the regiment (it was written in Arabic), the captain was good enough to conduct us to the Kasba, placing an orderly at our disposal during our stay in the city. As Kairouan is built on level ground, the Kasba does not dominate the city, as elsewhere, but consists merely

---

* Freiher von Maltzan, who visited Kairouan in 1869, was not permitted, any more than other infidels at that period, to enter the mosques. He recounts with some humour how the Arab official, arriving early in the morning to conduct him through the city, surprised him in his dressing-gown, and persisted in his retaining throughout the day that garment, as being, in his opinion, more dignified and less offensive to the inhabitants.

of a vast courtyard with a range of reservoirs underneath, and is surrounded by one-storied buildings now tenanted by French soldiery. It occupies an angle in the crenelated wall that encloses the city, and has an external gate communicating with the open country, without any bastions or outworks. Passing through the gateway we arrived, after five minutes' walk, at the remarkable double reservoir, said to have been constructed by a prince of the Aghlabite dynasty about the end of the eighth century. It has been restored at different periods, and although disused, is in sufficiently good preservation for the storage of fifteen million gallons of water. The reservoir consists of two large polygonal basins, 20 feet deep, the smaller one being 112 feet in diameter, and the larger one 414 feet. In addition there are two vaulted filters communicating with the large cistern, and the remains of covered galleries over them, for the purpose of keeping the water cool, as well as of sheltering from the sun the inhabitants and pilgrims who came here to draw it. The arrangement of these cisterns, as well as their construction, differs so much from those generally assigned to the period of the Arab occupation of North Africa, commonly called *feskias*, which are invariably of a square form and of rude construction, that one is tempted to discredit the statement of El-Bekri, an Arab writer of the eleventh century, attributing them to the Aghlabites. There is no other authority for the statement which has been handed down, uncontradicted and unverified, through eight centuries. There are many features in these cisterns in their present condition that point to an early period of the Roman occupation, probably the second or third century; and as they are of the same form as many others in the country that are undoubtedly Punic, it is reasonable to suppose they owe their origin to some Carthaginian settlement prior to the commencement of the Christian era. The remains of an octagonal tower in the centre of the larger basin, that in El-Bekri's time was crowned by a pavilion with four doors, leads one to conjecture that it was surmounted by the statue of a Roman Emperor, who had rebuilt or restored this public work. Again, the inside of the smaller basin is embellished with a series of eighteen circular-headed niches, evidently intended for statues of nymphs or water-gods; but of these it must be admitted there are no indications. The buttresses also of the walls of both basins are of a form peculiar to Punic times, and were adopted by the Romans in numerous reservoirs, of which there are many remains in other parts of the Regency.

Without entering further into the question, one may assume that some Aghlabite princes, desirous of promoting the welfare of the inhabitants of Kairouan, restored these cisterns, and probably built several of the other reservoirs outside the walls. mentioned by El-Bekri, of which there are the remains of four, long since neglected and disused. Any one, travelling over the great plain that isolates Kairouan from any other settlements, will see at a glance that the storage of water in a country where there is frequently no rainfall for more than twelve months was not neglected by its earlier rulers, and that the extraordinary fertility of the soil, recognised by most writers, was due in a large measure to the construction of reservoirs and a proper system of irrigation. Perhaps the existence of this abundant water storage may have influenced Okbah in his selection of this site for his capital, and that the town may have been, so to say, built up to the reservoir. There are no springs in the neighbourhood, and there is only one well outside the walls; every mosque, every house, has its tank in which to store the rainfall, so that a work of this kind and magnitude was of the greatest importance, not to say necessity.

The general aspect of Kairouan is that of a military rather than of a sacred city, bearing some resemblance to Peking, though on a much smaller scale. It is enclosed by a crenelated wall, having seven irregular sides, about 30 feet high, and varying from 6 to 8 feet in thickness, built entirely with small, well-burnt bricks, 2 inches thick, made from earth in the immediate suburbs. It is strengthened by square and round towers at intervals, of the same height as the wall, and although formidable enough in appearance, would be entirely useless at the present day as a place of defence. Inside the wall is a terraced walk all round, from 4 to 5 feet wide, just below the crenelations, and the foot of the wall is kept clear of buildings, so that there is free circulation all round on both sides. There are five principal gates of a somewhat similar form, and three posterns called *khaukhat*, which are nothing more than low winding passages, 5 feet high, and not wide enough to admit any but the thinnest of mortals. These are not closed either by day or night, and there are no indications of either doors or shutters ever having been attached. The Bab-el-Tunis, or Tunis gate, like the others, has an arch within an arch, the outer one resting on marble shafts, and the inner one having voussoirs of black and white marble. The spandrils are framed in marble, and two framed marble slabs covered with inscriptions adorn the filling-in between the two arches. These have the appearance of being modern, replacing others similarly inscribed. The writing on these gateways is in praise of the structure. 'Hasten to behold

BAB EL-TUNIS, KAIROUAN

it,' says the inscription on the Tanners' Gate; 'Beauty has placed its mark on the Gate of the Tanners.'

The history of Kairouan, from its foundation by Okbah in the year 667 through its four centuries of wondrous prosperity, followed by a long period of corruption, and finally by inevitable decay, has been so well traced by Mr. Broadley in his *Tunis Past and Present*, that it would be superfluous to enlarge on the subject here. It is sufficient to state that the Arab historian Novaïri, from whom later authors have mostly derived their information, tells us that in 55 A.H., or 675 of our era, Okbah selected the site for his city, the whole country being at that time an impenetrable forest, so infested with venomous serpents and wild beasts that his followers murmured at his choice. Upon which the religious commander, after addressing himself to Allah, ordered these enemies of the human race to retire. When he had ceased speaking, continues Novaïri, the Mussulmans saw with astonishment during the whole of the day the venomous beasts and wild animals retire in the distance, taking their young with them—a miracle which converted a great number of Berbers to Islamism. Then Okbah, planting his lance in the ground, exclaimed, ' Here is your Kairouan '—caravan or resting-place.

As no stone for building purposes is to be obtained within a reasonable distance, brick is the material most frequently used: a manufacture still carried on in the immediate outskirts of the city. The dwelling-houses are low, generally of one-storey, mean, and unimposing, each being provided with an underground water-tank. It need scarcely be said that these are mostly choked with dirt and the impurities of many centuries. Even the sacred edifices, the glory of Kairouan, are not attractive when seen from the streets, although the cupolas are more ornamental than those generally found in Tunisian towns. They are invariably fluted, or ribbed like a melon, and have been described as consisting of a series of 'vertical ribs converging towards the top, so that they are not unlike the knob of a keyless watch.' In common with other towns in North Africa, Roman shafts and fragments of Roman ornamentation are to be seen at the corners of streets, forming the quoin or prop of some ill-constructed Arab wall. The four principal streets are wide and fairly-well paved, but the by-streets and alleys are filthy and tortuous, and as ill-kept as in other Arab towns. The bazaars are similar to those of Tunis, and scarcely less animated, but the wares exposed for sale are neither so rich nor so varied, and the costumes of the inhabitants, almost entirely Arab, are less pleasing to the eye than the more ornate garments of the Moor or Jew. The industries are confined principally to the working of leather, the trade in horse-trappings being considerable. Slippers made at Kairouan are also much esteemed, their bright canary-coloured dye being as celebrated here as it was at Cordova in the days of its prosperity. Carpets also are made here, but the trade is not very considerable. The interest in Kairouan may be said to be centred in its mosques and *zaouias*. You may count fifty of the latter, and at least twenty mosques, but there are only six deserving special notice.

The great mosque, known as Djamäa-el-Kebir, occupying the north-east angle of the city, close to the ramparts, was built, as tradition informs us, by Sidi-Okbah, the companion of Mahomet and the founder of Arab rule in North Africa.* This was the man who, at

---

* In *La Civilisation des Arabes*, by Dr. Gustave Le Bon, will be found views of the mosques of Sidi-Okbah and of Sidi-Amar-Abada, as well as of the mihrab of the mosque of Sidi-el-Habib.

A STREET IN KAIROUAN

the head of a band of warriors, as fierce and daring as himself, passed like a whirlwind over the land, and when he arrived at the borders of the Atlantic upbraided his Creator for having stopped any further conquests. Of the original mosque little remains. Indeed, there are very few parts that do not indicate reconstruction or enlargement. El-Bekri tells us the mosque was entirely rebuilt by Hassan, A.H. 84, with the exception of the mihrab, and seventy years later it was again taken down and rebuilt. Many alterations have been made since that date, even to a very recent period. The arrangement of this mosque differs but little from that of Damascus, or the greater work at Cordova, of which it was the undoubted prototype. In each case there are the prayer-chamber, consisting of a series of aisles separated by marble columns, the mihrab surmounted by a dome, and the *kibleh*, or shrine. Without is a large quadrangle surrounded by a colonnade, the back-wall forming the enclosure of the mosque, and in the centre of one end of the quadrangle, facing the central aisle of the prayer-chamber, is the *minar*, or minaret. The entire mosque is in the form of an irregular oblong, the longest side measuring about 425 feet and the shortest about 250 feet. The prayer-chamber, 250 feet long, and 120 feet wide, has a central aisle 20 feet wide, and a series of eight aisles, each of eight bays, on either side. These are separated by marble shafts of great beauty and varied colouring, with capitals and bases mostly of white marble, the spoil of the chief buildings of Roman Carthage and other towns in North Africa. The columns of the central aisle, as well as of the bays nearest the back or eastern wall of the mosque, are grouped together in pairs, and in some cases in threes. Their height is a little over 22 feet, those in the aisles varying from 15 to

16 feet. Above the shafts rise horse-shoe arches, and these carry a flat trabeated ceiling, enriched with gold and colour. The mihrab is crowned by a cupola vaulted in stone, richly glazed, and supported on the north side by two groups of three shafts each, and on the south side by engaged shafts. In each of these groups is one of the two columns of red porphyry, mentioned by El-Bekri as having been brought from Cæsarea (the modern town of Cherchel, in Algeria), and reputed to have been worth their weight in gold. The mihrab niche, flanked by columns of porphyry, with capitals of white marble removed from some Christian basilica, is of semicircular form, gorgeously decorated with lapis lazuli and inlays of mosaic and white marble. About midway up the recess runs an inscription: 'God is the Lord, God is from the beginning and has not been begotten. There is none equal to Him. Mahomet is His prophet. May God bless him and grant him eternal salvation!' On the left of the niche is a slab of white marble framed in a broad band of green marble, forming a memorial of the founder. On it are written the words, 'The Creator—The Praised —the Glorious—The Giver of Life.' On the right is the *mimbar*, or pulpit, made of some dark wood, almost black with age, and elaborately carved after the manner of Cairene work, the panels being all different. Close to it is the *maksourah*, a kind of resting or retiring-place for the *Imaums*, but formerly used, as El-Bekri informs us, as a tribune or gallery for women. It is screened off from the prayer-chamber by a framing of Cairene work of great excellence. The floor of the mosque is paved with irregular slabs of white and other marbles, and fitted together very roughly. The side of the prayer-chamber facing the court is enclosed by a series of great doors, corresponding with the aisles, the central door,

DJAMAÄ EL KEBIR.

opening direct into the nave, being of larger dimensions and more richly carved. The colonnade surrounding the court or patio is formed by a double arcade, 20 feet wide, the front arches being of horse-shoe form and resting on coupled shafts of greyish marble, with white marble capitals of various designs, but mostly from some destroyed Roman edifices. The central archway of the southern façade, forming the main entrance to the prayer-chamber, is called 'The Beautiful Gate,' and has an archway of larger proportions, flanked by two smaller ones and surmounted by a cupola. The shafts supporting these arches are grouped in pairs, all monoliths of rare marbles, with richly carved composite capitals of white marble. Nearly in the centre of the northern side of the court rises the minar, which replaced the one attributed to Hassan, and of which there are vestiges at the south-west angle. It is a massive tower, clumsy in form, slightly tapering, and about 60 feet high. Above the parapet is a lantern of stone, crowned with a cupola on a vaulted arcade of good design, but so coated with whitewash that the lines of the architecture are almost effaced. Access is obtained by a flight of 125 steps within the tower, all made with slabs of marble of various colours, ill-fitted, as usual with the Arabs in adapting the materials of more ancient buildings. The view of the city from the top of the minar, and the aspect of the great plain bounded by an horizon of mountain and hill, is better seen than described. The panoramic view is marvellous. In El-Bekri's time there were ten gates or entrances to the mosque; at present there are five entrances to the great court, but one only is used. There is also an entrance direct into the prayer-chamber from the east side, which is still used by the Grand Mufti, the Archbishop, as it were, of Kairouan. Under the open court, which is mostly paved with large squares of white and grey marble, now in a dilapidated condition and overgrown with weeds, are immense cisterns. Marble bases of Roman shafts cover the approaches. There are also two sun-dials, one horizontal and one vertical, serving to fix the exact hour of prayer. On the north-east side of the mosque, between the entrance and the ramparts, is a large area of open ground; intended, no doubt, by the original founder, as a resting-place for pilgrims within the walls. Here is the sacred well of Kafayat, or 'It is enough.' It appears to have existed before the foundation of Kairouan, and has never been known to fail. It is enclosed by a rough wall faced with slabs of marble, stained and yellowed by age and neglect, and worn into furrows through long usage.

The Mosque of the 'Three Gates,' situated nearly in the centre of the town, is venerated by the Arabs on account of its antiquity. It consists of only one small chamber, the roof being supported, as usual, by Roman shafts with capitals of various designs and of beautiful workmanship. The minar is a poor edifice, but, as usual with the mosques of Kairouan, there is an inscription in raised bricks on the surface of the wall. The stone carving on the façade, in bands of foliage and Arab characters, is beautifully chiselled, showing that this branch of art was encouraged in Kairouan during its period of prosperity. Among the numerous zaouias or mosque-tombs within the walls, the burying-place of the Mourabet family, one of the oldest in Kairouan, built in the fifteenth century, is the most noticeable. A great arch nearly 40 feet high, flanked by marble shafts, and filled in with a doorway of white marble and a window covered with a bronze grille, forms the entrance to the vestibule. The court within has two storeys of arcades,

a marble basin in the centre, and is paved with slabs of black and white marble in geometric patterns. The shafts of the colonnade, which are of Moorish design, are of marble, but the arches are of stone. There are chambers at the angles, three of which contain tombs. Facing the entrance in the far side of the court is a small mosque, or family chapel as we should call it, where there is some excellent carving in marble in Kufic characters. The roof of the mosque is flat and trabeated, supported by sixteen Roman columns and arcaded over. South of the city, close to the ramparts, is the mosque-tomb of Sidi-Amar-Abada, the most conspicuous, as well as the most picturesque, of all the buildings in Kairouan, and, strange to relate, of very recent construction. It is crowned with six fluted domes, and was to have had seven. Internally it is very plain. In the vestibules are several wooden tables carved with inscriptions, and around most of the domes are broad bands of inscriptions in raised brickwork. This personage must have been a bit of a wag. His tomb has three cannon balls at his head and three at his feet. Huge swords covered with inscriptions adorn the walls, and a large pipe and tobacco-bowl are suspended over his remains. He died in Tunis about thirty-five years ago.

The Mosque of the 'Olive Tree,' a favourite designation in Tunisia, owing to the custom of planting a tree in the centre of the court, is outside the walls. This we did not visit, owing to the continuance of bad weather and the deplorable condition of the roads in the immediate vicinity of the city.

Outside the city walls are two large suburbs—mean, dirty, and devoid of interest, and here and there great mounds of *débris* and rubbish, heaped up higher than the ramparts, an accumulation of broken pottery, bones, and vegetable matter cast out of the city for many centuries past. Nothing in all Tunisia bears stronger testimony to the neglect and inherent stupidity of the Arab than these enormous piles of decayed rubbish exposed to the rays of a tropical sun. Even the very cemeteries, where one might have expected a show of veneration for the remains of thousands of poor pilgrims, who have sought at Kairouan a last resting-place, are nothing but huge excrescences on the flat plain, the heaped-up bodies of twelve centuries.

To describe the numerous places of sepulture of the learned and pious men who have been attracted to Kairouan as one of the great cities of Mohammedanism, would involve constant repetition. Their tombs, many of them still highly venerated, are to be seen everywhere, both within and without the walls, dotting the landscape with their whitened koubbas, invariably of the same pattern, and, with few exceptions, devoid of interest to the observer. But any description of the monumental works of Kairouan would be incomplete without something more than passing reference to the tomb of Sidi-Sahab, 'the holy companion and friend of the Prophet,' more generally, though incorrectly, styled 'The Mosque of the Barber.' The remarkable series of buildings that have clustered round this sepulchre, embracing the tomb itself, a mosque, and a college for instruction in the Koran (a *medressen*), were formerly within the walls; the city, according to all accounts, being so extensive in the days of its prosperity that children had little placards suspended from their necks, indicating the quarter where their parents resided. At the present day this mosque is more than a quarter of a mile from the ramparts. The entrance is through a courtyard and under a Moorish archway forming the bottom storey of a minaret, the upper stages of which are faced

DJAMÂA SIDI AMAR ABADA, KAIROUAN

with tiles of enamelled earthenware of great beauty of colouring and of varied design. The vestibule within, of square shape, is crowned by a dome, its surface covered with elaborate stucco-work, and the walls have a dado of old Persian faience, surmounted by plaster fretwork in the form of panels. Seats are ranged round the chamber. A short flight of stairs leads to an arcaded cloister of seven bays, ranged around a narrow open court. The shafts here are of white marble of Arab design, with the exception of two which have been taken from some Roman edifice, and the voussoirs of the arches are painted black and white alternately. The floor is paved with highly glazed black and white tiles, some octagonal, and some zigzag pattern, and the walls are finished like those in the vestibule. But here, as throughout this series of buildings, which have been added to, altered and patched at various times to a very recent period, the tile-work is a strange mixture of good and bad. Broken pieces have been replaced by bits of Italian manufacture of gaudy colouring, or by native faience so badly fabricated that the glaze drops off the body of the tile. The ceilings of the cloister are flat and trabeated, painted in sombre colours, and quite in harmony with the older parts of the work. From the cloister you pass through a vestibule into a large open court, with a colonnade all round, the centre of one side being the entrance into a chamber about 20 feet square. This is the tomb of 'The Companion.' A subdued light through a series of thick stained-glass windows in the domed roof reveals the wooden sarcophagus in the centre, covered with palls, the upper one being of green velvet, embroidered with silver thread. Around it is a high bronze lattice, to which stones, gilt balls of earth from Mecca, and native ostrich eggs, are attached. Banners and standards of rich fabrics are spread aloft, Eastern carpets, new and old, grace the floor, and from the centre of the richly decorated cupola is suspended a great chandelier of Venetian glass, with iron lances grouped round it. Persian faiences cover parts of the walls, the rest being in plaster arabesques, painted black and white. The door of the chamber, with its two little grilled windows on either side, is of Italian design and of recent date. The casings are of white marble, inlaid with panels of griotte, the symbols of the Prophet being carved over the openings. The material of these casings is rich, and the work is good, but it does not harmonise with the more sober colouring of the parts that are purely Arab.

From this large upper court, which is of the same character as the cloister already referred to, but much larger, you pass by a flight of steps to a lower court similarly planned. Here the shafts of white marble are of a more decorative character, but the rest of the work is simpler in design. This is the court of the College, consisting of a few offices, offensive to the eye as well as to the nose, and a series of small chambers or cells where the students reside. The instruction given here is confined to the study of the Koran and the Arabic language. Education, as understood amongst European nations, is unknown to these unprogressive people, and consequently ignorance and fanaticism, bred in such establishments as these, go hand in hand in upholding the tenets and superstitions of an unprogressive creed. The mosque attached to these buildings is small, and has no features of interest. It is of basilica form, with nave and aisles, columns of stone with plain capitals separating them, and with the mihrab at the end, the niche being flanked by two marble shafts.

ZAOUÏA SIDI-SAHAB

If this tomb of 'The Companion' is the most venerated of all the holy places of Kairouan, it is also the most interesting from its associations, as well as from the pure style of its architecture, and its characteristic adornments. 'Sidi-Sahab,' says the legend, 'attended the Prophet in all his expeditions, and lived in his tent. One day, while being shaved, Mahomed gave him three hairs from his beard, which the faithful Companion religiously preserved all his life. Proceeding to Cairo at the death of the Prophet, he accompanied the warrior Okbah to Kairouan, where he died. Then, following his instructions, one of these hairs was placed on his tongue, the other two on his eyes.'

The interest attached to Kairouan, second only to Mecca as a seat of Mohammedan fanaticism, and the mystery overshadowing its isolation of twelve centuries, is centred in the great mosque of Okbah, its founder, rather than in the group of buildings consecrated to Sidi-Sahab, the companion of the Prophet. Any one intimate with the Mosque of Cordova, occupying nearly five times the area of its prototype at Kairouan, its forest of marble shafts, the wondrous intricacies of perspective, the lace-like walls, the gorgeous mihrab, and the beauty of its mosaic ornamentation, will experience a feeling of disappointment on entering the prayer-chamber of the African mosque. The beautiful shafts of marble and porphyry, with their varied capitals of white marble, are not wanting; but of the delicate stucco ornamentation, the *nuksh hadida* of the Arabs, so beautiful at Cordova, there are no traces here. The mihrab niche is on a small scale, and the tile-work, of which there are a few exquisite specimens, have been so injured and pierced through frequent reconstructions that the beauty of the whole suffers accordingly. The builders' art must have been at a low ebb when the latest rebuilding of the mosque took place: columns and capitals ill-fitting are wedged up on a poor foundation with bits of olive-wood; arches are tied together with beams of wood, innocent of either plane or chisel; and the floor is paved with broken slabs of marble and stone, shape or pattern being wholly disregarded. Neglect has much to answer for, and waning enthusiasm, so noticeable in all the religious edifices of Tunisia, will not suffice to maintain these holy places or save them from inevitable ruin. It is to be hoped that the mosque of 'The Companion,' so complete in itself as a specimen of native workmanship, and so thoroughly in harmony with Arab ways, will at least be spared, and a fund for its maintenance be some day forthcoming.

How entirely changed is the aspect of the surrounding country! The forest of which the historian speaks has totally disappeared, and the entire plain is treeless and without shelter. Kairouan has neither wells nor fountains, and the absence of running water, so refreshing to the senses in any Eastern town, produces a depressing effect that cannot fail to influence the character as well as the health of the inhabitants.

The population of Kairouan, which may amount to some 10,000 souls,[*] was entirely Arab till the city came under the French protectorate. Jew traders, as well

---

[*] In a country where no census exists, estimates of population must be conjectural. The number of the inhabitants of Kairouan has been very differently given by various writers. The Chevalier de Hesse-Wartegg, writing in 1882, fixes the population at 30,000; M. Victor Cambon, 1885, at 25,000; M. V. Guérin, 1862, at 12,000; Lieut.-Col. Sir R. L. Playfair, 1877, after considering the reports of Mr. Wood, Consul-General at Tunis at that date, at 15,000; M. Pellissier at 12,000, adding, 'I should be inclined to put it down at considerably less than 10,000.'

as a few Maltese, were not long in following the footsteps of the French soldiers, and before long will establish themselves here as permanently as in other towns in the Regency.

From their custom of intermarriage, the sedentary nature of their occupations, and their general want of activity, from their alleged immorality, if not from other causes, they are neither a handsome nor a hardy people. In spite of their fanaticism and exclusiveness, they offered no resistance whatever when the French took their city; and they now suffer the yoke of the infidel with a meekness and resignation scarcely to be expected from a people at one time so arrogant and uncompromising.* Nearly every traveller to Kairouan has spoken of the averted looks, the imprecations, the insults, even the stone-throwing, to which he was subject at the hands of the people, both children and adults. We experienced no annoyance of any kind, although generally alone, unaccompanied even by our servants, penetrating without hesitation into some of the narrowest and least-frequented alleys. Far from this being the case, we were favoured on many occasions by much attention and courtesy. While sketching under a doorway, where we had taken refuge out of the rain, the proprietor of the house brought us a seat and a cup of coffee, presenting them with a graceful salute. Again, while inspecting the

---

* 'Like so many other cities, Kairouan is also one of the most corrupt; and the class of Tunisian dancing-girls is recruited in a great measure in that town of mosques and religious fraternities. The inhabitants of the city of Okbah pride themselves on living as parasites, at the expense of the faithful; consequently they are very degenerate, and have generally impure blood. Cancers, scrofula, all kinds of infirmities, give the inhabitants a repulsive appearance; they are wanting in strength for work, as they were in energy for resistance on the occasion of the French occupation.'—*Nouvelle Géographie Universelle*, xi. 232.

interior of the Grand Mosque, notwithstanding it was on a Friday, the numerous worshippers paused in their devotions, and without a murmur or an angry look suffered us to pass between them and the kibla. The native attendant, a servant of the mosque, who acted as our guide, merely turned up a corner of the rich carpet with which the floor of the kibla was covered, as a hint that it was not to be defiled by the tread of the infidel.

Rain had not ceased falling during the whole of our last day at Kairouan; but towards sundown a thunderstorm burst over the city, accompanied by such a downpour that we were fain to content ourselves with the four bare walls of our miserable lodging, and went to sleep with grave apprehensions for the morrow.

CHAPTER XIX.

KAIROUAN TO SBEITLA.

November 22nd and 23rd. Distance, 111 kilomètres.

TEDIOUS TRAVELLING—MORE RAIN—A DREARY PLAIN—DJEBEL TROZZA—WANT OF POPULATION—THE CAMP AT HADJEB-EL-AÏOUN — KIND RECEPTION—FIRST NIGHT IN A TENT—A RUINED CHRISTIAN TOWN—OUED GILMA — NUMEROUS NEGLECTED WATERCOURSES — INNUMERABLE RUINS—BIRDS—FIRST VIEW OF SBEITLA—WE STICK IN THE OUED—A SEARCH FOR A RESTING-PLACE IN THE DARK—A WALK AMONG THE RUINS BY MOONLIGHT.

THE distance from Kairouan to Hadjeb-el-Aïoun, where the French are establishing a strong camp, and where we had arranged to seek shelter for the night, is 66 kilomètres. We left Kairouan at 8.30 a.m., and did not reach our destination until 7.30 p.m.—eleven hours constant travelling, our four little horses trudging on bravely, without food, and with only one drink of water. The endurance of these miserable-looking, galled beasts, one with swollen fetlocks, seemed marvellous. Their only reward was the whip, both butt and lash, and their stall for the night was the open sky. Of Mohammed's instructions concerning kindness to animals the modern Arab takes no notice.

The morning of November 22nd was dull and cloudy. Scarcely had we passed the city gate when the rain began again, and continued to fall steadily until mid-day. We consulted our coachman, an intelligent dark-skinned Arab from the desert, whether we should return to the city, but as he was of decided opinion that the weather would clear we pressed steadily forward through the mud and slush.

If the route from Soussa to Kairouan was dull, that further west* was still more depressing—an absolute flat, devoid of cultivation, traversed by occasional marshes, and dotted with low bushes and scrub, covered by millions of small white snails, which at the distance looked like blossoms. The bushes frequently grow on small mounds, similar to those we had noticed a few days before. For four hours we journeyed slowly on over this melancholy plain, with nothing more diverting than the occasional crossing of an oued, until about mid-day, when, lunching in our carriage *en route*, we were delighted to find ourselves once more in the vicinity of hills. The roads were deep in mire; the rain, which had so far continued to fall steadily, now ceased, the clouds broke, and the prospect of reaching Hadjeb-el-Aïoun that evening looked encouraging. Djebel Trozza now towered up to our right, and the scenery on either side the track was inviting. At two o'clock we pulled through a small stream issuing from the Ain-el-Kraib, once spanned by a bridge, the remains of which still exist, and close to the spot where stands a square stone-built fondouk. This is the western boundary of the plain, at least sixty miles across, with Kairouan as its centre. Here the scenery is very weird, huge masses of rock peeping above the rough verdure, indicating by their stratification some

---

* In April, 1876, Lieut.-Col. Sir R. L. Playfair performed the journey from Kairouan to Sbeitla, passing over almost the same ground. He has given an interesting account in Chapter XX. of his *Travels in the Footsteps of Bruce*. The volume contains two views of Sbeitla from drawings by Bruce, viz. the Entrance to the Hieron, and the back wall of the Three Temples.

violent disturbance at the surface at no remote period. A few miles further we entered another plain, varied by occasional undulations, and gay with arbutus, bushes of juniper and different sorts of dwarf pine, with here and there a solitary olive-tree. The sun now set with a wild splendour, and the whole sky was lit up with gorgeous colouring. Fortunately a rising wind helped to dry the muddy track, and a welcome moon, shining forth with unwonted clearness, befriended us in the hour of need. In spite of the rain which had fallen during the morning and previous day, we had not been inconvenienced by the swelling of the oueds; indeed, many of them were comparatively dry, although we experienced considerable difficulty in crossing a marsh nearly a mile wide before reaching the rising ground, on the summit of which the French camp was temporarily pitched.

We had accomplished the entire distance from Kairouan to Hadjeb-el-Aïoun without passing either town or village; indeed, with the exception of the solitary fondouk already mentioned, there were no signs of any settled population. A few gourbies here and there, and flocks of sheep and goats visible on the rising ground, indicated the presence of Bedouin tribes, moving from place to place.

Captain Perronell, the chief officer of the camp, to whom we were furnished with an introduction, received us most cordially, placing a tent (a very dilapidated one, it must be owned) at our disposal. A frugal supper, composed of the provisions we had brought from Soussa, supplemented by a regulation loaf from the canteen, was quickly prepared and more rapidly dispatched, and wearied out with our day's journey we soon fell asleep. The wind had fortunately subsided; otherwise the rents in the canvas would have admitted more air than would have been agreeable. As it was, the temperature in this exposed and elevated position became very chilly as the night advanced, and both overcoats and wrappers were welcome coverings.

At the time of our visit the camp of Hadjeb-el-Aïoun was in process of construction, and the necessary installations were not yet completed. Hitherto the French head-quarters of the district had been on the banks of the Oued Gilma, or Djilma, a spot selected on account of the abundance of the water in that part of the stream. The position being low and unhealthy, and the water found to be injurious to health, the troops were removed to the site of the present camp, occupying the plateau of a small hill, at the foot of which is a copious spring of the purest water. The position is altogether admirable, and the panoramic view most extensive.

The state of our tent, with its tattered canvas, was so little conducive to protracted slumber, that we were up before sunrise and about the camp, watching the soldiers under the light of the waning moon perform their early duties, and giving instructions for our start.

By eight o'clock we were on the track again, passing over a pleasant stretch of green sward, where large flocks of sheep and goats were finding abundant pasture, and five miles further on we noted to our right some Roman ruins on rising ground. Blocks of hewn stone were still standing, but no buildings were traceable. We then traversed a wild, uncultivated plain, covered with scrub, the mountains rising majestically right and left. At about a hundred yards from the road we reached, at ten o'clock, the ruins of a town of great extent. On examining the remains we observed (1) a rectangular enclosure of Christian origin, twenty-five paces long by fifteen paces broad, built of horizontal and vertical stones alternately, the interspaces being filled in with rubble. This system of constructing walls, frequently employed by the Romans in the later days of the Empire, was introduced by them into Britain, and afterwards adopted by the Saxons, of which we have several examples existing at the present day. The wall of this structure was strengthened by square buttresses two feet wide on three sides. There were small windows between the buttresses, an apsidal end, and the substructure of an arcade dividing the nave and aisles. There were two doorways, one to each aisle. The plan of this early Christian basilica, of which there are numerous examples in North Africa, is familiar to us in the plan and arrangement of churches in our own country. (2) A vaulted construction, probably the remains of the baths, but too ruined to judge of the extent and outline of the building. All the buildings showed indications of having been reconstructed with the materials of former edifices. There are numerous foundations of other buildings which have now disappeared, but no inscribed stones were discernible.

For a full hour we journeyed over a vast plain, literally strewn with stones, the remains of former habitations, but where at present there are neither houses nor tents, nor any attempt at cultivation. At mid-day we reached the abandoned French camp on the Oued Gilma, and lunched in one of the few huts yet standing. As wood is so scarce in these parts the buildings were being gutted, and the materials, such as roofs, windows, doors, &c., were being transported to the new establishment at Hadjeb-el-Aïoun. The distance from Hadjeb-el-Aïoun to Oued Gilma is computed at 21 kilomètres.

At a quarter-past one o'clock we left our halting-place, crossing the oued exactly at the point where a

Roman aqueduct, level with the ground, but now in ruins, spanned the stream, bringing the water to a cistern of some magnitude a mile or so distant. This indicated a former settlement, of which, as far as we could judge, no other vestiges remain.

From Oued Gilma to Sbeitla, a distance of about twenty-five kilomètres, we crossed the beds of watercourses no less than seven times. They were fortunately dry, or nearly so, but as they fill very quickly after rain, and as there is not a single bridge, the traveller will do well not to attempt a visit to Sbeitla except during the dry season. He may reach his destination, but it is doubtful whether he would be able to return.

The whole district is literally strewn with Roman remains, giving the country the appearance of a vast cemetery. Scarcely a mile is passed without the presence of some ruined structure or groups of chiselled stones, requiring time and careful study to form conclusions as to their value. Here huge blocks of hewn stone half buried in the ground stand upright in pairs, surmounted by a lintel; there a cistern, of which the vaulting has fallen in, filling the space with a mass of *débris*. At other places the foundations of a fortress, or a basilica adapted to the performance of Christian rites, or the solid substructure of a Roman bath. What a field of study for the archæologist! what a melancholy page for the historian! Here must have dwelt formerly a numerous and active population. These innumerable and apparently unconnected oueds, at one time of the year beds of stones without a trace of water, at another rushing torrents swollen and impassable, were once running streams, embanked and spanned by bridges, filling the cisterns, and fertilising the soil. This barren, trackless plain, was formerly cultivated and intersected by good roads. A few shepherds, mostly Bedouins, were the only human beings we had met during the whole day; not a single habitation as far as the eye could compass. On the other hand we observed a great number of birds —magpies, partridges in great quantities, innumerable crested larks and other small birds, besides bustards, hawks, and birds of prey of larger kinds.

The sun was sinking behind the hills as we caught the first glimpse of the ruins of Sbeitla. The fatigue of a long day's journey was forgotten, and pressing on as quickly as our tired animals would permit, we arrived on the sandy margins of the river to which Sbeitla owes its name. Animated by the voice of their driver the horses dashed into the stream, struggled, and then stuck fast in the sandy bed. To add to the dilemma, one of the horses, by the violence of his efforts, had snapped the traces, and quietly walked away from the carriage, slaking his thirst as he went. The position was not pleasant, darkness was coming on, and Sbeitla was still at some distance. In an instant boots were off, trousers tucked up, and we were above our knees in the water. We were four, including our coachman and the servant. With a good will we went to work, and after half-an-hour's exertion were fortunate in reaching the other side of the stream.

There is no accommodation of any kind at Sbeitla. This we knew, the difficulty being to find in the dark (for the moon had not yet risen, and twilight is unknown in these latitudes) a resting-place for the night. Each of us started in a different direction to explore the dilapidated edifices of which the dim outlines loomed forth in the obscurity, stumbling as we went over the countless stones with which the surface is everywhere encumbered. A modern vaulted structure was at last discovered without door or windows, and here we determined to take up our quarters. Dinner over, and the arrangements for the night completed, we sauntered among the weird ruins that rose ghostlike over the far-stretching plain. The moon was up in all its splendour, and the stillness of the air was broken only by the bubbling waters of the river we had just crossed, and the occasional screech of an owl, whose 'ancient solitary reign' we were disturbing.

CHAPTER XX.

SBEITLA, THE ANCIENT SUFETULA.

November 23rd to 26th.

SUFETULA PAST AND PRESENT—ITS REMAINS—THE THREE TEMPLES—
THE MONUMENTAL ENTRANCE TO THE HIERON—THE TRIUMPHAL
ARCH—THE AQUEDUCT—EXPLORATION NECESSARY.

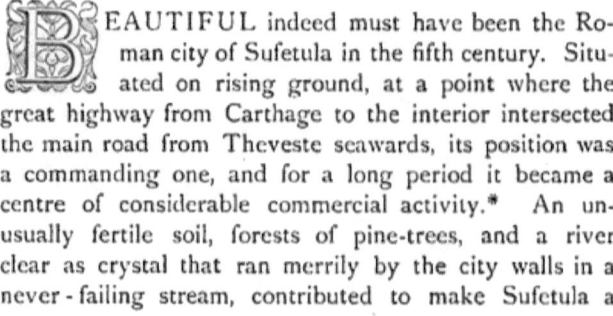EAUTIFUL indeed must have been the Roman city of Sufetula in the fifth century. Situated on rising ground, at a point where the great highway from Carthage to the interior intersected the main road from Theveste seawards, its position was a commanding one, and for a long period it became a centre of considerable commercial activity.* An unusually fertile soil, forests of pine-trees, and a river clear as crystal that ran merrily by the city walls in a never-failing stream, contributed to make Sufetula a

---

* 'In the neighbourhood of Sbeitla the bed of the river is of compact limestone; on either side of it numerous tepid springs are seen bubbling up from the earth, accompanied by free carbonic acid gas. These unite into one stream, of volume sufficient to supply an immense city, quite as large as the fountain of Zaghouan, and for more than a mile it thus flows in a clear and beautiful stream, never dry even in the hottest part of summer. The temperature is just high enough to make it slightly warm in winter, but quite sufficiently cool in summer.'—Lieut.-Col. Sir R. L. Playfair, *Travels in the Footsteps of Bruce*, p. 180.

place of delight for the wealthy colonists of North Africa.*

To-day all is changed—a solitary shepherd tending his flock is the only human being one is likely to meet where 'merchants once did congregate;' the trees are gone, the plains are arid or clothed with rough herbage, and all signs of habitation have been swept away. The river alone continues to flow as of old, lost some few miles lower down in the arid sand, and coming to the surface again at some lower level, like most of the neglected streams of this country.† Yet, in spite of prevailing desolation, this spot, so far removed from human dwellings—its ruined fanes outlined sharp and

---

* The spot reminds one of the so-called 'marble rocks' of Jubblepoor, though on a much smaller scale.

† 'My brethren have dealt deceitfully as a brook, and as the stream of brooks they pass away.'—*Job*, vi. 15.

Edrisi, the Arab geographer of the twelfth century, writes:— 'Sobeitala was, before the Arab invasion, the town of Gerges (Gregory), king (prefect) of the Romans of Africa; it was remarkable for its extent as well as for the beauty of its situation, for its abundant water, for the mildness of its climate, and for its wealth; it was surrounded by orchards and gardens. The Musulmans conquered it during the first year of the Hegira, and put the great king Gerges to death.'

Other writers inform us that Gerges, sometimes written Gregorius, had revolted from the Byzantine Empire, and, with the assistance of native tribes, had made himself ruler over a large territory, of which Sufetula was about the centre. With the appearance of the Arabs in this remote corner of North Africa commenced the struggle for supremacy between the representatives of Christianity and the followers of Mahomet. The city, having no walls of defence, soon succumbed to a horde of invaders. Gregorius was slain, and the treasuries of a wealthy population were seized by the victorious army. So great was the plunder, we are told, that every foot-soldier received 1000 dinars, and every horseman 3000 dinars, equal to more than 80*l*. of our money. The records of Sufetula cease with this calamity, by which one of the chief strongholds of the Christian creed was destroyed, and Christianity in Africa may be said to have received its final blow.

RUINS OF SUFETULA

clear against the sky, its weird stones standing ghost-like on the outstretched plain, the stillness of the air broken only by the babbling of the waters—has much to charm the eye and quicken the imagination.

The exact boundaries of Sufetula would be difficult to determine, as there are no remains of any outer walls. The lines of streets and foundations of numerous buildings, public and private, are still traceable for nearly a mile in one direction, and somewhat less than half a mile in another; and several noble edifices of a monumental character, partly ruined, bear testimony to the extent and ancient prosperity of this remote town. Indeed, its very remoteness has been the best protector of its monuments, for there is little doubt that if any settled population had existed within a radius of twenty miles, and any means of transport over a country now difficult of access at most seasons, the few buildings still remaining would long since have been overthrown. It is worthy of note that some twenty years ago the late Sidi-Mustafa-ben-Azooz, of Nefta (an oasis south of Sbeitla), selected this spot as a site for a town, and actually commenced building operations here, using the materials of the ancient city. Fortune did not favour his enterprise; work soon ceased, and the place was once more abandoned. Had the scheme succeeded, scarcely a monument would now be standing to mark the site of old Sufetula.

It is not our intention to enter into elaborate details of the monumental remains. We limit ourselves to a general description of the few structures illustrated on these pages, sufficient to show what Sufetula must have been in the days of its prosperity. The buildings, with few exceptions, were constructed with a very hard, compact limestone, quite white when quarried, but acquiring a rich golden hue after long exposure to the sun. The other facing materials were limestone also, but of different shades of colour, from pale rose to deep red, from light grey to dark slate.

The principal monument that has withstood the ravages of time and the neglect of more than twelve centuries consists of a range of three temples, placed side by side and partly attached. This may be assigned to the reign of Antoninus Pius, A.D. 138–161. The porticoes, forming the fronts, were within a large walled enclosure measuring about 240 feet by 200 feet, to which access was obtained through a monumental gateway facing the temples. The back wall of these edifices, still in fair preservation, was the back of the enclosure, and behind this ran one of the streets of the city. It will be sufficient to state that the central temple was of larger proportions than the two that flanked it, that it was of the Composite order (a mixture of the Ionic and the Corinthian, invented by the Romans and very largely used in the embellishment of buildings during the Empire), and that the side-temples were of the Corinthian order. The porticoes are entirely overthrown; the broken shafts, which were all monoliths more than thirty feet long, the enriched capitals, and huge fragments of sculptured ornamentation, lie piled up one on the other in a majestic and imposing mass. The whole enclosure was paved with immense slabs of stone, and from the general appearance of the remains it is reasonable to suppose that there were other temples or monumental edifices within the enclosure. The gateway above mentioned, dedicated, as the inscription states, to Antoninus Pius, consisted of a large central arch and two lateral ones; within the gateway was a portico communicating with a colonnade, which appears to have been

THE THREE TEMPLES AT SBEITLA

carried round three sides of the enclosure, abutting against the side-walls of the temples. The gateway was evidently intended to face the central temple, but, for some reason difficult to account for, it is fully twenty feet to the west of the central line or axis of the enclosure.

The custom of enclosing sacred edifices with walls of defence originated at some remote period, when temples were used as depositories for the treasure of the city, as well as affording shelter to women and children in times of invasion. There was an instance of this at Carthage, where the Temple of Æsculapius, the largest in the city, stood within the citadel. The Parthenon at Athens was within the walls of the Acropolis, and the Temple of Jupiter in Rome was in the Capitol. At Balbec also there is an enclosure commonly called the Hieron, bearing some resemblance, though on a larger scale, to this one at Sufetula.

The next monument in importance is a triumphal arch on the south-east side, forming the principal entrance to the city from the great highway that communicated with the coast. It appears to have been built at the close of the reign of Maximianus and the first of the reign of his successor, Constantine the Great. An inscription over the arch records the dedication of the monument to both these Emperors, A.D. 305-306.

Sufetula is bounded on the north-east side by the precipitous banks of a ravine, through which flows the river now known as the Oued Sbeitla. The retaining walls on this side of the city have entirely disappeared, and the bridge which appears, from the mass of *débris* below, to have spanned the river at this point and formed a communication with a suburb on the opposite bank, has been washed away. Some hundred yards higher up the stream a partially ruined construction, serving the double purpose of an aqueduct and a foot-bridge, but now disused, crosses the river. It is of comparatively modern construction, and, though it possesses no merit of design, forms a pleasing and picturesque feature in the landscape.

The explorations at Sbeitla (for in the main Sbeitla is Sufetula in ruins, and nothing more) have not hitherto been conducted in a systematic way. The French authorities, however, taking note of the remains, which are very numerous, have set up a series of stones to mark the lines of the principal streets, and made a few excavations, with a view to discovering the levels of the old city. Anyhow it is satisfactory to note that the *Société des Monuments Historiques* is keeping a watchful eye over these remarkable ruins, and that several inscribed stones, throwing much light on the history of Sufetula, have been recently unearthed.

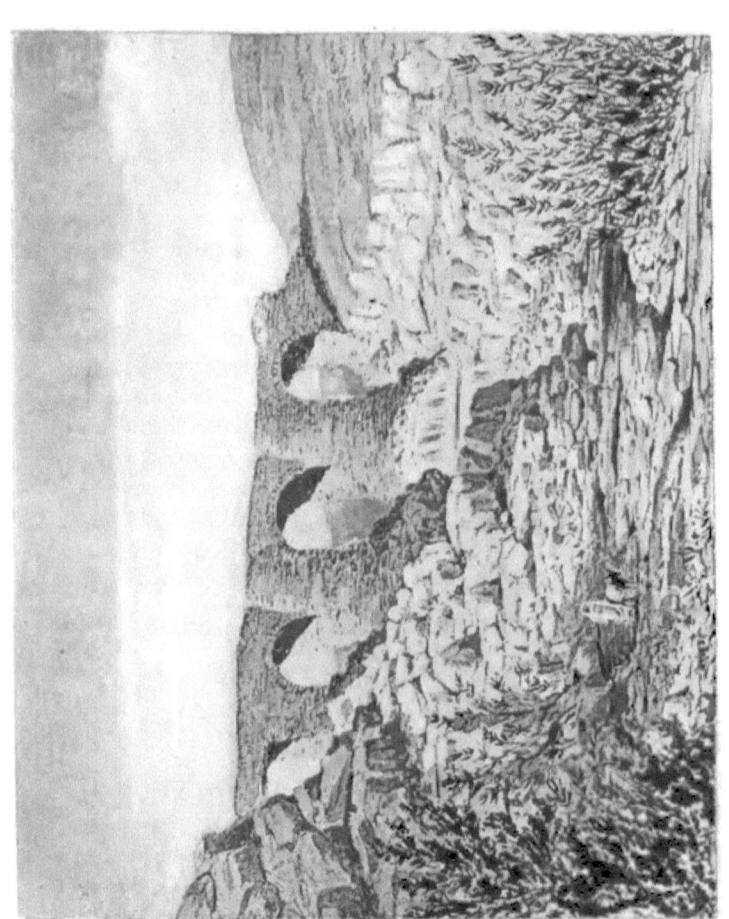

THE RIVER SBEITLA

CHAPTER XXI.

KASSERINE, THE ANCIENT COLONIA SCILLITANA, OR SCILLIUM.

JOURNEY MODIFIED—START FOR KASSERINE—ROMAN RUINS—ESPARTO GRASS—THE SITE OF SCILLIUM—ITS IMPORTANCE—MODERN KASSERINE—THE TRIUMPHAL ARCH—THE MAUSOLEUM.

OUR intention was to journey southward to Feriana and Gafsa, where we had letters of introduction; but the objects of interest in these remote parts of North Africa are too few and insignificant to compensate the traveller for successive days of fatigue and inconvenience. We resolved, therefore, to proceed to Kasserine, a distance of nearly thirty-five kilomètres, and return to Sbeitla the same day. A plunge into the tepid waters of the river while the moon was still up, and before the sun had risen, was a good preparation for ten hours' dusty journey. At daybreak we were off, entering a tract of country traversed by numerous oueds and entirely devoid of cultivation. Remains of Roman towns, villages, and farm-houses innumerable, were visible on either side the tract, and tufts of esparto grass, abundant over a portion of the plain, broke the wearying monotony of miles of scrub and stunted bushes.

Without halting (for we had lunched in the carriage),

we arrived soon after 11 a.m. on the banks of the Oued El-Darb, which was crossed without difficulty, and in a few minutes we reached the foot of the hill on the top of which stood the city of Scillium, or Scillitana Colonia of the Romans, but now better known as Kasserine.

The site of Scillium was well chosen. Placed on the verge of a rocky plateau and commanding a grand sweep of fruitful country, the situation was as strong for the purposes of defence as it was pleasant in its aspect. The mountains of Nouba and Selloum on one side, and the Chambi range on the other, contributed by picturesqueness of outline to the beauty of the landscape, and a river of water, clear as crystal, skirted the city wall and irrigated the great plain. To judge from the long lines of streets, still easily traceable, from the solid and extensive foundations of buildings now entirely demolished, and from the enormous blocks of white stone scattered over a vast extent of ground, the city must have been one of wealth and importance.

To-day the once beautiful river is neglected, and its never-failing stream, which forces itself with difficulty through the narrowed channel amid luxuriant oleanders, is soon lost in the region of sand. The site of the once flourishing Colonia Scillitana is perfect desolation. Two whitened koubbas, which have been stuck up among the ruined monuments, stamp the nationality of the present desecrators, and a hut or two, surrounded by a few miserable gourbies, are all that answer for the town of Kasserine, as marked on modern maps.

Of the monuments of Scillium, two only of importance have escaped the ravages of time: (1) A Triumphal Arch forming the entrance to the city on the south-east side, in connection with the highway to Sufetula and Carthage. This is an imposing monument, more remarkable for its

REMAINS OF A MAUSOLEUM AT KASRIN

solidity of construction than for any grace of outline. (2) Below the city, and near the river bank, a mausoleum, still in fair preservation, forms a conspicuous feature in the landscape. In spite of the numerous descriptions of this monument, often, as Guérin (I. 319) justly remarks, in terms so hyperbolical as to touch the ridiculous, we cannot pass it by without notice.

This mausoleum, three stages in height, and standing on a pyramid of steps now mostly covered by the ground, was erected by M. Flavius Secundus in honour of his parents and other members of his family, who are fully described in one of the lengthy inscriptions that nearly covers one entire face. In addition, there are no less than ninety hexameters and twenty elegiacs, in which the charms of the city and the neighbouring country are the subject of verse. The height of the monument was about fifty feet. At the summit was fixed a bronze cock, placed, as the quaint inscription below further informs us, ' above the clouds, and so near to heaven, that if nature had given it a voice it would have compelled all the gods by its morning song to get up early.' *

At two o'clock we took our departure from Kasserine, and regained Sbeitla at 7 p.m.

---

* M. Pellissier, an intelligent traveller in this country, has remarked, with reference to the monuments of Kasserine, that if those 'still standing in a country now desolate attest a former prosperity which confounds our imagination, these verses, composed in a remote town scarcely known to history, prove how the civilising influence of Rome had awakened the intelligence and rural nature of a people once numerous and wealthy, but to-day without either art or literature or even settled inhabitants. It may fairly be assumed, that at the time of the Antonines the flourishing cities of Byzacene, of which Scillium was a remote town, were peopled with Romanised Africans and supplied with schools capable of rivalling those of Italy.'

CHAPTER XXII.

SBEITLA TO SBIBA.

November 27th to 29th.

OUR HABITATION AT SBEITLA—WE LEAVE WITH REGRET—NUMEROUS BIRDS—DELICIOUS SOLITUDE—OUED-GILMA—HADJEB-EL-AÏOUN—A DAY IN CAMP—THE DOCTOR AND HIS PATIENTS—OUR EQUIPAGE—WE START—DJEBEL MERILAH—CARAVANS—HOW FAR TO SBIBA?—WE SLEEP IN A GOURBI—A BAD NIGHT'S REST.

THE rough vault that sheltered us during our sojourn at Sbeitla was a portion of an Arab dwelling commenced about twenty years ago, and to which reference has already been made. All else was in ruins. Rough masonry blackened by smoke, an earthen floor, dirty and uneven, a chamber with one opening but without either door or window, is not an exaggerated description of what we jokingly called our 'Grand Hôtel.' The soft air of this favoured region and the extreme beauty of the weather on the occasion of our visit did more than compensate for the discomfiture of such rough quarters.

Before the first morning broke, the Arabs in the neighbourhood had heard of our presence, and a couple of fowls and a score of eggs were tendered and paid for without much unnecessary bargaining. This addition to our modest larder afforded our servant-interpreter an opportunity of displaying his powers of cookery, at which, to our agreeable surprise, he was no novice; and with the help of a tin of Swiss milk and another of vegetables, a potfull of *poulet à la chasseur* formed an excellent stock-dish at the evening meal. It was with very great regret —indeed, with reluctance—we bade farewell to pleasant Sbeitla on the afternoon of November 27th. The three days spent there had been days of real enjoyment. Undisturbed by Arabs, we were at full liberty to explore the site of the ancient city, to make sketches of the principal monuments, and with tape and rule to measure the stones one by one, with a view to making such restorations as are annexed to these pages. Day and night succeeded each other in the same calm beauty. The moon was up, and but for the flittering of bats and owls among the ruined temples, the stealthy movement of an occasional jackal, or the hoarse bark of an Arab watch-dog, silence reigned supreme.*

Soon after 1 in the afternoon we left Sbeitla, recrossing the river without difficulty, and reaching the deserted camp at Oued-Gilma in four hours, where we found accommodation.

At 7.30 the following morning we started for Hadjeb-el-Aïoun, where we arrived at 10.15. About half way we had the pleasure of greeting Captain Perronell on his way to the abandoned camp, who had courteously left instructions with M. Lapeine of the ' Bureau de Renseignements' to render us every assistance. With-

---

* No one fond of sport should venture into the interior of this country without a gun. Tunisia abounds in game. Coveys of partridges, tame as domestic poultry, eagles and hawks, the lesser bustard, commonly known as the *poule de Carthage*, crested larks, thrushes, and other small birds, are innumerable. The gazelle as well as the wild boar haunts the plains; the panther and the hyena are as yet far from exterminated.

out this friendly aid further movements would have been almost impossible. M. Lapeine's perfect knowledge of the country made it clear that we could not advance northward in a carriage, but that the journey must be accomplished in the saddle. In spite of every endeavour on the part of our kind friend to procure at once the necessary guides and cattle, we could not start before the following morning.

The day in camp, thanks to his hospitality and the good fellowship of the doctor of the regiment, was spent most agreeably. It happened to be a reception-day for the sick of the neighbourhood, and about a dozen or more natives of both sexes soon arrived. The jovial doctor, cigar in mouth, examined them in the hospital enclosure; and if his remedies were not of the greatest efficacy, he had a word of kindness and encouragement for each sufferer, as male or female passed from his hands. The scene was more curious than pleasant. The first patient was a little girl of ten or twelve years, whose emaciated and ulcerated body clearly indicated that she was suffering from the misdeeds of her parents. Then came two women, the one troubled by the common malady, ophthalmia, the other rheumatism. The doctor gave them something to rub themselves with; probably a bath would have been more efficacious. As they were leaving, one of the women, about forty years of age, and red haired, returned abruptly, and begged the doctor to give her something that would enable her to bear children. The native attendants hurried her away. It was altogether a melancholy sight. Cleanliness and good water were what these poor people most needed.

At 7 a.m. on the following morning the beasts and attendants, a motley collection, were before our tent.

The guide selected for us (son of the owner of most of the animals, and quite a dandy in his way) was mounted in true Arab fashion on a good-looking native nag, equipped with high-backed saddle, stirrup-irons resembling small square tea-trays, a bridle of embossed leather, and an enormous and uselessly cruel bit. Our domestic was provided with a rather broken-down old pony similarly equipped. For ourselves there was a small mule with a pad, and a very disreputable pony, that might have been taken from the plough, with an old military saddle much the worse for wear. A large white donkey, by far the most capable and energetic beast of the collection, carried our provisions and scanty baggage, with a pack on his back and his head free of bit or bridle. It followed the guide's horse with exemplary steadiness and exactitude—a model donkey. Our cavalcade was completed by a nondescript man with little clothing, and that little exceedingly dirty; he rode a grey mare, whose only trappings were a halter and a sack; who he was or why he had joined our party we could not make out; it could scarcely have been for the sake of the scenery, and it is certain that he took no interest in ruins. We hazarded many rough guesses as to the object this gentleman had in view in travelling so far from home, and at last came to the conclusion that he wanted to sell the grey mare.

Half an hour sufficed for the labour of loading the donkey and other arrangements, and at 7.30 a.m., bidding adieu to the officers who had done us such good service, we started northward under a cloudless sky and in the best of spirits. Had we abandoned our carriage on our previous arrival at Hadjeb-el-Aïoun, and proceeded to Sbeitla on horseback, we should have been able to ride thence direct to Sbiba without having to retrace our steps, and thus avoiding the ascent of Djebel Merilah.

The distance from Hadjeb-el-Aïoun to Sbiba is about 50 kilomètres. The road we were told was easy, and, furnished as we were with a letter to the Caïd, we felt no misgivings as to reaching the place before sundown, and finding some accommodation on our arrival.

After nearly four hours steady travelling over a dreary scrub-covered plain, intersected by two or three dry oueds, we reached the hills. Viewed from afar, the Tunisian hills in the interior are not inviting, and do not improve on closer proximity.

In another half hour we entered the wild and rugged pass through Djebel Merilah, and after a short descent on the northern slopes approached the banks of the river Hatob, a stream of some importance. A large caravan was in the act of crossing; the women and children were bathing and washing their clothes, while the men were urging the camels and donkeys with shouts and threats as they lingered to enjoy the refreshing stream. Curiosity and the sight of a few sous soon brought the children around us. Among them was a girl of about twelve years with a bundle on her back, which on examination proved, to our surprise, to be her own baby. Crossing the river, we dismounted for lunch, and enjoyed an hour's repose and shelter from the sun under the welcome shade of a bank luxuriant with oleanders.

Our guide, whose intellect was of limited capacity, made up for his stupidity by extra devotions, and our repose was enlivened by watching his fervent prayers and energetic prostrations, his forehead touching the ground at frequent intervals.

Before 2 p.m. we were once more in the saddle,

and in a quarter of an hour crossed the same river again. A still more numerous convoy, composed entirely of camels, was revelling in the stream or stealthily endeavouring to roll in the cool waters, to the detriment of the merchandise on their backs. Some of the women and children were mounted, the latter bare-headed, without any protection from the glaring sun, and firmly tied on the animals' backs.

The Hatob again crossed, we found ourselves on a plain clothed with arbutus, and in an hour and a half entered another plain, of greater extent and redolent with wild thyme.

'Is Sbiba yet far distant?' we inquired of our guide, whose ignorance of the country we had suspected for some time.

He made no reply, but leaving us, galloped to some rising ground, whence he could better survey the surrounding country. On his return he led us to a cluster of gourbies in the valley.

'Here we have to sleep,' he said.

'How far are we from Sbiba?' we repeated.

'Too far off to reach it to-night.'

This indefinite reply was very unsatisfactory; and putting the same question to an Arab who, preceded by the usual pack of yelping curs, came from one of the gourbies to ascertain what we wanted, the answer was, 'Two kilomètres.'

'Then we will go on!' and, in spite of our guide's protestations and reluctance, on we went accordingly. It was now getting dark. Another lot of gourbies was struck, out of which came the customary welcome of growling and barking dogs.

'Is this Sbiba?'

'Yes; the whole district is Sbiba.'

'Where does the Caïd reside?'

'Over yonder hill, a long distance off.'

'We have a letter which we wish delivered to him at once.'

No one volunteered as messenger. Threats were useless; but the promise of a coin at last induced one of the Arabs to undertake the errand. That he would do so forthwith was by no means certain. The darkness of the night and the exhausted condition of our animals prevented further progress. Our vexation was augmented by knowing that under the Caïd's protection our quarters would have been secure, if not comfortable, whereas at this spot there was no accommodation whatever.

Resigning ourselves to our fate, there was no alternative but to accept the shelter of a gourbi, or, rather, part of one, which a member of the tribe placed at our disposal. The gourbi, or Arab tent, is about as uncomfortable inside as it is ugly from without. The covering, or cloth of camel's hair, dark grey in colour, is pitched so low that it is impossible to stand upright under any part of it. In the hope that our letter to the Caïd might yet procure more comfortable quarters we waited in patience.

No messenger arrived, and supper being announced, we crawled under the covering and made such arrangements for the night as the limited floor-space would admit. The part of the tent allotted to us was that in which the proprietor kept his harness, agricultural implements, sacks, &c., and in which his dog and poultry were accustomed to pass the night. The former had been put as closely as possible together in a heap; the latter turned out, and a piece of coarse sackcloth had been suspended across the tent so as to form a partition between us and the Arab and his wife and child in the other half. The floor of the tent was, of course, the bare earth. A large fire was lit outside, around which sat our servants and some Arabs; our horses were picketed in a row, with their forefeet all tied to a rope, the ends of which were staked to the ground.

Just as we were lying down to rest a dog, probably the one whose resting-place we had usurped, forced his way through the brushwood occupying the foot or so of space between the tent-cloth and the ground, and regarded us for a few moments with anything but a pleasant eye. Sticks being fortunately ready at hand, he did not wait to try their effect. Amid the squalling of the baby on the other side of the partition, who seemed to be aware that something unusual was taking place, the barking of the dogs without, and the talking of the Arabs we at last, from sheer lassitude, fell asleep. Slumber was of short duration, for long before daylight two cocks (one immediately over our heads, the other in a neighbouring gourbi) commenced a duo, which they continued with such energy and regularity as to put an end to further repose.

CHAPTER XXIII.

SBIBA TO ZANFOUR.

About 80 kilomètres. November 30th to December 1st.

THE CAÏD OF SBIBA—AN EARLY MORNING WALK—SUFES AND ITS GARDENS—THE RUINS—A HOSPITABLE SHEIK—COUSCOUSOU—A NIGHT IN A COWHOUSE—WANT OF POPULATION—FILTHY KSOUR—FIRST SIGHT OF ZANFOUR.

WHEN, at 5 a.m., in the waning moonlight, we crawled out of the gourbi, unrefreshed and benumbed by the cold air which had been blowing in upon us all night from under the tent cloth, we were informed that the Caïd had already arrived, and was awaiting our pleasure. On being conducted to his presence, we found him seated upon a mat on the slope of the mountain before a blazing fire, which two of his attendants were feeding with brushwood. The scene was very impressive. He was a portly man of handsome features and commanding aspect, and his greeting was stately yet graceful. The usual salutation was gone through—we shook hands, and then each carried to his lips the hand which the friend had just pressed. 'Would the Caïd honour us by drinking a cup of tea in our tent?' The invitation was accepted, and while the Caïd sipped the beverage and crunched some English biscuits, which he seemed greatly to relish, we endeavoured to get from him some information concerning the ruins of Sufes, to which he kindly offered to accompany us. Our beasts had yet to be saddled and burdened, and as the air was very chilly we begged to be allowed to proceed on foot—a request which appeared to astonish our conductor, who mounted his mule, and, accompanied by his two attendants, led the way. The ruins were yet a good two miles distant, and we reached them just as the sun appeared above the horizon.

Sufes, or Colonia Sufetanæ, but now known as Sbiba, must have been a place of considerable importance. Guérin estimates the outer wall at six kilomètres in extent. Like most Roman towns in North Africa, it occupied the foot of a hill, or rather the spurs of several hills, and extended some distance on to the plain. An abundant stream, which we crossed more than once as we approached the spot, ran through the town and irrigated the surrounding country. The whole district, even when El-Bekri visited it in the eleventh century, was covered with gardens, and produced saffron of the finest quality. The town itself contained a college and several baths. The Oued Sbiba is now lost in the arid soil at a short distance from its source; cultivation is entirely neglected, the site is absolutely deserted, and the buildings are so completely ruined that careful study and excavation would be needed for their identification. One huge mass of rubble walling, the remains of the ancient Thermæ, still stands up boldly from among the countless stones which encumber the soil.

The Caïd pressed us to spend the day at Sbiba, and begged to be allowed to prepare a good dinner. We declined with thanks his proffered hospitality, but gratefully accepted the services of one of his attendants, whom he placed at our disposal to guide us on our way. At

8 a.m. we took our leave of the kind Caïd and continued our route. Among the ruins we observed a great number of pigeons and some large crows. The distance from Sbiba to Ksour is about fifty-six kilomètres. Our road lay at first over a vast uncultivated plain, Djebel Reukaha being on our left, and Djebel Djiljie on our right. At 10.15 we passed a handsome koubba, called Sidi-Mehrani, with a fluted dome, and shortly afterwards Roman ruins on both sides of the track. There was more cultivation than usual in this district, and gourbies were numerous. Threshing was being done, as in the days of the Israelites, by horses trampling out the corn.

At midday we struck the Oued Sgiff, which flowed on the right of our path. We did not cross the river, but passed between it and a koubba, Sidi-Ahmed-Zei, on our left. On the other side of the stream we observed another koubba, called Sidi-Monella. Here we lunched.

At one o'clock we were again in the saddle, and for an hour saw no landmark other than a small koubba to our left, and a few Roman remains utterly ruined amid a desolate country.

At 2.30 we crossed a dry oued, and noticed Roman remains to our left. We now traversed a wild and romantic country, among barren rocky hills covered with stones, passing at 3.30 an extensive ruined Roman post on elevated ground, while a few gourbies were observable in the valley.

It was now past four o'clock, and it was evident we could not reach Ksour that evening. Some stone buildings surrounded by gourbies, occupying what seemed to be the site of a Roman settlement, appeared to our left. It was the habitation of a sheik, and we resolved to beg his hospitality for the night. The sheik, a fair-haired man of prepossessing appearance, was seated cross-legged on the ground in front of his gourbi, watching the ploughing and other agricultural pursuits in the valley below. He rose at our approach, and received us with great politeness. When our interpreter communicated to him our request, he placed his hand on his breast, and with a graceful bow intimated that his dwelling was at our disposal. 'Would we prefer to sleep in a gourbi or in a stone building?' We chose the latter, which, upon inspection, proved to be a small cow-house. Some calves, awaiting the return of their mothers, were removed to make room for us, the sheik's best carpet was spread on the ground, and we were soon comfortably installed. Our host, whose energy was on a par with his urbanity, now begged permission to provide our evening meal,—an offer which we thankfully accepted. 'Should the couscousou be of chicken or of mutton?' As we had for the last few days been living chiefly on poultry and eggs, and as the Arabs who surrounded their chief seemed to desire mutton, we pronounced for the latter. The reason why the sheik's retainers desired mutton may be explained in a word. An animal had to be killed for the dish, of which what we left became their perquisite. The couple of fowls, which would have sufficed had we chosen poultry, we should pretty well have consumed, and little would have remained for them; but, hungry as we were, we could scarcely have been able to clear off a whole sheep, or even a lamb or kid. We had to wait some time for our repast, which had to be prepared from the very beginning, but it came at last. On a huge, shallow wooden bowl, filled with couscous, a meal prepared in a manner peculiar to the Arabs, lay an entire lamb or kid; a small one it must be owned, yet the whole animal, less the head, was there. A smaller bowl contained gravy. No utensils of any kind accompanied the dish. Fortunately we had our own plates, knives, and forks, otherwise we should have been embarrassed. We cut off the parts which appeared to us the most delicate, or the easiest to get at, and made an excellent repast, for the food was really, in its way, well cooked. Our servant then removed the dishes, which were speedily cleared off by the Arabs, who were eagerly awaiting the moment when our hunger should be appeased and the remains fall to their share. No wine was, of course, offered, nor even a cup or glass of any sort to drink water.*

On the following morning our host was already at the opening of our habitation (opening is used advisedly, as there was no door) when we arose. He willingly joined us in a cup of tea, and, as his men were all busy, mounted his mule and escorted us himself to Ksour. We started at 7.30 a.m. Our way lay over undulating ground,

---

* 'The roasted sheep is a dish worthy of introduction into the most civilised society. The animal is skinned and cleaned within a few moments of his death; a stake six feet long is passed through his body, entering at the mouth, and a large fire having been prepared beforehand and allowed to subside into a state of hot embers without flame, the animal is laid across it, supported on two posts, constantly turned round, and basted with butter till sufficiently cooked; it is then served up by the stake being stuck upright in the earth, or supported transversely on big stones; and then it is consumed with the aid only of Nature's knives and forks. It requires some little education to know exactly where to search for the best morsels; but our hosts were always courteous enough to tear these off and present them to us.

'Couscousou well prepared is by no means a dish to be despised. The raw material is simply semolina of hard wheat, the grains of which are large, carefully sifted from the flour, and prepared in a peculiar manner by the ladies of the household, who roll it about and turn it over with their hands in large wooden dishes. When this has to be cooked it is placed in a small earthen dish pierced with holes, on the top of another, in which a soup of meat and vegetables is prepared. The steam causes the grain to swell and soften without rendering it sodden. When the couscousou is sufficiently cooked it is placed in a

across well-cultivated fields,* and in an hour and a half we reached Ksour.

Since we left Kairouan we had seen neither town nor village, and excepting the French hut encampment, no permanent human habitation. Ksour, which possesses a mosque and two or three koubbas, may contain 400 or 500 inhabitants. Although a mountain stream passes through it, the town is, as usual, filthy in the extreme; and the stream, the banks of which are encumbered with dung and refuse of every kind, is befouled before it reaches the dwelling-houses. In spite of every exertion, we were not able to procure a piece of bread anywhere in the town.

We tarried no longer than the time needed for the sheik of the district to be apprised of our presence. On his arrival our kind conductor bid us adieu and returned home.

In a journey through the interior, where hospitality and other services cannot be repaid with coin, the traveller will do well to provide himself with articles for

---

large flat dish; the soup, highly seasoned with red pepper, and thus called *mergäa*, is poured over it; the meat or fowls and vegetables, if any are procurable, are placed on the top, perhaps with a morsel of butter; and thus prepared, in the tent of an Arab of rank and means, it is as palatable a dish as a hungry traveller need ever desire to have set before him. Sometimes, instead of the meat and soup, sugar or honey, raisins and milk are substituted. The only thing I can suggest as better than either of them is both in succession.

'When the guests have finished their repast the dishes are passed on to the higher retainers, and so on to the various ranks and classes, till nothing remains.'

* 'The wheat of this country, little different from ours, does not, however, produce a pure and nutritive flour. The meal, obtained by grinding between two portable millstones, is coarse.'—ABBÉ POIRET, *Travels through Barbary*, 1785-86.

presents. Cutlery or bright-printed handkerchiefs are always acceptable.

Soon after leaving Ksour, the distance from which place to Zanfour is about 24 kilomètres, we observed some Roman remains, but of no great importance, on a hill to our left.

At 11 a.m. we passed through a wild and romantic gorge, where women were washing in the stream, although we perceived no habitations in the vicinity.

Two more hours of steady travelling were needed before we caught sight of the ruins of Zanfour. The view from the hill at the foot of which Zanfour is situated is very fine and of great extent. We made straight for the shady banks of the river, where we lunched and rested our beasts, whose impatience to roll in the stream threatened to deprive us of our provisions and ruin the harness.

CHAPTER XXIV.

ZANFOUR TO AIN-HEDJAH.

December 2nd. Distance about 85 kilomètres.

FINE SITUATION OF ZANFOUR — BLED-ES-SERS — GLORIOUS SUNSET — SOUK-EL-TLETA—WE STICK IN THE MUD OF OUED SIDI-HAMI—SIDI-BOU-ROUIS — DEFILE OF DJEBEL DOU-KOHIL — DIFFICULT TRACKS — BORDJ-MESSAOUDI, ANCIENT THACIA — GARAT-EL-KERIB — SIDI-ABD-ER-REUBBOU, ANCIENT MUSTI — AN INSCRIPTION — OVERTAKEN BY DARKNESS—SHOULD WE SLEEP IN A KOUBBA?—WE PUSH FORWARD —THE FONDOUK AT AIN-HEDJAH—FELINE VISITORS DISTURB REPOSE.

HENCHIR ZANFOUR covers the site of the Roman city of Assuras. Built on a plateau raised above the level of the plain, and watered by a river which rises among the surrounding hills, Assuras boasted a situation equal to its importance. A terrible convulsion of nature must have been the chief cause of its destruction. Huge stones, split and broken by superhuman agency, lie scattered over the site. Among the ruins of many stately monuments, the remains of three triumphal arches are still conspicuous, one only retaining traces of architectural detail. There are also three walls of the cella of a temple, the columns of its portico, no doubt, still lying far below the present surface.

Patient and systematic exploration of the site would probably bring to light many objects of historical value. No time, however, should be lost, for at the moment of our visit some Arabs with asses, and provided with hatchets and shovels, were actively filling their panniers with broken stones. They even offered to break off any piece of carving or other ornamental work we might covet, and to transport it at our pleasure. It appeared that these stones were being removed to an adjacent plain for constructing a French military post

The fondouk of Souk-el-Tleta, our destination for the night, being plainly visible from Henchir Zanfour and within a short hour's ride, we had ample time for a careful inspection of these wide-spread ruins. Just before sunset we started, crossing the river, where are the remains of a Roman bridge, and entering the Bled-es-Sers, a low-lying plain of great fertility, but rendered swampy in many places by the uncontrolled waters of the Oued Zanfour, which are lost below the surface a little further down. An unusual quantity of cattle were grazing in the rich pasture, and numerous gourbies dotted on the plain indicated the presence of a considerable population.

As we neared Souk-el-Tleta a sunset of unusual magnificence, even in these regions, where sunset effects are marvellously beautiful, illumined the whole sky with most gorgeous hues. Every point of the compass seemed ablaze, and hill and mountain caught up the reflected light. But the peculiarity of this glorious phenomenon was that in the west the colours were the least intense. Short was its duration. The fairy-like tints faded away before one had time to realise them, and the whole landscape was, as it were in a moment, enveloped in obscurity.

The fondouk of Souk-el-Tleta was in process of reconstruction, or, rather, the dens which had hitherto been allotted to human beings had been given up to quadrupeds, and a kind of café, which was in future to serve that purpose, was not yet completed. We had to make the best of it, surrounded by half-mixed mortar and heaps of building materials. The dogs from the neighbouring gourbies, the great nuisances of this country, surrounded us, barking and snarling while the keeper of the establishment went for his key to unlock the door. Nor did they discontinue their howlings the whole night long.

Dawn was a welcome termination of an unpleasant night. We were in the saddle as the sun was rising, but unable to start, owing to the non-arrival of the guide, whom we had demanded over-night from the sheik of this district. At last he appeared, mounted on a mare with a foal by her side. A long morning's work could not be done in this fashion, and we had not proceeded far before he galloped off in order to change his mount. A slight mishap occurred, which still further delayed our progress. The track crossed the Oued Sidi-Hami, a winding stream which ran between banks of slippery mud. Our guide, who was some distance ahead, had already crossed, but at what exact point we had failed to note. The steed of one of our party feeling himself sinking in the mud, made a desperate plunge, and in so doing gained the opposite bank, but threw his rider. The sumpter donkey, a brave beast who was always well to the front, now attempted to cross, but, being heavily burdened, stuck fast in the mud up to his girth. Our guides and servant dismounted, and their united efforts were required to extricate the poor ass from this 'slough of despond.'

Owing to these little accidents, we were not clear of the marshes of Bled-es-Sers until 8.25 a.m., although we had started before 7. The track now took a north-easterly direction over the slopes of Djebel Trisha, commanding some fine stretches of scenery. In two hours our guide had reached the confines of his district, and at Sidi-bou-Rouis, where there is a koubba and a small Arab cemetery, departed, leaving us in charge of the sheik of that place.

Crossing the Tessa, a charming stream, where we watered the horses and filled our bottles, we reached at 11 a.m. some unimportant Roman remains on our left hand. For half an hour the route lay over a well-cultivated plain, and then ascended Djebel Bou-Kohil. Here commenced a wild defile, formerly spanned by a Roman bridge, the masonry of the abutments being still undisturbed. Along the whole of this route as far as Bordj-Messaoudi, which we sighted at midday, the scenery is very grand. The mountains, although treeless, are well covered with green shrubs, and the passes are abrupt, startling, and most picturesque. There is no attempt at road-making in this region, and our sure-footed little animals had frequently to pick their way round the precipitous mountain-sides, among rolling stones, and along paths a couple of feet wide, formed of mud, now, fortunately, dry and hard. Locomotion after rain must be dangerous, if not impossible.

Bordj-Messaoudi, 3 kilomètres distant in the valley below, and built on the site of the Roman town of Thacia, consists at the present day of a single house and a fondouk, of which the white walls shone forth like jewels in the bright sunlight as we descended the northern side of the mountain. Here we lunched and rested our cattle. There are many remains scattered about in the vicinity of Bordj-Messaoudi, but nothing of any special interest. The house above mentioned is supported by Roman shafts, while carved stones and other relics decorate the garden.

At 1.45 p.m. we left Bordj-Messaoudi in the direction

of Teboursouk. The sheik who had accompanied us thus far bid us adieu, directing us to follow the telegraph wires which communicated with that town.

For several miles the track passed over a grassy plain called Gorat-el-Kerib, lying between the hills of Jouaouda and Sidi Abdallah-ech-Cheid. Roman remains, either of villages or farm-houses, are visible at frequent intervals.

At 3.30 p.m. we traversed Sidi-Abd-er-Reubbou, the site of the Roman town of Musti. Here a koubba and several Arab hovels disfigure the monumental remains. Among these a gateway of some importance stands conspicuous, but devoid of any special architectural merit.*

The town stands on high ground, a pretty stream in which we watered our horses flowing through it. More Roman remains were visible on the plain at some distance, and shafts and carved stones thrown down and half-buried in the soil arrested our attention all along the road.

It was now 5 p.m., and the sun was nearing the horizon. We had no local guide with us, and the young Arab who had accompanied us from Hadjeb-el-Aïoun, and who was quite ignorant of the country, began to express a doubt whether we should reach our destination at Ain-Hedjah that night. He reined up his horse and proceeded to shout at the top of his voice, in order to attract the attention of an Arab settlement at a little

---

* An inscribed stone lying close by appears to have escaped the observant eye of V. Guérin, but was noted by Berbrugger:—

    VAEPROMISER .T
    CTIONEMMVS ITANIS
    DEDICAVIT DATIS
    SIS . PON . . . ARIBVS.

distance from the track. Several men soon arrived; but not being able to get any definite information, we left them talking, and proceeded to explore a ruined koubba close to the roadside, with a view to ascertaining whether in case of need we might find a shelter there for the night. It appeared to be a mausoleum, approached through a courtyard planted with trees. There were two other chambers besides that in which reposed the relics of the marabout, or, rather, marabouts, for there were two tombstones.

We had already been quartered in such strange and uncomfortable places that it was a matter of indifference whether, for once in a way, we should sleep alongside the bones of saintly Mohammedans. Perhaps the Arabs, little as they regarded the sanctuary crumbling to decay, might have objected to its desecration by conversion into a lodging-house for infidels. Under stress of circumstances, and the prospect of sleeping *à la belle étoile*, we should probably have overstepped these objections, had not our interpreter at last informed us, as the result of much parleying with the Arabs, that the fondouk of Ain-Hedjah was only two kilomètres distant. It was well that we pressed forward as fast as the wearied condition of the horses would allow; for the sun had set, darkness was closing around us, and some awkward ravines had still to be passed. Another cluster of gourbies, visible at a distance by the fires ignited before them, was a welcome sight. Here we obtained a guide to the fondouk, which we reached at half-past six, thoroughly tired out.

The fondouk of Ain-Hedjah is a modern addition to one of the vast edifices still standing, but partially ruined, of the ancient city of Agbia. A more miserable place it is difficult to conceive. The chamber placed at our disposal was a dilapidated café, the walls of which were blackened with smoke, and the earthen floor strewn with rubbish. Through two openings in the wall, intended, probably, for windows, but now partially blocked up by loose bricks, and through a door impossible to close, the dust of the surrounding country and the filth from the adjoining caravansera were blown in by every gust of wind. Rough stones encumbered the earthen bench on which we had to sleep, and broken Roman shafts, unchopped firewood, and other *débris*, constituted the furniture of this lordly establishment. On our arrival a couple of Arabs, dozing away in a corner, were turned out unceremoniously by the proprietor, who informed us that the entire apartment was now at our disposal. Some live embers in the fireplace accelerated the preparation of our evening meal, cheered by the presence of all the domestic animals belonging to the establishment. The most persistent of these visitors were two half-wild cats, who made free with the place during the whole night, frisking among the pots and kettles, upsetting everything, jumping over our bodies, and making continuous slumber impossible. A shot from a revolver only made them more lively.

The approximate distances accomplished to-day were: Zanfour to Souk-el-Tleta, 8 kilomètres; Souk-el-Tleta to Bordj-Messaoudi, 56 kilomètres; Bordj-Messaoudi to Ain-Hedjah, 21 kilomètres.

CHAPTER XXV.

AIN-HEDJAH AND DOUGGA.

December 3rd.

THE CITADEL—DOUGGA—FINE SITUATION—THE TEMPLE IN THE DISTANCE—FILTHY CONDITION OF DOUGGA—THE CISTERNS AND OTHER REMAINS—THE TEMPLE—THE TRIUMPHAL ARCH—THE MAUSOLEUM—INSCRIPTION REMOVED TO THE BRITISH MUSEUM—THE SHEIK OF DOUGGA—DEPARTURE FOR TEBOURSOUK.

THERE are few visible remains here of any special interest of the old Roman town of Agbia that covered the site of the modern Hedjah. An immense Byzantine fortress, with square towers at the angles, constructed entirely with the stones of older buildings, is the only edifice now standing, and from its large dimensions is a conspicuous object.*

Leaving our men to saddle the animals and follow us at their leisure, we started early the following morning

---

* These fortresses are a marked feature in North Africa, and have a peculiar interest to archæologists as the prototype of the mediæval castle. The strongholds erected by the Romans during their five centuries of occupation of the country were destroyed by the Vandals, with the exception of the citadel and walls of Carthage; so that, when the armies of Justinian landed on its shores, this imprudent race was left without defences. The Byzantine generals in their turn not only reinstated the defences, but constructed fortresses and strong enclosures in nearly every Roman town in the interior, destroying the principal public buildings that had survived the destructive sway of the Vandals, and using up stone and marble indiscriminately in their works of defence.

for Dougga, an uphill walk of about an hour, under the guidance of an old Arab.

Thugga, as it was called by the Romans, but now known as Dougga, occupies one of the finest sites in the interior of North Africa, and must have once covered an area of nearly three square miles. The hill on which it stands rises boldly from a plain of great fertility, over which Thugga looked in three directions. The ruined portico of a temple dedicated to Jupiter and Minerva, still erect when nearly everything else has disappeared, stands out on the crown of the hill, a structure of great beauty. A more lovely spot than Dougga, even in its present condition and when seen at a distance, it is not easy to picture. The temple forms the main feature of a cluster of buildings which spring, as if by magic, out of a luxuriant olive-grove. But 'distance lends enchantment to the view'; the enchantment is dispelled as soon as the first Arab habitation is reached, and modern Dougga in its degradation and dirt stands before one. We had become accustomed to the squalor and neglect of Arab towns, but the aspect of Dougga fairly startled us. Mud, over a foot deep in many places, rendered the narrow streets and lanes almost impassable even at this dry season, and heaps of dung and refuse, festering under the hot sun and emitting loathsome stenches, encumbered every corner. The temple, so beautiful at a distance, is befouled by ordure, and rude stone walls of miserable dwellings are clustered round its noble remains. The rivulet which we observed at the foot of the hill on our approach, appears to have been insufficient for the requirements of the inhabitants in the days of its prosperity, for Thugga was provided with a series of spacious cisterns, now almost entirely ruined. Carved and inscribed stones are built into the walls of Arab houses, and the remains of three triumphal arches, a second ruined temple, a theatre, and two fountains, that were embellished with colonnades like those at Zaghouan bear some testimony to the magnificence of the ancient city. The ruined monuments which still command admiration, viz.—(1) the Temple of Jupiter and Minerva ; (2) a Triumphal Arch ; (3) a Mausoleum once bearing the famous bi-lingual* (Libyo-Punico) inscription removed by the late Sir Thomas Reade, and now in the British Museum, are scattered over the hillside.

(1.) The temple appears to have been built during the reign of Marcus Aurelius and his colleague L. Aurelius Verus, between A.D. 161 and 169, at the expense of two brothers of the name of Marcius, whose names were inscribed on a pedestal raised in their honour. The columns of the portico, with one exception, are monoliths, and, including the capital and base, are 33 feet high. The doorway of the cella, which is still standing, is of immense proportions. The jambs are 27 feet long, each in one stone, and the lintel is 22 feet long. For elegance of design, this portico will compare favourably with any of the better-known examples in Rome or elsewhere.†

---

* The Libyan tongue was spoken by the native tribes of North Africa, Punic being confined to the citizens of Carthage and of the coast towns. The language of diplomacy was Greek. Hannibal, we know, wrote in Greek.

† 'Bruce states that the material of which this temple is built is white marble. If this is not actually the case, it is a very compact and crystalline limestone, full of fossil-shells, and susceptible of receiving a high polish. When new, it must have been even more effective than the finest description of marble. I am inclined to believe it is none other than the *Lumachella antica*, one of the lost Numidian marbles, of which only two or three specimens are known to exist.'— Lieut.-Col. Sir R. L. Playfair, *Travels in the Footsteps of Bruce*, p. 220.

TEMPLE AT DOUGGA

(2.) The remains of the one triumphal arch still standing do not demand any lengthened notice. The upper portion, long since overthrown, lies buried under the soil; its shafts, white like marble, have almost disappeared, and decorative fragments peep out above the grass or between the roots of an adjoining olive-grove.

(3.) The ruined mausoleum, commemorative of a distinguished Numidian who lived before the commencement of the Christian era, has attracted a larger share of attention than many of the more important monuments of North Africa, and not undeservedly. Apart from the beauty of its position on the hillside, and in the middle of an olive-garden, the structure itself, to judge by the remains, possessed considerable architectural merit. Fifty years ago it was in fair preservation, and was only deficient in the pyramid of graduated steps forming the crowning portion of the edifice. To-day the lower stage, forming a square of about twenty-two feet, and the steps forming the base, are all that remain. The story of its demolition some forty years ago is not pleasant to relate. It appears that Sir T. Reade, at that time British Consul-General at Tunis, obtained permission from the Bey to remove from the monument two stones, bearing the remarkable bi-lingual inscription above referred to, the only known example of a dedication in the Libyan and Punic tongues, and consequently esteemed of great value. Instead of personally superintending the operation, the Consul appears to have ordered the removal of these inscribed blocks, without instructing the workmen how it was to be done. The mausoleum is of solid construction, built with immense blocks of cut stone, and consequently the removal of any of the lower facing stones would require unusual care. The modern Arab workman is neither renowned for skill nor ingenuity, and his clumsy tools and primitive appliances are ill-adapted for any delicate building operations. In this case he commenced at the summit, throwing down every stone till he arrived at the two bearing the inscription. These were purchased by our Government at the sale of Sir T. Reade's collection, and may be seen, in excellent preservation, in the British Museum.

In a small open space among the wretched hovels which compose the modern village of Dougga, we perceived some five or six Arabs squatting on a dungheap, and basking in the sun, in apparent silence and unconcerned indolence. These men, as we afterwards learned, were the sheik of the place and his friends or attendants. They observed our movements with apathy. On our addressing the sheik, however, through the interpreter, he responded courteously to our demands, sending a man to point out the ruins, and furnishing us with a guide to Teboursouk.

Teboursouk is but an hour's journey from Dougga, the road passing by the most part through olive-groves, among which numerous white koubbas are conspicuous.

CHAPTER XXVI.

TEBOURSOUK TO TUNIS.

December 4th.

TEBOURSOUK — CONTAINS LITTLE OF INTEREST — DEPARTURE — PIC-
TURESQUE COUNTRY — AMONG THE MOUNTAINS — CROSSING THE
MEDJERDAH — RETROSPECT — TUNIS AGAIN.

AFTER the dirty condition of Dougga and its utter lifelessness, Teboursouk appeared to us a tolerably clean and lively town. If the by-streets are dull and sparsely populated, the main street at any rate is animated, fairly-well paved, and, as Arab towns go, decently kept.*

Teboursouk, the ancient Thibursicum, possesses

---

* 'It did not present itself in the same light to M. Guérin, who thus describes it: 'The interior of the town bears the appearance of great misery and complete decay; at least half the houses are abandoned and in ruins. The streets are revoltingly filthy, and it is surprising that the plague does not yearly decimate the inhabitants. As it is, the population is reduced to 2500 souls. No public monument, externally at least, merits the traveller's attention. Only a few fine relics of antiquity are to be found here and there (generally mutilated and disfigured by layers of whitewash) in Arab buildings, which are themselves falling into ruins. The upper quarters of the town are nearly deserted, and the few inhabitants one meets seem to wander like phantoms in the solitary streets, obstructed at intervals by heaps of refuse. The lower quarters are more peopled; not even so thickly, however, as of old, for I was told—in 1862—that the depopulation had greatly increased during the last fifteen to twenty years.'—*Voyage, II.*, 114.

many of the requirements of a flourishing place. It is situated on high ground, in the midst of a fertile country, and has an abundant supply of water. It is enclosed by a wall of defence, with square towers at intervals, constructed by the Byzantines with the materials of the old Roman town. Apart from this indication of former strength and importance, Teboursouk has no vestiges of architectural monuments.

Not finding any objects of special interest to detain us, we took our departure at midday for Beja, or rather for the railway-station of that name, where we had arranged to take the train for Tunis, under the guidance of a mounted Arab, whom the sheik was good enough to place at our disposal.

For a considerable distance we rode under the pleasant shade of olive-trees, and then crossing the Oued Falhar or Khallad, entered a region of hill and dale, clothed with verdure and abounding in picturesque scenery. At 1.15 we traversed a valley, in which many Roman remains were discernible near the track, while others dotted the sides of adjacent hills. These ruins are called Henchir Ain-el-Caïd. By two o'clock we had entered the splendid defile between Djebel Mahia and Djebel Kabika, and while winding round the picturesque slopes of these mountains at a great altitude, caught occasional glimpses of the distant and fantastic peak of Zaghouan. Until 3.30 the track, quite imperceptible except to an experienced guide, steep and dangerous in some parts, and at others encumbered with huge lumps of rock, lay among the mountains. It was with a feeling of thankfulness that we at last attained the summit, and looking down the northern slopes saw the great plain of the Medjerdah, with the railway-station, indicated by a white spot in the far distance, lying at our feet.

After an hour or more of gradual descent, an unexpected difficulty presented itself. Between the foot of the mountain and the railway-station flows the serpentine Medjerdah, a bridgeless stream, capricious at all seasons, and after heavy rains impassable. At this point it is pretty wide. Weary of the saddle, we had dismounted and walked down the hill, leaving our horses to the care of the Arabs. Somehow or other the animals, following in single file, had got loose, and making straight for the water, were soon up to their girths in mid-stream. To increase the unpleasantness of the situation, the guide who had conducted us from Teboursouk had gone back, after having safely piloted us through the mountains, and our own men, one of whom called himself the guide, had no knowledge of the river, nor of any spot where it was fordable.

After the exercise of much patience and the use of a little violent language, of which, fortunately, our stupid Arabs did not understand a single word, the animals were at last brought safely to the bank; and, as a piece of good luck in a part of the country where scarcely half-a-dozen people may be seen in the course of a whole day, an Arab happened to be passing on the opposite side. A fordable spot higher up the stream was indicated, and we got safely across.

Scarcely had we reached the station when the train, the last and only one, steamed in. We had barely time to settle for our horses and book our luggage. Looking out of the carriage-window as our train moved off, we observed, with considerable amusement, the commencement of a dispute amongst our Arabs about the division of the sum of money they had just received. A goodly pile of dollars had to be counted and divided proportionately between them, according to an arrangement best known to themselves. A financial settlement such as this—a matter of easy adjustment among any civilised people—would be the subject of deep deliberation with such primitive folk : much counting and weighing the pieces of silver, and perhaps a final settlement after several sittings.

At 8.30 p.m. we were back again in Tunis. We had thus, in fourteen days from the date of leaving Soussa, accomplished a somewhat difficult journey without misadventure. Favoured by most beautiful weather, unvaried except by the one important downpour before leaving Kairouan, we had been enabled to traverse parts of the country that would be inaccessible after heavy or continuous rains. The innumerable oueds that intersect most parts of Tunisia, especially in the vicinity of Sbeitla and Kasserin, and the defiles between Ksour and the mountains bordering the plain of the Medjerdah, will always be a source of risk and inconvenience to travellers in the absence of fine weather. The time we had devoted to this journey, so full of interest, was, on retrospection, too short. It would have been pleasant to have loitered longer on the road, to have stepped a little further from the track to examine more distant monumental remains, to have lingered during the heat of midday by the banks of some of the pleasant streams, or stopped to note more fully the beauty of a mountain pass or a distant landscape. Impossible ; our only resting-place for the night was often so many kilomètres distant, and it was imperative to reach it before sundown, at the risk of finding ourselves shelterless as night set in, and when darkness would render locomotion, especially among the mountains, absolutely impossible. Hot as was the mid-day sun, the nights were frequently chilly, and, in default of a well-closed room, all our wrappers were needed to keep out the cold. It may be as well to mention that waterproof sheeting, air-pillows, and a couple of rugs each, constituted our bedding. We found these quite sufficient. They were very portable, and when rolled up inside the india-rubber covering occupied but little space. For any lengthened stay in the interior of this country a tent is indispensable. This necessitates an extra baggage animal.

CHAPTER XXVII.

LA CALLE TO EL-KEF AND CHEMTOU.

March 7th to 16th.

LA CALLE—BEAUTIFUL SCENERY—TABARCA—THE KHOMAIR COUNTRY—AIN-DRAHAM—FERNANA—BULLA REGIA—SOUK-EL-ARBÂA—HIGH LATITUDES—EL-KEF—A STORM—CHEMTOU AND ITS QUARRIES OF MARBLE—CROSS THE FRONTIER INTO ALGERIA.

A FEW years hence an excursion through the country of the Khomair* may be of everyday occurrence. Less than ten years ago, no European would have ventured to ride through the heart of this wild mountainous region except with a powerful escort; and even the soldiers of the Bey regarded its inhabitants with so much dread that they hesitated to pass certain well-defined spots on the line of frontier. No region of North Africa was less known to the outside world. It was left as a blank space on most maps, and the fierceness and brutal habits of the untamed tribes that formed the Khomair population, though probably much exaggerated, contributed more than anything else to secure for them entire control over the territory they occupied. Guide-books up to this date say little about a comparatively unknown district; but since the French protectorate of Tunisia, and the consequent disarming of the population, there is no reason why Europeans should not visit every corner of

---

* Generally written Kroumir. Sing. Khomiri ; Plur. Khomair.

it without more risk than in other thinly inhabited parts of North Africa.

It was our good fortune to ride through the Khomair country in the month of March, 1885, when vegetation was bursting forth in all the luxuriance of early spring, and when the verdure of winter herbage had not yet been parched by the scorching rays of a tropical sun.

The best approach is by way of La Calle,* a small coast town about three hours' journey by steamer from the port of Bône. There is no harbour nor safe anchorage, and as landing is impossible in bad weather, it is advisable to ascertain before leaving Bône whether the steamer will land passengers at La Calle.

The weather being favourable for landing, there was little difficulty in reaching the shore, clean lodging and good food being obtained at a modest little establishment styled Hôtel d'Orient. From the proprietor we obtained two horses and the services of an intelligent Arab, and on the following morning left by the new carriage road, then in formation, for Tabarca, the first town on the Tunisian frontier. Our baggage consisted of knapsacks, convenient for slipping over the back of an animal, rugs, umbrellas, and revolvers.

---

* The French name of this town serves as a memorial of the settlement at Cape Negro, some miles eastward, of a few merchants from Havre, for the purpose of opening up a trade in coral, transferred 150 years later to La Calle. It is now a small town, chiefly inhabited by Italians who, till recently, carried on a considerable trade in sardine-salting as well as in coral fishery. But the coral banks have either shifted or, more probably, have been exhausted, and the sardines have found other quarters on the coast, where they are left undisturbed. The old method of fishing is still pursued. 'They fish,' says Edrisi, the geographer of the twelfth century, 'by means of implements to which a number of hempen bags are attached. These are put in motion, the threads become entangled in the coral, upon which the fishermen draw up the instruments and extract the coral in great abundance.'

After passing through a forest of magnificent cork trees and oaks the track skirted the Guerra el-Hout, or Lake of Fish, at that time of the year a sheet of water, but in the summer months converted into a marsh of a pestilential nature. Beyond are some valuable lead mines worked by an English company, and near here a lower road branches off to the right by way of the Col de Babouch to Ain-Draham; an upper one that we followed proceeding in a north-easterly direction through a mountainous country, embracing some of the finest scenery in Tunisia. Hill and dale here succeed each other, clothed with wild luxuriance of vegetation; a jungle of brushwood and myrtle, rose-laurels and heath, narcissus and daffodil, and wild herbs, sweet to the smell and agreeable to the eye. After passing the frontier some ten miles from La Calle the road turned northward and approached the coast line. A few miles further a white speck near the long stretch of indented shore marked the little island of Tabarca, rising some 400 feet above the sea-level and crowned by its weird castle, outlined sharply against the clear sky. After nearly eight hours in the saddle, the heat of midday preventing rapid locomotion, the small military station at Tabarca, on rising ground above the town, was reached by a zigzag path, and then, descending the hill on the other side, we drew up at an isolated cottage, dignified by the name of the Hôtel Tiret.

The aspect of Tabarca is not cheering. A few stone houses and a number of wooden shanties half finished, and many of them untenanted, do not give indications of progress or prosperity. But the inhabitants—a mixed assemblage of Europeans of many nationalities and a sprinkling of natives—are hopeful of the future. A concession by the Government of the Bey to an influential company to work some extensive deposits of iron and copper ore at Ras-er-Rajel, eight miles eastward, will promote the employment of a large number of men. The construction of a harbour and a railway to the mines, now commenced, will open up an increased trade with the interior, and cannot fail to make Tabarca the commercial port for a considerable tract of country.

The remains of the Roman colony of Thabraca, as it was then written, are very insignificant, and consist of the ruined baths near the shore, and masses of walling that bear evidence of subsequent reconstruction. All interest is centred in the ruined castle or citadel, erected by Charles V. on the island after his memorable expedition against Tunis in 1535—a picturesque group of walls and towers, bleached by sun and wind, and perched on the very edge of a precipitous rock rising vertically out of the sea. Under the courteous guidance of the officer in command of the station we made a tour of inspection of this dilapidated citadel, with its great vaulted chambers, successively occupied by the Spaniards, the Genoese, and, till recently, by the soldiers of the Bey. By a concession to the mining company before mentioned, the stones on the island may be employed in the construction of the new harbour works. It is to be hoped that this old castle may still be preserved as the most picturesque object along the whole northern coast of Tunisia.*

---

* ' Bruce visited the island after he had left Africa in 1765, and proposed to the ministry of the day to obtain possession of it as a station for the British trade in the Mediterranean. "The mountains opposite Tabarca," he says, "are covered with oak-trees of immense size, where, I think, the Mediterranean ports might be easily supplied with timber for construction."

' M. Desfontaine, who travelled in Tunis from 1783 to 1786, was

On the morning of March 10th we left our comfortable quarters at Tabarca for Ain-Draham, thirty-one kilomètres direct south, and in the centre of the Khomair country. A road is in course of formation, but it will be some years before it is practicable for carriages. The track followed the banks of the Oued el-Kebir, or River of Oak-trees, the old Eastern boundary of Numidia, and lying in the centre of a broad and beautiful valley about eight miles long. Here the soil is remarkably fertile, and only requires a better system of drainage and improved methods of agriculture to render this locality a centre of great prosperity. At a distance of five kilomètres a ruined building of some pretensions attracted our attention. It appears to have been the dwelling of a rich Roman proprietor, but the absence of inscriptions forbade any clue to its ownership. At eighteen kilomètres we crossed the Oued Kerma, or River of the Fig-tree, a pleasant resting-place, its banks clothed with olive and oak—a spot to charm the eye of poet or painter. Here were several women engaged in washing. Either through fear or natural modesty they removed to a distance, watching our movements with much astonishment, and showing by their gestures that we were not to gratify curiosity by approaching them. The appearance of the inhabitants of this wild country may be expressed in one word—poverty-stricken. Centuries of dogged independence and severance from other tribes, and an occasional raid across the frontier levying black-mail whenever pressed by want,

---

equally desirous that this island should be taken possession of by the Government of France, and expressed his conviction that, were it occupied, France would be able to lay down the law throughout the Mediterranean, and that England would be excluded and lose the Levant trade.'—Lieut.-Col. Sir R. L. Playfair, *Travels in the Footsteps of Bruce*, p. 250.

have made these people as far removed from civilisation as the inhabitants of any country that we should designate as barbarous. The race is stalwart; the men are, as a rule, of tall stature, with features belonging rather to the Moor than to the Arab, the look of the warrior rather than of the agriculturist. Those we met on the track, whether mounted or not, returned our salutations with courtesy, and passed on without the slightest interest in our movements, or even stopping to parley with our guide. Once only in the course of that day we had the slightest cause for anxiety. In riding single file through a wood we suddenly met, at a sharp turn in the track, a mounted Kroumir, armed to the teeth. With wondrous dexterity he spurred his horse into the thick scrub, as though preparing for attack. But a glance at his saddle-bags explained everything. He was the military courier, and was conveying the mails to the camp at Tabarca.

The dwellings of these folk are as squalid as they are themselves, chiefly made of branches of trees, and layers of dried grass daubed over with a little mud. An inventory of the contents is soon taken: a flat bank of earth for a bed, covered by a mat or a few handfuls of straw, some rough earthenware vessels, a wooden bowl or two, a goatskin for churning butter, and a couple of portable millstones, these constitute the ordinary contents of a Khomiri dwelling.

The dress of the men consists of a long shirt reaching to the knees, and a bernous over it, either of dark camel's hair, or white, if they can afford it. A red fez cap with a white turban wound round it constitutes the headgear. The women's garments are very similar to those of the Bedouin tribes. A large square piece of blue woollen material, neither shaped nor sewn, is wound about the body in a very ingenious way, and tied round the waist with a cord. It cannot be said to cover the figure, for it is quite loose above the waist, forming a sort of large pocket, in which provisions and other articles are carried when they are on the move. Like the Bedouins also, they enjoy more privileges than their Arab sisters, for their faces are never veiled, and they may be seen talking to the men with European freedom.

At twenty-six kilomètres from Tabarca, still in the midst of beautiful scenery, we reached the Col de Babouch, the junction with the road mentioned before as forming the more direct route between La Calle and Ain-Draham, and where a frontier custom-house has been established. Here the carriage-road is completed, and for the next five kilomètres winds round the mountains to a higher level in the midst of a forest of corks. The magnificence of these trees, fully sixty feet high, with trunks varying from ten to fifteen feet in girth, and lateral branches clothed with moss and sprays of luxuriant ferns, is unsurpassed in North Africa. The trees are barked in the summer months, at intervals of about every ten years, and are a source of considerable revenue to the Government. Turning an angle of the wooded slope, the huts and rough tenements that constitute the newly-built village of Ain-Draham appeared on the hillside, perched high up and apparently inaccessible. The altitude is somewhere about 2600 feet above the sea-level. In a few minutes we dismounted in front of the Hôtel des Pacificateurs, as it is styled, where we found indifferent food and very rough lodging. Ain-Draham is nothing more than a military station established after the subjugation and disarming of the Khomair, and around it are clustered the rough dwellings of small traders, who have been attracted here in the hope of doing business with the officers and men of the French army of occupation.

Through a letter of introduction to the proprietor of the principal store we were able to obtain a carriage and a pair of good horses for continuing the journey. Sending our saddle-horses back to La Calle by the guide, we started early the following morning on an excellent road for Souk-el-Arbâa, in the Medjerdah valley. For many miles the road gradually descended through a forest of cork-trees, followed by an open undulating country, partly covered with heath, and partly under cultivation. A Roman miliary column, set up in a meadow on the left of the track, six kilomètres from Ain-Draham, marks the course of the old Roman road. An inscription on the shaft, which is about five feet high, fixes the date at about A.D. 320. At a distance of twenty-six kilomètres we drew rein at the rest-house of Fernana,* where food can be had, but no lodging. This is a bleak spot, commanding an immense sweep of undulating plain, thinly cultivated. It derives its name from a cork oak close by, of gigantic size, the only tree visible for many miles. The girth of the trunk exceeds twenty feet, and the spread of the branches 120 feet. Fifteen kilomètres further on we quitted the main road and entered a track branching off to the left, for the purpose of visiting the ruins of Bulla Regia. In fine weather the track is practicable for carriages, but is not recommended after heavy rains. It is full of ruts, the surface is very uneven, and the coarse

---

* 'Fernana is on the boundary of the Khomair country, and used to be the extreme limit to which the Bey's camp was permitted to come in its annual circuit for the collection of taxes. Here the chiefs used to meet it, and hand over such sums as they felt disposed to pay. If the Tunisian soldiery advanced a step further the taxes were paid with powder and lead, and these brave warriors never dared to follow their assailants within the limits of their mountains and forests.'—*Consular Report* by Lieut.-Col. Sir R. L. Playfair, July, 1884, p. 6.

herbage that almost conceals it in some places is very obstructive to wheels. It is better, under these circumstances, to go on direct to Souk-el-Arbäa, and to visit the ruins from that station, either on foot or on horseback.

The site of Bulla Regia, now called Beni-Mazeu, covering an area of about a mile in length, was unknown a few years ago. At the present day it is so choked with weeds and coarse grass, and its ruined monuments are so buried under the surface, that identification of the public buildings is no easy task. The walls of the great Thermæ are still partly standing, surrounded by huge masses of stone and rubble, piled up or thrown down in endless confusion. The theatre, built of great blocks of finely-cut limestone, is filled up with earth almost to the top of the auditorium, and the spring, which bears indications of having been embellished with arcades, after the manner of the springs at Zaghouan, is now half-concealed in the long grass. A triumphal arch and other monumental remains, which existed here a few years back, have been wantonly destroyed, and the materials used in the construction of the Tunisian railway, which crosses the plain some four kilomètres distant. What might have been the appearance of this royal city in the days of its prosperity is a matter of pleasant conjecture. Looking down from the higher ground on this assemblage of stones and half-buried remains, the eye can see at a glance that the site was well selected. A large extent of fertile country lay at its feet, and the supply of pure water from the mountains that screened it from the north was abundant and never-failing. It is to be hoped that the site of Bulla Regia may some day be explored.

Regaining the road we crossed the river Medjerdah over a modern bridge, and at 6 p.m., much fatigued by the heat and exertions of the day, reached the buffet

RUINS OF BULLA REGIA

adjoining the railway station at Souk-el-Arbäa. Here we obtained comfortable lodging, and good food and attendance.

Our intention was to dismiss the carriage here and to proceed to El-Kef, forty-six kilomètres, on horseback; but our driver, an Italian, was so anxious to visit some friends there that we were persuaded to continue the journey with him. There is a small mail-cart running daily to El-Kef, but it is a rickety sort of vehicle and not well horsed, and, as the road is only completed for about two thirds the distance, this mode of conveyance is not recommended.

Leaving early the following morning direct south, a sharp trot of nine kilomètres brought us to the banks of the Oued Mellegue, where there is a ferry. The long drought, however, had made the stream quite fordable. Ascending the mountain range forming the southern boundary of the Medjerdah valley, and then traversing a large extent of heathland, partly cultivated and affording good pasturage for numerous flocks of sheep and goats, we drew up at the rest-house of Nebour, a distance of twenty-eight kilomètres. The panoramic view from this elevated region is most extensive, and the scenery picturesque. Below lies the pretty little village of that name, with its white-domed koubbas nestled in olive-groves, and framed by the long range of Numidian mountains. There are two roads from Nebour to El-Kef: the one by the plains, of easy ascent, thirty-eight kilomètres, the other over the mountains, very steep, eighteen kilomètres. Our driver, over-confident of the strength of his animals, chose the latter. With great difficulty they were urged up the sharp ascent, and only succeeded in reaching more level ground after a heavy pull of nearly two hours. Finding they were thoroughly ex-

hausted we alighted and walked on till the walls of El-
Kef came in view. The wild grandeur of the scenery at
this high altitude is very striking. In so clear an atmosphere the range of vision seems illimitable, and distant
objects, that in other climates would not be perceptible,
are here outlined with a sharpness that is quite remarkable. A long range of precipitous limestone cliffs, rising
in some parts nearly 200 feet, skirts the road for a long
distance. Here, at the most prominent angle, the French
have established a signal-station for military purposes.
After forty-six kilomètres, the road wound round to the
right, and the walls of the town and its Kasba came into
view. Getting into the carriage again for the sake of appearance, we drove through the upper gate, in a long line
of crenelated wall that followed the slope of the mountain,
and having satisfied the sentry, we dashed along the
narrow tortuous streets to the delight and astonishment
of the inhabitants. The less said about accommodation
here for European travellers the better. It is sufficient
to state that the two houses dignified by the name of
Hôtel are both dirty, and their culinary powers of the
most limited description.

The town or city of El-Kef,* signifying the Rock,
is of irregular shape, built on the side of a steep rock
facing south-west, and enclosed by a loop-holed wall
having six gates. It contains a population of about
4000 Arabs and Jews, and a few score of Europeans,
mostly Maltese. Like all Arab towns, it is dirty and ill-
paved, and except for its situation and some remains of the

---

* 'It is probable that this town, known as Sicca Veneria, owed its
foundation at a remote period to a colony of Phœnicians, who introduced the worship of the Asiatic Venus, worshipped in Assyria, and
most probably also in Syria and Phœnicia, under the name of Succoth-
Benoth.'—V. GUÉRIN, *Voyage*, II. 57.

older Roman town of Sicca Veneria, with the materials of which it has been built, it has no special interest. El-Kef has six mosques, of poor appearance externally, neither remarkable for grace of outline nor for any of that delicacy of ornamentation so frequently found in Arab work. Of the interiors it is impossible to speak, as entry is forbidden to the infidel. There is an absence of prosperity in the town; many of the houses are unoccupied, and some of them deserted and unroofed. The Kasba, occupying the most prominent position, is built, as in many other Arab towns, in an angle of the enclosing walls, but as it is commanded by a plateau of rock at a higher level it has little value as a citadel. The fragmentary remains of a great temple dedicated to Hercules are built into the walls of an European house, and portions of a basilica or palace in the centre of the town, constructed with huge blocks of masonry, stand out majestically amongst a mass of *débris*, the vaulted apse of one of the chambers, now blackened by smoke, forming the residence of an Arab. The principal advantage at El-Kef is an abundant and never-failing supply of pure water. It comes bubbling up from a spring in the rock that overhangs the town, and rushes into a conduit at the rate of many tons a minute. A monumental fountain erected by the Romans at the end of this conduit is still in fair preservation, and men, women, and children, camels and cattle, may be seen here at nearly all hours of the day, luxuriating in the beneficent flow of cool water, while the waste from the troughs passes down the slope to irrigate and fertilise the plains below. Thirteen great Roman cisterns, side by side, almost as perfect as on the day they were built, were used as storehouses for water in case of drought, but they have long since been disused. At the present day the French soldiers, occupying some hut-barracks outside the town, use them for gymnastic purposes, and 'Salon de billard' and 'Salle d'escrime,' written on the wall in rough pigments, seem to indicate the purposes to which they are or may be applied.

To those who are interested in epitaphs or inscriptions, whether relating to the Romans, or to the early Christians who formed an important community here in the fourth or fifth centuries, El-Kef must be a treasure-house of instruction. There is scarcely a house which does not possess one or more of these inscribed stones built into the walls, and votive pedestals and tumulary pillars in stone or marble are more numerous here than in any other town of the Regency. In the little burial-ground outside the walls, appropriated to the Jews, the memorial stones consist mostly of Roman altar or votive pedestals laid flat over the graves, coated thickly with whitewash, and the lettering, commencing with the pagan 'D. M. S.', not even erased. Reverence for the dead does not appear to stand very high among these primitive people. The exploration of El-Kef has not yet been conducted in any systematic way, but there is little doubt that valuable remains of the older Roman town, and probably of its Punic predecessor, may some day be brought to light. Three statues of white marble were unearthed less than two years ago near the site of the Temple of Hercules, and many objects of interest to the antiquary are constantly found whenever the surface is disturbed a few feet in depth.

A pleasant breakfast in the patio of the house of M. le Maire, who received us with great courtesy, brought an agreeable visit to a close, and at 2 p.m. on the second day we started on the return journey to Souk-el-Arbāa. Our intention was to have dismissed the carriage and to proceed in the saddle to Zanfour, but the difficulty in obtaining horses for any cross routes, and the absence of reliable information as to distances, made it unadvisable to journey further south. It was as well we did not venture into a part of the country where accommodation was difficult to obtain, for while descending the mountain, the clouds gathered, and a pitiless downpour of rain soon drenched us to the skin. By sheer good luck we managed to cross the Oued Mellegue before the storm-waters had rendered it impassable, and at 8 p.m. we reached the Hôtel buffet at Souk-el-Arbäa.

At 11 a.m. the following morning we left by train for Oued-Meliz, a station twenty-three kilomètres further west, for the purpose of visiting the ancient marble quarries at Chemtou. Leaving our light baggage in charge of the station-master, we started across the heath for a walk of about five kilomètres, forgetful at the moment of the presence of the river Medjerdah, which lay between us and the quarries. This remarkable river, one day almost dry, at another a rushing torrent of water, yellowed by sandy mud, has been already referred to, and its dangers have not been exaggerated. 'Can the gentlemen swim?' said a female voice in Italian at a side-window of the whitened hut that served for a railway-station (evidently the wife of the station-master). 'Oh, yes!' we said. 'You'll get across,' added the husband; 'the waters are not up yet.' The contemplation of the landscape, the beauty of the heather, and the gorgeous colouring of the wild flowers that dotted the plain, drove away all thoughts of the river in front of us. In half an hour we suddenly came to the edge of a steep bank, with the troubled waters below. To strip and pile our clothes on the top of our heads was a matter of unpleasant necessity, but there was

O

no alternative, except to retrace our steps. By good fortune we reached the opposite bank without mishap, and in half an hour arrived at the cluster of cottages occupied by the workmen engaged in the quarries. Under the courteous guidance of the resident director we made the circuit of the old Roman city that stood here under the name of Simittu Colonia, on the highroad from Carthage to Hippo Regia (Bône). Its situation on the lower slopes of the Djebel Herrech, commanding a magnificent sweep of the fertile Medjerdah plain, was well chosen. A great bridge over the river gave direct communication southward with Sicca Veneria, and another northward through the Kroumir country conveyed to the port of Thabarca, for shipment to Rome, the rich products of its quarries. With the exception of a portion of an aqueduct built with waste marble, and bearing evidences of reconstruction, no single monument is now standing. Trajan's bridge across the Medjerdah, overthrown by an earthquake, is a confused mass of stone and marble, and Roman remains peep out in all directions above the rough scrub that covers the surface. The quarries are much in the condition in which the Romans left them on the irruption of the Vandals in the fifth century. There are great yawning chasms in the mountain side, half-quarried blocks of giallo-antico, and rose-coloured marble, and slabs of breccia, intended perhaps for the embellishment of some temple or palace in Imperial Rome. A concession of these quarries to a Belgian company is likely to be attended with success. There is branch communication by rail with the Tunisian line, and easy transport either to Bône or Tunis.

As there is no accommodation for travellers at Chemtou we were obliged to return to the railway station the same evening. 'How did you arrive here?' we were asked at the quarries, and, on describing our river experiences, were told on all sides we might have been drowned. To return by the same route was impossible, as the waters, owing to the storm of the previous day, were rising rapidly. However, by following the branch tramway from the quarries to a point on the main line, some three kilomètres lower down the valley, indicated by a white cottage in the far distance, and crossing the river by a railway-bridge, we were enabled to reach Oued-Meliz in time for the evening train to Souk-Ahras on the Algerian side of the frontier.

CHAPTER XXVIII.

DOMESTIC LIFE.

DIFFICULTY OF OBTAINING INFORMATION CONCERNING DOMESTIC LIFE IN TUNISIA—WOMEN CLASSED UNDER THREE HEADS: MOORS, BEDOUINS, AND JEWESSES—MOORISH FEMALES SELDOM MET IN THE STREETS—THE YOUNGER ONES KEPT STRICTLY WITHIN DOORS—THEIR FACES ARE ALWAYS HIDDEN—HEAD-GEAR—POLYGAMY ON THE DECLINE—VISIT TO THE INTERIOR OF A HOUSE IN TUNIS—THE MYSTERIOUS SHEET—INMATES OF THE HAREM—PUNISHMENT OF THE CORSET—BEDOUINS DO NOT CONCEAL THEIR FACES—THEIR APPEARANCE, GARMENTS, AND JEWELRY—FALSE HAIR—JEWESSES SEEN ONLY IN TOWNS—THEIR CORPULENCE ARTIFICIALLY ENCOURAGED—THEIR BEAUTY—JEWISH HOSPITALITY—LAX MORALITY.

THE pertinacity with which dwelling-houses are closed against Europeans, and the jealousy with which strangers are regarded, are a bar to any intimate acquaintance with the domestic life of the people. It is, therefore, a difficult task for those whose residence in the country has been of short duration to contribute anything of value on the subject of harem life. It would, however, be a grave omission in a work on Tunisia not to make any mention of the social life of the female population, which, especially in the towns, has been less affected by European influences than in any other Mohammedan centre.

It is not within the scope of these notes to discuss the vexed question of polygamy, or to inquire whether the condition of the inmates of a harem is preferable or

not to the lot of women of more civilised countries—
the former relieved of all care and responsibility so long
as they obey one master; the latter burdened with the
vagaries of fashion, the cares and exactions of the household, the consequences of excessive education, or, in the
case of the less fortunate, subject to the thraldom of
domestic service with the risk of capricious dismissal,
to be followed by the almshouse or union when they
can work no longer.

The women of Tunisia may be roughly classed under
three heads: the townswoman, generally of Moorish extraction; the Bedouin nomad; and the Jewess. Moorish
women, especially of the higher class, are rarely seen
in the streets, although a few may be found passing
through the bazaars before noon. In this respect there
is a marked difference between Tunis and other great
Mohammedan capitals like Constantinople or Cairo,
where women of the higher grades enjoy a greater
amount of personal liberty, and, consequently, are far
more numerous in the public thoroughfares. As their
faces are invariably hidden and the outlines of their
forms enveloped in the folds of their garments, it is
difficult to arrive at an opinion as to their ages, especially
as there is an absence of elasticity in their movements.
It would seem, however, that the privilege of walking
abroad, either to make purchases or to go to the bath,
is confined to those who are past middle age, and that
the younger women are kept at home. The covering
of the face differs from that used in Turkey or Egypt,
and consists of two bands of black plaited horsehair, or
white material (generally the former), bound horizontally
across the face, and leaving the eyes only uncovered.
Sometimes the black yashmak, as it is called, mostly
of silk and richly embroidered, such as is worn by the

higher grades, constitutes a veil as well as a mantle. Both modes of head-gear are exceedingly ungraceful, and appear to have been designed to render their wearers as repulsive as possible. Harems containing many women are not so frequent in Tunisia as formerly, most likely from reasons of economy. Men of position content themselves with one, or at most two, wives, and those of the lower orders are invariably the husbands of one only. For information concerning the inner life of a harem, one must be beholden to European ladies.* Admission is never granted to men, nor would it be discreet to question an Arab about his domestic arrangements; any inquiries after a man's wife and family, so usual with us, would be regarded by him as a gross impertinence. Only once, however, were we able to inspect a house in Tunis occupied by a Mohammedan and his family, accompanied by a friend who contemplated purchasing the house, and who had announced his visit beforehand. We passed through the vestibule into the patio, where the proprietor received us. Room after room was entered without a glimpse of a female form. At length, in the corner of one of the dimly-lighted apartments we perceived a large sheet, concealing something which appeared to move. Directing our gaze in an opposite direction but still mindful of the sheet, we turned suddenly round, and saw, as we anticipated, bright eyes peering at us from underneath the folds.

---

* An interesting chapter upon Tunisian domestic life and the habits of the women will be found in *La Côte barbaresque*, by Le Prince J. Lubomirski, together with the narrative of a visit made by the Princess Lubomirski to the Beya at the harem of the Bardo. The same account is given, translated, but without any recognition of authorship, by Herr von Hesse-Wartegg, in chap. viii. of his work on *Tunis*.

The wary Arab had hit upon this simple expedient for the temporary concealment of the female portion of his household.

In conversation with a French lady resident in Tunis, who had just visited one or two harems of that city, we learnt that the inmates are as a rule plain, ignorant, and trivial. What most interested them was her own dress, and they persisted in divesting her of her garments one after another, and examining the lines of stitching with eager curiosity. When they came to the corset, one of them exclaimed, 'You must be a very wicked woman!' and then begged to know how she could have offended her husband to such a degree that he should have inflicted upon her so severe a punishment.*

The Bedouin women, seen only in the interior of the country, do not cover their faces, but seem proud of their red skins, face, neck, and chest tattooed with all sorts of quaint devices. Their countenances are expressive of intelligence, if not of beauty, and their sprightly movements and quick steps indicate that nomadic life, in spite of much drudgery, is more enviable than the monotonous unvarying lot of their Arab sisters in the towns. They affect garments of bright colours, and wear a profusion of silver jewelry (the investment of their earnings), to be valued rather by weight of metal than by delicacy of workmanship. Amongst the profusion of chains, fibulæ, and bangles, one is sure to notice some one or more pendent talismans, believed to be charms

---

* In a letter to Lady Rich, dated Adrianople, April (o.s.), 1717, Lady Mary Wortley Montagu describes a visit to the Bagnio, and showing her stays; she adds that the inmates 'believed I was locked up in that machine, and that it was not in my power to open it; which contrivance they attributed to my husband.'

against the evil eye. In some districts they cover their heads with false hair, arranged in small ringlets. These nomads are by no means shy, and do not object to approach a stranger, subject to the permission of their men, or when they feel certain of not being detected. Unlike his co-religionist of the towns, the Bedouin has several wives, which to him become a source of gain, as they supply him with cheap labour.*

Jewesses are seldom met with in the country, but in the principal towns form a conspicuous as well as an interesting portion of the population. In the account of our visit to Sfax we made special note of their curious and picturesque appearance. Young or old, they are nearly always fat—to an extent indeed which would be deemed incredible by one who has not seen them; and as obesity is in the eyes of their relations and admirers their chief attraction, art is employed to assist nature in augmenting the volume of their charms.†
They hide neither face nor form, for their tightly fitting

---

* We had been told that the greatest compliment an European could pay to a Bedouin parent was to spit deliberately into the faces of any of his children. Many travellers have noted the incredible value of spittle, as recorded in Biblical times. We need scarcely say that when an opportune moment arrived for testing the value of the recipe we shrank from the experiment.

† This strange practice is not confined to the Israelites, but prevails also among the Mohammedans. Macgill (*Account of Tunis*, 1816, p. 90) thus describes the process: 'The Tunisines have a curious custom of fattening up their young ladies for marriage. A girl, after she is betrothed, is cooped up in a small room. Shackles of silver and gold are put upon her ankles and wrists as a piece of dress. If she is to be married to a man who has discharged, dispatched, or lost a former wife, the shackles which the former wife wore are put upon the new bride's limbs, and she is fed until they are filled up to the proper thickness. This is sometimes no easy matter, particularly if the former wife was fat and the present should be of a slender form. The food used for

AN ARAB WOMAN AND A BEDOUIN GIRL.

garments permit an exact estimate of the outlines of their persons. In youth they are frequently of great beauty—big, lustrous eyes, finely cut features, delicate, transparent skins, and, due allowance made for the bulkiness of their forms, well-proportioned and well-formed limbs. Unlike the dwellings of Mohammedans, the Israelitish houses are not closed to strangers; on the contrary, the proprietors, on the occasion of a marriage* or other family festivity, are given to hospitality, and extend a cordial welcome to the stranger, even though his visit be one of mere curiosity. The men appear to be devoid of that jealousy which with the Mohammedan amounts to fanaticism, and in the lower ranks of life permit their women to pursue, with impunity, a calling which is considered by Europeans as the lowest step of the social ladder.† The evil is not confined to the Jewish portion of the population, but is equally practised by the followers of Mohammed—in their case, however, to the entire exclusion of Europeans.‡

this custom, worthy of barbarians, is a seed called *drough*, which is of an extraordinary fattening quality, and also famous for rendering the milk of nurses rich and abundant. With this seed and their national dish, "*cuscusu*," the bride is literally crammed, and many actually die under the spoon.' This account is endorsed by both M. Léon Michel and Herr von Hesse-Wartegg, who further affirm that the girls are shut up in dark, damp places, and that such delicacies as the flesh of young dogs and horse-livers are added to their diet.

* The proceedings have been so frequently described that we hesitate to offer any account of our own, preferring to refer our readers to the pages of Herr von Hesse-Wartegg, M. Léon Michel, and others.

† Those desirous of pursuing the subject will be able to satisfy their curiosity in *Les Français à Tunis*, Pierre Giffard, p. 128.

‡ Consult, *inter alia*, *La Côte barbaresque*, par Le Prince J. Lubomirski, p. 68.

CHAPTER XXIX.

CONCLUSION.

ADIEU TO OUR FRIENDS — FRENCH AND ARAB COURTS OF JUSTICE — NOAH'S ARK — DEARTH OF LITERATURE IN TUNIS — A SHAKSPEARIAN READING — DEPARTURE.

THE couple of days which remained before our return to England by the next steamer from the port of Tunis, was pleasantly occupied in a round of visits to those whose acquaintance we had the good fortune to make on previous occasions, and who had rendered us much courteous assistance.

A visit to the Gouletta, under the friendly guidance of Mr. S. R. Pariente, an old and respected resident in Tunis, who placed a carriage at our disposal, took up the best part of a day. Although the port bearing that name has an important bearing on the history of North Africa, having been several times captured, destroyed, and rebuilt, it demands no lengthened description. As the commercial harbour of Tunis, separated from the city by El-Bahira, or the lake of Tunis (mentioned in the first chapter), it is essentially a busy place; its inhabitants, half Oriental half European, being of that nondescript character peculiar to other maritime towns of the East. The narrow channel, the Gouletta proper (a corruption of the Arabic words, Halk-el-Oued, or Throat of the Canal), that links the Mediterranean with the lake, is an artificial cut of great antiquity, having been in existence as far back as the brightest epoch of Carthaginian rule. Of the buildings that constitute the town on either bank of the canal little need be said. They owe their origin to ruined Carthage, and if stones could speak another chapter might be added to the sad tale of the last Punic war. The summer palace of the Bey on the sea-shore, with its luxuriant gardens—a tangled undergrowth of tropical plants—has long since been deserted. The villas of wealthy Tunisians who resort here during the summer months are simple and unpretentious, and the shops and cafés that line the main street are mostly one storey high, mean, and unpicturesque.

An agreeable morning and a *déjeûner* with M. Lemarchand, one of the judges of the French Court recently established in Tunis, was followed by a visit to the Court, where justice was administered in conformity with French law. One might, as far as appearances went, have been in France; the judges and pleaders in their robes and *toques*, speaking pure Parisian dialect, and the assistants, with few exceptions, European. Two years previously we had paid a similar visit to the Court of justice here, that of the Cadi, where Arab laws prevailed and Arab customs were observed. The Court, on that occasion, had just opened, and the Cadi's richly-caparisoned and well-kept mule was standing in the open street, tethered and unattended. Passing through the gateway, and into a spacious patio, where some thirty or more natives were congregated, awaiting their turn, we reached a small door, giving access to a chamber, scarcely twelve feet square. Here, on a cushioned bench, occupying one side of the apartment, was seated, cross-legged, the Cadi, a man of some sixty years, whose benevolent countenance displayed intelligence and the habit of command. In front of him, their knees almost touching his couch, sat the persons whose case he was considering—plaintiff and defendant —both on the same seat, elbow to elbow. A minute or two sufficed to decide each case, and the disputants left the court, apparently satisfied with the judgment so hastily pronounced. A running clerk, attached to the court, delivered the judgment to the registrar, whose office was on the other side of the patio.

As we were leaving the court, the usher or secretary, a man of some seventy years, who had been noting the Cadi's judgments, followed us. 'Were the strangers Englishmen?' he demanded of our interpreter. 'And, if so, could he ask them a question?' On receiving an affirmative reply, his serious, unanimated countenance brightened, and after a pause he said: 'I know well how powerful the English are on the sea, and I have heard that they have discovered Noah's ark. Is it true?' The question fairly took us aback, and great was the inclination to laugh; but stifling our hilarity, which would have wounded the old man's feelings (for he spoke with earnestness), we replied, with as much seriousness as we could assume, that his estimate of British naval prowess was as correct as it was flattering, but, so far as we knew, Noah's ark had not yet been found.

There is probably no Eastern country, equally conspicuous for its long history, as well as for its commercial importance, where every branch of literature has been less encouraged than in this corner of North Africa. Under the sway of the Roman Empire, and during the many centuries of Arab occupation, no great work of literature has ever issued from this old-world city. Setting aside the notes by travellers of all nations during the last century, the history of literature in Tunis may be recorded as blank. It is true that the Sheik Nefzaoui, who flourished in the sixth century, made it his home, and probably wrote within its walls that very remarkable work on the social and domestic manners of his countrymen, which has lately been introduced to the curious of both Paris and London. And we may also note that John Howard Payne, author of 'Home, sweet Home,' died at Tunis, April 10th, 1852. The United States Government has erected a monument over his remains in the cemetery of St. George, and the Protestant church is embellished with a memorial window.

With this dearth of literature in a country where bookstalls are unknown, and books at a discount, it was an agreeable surprise to receive an invitation for the last evening of our stay in Tunis to a Shakspearian reading at the British Consulate. The other guests were for the most part members or friends of the diplomatic body. Among the readers (audience there was none) the Italian Consul was conspicuous, and some young ladies from the German Consulate also took parts. This pleasant evening, one of many passed under the hospitable roof of our esteemed Consul, seemed to assure us that, however much the political influence of Great Britain has been allowed of late to decline in these parts, her literary influence is as strong as ever.

To the expression of gratitude to Mr. T. B. Sandwith, C.B., whose kindness and attention contributed so largely to the pleasure and profit of our journey, we would add our thanks to Messieurs Carbonaro, father and son, for numerous valuable services unsparingly rendered.

The 5th of December, the day fixed for our departure, had arrived. Our good friend, Mr. S. R. Pariente, whose attentions had been unceasing, accompanied us to Gouletta, where we spent a pleasant hour in his villa by the seashore, and at 5 p.m. embarked in the *Ville de Rome* for Marseilles.

As the Tunisian shores receded from our view, and our thoughts reverted to the home we were now so rapidly approaching, its comforts contrasted with the rough food and rougher lodging of the past few weeks, and we were constrained to acknowledge the vein of truth pervading the words of Touchstone, which we had read on the previous evening : 'Ay, now am I in Arden : the more fool I ; when I was at home, I was in a better place: but travellers must be content.'

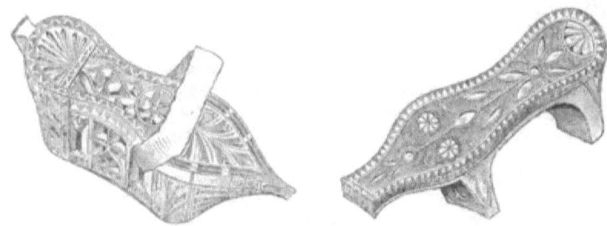

GLOSSARY OF ARABIC TERMS & WORDS USED IN THE BOOK.

Abd (âbd), a slave.
Ain (âin), a spring or fountain; lit. an eye; plur. *òyún*.
Arba (arbaâ), four. Ex. *Souk-el-arbaâ*, the market of the fourth day of the week, *i.e.*, Wednesday.
Arbâl (arbal), a quarter or district of a town or suburb. Sp. *Arrabal*.
Areg, sand-hills.
Attar (âṭṭár), perfume. Ex. *Souk-el-âttarin*, market of the perfumers.
Bab, a gate or doorway; plur. *Bibán*. Ex. *Jâmi ath-thalatha-bibán*, the mosque of the three gates.
Bahíra (baḥirah), a plain or flat surface.
Bahr (baḥr), the sea.
Bahira (buheyrah), a little sea, a lake, Sp. *Albufera, albuhera*.
Bakha, generally el-Batchah, equivalent to Sp. *patio*, signifying an uncovered space in the centre of a house.
Baracan (barakan), a cloak or covering, generally of camel's hair, of the same form as the vestment worn by our Saviour. Sp. *Barragan*.
Beit (beyt), a hall, a reception-room. Ex. *Beit-el-Belâur*, or the hall of glass in the Bardo palace.
Ben (ebn, ibn), son; plur. *bení*.
Bernous (bornús), a large mantle or shawl in one piece, with a hood. Sp. *Albornoz*.
Bey, a governor-general, owing allegiance to the Sultan.

Bindir (bender), a sort of drum or timbrel. Sp. *Pandero*.
Bir, a well.
Bordj (borj), a castle or fortified structure. Sp. *Borje*.
Bou (bú, for abú or abí), a father.
Chachia (shashia), a red skull-cap.
Chott (shott), a salt-lake.
Couscous, Couscousu (kuskusú). Sp. *Alcuzcuz*, a farinaceous food.
Dar, a stone-built house.
Dey, a supreme ruler.
Djamaä (Jamâ), a mosque. Sp. *Aljama, aljamia*.
Djebba (jebba, jubba), a kind of petticoat worn by women, also a vest for men.
Djubba, a vest; whence Sp. *Aljuba, jubon, chupa*. Fr. *Jupon*.
Djebel (jebel), a mountain. *Djebeli* (jebelí), mountainous.
Djerid (jeríd), the dry country, the desert.
Dib (dhîb), a jackal. Sp. *Adive*.
Diffa (dhayffah, dheyffah), a repast prepared for guests. Sp. *Daifa*. Eng. *Tiffin* (?).
Dríba (diriba), a wigwam, or enclosure formed with bamboo and palm branches.
Douar (dowar), plur. of *dâr*, a group of Arab tents or families representing a tribe; also round. Ex. *Hisn-ad-dowár*, the 'round tower.'
El (al), the, being the article prefixed to all nouns, sing. or plur.

Fondouk (fondak), an inn, a caravansary. Sp. *Alhondiga*.
Gandoura (ghandora), a large robe, covering the limbs down to the ankle. Sp. *Alcandora*.
Gimbrik, a native stringed instrument.
Gourbi (gurbí), a native tent.
Guera, a pond.
Hadar (ḥadhrí), an Arab living in a town ; the counterpart of *Beydawi*, a Bedouin.
Hajd (ḥajji), one who has made a pilgrimage to Mecca.
Haik (ḥaik), a piece of thin material, about a yard wide and four yards long, going round the body, and covering the *chachia*, or skull-cap, the whole being secured round the head by a camel's-hair rope. Sp. *Haique*.
Hammám (ḥammah ; plur. ḥammám), hot spring or bath. Ex. *Hammam-el-enf*, the bath of the nose, from the outline of the adjoining hill resembling that organ. Sp. *Alhama*, hot bath.
Hasheesh (hashishah). Sp. *Alexixa*.
Hegira, *Hadjira* (higra), the flight of Moḥammad from Mecca to Medina, from which the Mohammedans begin their calendar.
Henchir, ruins or remains of antiquity.
Hout (hut), a fish. Ex. *Guera-el-hout*, the fish-pond.
Imám, a leader.
Jehád, the holy war against the infidel.
Kadi (kádhi), a judge. Sp. *Alcaide*.
Kaid, a chief, the governor of a castle, a captain. Sp. *Alcaide*.
Kantara, a bridge on arches. Sp. *Alcantara*, *Altantarilla*.
Kasba, *Kaṣbah*, *Kaṣába*, a citadel. Sp. *Alcazaba*.
Kasr (kaṣr), a fortress, or fortified palace. Sp. *Alcazar*.
Kasserin, the two fortresses.
Kebir, great.
Kelb, a dog.

Kindja (Kamija), an undergarment. Sp. *Camisa*. Fr. *Chemise*.
Kibleh (kiblah), the shrine of a mosque looking to Mecca. Sp. *Alquibla*.
Kot (koṭu), cotton. Sp. *Algodon*.
Koubba (kubba), a dome ; the tomb of a marabout or Mohammedan saint, invariably surmounted by a cubba, or cupola ; also a bed recess. Sp. *Alcoba*. Fr. *Alcôve*. Eng. *Alcove*.
Legma (leḥma), the sap of the palm-tree, an intoxicating liquor.
Medrassen (midrasa, madrisa), a school, college, or university.
Maksoura (makṣúrah), a vestiary or vestry in a mosque.
Mansoura (mansúrah), the city of the victorious or conqueror.
Marabout (marbút), a man who devotes his life to contemplation and religious exercises.
Melah (melaḥ), salt. Ex. *Chott-el-Melah*, the salt-lake.
Membar (mimbar), the pulpit in a mosque. Sp. *Almimbar*.
Mersa, *Marsa*, a port, an anchorage. Ex. *Marsa-el-quibir*, the great or capacious port. Sp. *Maçarquivir*.
Mihrab, the niche or recess in a mosque indicating the position of the kibleh.
Minar, a tower attached to a mosque. The Moors call such towers *ṣômah*. Sp. *Minarete*.
Mesdjid (mesjid), a mosque, a house of prayer, from *sajada*, to prostrate oneself. Sp. *Mezquita*.
Moghreb (magrib), the west, the sunset. Sp. *Almagreb*.
Mokaddem (maçaddam), a head man, a chief, or captain. Sp. *Almocaden*.
Muezzin (muedhen), attendant at a mosque, who calls the faithful to prayer. Sp. *Almuedano*.
Mufti, a spiritual governor, a bishop exercising magisterial functions.
Oued (wad, or wadi), a watercourse, a river ; also a valley traversed by a river. Sp. *Guada*. Ex. *Guadal-*

GLOSSARY.

quivir, the great river; *Guaroman*, the river of the pomegranates; *Guarrazas*, the river of lead; *Guadarama*, the sandy river, &c.

Oulad (ulad), sons; plur. of *wald*, son. It is often used as the equivalent of *Benu* or *Beni*, to designate a tribe or family. Ex. *Beni Menú, Beni Idrís, Beni Ummmayah, &c.*

Oust, middle, applied to the central court, or *patio*, in the middle of a Moorish house.

Ras, a head, a cape or promontory. Sp. *Rés.*

Resás (raṣás), lead. Ex. *Djebel Resás*, the mountain of lead; *Guada Resás*, the river of lead.

Roumi (Rumí), literally a Roman, but generally used by Arabs throughout the East to designate strangers of Christian origin. Ex. the great sepulchre of the Mauritanian kings west of Algiers, known as the *Tombeau de la Chrétienne*, is in Arabic *Kabr-er-Roumia* (masc. *Roumi*, fem. *Roumia*).

Sabbat, shoes. Sp. *Zapatos*. Fr. *Sabot* and *Savate*.

Sahel (saḥl), the coast.

Sahib, Saib (sáḥib), a companion, a friend, a master or lord, the author of a book.

Sebkha, a salt lake or a marsh.

Sebb (Sebâ), the seventh day, *i.e.*, Saturday.

Scherif (sharíf, sherîf), a supposed descendant of the Prophet, conspicuous by wearing a green turban. Sp. *Xarife.*

Sheikh (shekh), the chief of a tribe. Sp. *Xeque.*

Sid, lord. *Sidi*, my lord. Sp. *Cid* and *Cidan.*

Silos (síl), subterraneous granaries for corn. Sp. *Silo.*

Skiffa, the vestibule of a Moorish house. Sp. *Acequife.*

Smala, a fortified camp occupied by Spahis; also an army.

Sof, a league or brotherhood bound by the same laws, hence the *Sufis.*

Souk (súk), a market. Sp. *Zoco.*

Sura, a chapter of the Koran. Sp. *Azora.*

Zab, an oasis watered by a river.

Zaouia, a college or place of refuge for poor scholars or religious mendicants.

Zeituna, an olive-tree. Sp. *Azeituno*, the fruit itself being *Azeituna*.

As French scholars in Oriental languages have not yet fixed on any one of the various systems of orthography used in Europe, the different Arabic names in brackets have been written in accordance with the rules established by the Asiatic Society of Great Britain. Some of the letters, however, must be distinguished by points or dots, â ḥ ṣ ṭ, if their full value is to be given. To those words which have left their mark on European languages (chiefly Spanish) we have added their derivatives, in the hope that this may be found useful to Europeans not thoroughly acquainted with Arabic.

Introductory Note to Bibliography.

THE following Bibliography comprises:—(1), Books on Carthage and Utica, with their history and archæology; (2), Books on Tunisia, or on towns or separate districts of that country; (3), Books partly on Tunisia; (4), Books on the Barbary States (when Tunisia is included) and their piracies; (5), Articles in Societies' Transactions, Collections of Travels, Encyclopædias, Magazines, and other periodicals; (6), Dictionaries and Manuals of Conversation in the Arab language; (7), A few books not specially on Tunisia, but illustrating indirectly the religion, customs, antiquities, or language, ancient or modern, of that country; (8), Some works of the imagination.

The Bibliography is neither descriptive nor critical; *i.e.*, we have not attempted to follow the books noted through their several editions, to indicate their typographical or iconographical peculiarities, or even to analyse their contents; occasionally, however, we have appended a short note to an important or specially useful work. Our object has been to offer, in as concise and portable a form as possible, a list of the principal authorities on the subject.

For the works which have not passed through our hands we are indebted to the following publications:—

Bibliographie carthaginoise, par E. de Sainte Marie, Paris, Jourdan, 1875. 8vo. The same appears in 'Recueil des Notices et Mémoires de la Société archéologique du Département de Constantine,' xvii., 69-110. Severely noticed in 'Litterarisches Centralblatt,' May 20, 1876. M. de Sainte Marie was Premier Dragoman du Consulat de France à Tunis.

Essai de Bibliographie tunisienne, ou Indication des principaux ouvrages publiés en France sur la Régence de Tunis, par A. Demarsy, Paris, 1869. 8vo.

Bibliothèque asiatique et africaine, ou catalogue des ouvrages relatifs à l'Asie et à l'Afrique qui ont paru depuis la découverte de l'imprimerie jusqu'en 1700, *par H. Ternaux-Compans,* Paris, 1841. 8vo.

Bibliographie des Ouvrages relatifs à l'Afrique et à l'Arabie. Catalogue méthodique de tous les ouvrages français et des principaux en langues étrangères traitant de la géographie, de l'histoire, du commerce, des lettres, et des arts de l'Afrique et de l'Arabie, par Jean Gay, San Remo, chez J. Gay & fils ; Paris, chez Maisonneuve & Cie. 1875.* 8vo., pp. xi. and 312, double cols.

Bibliographie d'Ouvrages ayant trait à l'Afrique en général dans ses rapports avec l'exploration & la civilisation de ces contrées depuis le commencement de l'Imprimerie jusqu'à nos jours, précédé d'un indicateur par Gabriel Kayser, Propriété de l'Auteur, Bruxelles, 1887. 8vo., pp. xv., 176.

A Bibliography of Algeria, from the Expedition of Charles V. in 1541 *to* 1886, *by Sir R. Lambert Playfair, K.C.M.G., H.M. Consul-General for Algeria and Tunis, &c.* (Published by the Royal Geographical Society of London.)

Bibliotheca Geographica. Verzeichniss der seit der Mitte des vorigen Jahrhunderts bis zu Ende des Jahres 1856 *in Deutschland erschienenen Werke über Geographie und Reisen mit Einschluss der Landkarten, Pläne und Ansichten. Herausgeben von Wilhelm Engelmann. Mit einem ausführlichen Sach-Register.* Leipzig, W. Engelmann, 1858. 8vo., pp. vi. and 1225. A most useful and carefully executed compilation.

Classified Catalogue of the Library of the Royal Geographical Society, to December 1870, London, John Murray, 1871. 8vo.

Bibliotheca Britanica; or, a General Index to British and Foreign Literature. By Robert Watt, M.D. Edinburgh, A. Constable & Co.; London, Longman & Co., 1824. 4 vols.

Catalogue général de la Librairie française pendant 25 *ans* (1840-1865) *rédigé par Otto Lorenz,* Paris, O. Lorenz, 1867-1880. 8vo., 8 vols.

Index to the British Catalogue of Books published during the years 1837 *to* 1857 *inclusive. Compiled by Sampson Low,* London, Sampson Low & Co., 1858. Vol. ii., 1856 to Jan. 1876 ; vol. iii., Jan. 1874 to Dec. 1880.

---

* Gay's compilation being based upon : *Biliographie de la France, journal général de l'imprimerie et de la librairie; Bibliographie des Ouvrages relatifs à l'Amour, aux Femmes, &c.; Catalogue des Accroissements de la Bibliothèque Royale,* Bruxelles, 1843; *Catalogue des Livres de la Bibliothèque de Grenoble; Catalogue de M. le Duc de la Vallière,* Paris, 1783, *Nouveau Dictionnaire historique portatif, &c., par une Société de Gens de Lettres,* Amsterdam, 1771; *Polybiblion;* and the works of MM. Barbier, Bouillet, Bourquelot, Brunet, Eug. Hatin, Peignot, Quérard, Van Hulthem, **Vapereau** and Walckenaer; those authorities have not been again consulted.

A Subject Index to the Modern Works added to the Library of the British Museum in the years 1880–1885. Compiled by G. K. Fortescue, Superintendent of the Reading-room, British Museum. Printed by Order of the Trustees, &c., London, 1886.

An Index to Periodical Literature by W. F. Poole, LL.D. Third Edition. Boston, J. R. Osgood & Co.; London, Trübner & Co., 1882. Large 8vo., pp. 1442.

Notes and Queries, London.

L'Intermédiaire des Chercheurs et Curieux, Paris.

Le Livre, revue du monde littéraire, Paris, Quantin.

And the excellent trade catalogues of M. Challamel aîné, and of M. A. Barbier, of Paris.

The arrangement is alphabetical, by authors' names;* publications, however, of which we have been unable to ascertain the authorship, will be found under the heading *Anonymous*, and these we have, in order to facilitate reference, subdivided, and arranged, as far as was practicable, chronologically.

We would indicate the following twenty works as sufficient for the purpose of the traveller:—

A. M. BROADLEY: *The Last Punic War* (p. 222, *post*).—A. DAUX: *Recherches sur l'origine et l'emplacement des emporia phéniciens* (p. 229).—Dr. N. DAVIS: *Carthage and her Remains* (p. 229).—DUREAU DE LA MALLE: *Recherches sur la Topographie de Carthage* (p. 232).—EL-BEKRI:

---

* We have experienced some difficulty in placing correctly and consistently the Arab writers: firstly, because their name system differs so widely from ours; and secondly, by reason of their names having been imported into European languages, with spellings dictated by the nationality or caprice of the translators or compilers. To offer a single example: A man known as *John, son of James, father of George, the Londoner, inhabitant of Manchester*, would evidently suggest difficulties as to his proper alphabetical position; when now *John* is suppressed, and the individual is known as the *son of James*, or as the *father of George*, or as the *Londoner* simply, the difficulty is augmented. Further, the prefixes *al* or *el, ebn* or *ibn*, are written either way indiscriminately, and the same sound in a name will be rendered by a *c*, a *g*, or a *k*, as the translator may think fit. We have been constrained, then, to copy the names as they are given in the books we have noted, and to adopt the arrangement introduced by our predecessors; in our alphabetical headings, however, we have invariably employed one and the same spelling for the same prefix, *e.g., el* not *al, ibn* not *ebn*, so that the Arab writers cited will generally appear under those prefixes, as *El-Bekri, El-Edrisi, Ibn-Haukal, Ibn-Khaldoun*, &c.

BIBLIOGRAPHY.

Description de l'Afrique (p. 233).—EL-EDRISI: *Commentatio de Geographia Africæ* (p. 233).—V. GUÉRIN: *Voyage archéologique* (p. 239).—Comte D'HÉRISSON: *Relation d'une mission archéologique en Tunisie* (p. 242).— E. VON HESSE-WARTEGG: *Tunis: Land und Leute* (p. 242).—IBN-KHALDOUN: *Histoire de l'Afrique* (p. 243).—LEO AFRICANUS: *Totius Africæ Discriptionis* (p. 248).—MARMOL: *Descripcion de Africa* (p. 252).— E. PELLISSIER: *Description de la Régence de Tunis* (p. 256).—PEYSSONNEL et DESFONTAINES: *Voyages dans les Régences de Tunis et d'Alger* (p. 257). —Sir R. L. PLAYFAIR: *Travels in the Footsteps of Bruce* (p. 257).—Abbé POIRET: *Voyage en Barbarie* (p. 258).— Baron ALPHONSE ROUSSEAU: *Annales tunisiennes* (p. 264).—Dr. THOS. SHAW: *Travels* (p. 268).— R. BOSWORTH SMITH: *Carthage and the Carthaginians* (p. 269).—Sir GRENVILLE TEMPLE: *Excursions in the Mediterranean* (p. 271).

BIBLIOGRAPHY.

ABELUS, Mgr.: *Vie de St. Vincent de Paul*, Paris, 1839. 8vo. St. Vincent de Paul was enslaved at Tunis in 1667. Consult also: *Lettres de Saint Vincent de Paul*, Paris, 1880. 4 vols., 8vo.

ABU SA'ID, Capitaine: *Le Marabout de Sidi-Fat-Allah, Épisode de l'Insurrection tunisienne en 1881*, Paris, 1884. 12mo., pp. 278.

ADANSON. See DOUMET-ADANSON.

ADDISON, JOSEPH: *Cato; a Tragedy*. The scene is a large hall in the Governor's palace at Utica. See also DAMPMARTIN.

(AGUILAR, El Alférez PEDRO DE): *Memorias del Cautivo en La Goleta de Túnez, del Original en poder de Tyssen Amhurst, Esqre, de Didlington Hall, Norfolk. Publícolo la Sociedad de Bibliófilos Españoles*, Madrid, 1875. 8vo., pp. xx. and 314.

'We have here,' writes Señor Pascual de Gayángos in the Introduction, 'an original and extremely curious book, in which a Spanish soldier, a captive in Barbary and Constantinople, relates with simplicity and in prose mixed with verse the events, now prosperous now adverse, of which he was witness; his own adventures of love and fortune, his campaigns against the Moors of Alpujarras, and, finally, the loss of the Goleta of Tunis, from which he dates the loss of his own liberty.' The volume contains, *inter alia*, the description and origin of Tunis; an account of the island of Estaño, or Estanque, three miles distant from Tunis; poems on the loss of the Goleta, of the loss of Tunis, and of the island of Estaño; and *Relacion de Don Joan Zanoguera* hecha á el Señor Don Joan (of Austria) *del Suceso de La Goleta y Fuerte de Túnez y Isla del Estaño*. Although the original MS. has neither title nor name of author, Señor Gayángos does not hesitate to attribute it to Pedro de Aguilar, the friend mentioned by Cervantes in his *Novela del Cautivo*.

AGUILERA: *Chronica y Recopilacion de varios Succesos de Guerra que han acontecido en Italia y paites de Levante y Berberia, desde que el Turco Selin rumpio con Venecianos*, Çaragoça, 1579. 4to.

AILLY, Baron D': *Sur une Médaille inédite de Leptis*, art. in 'Revue Numismatique Française,' série 1, vi., 349.

ALIX: *Le Dromadaire tunisien*, art. in 'Science et Nature,' Oct. 3, 1885.

ALLEMAND-LAVIGERIE, C. M. See LAVIGERIE.

AMARI, M.: *I Diplomati arabi del reale archivio fiorentino*, Firence, Lemonnier, 1863. 4to.

A work to be consulted, says M. A. Demarsy, on the history of Tunisian diplomacy.

AMBERT, Général: *Tunis et Carthage*, art. in 'Univers,' August 25, 1881.

AMEILHON, H. P.: *Mémoire sur une Inscription sur une plaque de cuivre trouvée à Tunis*, art. in 'Mémoires de l'Académie des Inscriptions,' 1789, xlix., 501.

ANDRÉ, M., Conseiller à la Cour d'Appel d'Alger: *Album africain, recueil de cartes, plans, vues, gravures, lithographies, dessins, aquarelles, etc.*, re-

présentant les sites, les événements, les personnages, les monuments, les mœurs et coutumes de l'Algérie et du littoral de la Méditerranée musulmane, recueillies par M. André, Alger, 1852, Fol. 3 vols. Tunis is contained in the third vol.

ANDREUCCI, F. See GALEOTTI.

ANGEL, FR. PIERRE: *Les Frères des Écoles chrétiennes à Tunis*, arts. in 'Œuvres des Écoles d'Orient,' Nov. 1871 and January 1873.

ANGVILLE, B. D'. See BOURGUINON.

ANTIAS, VALERIUS. See FRIEDRICH.

ANTICHAN, P. H.: *La Tunisie autrefois et aujourd'hui*, Paris, Delagrave, 1884. 8vo., pp. 298.

ANTINORI, ORAZZIO: *Lettere sulla Tunisia*, Firenze, 1867. 8vo.

—— *La Quistione Tunisiana*, Firenze, 1868. 8vo., pp. 39.

ANTONINUS, AUGUSTUS: *Itinerarium A. Augusti*, ed. G. Parthey and M. Pinder, Berlin, 1848. 8vo.

APPIANUS: *Romanarum Historiarum Punica, Parthica, etc., gr. et lat. cum annotation. Henr. Stephani, &c.*, Genevæ, 1592. Fol.

—— *Hoc in volumine continentur Bellum Carthag. Syr. Part. et Mithridat. in vulgare sermone (du Als. Braccio)*, Roma, Euch. Silber, 1502. Fol. There are translations into English, French, Spanish, Italian, &c.

APULEIUS: *Œuvres complètes d'Apulée, traduites en Français par Victor Bétolaud, &c.*, Paris, Garnier frères, 1883. 8vo. 2 vols. The Latin text is given at foot of the page. Speaks of Carthage in the time of Apuleius, and pronounces an eulogy on the city and its inhabitants.

ARCHINARD, Commandant. See RAMBAUD.

ARÈNE, PAUL: *Vingt Jours en Tunisie*, Paris, Lemerre, 1884. 'In-18 jésus,' pp. 300. Favourably noticed in 'Le Livre,' Oct. 1884, p. 634.

ARÈNE, PAUL: *Vingt Jours en Tunisie*, art. in 'Nouvelle Revue,' Oct. 1, 1883.

—— *Voyage à Kairouan*, art. in 'Science et Nature,' June 28, 1884.

—— *Une Mosquée à Kairouan*. Idem, July 26, 1884.

ARETINUS (or BRUNUS LEONARDUS): *Libro chiamato de la Prima Guerra Punica qual fo tra Romani et Cartaginesi, composto de . . Leonardo Aretino, prima in latino, poi in lingua materna*. 4to., 86 ff., 27 lines per page. Also as :

—— *Historia della Guerra delli Carthaginesi con gli Romani, composta nella Lingua Latina, e fatta volgare da un suo Amico*, Firenze, 1528. 8vo. The Latin version, printed later, is entitled :

—— *De Bello Punico Libri II. opus recens editum (per Bern. Magnoaldum Vindam)*, Augustæ-Vindelicor, 1537. 4to.

ARISTOTELES : *De Politica Carthaginiensium, gr. textum critice recognovit . . F. G. Kluge : accedit Theod. Metochitæ descriptio Republ. Carthagin. cum notis criticis*, Vratislaviæ, Max, 1823. 8vo. Extracted from Book IV. of the 'Politica,' of which there are translations into the chief modern languages.

ARNAULD D'ANDILLY, R. See VICTOR.

ARNOLD, THOMAS, D.D.: *The Second Punic War: being Chapters of the History of Rome. By the late Thomas Arnold, D.D. Edited by W. T. Arnold, M.A.* London, Macmillan & Co. 1886. Crown 8vo., 8 maps.

ARVIEUX, Chevalier d'. See LABAT.

AUBÉ, B. : *L'Église d'Afrique et ses premières épreuves sous le règne de Septime Sévère*, art. in 'Revue Historique,' Nov. 1879.

AUCAPITAINE, Baron HENRI : *Crocodiles de l'Oued Takmalet, dans le Sahara tunisien*, art. in 'Nouvelles

Annales des Voyages,' 1860. i., 232 to 234.

AVECIO, LÉONARD DE: *Livre des Batailles de Carthage.* Noted by Gay (art. 1397) as follows: 'Trad. en français l'an 1542 et dédié à Charles VII. roi de France. In-fol. Roman de chevalerie, manuscrit du XVe. siècle, sur papier. Au bas de la première page on lit l'inscription suivante : "*C'est livre des batailles de Carthage* . . 1584." (Archives du bibliophile, 1860, n°. 6776, 100 fr.).'

AVEZAC, M. A. P. D'., Membre de l'Institut : *Esquisse générale de l'Afrique, et Afrique ancienne*, pp. 272, in 'L'Univers Pittoresque,' Paris, Firmin Didot, 1844.

—— *Esquisse Générale de l'Afrique. Aspect et constitution physique, histoire naturelle, ethnologie, linguistique, état social, histoire, explorations, et géographie.* Paris, Dondey-Dupré, 1837. 12mo. pp. xii. and 132. Contains, *inter alia*, short sketches of : Races africaines septentrionales, Carthage, Rome, Christianisme, Vandales, Byzantins, Conquête des Arabes, Époque des Edrysytes et des Aghlabytes, Connaissances des Phéniciens et des Carthaginois, &c.

—— *Études de Géographie critique sur une partie de l'Afrique septent. Itinéraires de Haggy-ebn-el-Dyn-el-Aghouathy, &c.* Paris, 1863. 8vo., pp. viii. and 1881, map.

—— *Description et histoire de l'Afrique ancienne, précédée d'une esquisse générale de l'Afrique.* Plates. Paris, 1845, 8vo.

—— *Relation d'un Voyage dans l'intérieur de l'Afrique septentrionale, par Hhâggy-Ebn-Al-Dyn-El-Eghoûathy*, traduit et annoté par M. d'Avezac, publié dans le 'Bulletin de la Société de Géographie,' 2e série, i., 277 et 349; ii., 81 et 145, et appendice sur l'emploi de nouveaux documents ; iv., 347 ; et v., 144. 'Ce travail renferme une étude très-complète sur la géographie et les routes de la Régence de Tunis.' —A. Demarsy.

BACHE, E.: *Notice sur les dignités romaines en Afrique; cinquième siècle de J. C.*, 'Rev. Afr.,' 1862, vi., 135.

BAEDEKER, K.: *Italy. Handbook for Travellers.* Third Part, with Excursions to Tunis, &c. Leipzig, Karl Baedeker; London, Dulau & Co. 1887. Small 8vo. with a map of Tunis and its environs.

BALDUINUS. See BAUDOUIN.

BARABAN, L, Inspecteur des Forêts: *En Tunisie, Notes de Voyage*, arts. in the 'Revue des Eaux et Forêts,' 1886.

—— *A Travers la Tunisie, Études sur les Oasis—les Dunes—les Forêts —la Flore et la Géologie, Ouvrage avec carte et vignettes*, Paris, J. Rothschild, 1887. 8vo., pp. viii. and 227.

BARBE PATTERSON, Mme.: *Chips from Tunis*, London, Hachette & Co. 1885. 8vo. Favourably noticed in 'Saturday Review,' Dec. 26, 1885.

BARBIER, J. V.: *Algérie, Tunisie et Sahara central*, Paris, 1881, map.

BARBIER DE MEYNARD: *Rapport sur des Inscriptions arabes provenant de Mehdya, Régence de Tunis*, art. in 'Académie des Inscriptions et Belles-Lettres,' 1883.

—— *Marabouts et Khouan*, art. in 'Journal des Savants,' Dec. 1884.

—— *Exploration archéologique entreprise en Tunisie par M. Basset*, communication to 'Académie des Inscriptions et Belles-Lettres,' séance du 12 août, 1887.

BARD, Le Chevalier: *Voyage d'études de Tunis à Gibraltar par l'Afrique française.* Vienne, 1853, 8vo.

BARD, JOSEPH: *L'Algérie en 1854. Itinéraire général de Tunis à Tanger;*

colonisation, paysages, monuments, culte, agriculture, &c. Paris, 1854. 8vo., pp. 251, 1 plate.

BARGÈS, Abbé J. J. L.: *Temple de Baal à Marseille, ou grande Inscription phénicienne découverte dans cette ville en* 1845 *expliquée*, Paris, 1847. 8vo.

—— *Aperçu historique sur l'Église d'Afrique en général*, Paris, 1848. 8vo.

—— *Mémoire sur deux Inscriptions puniques découvertes dans l'île du port Coltion à Carthage*, Paris, 1849. 4to. Illustrated.

—— *Mémoire sur* 39 *Inscriptions puniques expliquées*, Paris, 1852. 4to.

—— *Nouvelle Interprétation de l'Inscription phénicienne découverte par M. Mariette dans le Sérapéum de Memphis. Examen critique de l'interprétation donnée par M. le duc de Luynes*, Paris, 1856. 8vo.

—— *Inscription phénicienne de Marseille, nouvelle interprétation*, Paris, 1858. 4to.

—— *Examen d'une nouvelle Inscription phénicienne découverte récemment dans les ruines de Carthage et analogue à celle de Marseille*, Paris (1868). 4to., pp. 31. One engraving.

BARTH, H., Ph.D., D.C.L.: *Wanderungen durch die Küstenländer des Mittelmeers, in* 1845-1847, Berlin, 1849.

—— *Reisen und Entdeckungen in Nord- und Centralafrika in den Jahren* 1849-1855, Gotha, 1857-58. 5 vols. Engravings. The work has been translated into French by Paul Ithiar, Bruxelles, 1859-61. 8vo., 4 vols. And into English:

—— *Travels and Discoveries in North and Central Africa: being a Journal of an Expedition undertaken under the auspices of H.B.M.'s Government in the years* 1849-1855, London, 1857-59. 8vo., 5 vols, maps and engravings, same as in the German edit.

BARTH, H., Ph.D., D.C.L.: *Idées sur les Expéditions scientifiques en Afrique.* Paris, 8vo., pp. 19. Extracted from 'Bulletin de la Société de Géographie,' 1872.

Several notices concerning Dr. Barth and his works will be found in *Zeitschrift für allgemeine Erdkunde*, Berlin, D. Reimer, 1853. 8vo., 6 vols.

BASSET, R. See BARBIER DE MEYNARD and HOUDAS.

BAUDOUIN, FRANÇOIS: *Historia Carthaginensis Collationis, &c.*, Paris, 1566. 8vo. Relates to the controversy between Catholics and Donatists.

—— *Delibatio Africanæ Historiæ Ecclesiasticæ*, Paris, 1569. 8vo.

BAYLE, PIERRE: *Hannon*, art. of 7 cols. in his 'Dictionnaire,' Paris, Desoer, 1820. See also HANNO.

BEAULIEU. See LEROY-BEAULIEU.

BEAUSSIER: *Dictionnaire pratique arabe français, contenant touts les mots employés dans l'Arabe parlé en Algérie et en Tunisie, ainsi que dans le style épistolaire, les pièces usuelles et les actes judiciaires*, Alger, 1871. 4to., pp. 764. Also Alger, 1873, pp. xvi. and 776. Both double cols.

BÉLIDOR, BERN.: *Sommaire d'un Cours d'Architecture militaire,civile et hydraulique*, Paris, 1720. 12mo.

—— *Architecture hydraulique*, Paris, 1737-53. 4to., 4 vols. In both works the situation of Carthage is considered.

BELLANGER, CH.: *Histoire et Géographie des Colonies de la France et des pays placés sous son protectorat, d'après les documents les plus récents*, Paris, E. Dentu, 1886. 18mo.

BELLERMANN, J. J.: *Phoeniciae Linguae Vestigiorum in Melitensi Specimen*, 1809.

BELLERMANN, J. J.: *De Phoenicum et Poenorum Inscriptionibus cum duarum Explicationis Periculo*, 1810.
—— *Bemerkungen über phönicische und punische Münzen*, 4 Stücke, 1812-16.

BENAIAD: *Deux Notes du général Mahmoud Benaiad à son Excellence Monsieur le Ministre des Affaires étrangères, accompagnées des pièces justificatives.* 1853. 8vo.
Le général Benaid, directeur de la banque de Tunis, fut accusé de concussion par son gouvernement; il se sauva en France et se fit naturaliser Français. Ces deux notes justificatives ont été écrites par lui au ministre des affaires étrangères de France pour réclamer son intervention auprès du gouvernement du Bey qui avait mis le séquestre sur ses biens.

BENICKEN: *Hannibal*, art. of 10 cols. in 'Allgemeine Encyclopädie von Ersch und Gruber,' Leipzig, 1828.

BER, E.: *Exposition tunisienne*, 1855, art. in 'Revue des Deux-Mondes, Bulletin annexe,' Nov. 1, 1855.

BERBRUGGER, A.: *Voyages dans le sud de l'Algérie et des États barbaresques de l'ouest et de l'est, par Al-Aliaci-Moula-Ahmed, traduits par M. Adr. Berbrugger,* Paris, Imp. Roy., 1846. In 'L'Exploration scientifique de l'Algérie.' See also EL-AÏACI.

—— *Projet d'Exploration dans la deuxième ligne des Oasis algériennes par Gabès, Souf, Tougourt, Ouargla, Golea, Touat, et retour par Metlili et le Ouadi M'Zab,* Alger, 1850. 8vo., pp. 3.

—— *Itinéraires archéologiques en Tunisie,* in 1850, arts. in 'Revue Africaine,' April, June, and Oct. 1856. These journeys are from Souk-Ahras to El-Kef and from El-Kef to Tunis; and to Nefta by way of Kairouan.

—— *L'Afrique septentrionale après le partage du Monde Romain en Empire d'Orient et d'Occident.* Idem, i., 81.

BERBRUGGER, A.: *La Polygamie musulmane, ses causes fatales et le moyen de la détruire.* Idem, iii. 254.
See also LEO AFRICANUS.

BERGE, A. DE LA. See LABERGE.

BERGER, PH.: *Lettres à M. Alex. Bertrand sur une nouvelle forme de la Triade carthaginoise,* in 'Revue Archéologique,' April, 1884.

—— *Note sur trois cents nouveaux Ex-voto de Carthage,* art. in 'Bulletin de l'Académie des Inscriptions et Belles-Lettres,' July, 1886.

BERGK, J. A. See MAYER, H. L.

BERNARD, GEORGES: *La Mer intérieure du Commandant Roudaire* (see that name), art. in 'Revue Libérale,' February, March, 1884.

BERNARD, JOSEPH. See LA FAYE.

BEROTIUS, JO.: *Diarium Expeditionis Tuniciæ, a Car. V. Imp. susceptæ,* Lovan, 1549. 8vo.

BERRIAT, JACQUES ST. PRIX, Docteur en Droit: *Annibal à Carthage, après la bataille de Zama, fragment lu à l'Académie de Grenoble,* le 6 Sept. 1805, in 'Magasin Encyclopédique,' 1806, vi., 344.

BERTHERAND, E. L. See PHARAON.

BESCHERELLE aîné, M., ET DEVARS, M. G.: *Grand Dictionnaire de Géographie universelle ancienne et moderne, &c.* Paris, Administration Générale, 1856-7. 4to., 4 vols. Contains following arts.: *Carthage,* 5 cols.; *Carthaginois,* 1 col.; *Tunis,* 5 cols.

BÉTOLAUD, V. See APULEIUS.

BEULÉ, CH. ERN., Membre de l'Institut: *Extrait d'une Lettre adressée à l'Académie des Inscriptions et Belles-Lettres,* in 'Nouvelles Annales des Voyages,' 1859. ii. 259.

—— *Fouilles à Carthage,* Paris, 1860. 8vo. Extracted from 'Revue Archéologique.'

—— *Fouilles faites à Carthage aux frais et sous la direction de M. Beulé,* Paris, 1861. 4to., pp. 143, 6 illustrations. Includes the excavations made in 1859 and 1860 at Byrsa, at the ports and necropolis of Quamart. Noticed by A. JAL (see that name). Translated into German, Leipzig, 1863.

BIGNAN, ANNE: *Monument de Saint-Louis à Tunis, Ode*, Paris, 1841. 8vo., pp. 16.

BILINTANO, POMPEO: *Affricano, nel quale si contengono le gesti e le victorie di Carlo V.*, Napoli, 1536. 8vo. Poem.

BIRAGO, J. B., Avogadro: *Istoria Africana della Divisione dell' Imperio degli Arabi, &c.*, Venezia, 1650. 4to. Translated into French by Michel De Pure:
—— *Histoire africaine de la Division de l'Empire des Arabes, &c.*, Paris, 1666. 12mo.

BISSON, LÉON DE: *La Tripolitaine et la Tunisie*, Paris, Challamel aîné, 1881. 8vo., pp. 147.

BIZEMONT, DE: *La France en Afrique*, art. in 'Correspondant,' February 25, 1883.

BLAKESLEY, J. W.: *Four Months in Algeria, with a visit to Carthage*, Cambridge, 1859. 8vo., maps and engravings.

BLANCARD, M. THÉODORE: *La Tunisie, notes sur le mouvement des troupes du quartier général*, art. in 'Revue du Monde Latin,' 1884.

BLAQUIÈRE, EDWARD: *Letters from the Mediterranean; containing a civil and political account of Sicily, Tripoli, Tunis and Malta; with Bibliographical Sketches, &c.* London, 1813. 8vo. 2 vols. Vol. ii. contains 133 pages on Tunis; general notices on Geography, Commerce, and Government. A German translation :
—— *Briefe aus dem Mittelländischen Meere*, forms vols. xxv. and vi. of 'Neue Bibliothek der wichtigsten Reisebeschreibungen,' &c., von F. J.

Bertuch, &c. Weimar, 1815-35. 8vo., 65 vols., maps and engravings.

BLED DE BRAINE: *Cours synthétique, analytique et pratique de la langue arabe, ou les dialectes vulgaires africains d'Alger, de Maroc, de Tunis et d'Egypte, enseignés sans maître*, Paris, 1846. 8vo.

BODDY, Rev. ALEXANDER A.: *To Kairwân the Holy; Scenes in Mohammedan Africa*, London, K. Paul, Trench, & Co., 1885. Post 8vo., maps and illustrations.

BODICHON, Dr. E.: *Tableau synoptique représentant les noms, les émigrations, les filiations, l'origine, les caractères physiques et moraux des races de l'Afrique septentrionale*, Nantes, 1844. Folio.

BOESWILLWALD, E. See SISSON, T.

BÖTTICHER, K. A.: *Geschichte der Karthager*, Berlin, 1827.

BOIS, MAURICE, Capitaine au 76° Régiment d'Infanterie : *La France à Tunis. Expédition française en Tunisie (1881-82), précédée d'une description géographique et historique de la Régence de Tunis*, Paris, Bardoin, 1885. 12mo., pp. iv. and 160.

BOISSIÈRE, G.: *Esquisse d'une Histoire de la Conquête et de l'Administration romaine dans le nord de l'Afrique, et particulièrement dans la province de Numidie*, Paris, Hachette, 1878. 8vo.

BOLLANDUS, J.: *Acta San.torum quotquot toto orbe coluntur, collegit, digessit, notis illustr. Joan. Bollandus, &c.*, Anturpiæ, &c., 1643-58. Fol., 56 vols. A necessary authority concerning the martyrs of the Church of North Africa, and particularly of Carthage.

BONNET, Dr. : *Les Médecins indigènes du sud de la Tunisie*, art. in 'Journal d'Histoire naturelle de Bordeaux et du Sud-Ouest.' Analysed in 'Globus,' xlix, 331.

BORGIA, Conte ETTORE: *Sopra un Viaggio scientifico di Camillo Borgia nella Reggenza di Tunisi*. Letter in 'Bollettino della Società Geografica Italiana,' Firenze, 1869, fascicolo 3, pp. 457 to 459. See ESTRUP.

BORHECK, AUG. CHR.: *Neue Erdbeschreibung von ganz Afrika, aus den besten ältern und neuern Hülfsmitteln gesammelt und bearbeitet*, Frankfurt a. M., Varrentrapp, 1789-91. Large 8vo., 3 vols.

BORZCERI, H.: *Abrégé de l'Histoire égyptienne des Carthaginois*, Gronda, 1776. 8vo. Written in French and Polish.

BOSSAY, P. DE. See GUÉRIN.

BOSSOLASCHI D'ALMÉRAS: *Excursion du Club Alpin de Constantine à Tunis et à Carthage*, 'Bull. Soc. Géogr. de Const.,' 1886, 3ᵉ ann., pp. 199-204.

BOUGAINVILLE, J. P., Membre de l'Académie des Inscriptions, &c.: *Mémoire sur les Découvertes et Établissements faits le long des côtes d'Afrique par Hannon*, with map by Robert de Vaugondi, art. in 'Recueil de l'Académie des Inscriptions,' 1759. See also HANNO.

BOUILLET, M. N.: *Atlas universel d'Histoire et de Géographie, &c.*, Paris, Hachette & Cie, 1877. 8vo. Consult arts.: 'Afrique et Numidie,' p. 906, and 'Régence de Tunis,' p. 1081.

BOUIN. See CUVILLIER.

BOUINAIS, Capt. See RAMBAUD.

BOURGADE, Abbé, Aumônier de la Chapelle de Saint-Louis à Carthage: *Les Soirées de Carthage, ou Dialogues entre un Prêtre catholique, un Muphti et un Cadi*, Paris, 1847. 8vo.

—— *La Clef du Coran, faisant suite aux 'Soirées de Carthage,'* Paris, 1852. 8vo.

—— *Passage du Coran à l'Évangile, faisant suite aux 'Soirées de Car*-*thage'* et à '*La Clef du Coran*,' Paris, 1855. 8vo.

BOURGADE, Abbé.: *Baal-Hah (maître de l'anneau, c'est-à-dire Mercure)*, Paris, 1857. 12mo. Includes two inscriptions reproduced in the following work:

—— *Toison d'Or de la langue phénicienne, recueil d'inscriptions puniques trouvées sur les ruines de Carthage et sur divers points de la Régence de Tunis, avec la transcription en caractères hébreux et la traduction en latin et en français*, Paris, 1856. Fol., 21 illustrations.

BOURGUIGNAT, J. R.: *Histoire malacologique de la Régence de Tunis*, avec une carte des environs de Tunis et une planche, Paris, 1868. 4to.

BOURGUINON D'ANGVILLE, J. B.: *Géographie ancienne abrégée*, Paris, Merlin, 1768. 12mo., 3 vols. Frontispiece by H. Gravelot, and maps. About 12 pages are given to Carthage. Reprinted in 1782. In English as:

—— *Compendium of Ancient Geography*, &c., London, J. Faulder, &c., 1810. 8vo., 2 vols., maps.

BOYÉ, M. MARIUS: A plan of Sbeitla and nine Roman inscriptions discovered during the excavations there, 1883-84, in 'Académie des Inscriptions et Belles-Lettres, Comptes rendus des Séances,' tom. 12, 1884.

BRAINARD, CHARLES H.: *John Howard Payne; a Biographical Sketch of the Author of 'Home, sweet Home,' with a Narrative of the Removal of his Remains from Tunis to Washington*, Washington, 1885. 8vo., pp. 144, 8 plates.

BRAINE. See BLED DE BRAINE.

BRAKEL, V. VAN. See VAYNES VAN BRAKEL.

BRANDIN, A. V.: *Considérations politiques, historiques, statistiques et hygiéniques sur le Royaume de Tunis*, dans ses *rapports avec l'état actuel de l'Algerie*, Paris, 1847. 8vo. See also ROUX DE ROCHELLE.

BREVES, FRANÇOIS SAVARY, Sieur de : *Relation des Voyages, tant en Grèce, Turquie et Egypte, qu'au Royaume de Tunis et Alger, avec un Traité fait en l'an 1604 entre le Roy Henry le Grand et l'Empereur des Turcs, et trois Discours du dit Sieur, le tout recueilli par S. D. C.* (*Du Castel*), Paris, 1628. 4to.

BRICARD, Le Sieur de : *Relation des Voyages faits à Thunis par ordre de sa Majesté*, in 'Arch. Cur. de l'Hist. de France,' Paris, 1834. 2ᵉ série, x., pp. 89 to 97.

BROADLEY, A. M. : *The Last Punic War, or Tunis Past and Present*, Edinburgh, W. Blackwood & Sons, 1882. 8vo., 2 vols. This is a well-written book.

BROECKHUYSEN. See DAN.

BROWNING, OSCAR : Carthage, art. of 7 cols. in 'Encyclopædia Britannica,' &c. Ninth Edition. Edinburgh, A. & C. Black, 1876.

BRUCE, C. L. C. : *Memoir regarding Bruce's Journies* (sic) *and Drawings in North Africa*, by C. L. C. Bruce. A. Spottiswoode, London, 1837. 8vo., pp. 24.

BRUCE, JAMES : *Travels to discover the Source of the Nile in the years 1768-1773*, Edinburgh, 1790. 5 vols., 4to. The first chapter contains a narrative of Bruce's journey through Tunisia. Translated into French by J. Castera, Paris, 1790-91. See also PLAYFAIR.

BRUN, GEORGES : *Civitates Orbis Terrarum*, Coloriæ, 1572-1618. Fol., 6 vols. Contains a description of Tunis, with two views. The same appear in 'Théâtre des Principales Villes de tout l'Univers.' Bruxelles, 1574. Fol., 2 vols. The fine engravings are mostly by Franciscus Hohenbergius.

BRUNETTI, E. See GALEOTTI.

BRUNIALTI, Il Dottor A. : *Il Mare Saharico e la Spedizione Italiana in Tunisia*, 1875, with several woodcuts, in 'Biblioteca di Viaggi,' Milano, Fratelli Treves, 1876. xxxvii., 193 to 213.

—— *Algeria, Tunisia e Tripolitania, studio di geografia politica sugli ultimi avvenimenti africani*, Milano, 1881. 12mo., map.

BRUNUS LEONARDUS. See ARETINUS.

BRUNZEN LA MARTINIÈRE : *Grand Dictionnaire géographique et critique*, La Haye, 1726. Fol.

BUCKE, CHARLES : *Ruins of Ancient Cities; with general and particular accounts of their rise, fall, and present condition.* In 2 vols. London, Thomas Tegg, 1840. Small 8vo. Contains (vol. i.) Carthage, pp. 215 to 237.

BURBAUD, ROGER : *Voies et moyens de communication en France, en Algérie et en Tunisie*, Paris et Limoges, 1886. 2 vols., 16mo. 'Petite Bibliothèque de l'Armée française.'

BUSSY, T. R. DE. See ROLAND DE BUSSY.

CÆSAR, CAIUS JULIUS : *Commentaries*, with the supplemental books attributed to Hirtius. Lit. transl. Bohn's 'Classical Library.' 1848. 8vo.

CAGNAT, R. : *Rapport sur une Mission en Tunisie* (1881-82), art. in 'Archives des Missions Scientifiques et Littéraires,' Paris, 1885, xi., 1 to 156, with map of the Gulf of Hammamet and eight illustrations.

—— *Explorations épigraphiques et archéologiques en Tunisie*, Paris, 1883-84. 8vo., 3 parts.

CAGNAT et REINACH : *Découvertes de Villes nouvelles en Tunisie*, art. in 'Bulletin de l'Académie des Inscriptions, &c.,' July, 1885.

CAGNAT et SALADIN: *Voyage en Tunisie*, in 'Tour du Monde,' 1885, and April 16-23, 1887. Noticed in 'Globus,' xlix., 249, 257, 273.
—— *Notes d'Archéologie tunisienne*, art. in 'Bulletin Monumental,' No. 2, 1884.
CAHUN, LÉON: *Les Aventures du Capitaine Magon, ou une exploration phénicienne mille ans avant l'ère chrétienne*, Paris, 1875. 4to.
CAIGNARD DE SAULCY, L. F. J., Membre de l'Institut: *Recherches sur la Numismatique punique*, Paris, Impr. Roy. 1843. 4to. Extracted from 'Mémoires de l'Académie des Inscriptions,' Nouvelle série, xv., 2 partie. Analysed by M. Defrémery, in 'Revue Numismatique Française,' 1844. 1 série, ix., 451.
—— *Recherches sur les Inscriptions votives, phéniciennes et puniques*, Paris, 1846. 8vo.
—— *Lettre à M. Lenormant sur un point d'Épigraphie phénicienne*, art. in 'Revue Archéologique,' 1846, p. 629.
—— *Rectification de la valeur alphabétique d'un Caractère de l'Écriture punique*, art. in 'Revue Archéologique,' 1846, p. 565.
—— *Nouvelles Inscriptions votives trouvées à Carthage et à Constantine*, Paris, 1848. 8vo., plates.
—— *A propos de deux Inscriptions bilingues trouvées à Leptis Magna et publiées dans le Journal Asiatique*.
CAILLAT, PHILIPPE, Ingénieur au service du Bey: *Notice sur l'ancien Aqueduc de Carthage*, Paris, 1837.
CAILLETTE DE L'HERVILLIERS, EDM.: *Étude de quelques Inscriptions chrétiennes carthaginoises*, Paris, 1863. 8vo.
CALVETE DE ESTRELLA, ALFONSO *La Conquista de Africa, en Berveria, escrita en Latin por Alfonso Calvete de Estrella*, Salamanca, Canova, 1558. 8vo.

CAMBON, VICTOR, Ministre résident à Tunis: *De Bone à Tunis, Sousse et Kairouan*, Lyon, Imprimerie du Salut Public, 1885. 8vo., pp. 191, with photogravures. Also Paris, 1886.
—— *Discours prononcé par M. Cambon, Séance du 1 Avril, 1884; Première délibération sur le Projet de Loi portant approbation d'une Convention conclue avec le Bey de Tunis*, Paris, 1884. 8vo., pp. 29.
'M. Cambon quitted Tunis Nov. 15, 1886; his speeches on that occasion, and the reply of the Bey, will be found reported in the 'Journal des Débats,' Nov. 15 and 16, and other French newspapers of same dates.
CAMPOMANES, PEDRO RODR.: *Antiguedad maritima de la Republica de Cartago*, Madrid, 1756. 4to. Illustrations. Analysed in 'Mémoires de Trévoux,' 1757, p. 1938. Contains a translation of the 'Periplus of HANNO' (see that name).
CAMPON. See DE CAMPON.
CAMPOU, LUDOVIC DE: *La Tunisie française*, Paris, Charles Bayle, 1887. 8vo. A map and 8 phototypes. Worthless according to 'Le Livre,' Sept., 1887.
CANINA: *Amfiteatro di Tisdro*, art. in 'Annale dell' Institi archit. di Roma,' 1852, p. 241.
CAPELLA, M.: *Martiani Minei Capellæ Carthaginensis de Nvptiis Philologiæ, & Septem artibus Liberalibus Libri Novem optime castigati*. Lvgdvni, apud B. Vincentium, 1592. 8vo., pp. 16 and 397.
CAPITOLINUS, JULIUS: *Vies d'Antonin le Pieux, de Marc Antonin le Philosophe, de Verus, de Pertinax, d'Albin, de Macrin, des deux Maximin, des trois Gordien, de Maxime et de Balbin, traduction nouvelle, par M. Valton*, Paris, C. L. F. Panckoucke, 1844. 8vo., pp. 383. Forms vol. iii. of

'Ecrivains de l'Histoire Auguste.' The Latin and the translation are given on opposite pages.

CARDON, EMILE: *Études sur les progrès de la civilisation dans la Régence de Tunis*, art. in 'Revue du Monde Colonial,' 1861, 2 série, i., 305, 378, and 487. Issued also in separate form.

—— *Le Progrès en Tunisie*, Idem, 2 série, vi., 345. 'Résultats des réformes amenées par la constitution promulguée en 1860.'—A. Demarsy.

CARDONNE, D. D.: *Histoire de l'Afrique et de l'Espagne sous la Domination des Arabes*, Paris, 1765. 12mo. 3 vols.

CARETTE, E., Commandant du Génie: *Origine de la division territoriale établie en Afrique par les Romains*. 4to., pp. 26, without place or date.

—— *Recherches sur l'Origine et les Migrations des principales Tribus de l'Afrique septentrionale*, Paris, 1853. 8vo. Published in 'L'Exploration Scientifique de l'Algérie.'

—— *Études des Routes suivies par les Arabes dans la partie méridionale de l'Algérie et de la Régence de Tunis, pour servir à l'établissement du réseau géographique de ces contrées*, Paris, 1854. 8vo., map. First published in 1844, Paris, 4to., 2 vols.

CAREY, H.: *D'Alger à Tunis*, Genève, 1886. 18mo., pp. 79.

CARLETTI, J. T. See ROUSSEAU, A.

CARTA, F.: *La Questione Tunisiana e l'Europa*, Roma, 1879. 8vo., pp. 29.

CASSE, ROBERT DU: *Un Mameluck tunisien général français*, art. in 'Contemporain,' January, 1880.

CASSON, EDMUND *A relation of the whole proceedings concerning the redemption of the captives in Argier and Tunis . . . together with a list of the captives' names redeemed, and the prices they cost there in the market*. Published by special authority. London, 1647. 4to.

'The list contains the names of 242 persons redeemed from slavery.'—PLAYFAIR.

CASTAN, F. F. J. A.: *Le Capitole de Carthage*, art. in 'Académie des Inscriptions et Belles-Lettres,' April, 1885.

CASTEL, DU. See BREVES.

CASTELLI, A. See GALEOTTI.

CAT, É.: *Excursion d'Alger à Tunis*, art. in 'Revue de Géographie,' Dec., 1882.

CHALON, HENRI: *La Tunisie, Chrétiens et Musulmans*, Paris, 1881. 12mo.

CHAMBERLEN, PAUL: *History and Antiquities of the Ancient Egyptians . . . . and Carthaginians*, London, 1738. Fol.

CHAMPLOUIS. See DE CHAMPLOUIS.

CHAMPOLLION et REINAUD: *Mélanges et Documents inédits*, Paris, Impr. Royale, 1843. The second volume contains treaties of peace, in the Catalonian dialect and in the Arab language, concluded in 1270, 1278, 1312, and 1339, between the Kings of Majorca and the Kings of Tunis and Algeria.

CHAPELET, AMABLE: *Voyage à Tunis*, in 'Tour du Monde,' Dec. 1864.

CHARENCY, H. DE: *La Régence de Tunis*, arts. in 'Revue Orientale et Américaine,' 1859, i. 297 and ii. 51.

—— *La Régence de Tunis*, Paris, 1859. 8vo.

'L'auteur, rendant compte du travail de M. Dunant (see that name), a donné un résumé aussi complet que possible des notions recueillies jusqu'à cette époque sur Tunis et son territoire. Des renseignements communiqués à M. Charency par M. Soliman el Haraïra, interprète du consulat général de France à Tunis, lui ont permis de compléter son travail et d'y joindre un certain nombre de détails nouveaux.'—A. DEMARSY.

CHARLES, Mrs.: *Lapsed, but not Lost; a Story of Roman Carthage*, London, Daldy, 1877. 8vo., pp. 304.

CHARMES, GABRIEL: *La Tunisie et la Tripolitaine*, Paris, Calman Lévy, 1883. 8vo. Treats of the French occupation.

—— *La Politique française en Tunisie*, art. in 'Revue Politique et Littéraire,' 1882.

CHARRIÈRE, E.: *Négociations de la France dans le Levant, ou correspondances, mémoires et actes diplomatiques des ambassadeurs de la France, &c. dans les États de Tunis,&c.* Publiés par E. Charrière, Paris, Imprimerie Nationale, 1848-1860. 4to., 4 vols.

This work, according to M. A. Demarsy, gives important details concerning the negotiations of France and Tunis to the xvith century, and reproduces several documents, among others the letters of Louis XI. to the King of Tunis, and that of the Count d'Anguillara on the victory of Charles V.

CHASSIRON, Baron CHARLES DE: *Aperçu pittoresque de la Régence de Tunis*, Paris, 1849. Fol., 37 lithographs.

CHATEAUBRIAND, Vicomte de: *Essai sur les Révolutions*, Chapt. xxx. *Carthage*, Chapt. xxxi. *Parallèle de Carthage et de l'Angleterre*, Chapt. xxxvi. *Influence de la Révolution grecque sur Carthage*.

—— *Itinéraire*, Part vii. *Voyage de Tunis*, chiefly concerning Carthage, *Mémoire sur Tunis*.

—— *Travels, &c.*, translated (from the above) by Frederic Shoberl, &c., London, Henry Colburn, 1835. 8vo., 2 vols. Two chapts. in vol. ii. 64 pages, are devoted to Tunis and Carthage.

CHATELAIN, Le Chevalier, Lieut.-Colonel de Cavalerie: *Mémoire sur les moyens à employer pour punir et détruire la piraterie des puissances barbaresques; précédé d'un précis historique sur le caractère, les mœurs, et la manière de combattre des Mussulmans habitant la côte d'Afrique, et* un coup d'œil sur les *expéditions françaises tentées contre eux à diverses époques*, Paris, 1828. 8vo.

CHAUX, PAUL: *Rapport sur les Fouilles faites à Tysdrus par Sir Grenville Temple* (see that name), art. in 'Bulletin de la Société de Géographie,' 1847, 3 série, vii.

CHAVANNE, J.: *Das Algerische-tunesische Binnenmeer*, in 'Deutsche Rundschau,' 1880.

CHERBONNEAU, A., Professeur d'Arabe à la chaire de Constantine: *Précis historique de la dynastie des Aglabites, traduit en français et accompagné de notes*, art. in 'Revue de l'Orient,' 1853, xiv., 417.

'The original is by Ibn-Oudrâne, and exists in the Djama Ez-zeitouna at Tunis.' —PLAYFAIR.

—— *Description de Tunis, d'après El-Abdery (Ad-Hari)*, art. in 'Journal Asiatique,' 1854, 5 série, iv., 163.

—— *Voyage d'El-Abdery à travers l'Afrique septentrionale au XIIIᵉ siècle*, art. in 'Revue de Géographie,' July, 1880.

—— *Un Recueil de Fables arabes*, art. in 'Journal Officiel,' August 1, 1880.

—— *Les Ruines de Carthage, d'après les écrivains musulmans*, art. in 'Annuaire Constantine,' 1885, i., pp. 28.

CHESTER, Rev. G. S.: *Notes on recent discoveries at Carthage*, art. in 'Archæol. Journal,' 1866, xxiii.

CHEVALIER-RUFIGNY, H.: *Mémoire sur l'affaire de 'L'Enfida' (Tunisie), propriété acquise de S. A. Kérédine Pacha*, Paris, 1881. 4to., pp. 64.

CHEVANNE, J.: An art. of his (which we have not seen) on the Inland Sea is noticed in 'Deutsche Rundschau,' April, 1880, and *ante*. See 'Le Livre,' i., 408.

CHIKHACHEV, P.: *Espagne, Algérie et Tunisie*, Paris, 1880. 8vo., pp. 595.

—— *Spanien, Algerien und Tunis*, Leipzig, 1882. 8vo., pp. 531.

Q

CHILDE, Mme. L. See LEE CHILDE.
CHOTIN, A. G.: *Les Expéditions maritimes de Charles-Quint en Barbarie*, Bruxelles, 1849. 8vo., pp. 292. Also Tournai, 1857. 8vo.
CHURCH, Prof. ALFRED J.: *Carthage*, London, T. Fisher Unwin, 1886. 8vo. One of the series of 'Stories of the Nations,' furnished with Maps and Indexes.
CIRCOURT. See GUÉRIN.
CLARIN DE LA RIVE, ABEL, Correspondant de la Société des Études historiques de la France: *Histoire générale de la Tunisie, depuis l'an 1590 avant Jésus-Christ jusqu'en 1883, avec une Introduction par M. P. Mignard*, Tunis, E. Demoflys; Paris, Challamel, 1883. 8vo., pp. lx. and 414.
CLARK KENNEDY. See KENNEDY.
CLERMONT-GANNEAU, M. CH.: *L'Imagerie phénicienne et la Mythologie iconologique chez les Grecs*, 1 partie la Coupe phénicienne de Palestina, Paris, Leroux, 1880. The author supposes the silver cup in question to have been brought from Carthage.
—— *Nouvelles Inscriptions phéniciennes*, art. in 'Revue Archéologique,' May, 1885.
CLESS, C.: *Utica*, art. of pp. 4 in 'Pauly's Real-Encyclopädie,' Stuttgart, 1852.
COGNAT: *Explorations épigraphiques et archéologiques en Tunisie*, art. in 'Revue Critique d'Histoire et de Littérature,' June 9, 1884.
COLLIGNON: *Les Ages de la Pierre en Tunisie*, art. in 'Matériaux pour l'Histoire de l'Homme,' May, 1887.
COLLOT: *Nouveau Voyage fait au Levant ès années 1731 et 1732, contenant les descriptions d'Alger, Tunis, Tripoli, de Barbarie, &c.*, Paris, 1742. 12mo.
COLUMELLA: A Roman writer on agriculture of the first century. He translated the 28 books of Mago the Carthaginian. Edition Panckoucke. 3 vols., 8vo. 1845-46.
COMELIN, F. See LA FAYE.
COOKE, G. WINGROVE: *Conquest and Colonisation of North Africa*, Edinburgh, Blackwood, 1860. 8vo.
COPPIN, R. P. JEAN, Consul des Français à Damiette, &c.: *Le Bouclier de l'Europe, ou la Guerre sainte, &c., avec une Relation de Voyages faits dans la Turquie, la Thébaïde, & la Barbarie*, Lyon, Antoine Briasson, 1686. 4to., pp. 496 and 16 unnumbered. In the 5th book the author describes the fortress of the Goulette, the town of Thunis, &c.
CORSI, T. See GALEOTTI.
CORTAMBERT, RICHARD: *Essai sur la Chevelure chez les différents Peuples*, Paris, Challamel, 1861. 8vo. For Tunisia the author is indebted to H. Duman. Extracted from 'Revue Orientale et Américaine,' iii., iv., and v.
CORY, ISAAC PRESTON: *Ancient Fragments, Chaldæan, Egyptian, Tyrian, Carthaginian, &c. With an Inquiry into the philosophy and trinity of the Ancients*, London, 1832. 8vo., pp. lix., 361, and 4.
COSSON, Dr. E. S. C.: *Le projet de Mer intérieure en Algérie*, art. in 'Revue Scientifique,' 1879.
—— *Nouvelle Note sur le Projet de création en Algérie et en Tunisie d'une Mer, dite intérieure*, art. in 'Comptes rend. Acad. des Sciences,' 1882, xciv.
—— *Sur le projet de création en Algérie et en Tunisie d'une Mer dite intérieure*, in 'Comptes rendus de l'Association Française pour l'Avancement des Sciences, Congrès de Blois,' 1884.
—— *Note sur un projet de création en Algérie d'une Mer dite intérieure*,

art. in 'Bulletin de la Société de Géographie,' January, 1880.

COSSON, Dr. E. S. C.: *Rapport à M. le Ministre de l'Instruction publique et des Beaux-Arts, sur La Mission botanique chargée, en* 1883, *de l'Exploration du nord de la Tunisie, par E. Cosson, membre de l'Institut (Académie des Sciences)*, &c., Paris, Imprimerie Nationale, 1884. 8vo., pp. 31.

—— *Compendium floræ atlanticæ seu expositio methodica plantarum omnium in Algeria. Flore des États barbaresques, Algérie, Tunisie, Maroc. Tome 1ᵉʳ, première partie: historique et géographique*, Paris, 1881. 8vo., avec 2 cartes coloriées.

—— *Illustrationes floræ atlanticæ seu icones plantarum novarum, rariorum vel minus cognitarum in Algeria nec non in regno Tunetano et imperio Marocano nascentium.* Fascicule i., Paris, 1883. Fol., avec 25 pl. gravées.

—— *Conspectus floræ atlanticæ seu enumeratio plantarum omnium in Algeria, regno Tunetano et imperio Marocano hucusque notarum exibens quoque diagnoses specierum novarum et annotationes de plantis minus cognitis.*

COSSON, Dr. E. S. C., and KRAKLI, M. L.: *Sertulum Tunetanum. Notes sur quelques Plantes du sud de la Régence de Tunis* (1847).

COURTANT.   See D'ESTOURMETTES DE.

COURTRAY DE PRADEL, EUG. DE: *Saint-Louis en Afrique, récit en vers*, Rochefort, 1827. 8vo., pp. 48.

COUSINÉRY, E. M.: *Essai historique et critique sur les Monnaies d'Argent de la ligue achéenne, accompagné de recherches sur les monnaies de Corinthe, de Sicyone et de Carthage, qui ont eu cours pour le service de cette confédération*, Paris, 1825. 4to., 5 illustrations.

CRAPELET, AMABLE: *Voyage à Tunis en* 1859, in 'Tour du Monde,' 1864, Nos. 262, 263.

—— *Viaggio a Tunisi*, with numerous woodcuts, in 'Biblioteca di Viaggi,' Milano, Fratelli Treves, 1876. xxxvii., 1 to 79.

CREULY, Général: *Sur diverses Inscriptions romaines de Tunisie*, Paris, 1858. 8vo. Published originally in 'Revue Archéologique,' 1858, xv., 285.

'Le savant épigraphiste,' says M. A. Demarsy, 'passe en revue une série de travaux sur les antiquités tunisiennes, publiés dans la Revue Algérienne, en avril 1857, par le capitaine Lewal, et en juin, par M. A. Rousseau.' See those names.

CROIX.   See DE LA CROIX.

CROZALS, M. DE: *Tunis*, art. in 'Revue Politique et Littéraire,' 1881.

—— *Le Collège Saint-Louis de Carthage, Le Cardinal Lavigerie* (see that name), Idem, 1882.

—— *Les Races primitives de l'Afrique*, art. in 'Revue de Géographie,' August, 1881.

—— *Bizerte, son passé, son présent, son avenir*, Idem, Sept. and Oct. 1881.

CUBISOL, CHARLES, Vice-Consul à la Goulette: *Notice abrégée sur la Régence de Tunis*, Bône, 1867. 8vo., 16 plates of inscriptions.

The author published in 1866, under the same title, an autographed pamphlet followed by the description of the products sent by S. A., the Bey to the Universal Exhibition of Paris. This notice contains statistics chiefly.

CUEVA, PEDRO DE LA: *Dialogo de la Rebellion de Tunez*, Sevilla, S. Truxillo, 1550. 8vo.

CUVILLIER et BOUIN: *Essai d'un Dictionnaire des principaux Ports et Mouillages du Monde connu*, Paris, 1845. 8vo.

CYPRIEN, Saint: *Histoire et Œuvres complètes de Saint Cyprien, Evêque de Carthage, Traduction française par M. l'Abbé Thibaut, &c.*, Tours, Gattier, 1868. 8vo., 2 vols. See also FREPPEL, HAVET, and POOLE.

DAIN, ALFRED, Prof. agrégé à l'École de Droit d'Alger: *Le Système Torrens. De son application en Tunisie et en Algérie, rapport à M. Tirman, gouverneur général de l'Algérie, suivi d'une traduction de 'l'Act-Torrens,' et de la loi foncière tunisienne, du 5 juillet, 1885*, Paris, 1886. Large 8vo.

DAMPIERRE: *Histoire de la Rivalité de Carthage et de Rome.*

DAMPMARTIN, A. H., Capitaine au régiment Royal: *Histoire de la Rivalité de Carthage et de Rome, à laquelle on a joint La Mort de Caton, tragédie, nouvellement traduite de l'anglais, de M. Addisson* (sic), Strasbourg, J. G. Treuttel, (1789). 8vo., 2 vols. See also ADDISON.

DAN, P. F. P.: *Histoire de Barbarie et de ses Corsaires, des Royaumes et des Villes d'Alger, de Tunis, de Salé et de Tripoli, où il est traité de leur Gouvernement, de leurs Mœurs, de leurs Cruautés, de leurs Brigandages, de leurs Sortilèges, &c.*, Paris, 1649. Fol. First published in 1637, Paris. 4to. Done into Dutch as:

—— *Historie van Barbaryen, &c.*, vertaalt door G. v. Broeckhuysen, vermeerdert door S. de Vries, Amsterdam, 1684. Fol., illustrations. Also Amsterdam, 1641. Fol., 2 vols.

    The author was for nearly half a century a Trinitarian father, engaged in the release of captives. His work is most interesting from an English point of view, as he gives an account of the Irish captives taken at the sack of Baltimore by the Algerines. See also Charles Smith's *History of Cork*, vol. i., p. 278.—PLAYFAIR.

DANA, C. A. See RIPLEY.

DANDOLO, TULLIO: *Studii sul Secolo d'Augusto, Libri Quattro*, Milano, P. A. Molina, 1837. 8vo., pp. 243, double cols. Contains an account of the Punic Wars.

DAPPER, OLIVER, D.M: *Nauwkeurige beschrijving der Afrikaansche gewesten van Egypten, Barbaryen, Libyen, Biledulgered, Negroslant, Guinea, Etheopien en Abyssiniën.* Amsterdam, 1668. Fol.

—— *Description de l'Afrique, contenant les Noms, la Situation et les Confins de toutes ses parties; leurs Rivières, leurs Villes et leurs Habitations, leurs Plantes et leurs Animaux; les Mœurs, les Coutumes, la Langue, les Richesses, la Religion et le Gouvernement de ses peuples. Traduit du Flamand.* Amsterdam, 1686. 4to., 'orné de 31 planches, 15 cartes et 54 figures dans le texte.'

DARCEL, A. *Notice des émaux et de l'orfèvrerie* (du Musée du Louvre). 'D. 764 et 765. Aiguière et plateau en argent ciselé . . . .' représentant la conquête de Tunis par Charles-Quint.

—— *Excursion en Espagne.* Indication, in the chapter devoted to the Alhambra, of paintings of the xvith century, in 'le cabinet de toilette de la reine,' representing the conquest of Tunis by Charles-Quint.

—— *Excursion à Malte.* One chapter contains a visit to Tunis and Carthage.

DAREMBERT: *La Salubrité publique à Tunis*, art. in 'Revue Scientifique,' July 5, 1884.

DARRÉ, Dr. See POINSSOT.

DAUMAS, Général: *Du chameau d'Afrique*, art. in 'Rev. de l'Orient,' 3 sér., i., 178. 1855. Originally addressed to the President of the Soc. Zool. d'Acclim.

DAUMAS, PHILIPPE: *Quatorze ans à Tunis*, Alger, 1857. 8vo.

DAUX, A., Ingénieur civil de Nîmes *Recherches sur l'origine et l'emplacement des Emporia phéniciens dans le Zeugis et le Byzacium, faites par ordre de l'Empereur*, Paris, Imprimerie Impériale, 1869. 8vo., pp. 313, 9 plates.

—— *Notice sur Utique*, in 'Tour du Monde.'

—— *Le Rovine d'Utica*, 1868, with many woodcuts, in 'Biblioteca di Viaggi,' Milano, 1876, xxxvii., 153 to 192.

—— *Achmet-pacha, Bey de Tunis, et des réformes récentes qu'il a faites, &c.*, art. in 'Revue de l'Orient,' 1848, 2 série, iv., 342.

D'AVEZAC. See AVEZAC.

DAVIDSOHN, R.: *Vom Nordcap bis Tunis*, Berlin, 1884. 8vo., pp. 175.

DAUIES, WILLIAM: *A Trve Relation of the Travailes and most miserable Captiuitie of William Dauies, Barber-Surgion of London, under the Duke of Florence, &c.* London, Nicholas Bourne, 1614. Small 4to., pp. 40, unnumbered. The 'Description and Discouery of Tunys' occupies chap. iii. Reprinted in 'A Collection of Voyages' (Churchill), London, T. Osborne, 1757, vii., 476 to 488.

DAVIS, Dr. NATHAN. *Carthage and her Remains, being an account of the excavations and researches on the site of the Phœnician metropolis of Africa, and other adjacent places, conducted under the auspices of Her Majesty's Government*, London, 1860. 8vo., pp. 640. Noticed in the 'Christian Observer,' lxi., 544. Translated into German, Leipzig, 1863.

—— *Inscription in the Phœnician character, now in the British Museum, discovered on the site of Carthage*, London, 1863. Oblong fol.

—— *Ruined Cities within Numidian and Carthaginian Territories*, London, 1863. 8vo., pp. xvi. & 391, map.

DAVITY, PIERRE, Seigneur de Montmartain : *Description générale de l'Afrique, seconde partie du Monde. Avec tous ses Empires, Royaumes, et Républiques, qui sont déduits et traités par ordre de leurs Noms, Assiettes, Confins, Mœurs, Richesses, Forces, Gouvernement et Religion; et la Généalogie des Empereurs, Rois et Princes souverains, lesquels y ont dominé jusqu'à présent. Nouvelle édition revue et corrigée par J. B. de Rocoles*, Troyes et Paris, 1660. Fol.

DE BISSON, L. See BISSON.

DE BIZEMONT. See BIZEMONT.

DE CAMPON : *Tunis et le Cardinal Lavigerie* (see that name), art. in 'Correspondant,' April 25, 1887.

DE CHAMPLOUIS, M. Nau, Capitaine au Corps Impérial d'État-major : *Notice sur la carte de l'Afrique sous la domination des Romains, dressée au Dépôt de la Guerre d'après les travaux de M. Fr. Lacroix, par ordre de S. E. le Maréchal Comte Randon, Min. de la Guerre*, Paris, 1864. 4to., pp. 46.

'The map in question is in two large sheets (2,000,000ᵐ), and includes the whole district between the Cyrenaica and the Atlantic. See also "L'Ann. Géogr.," t. iii. p. 110.'—PLAYFAIR.

See also LA CROIX F.

DEFOURNOUX, Dr.: *Du Maroc en Tunisie*, in 'Comptes rendus des Séances de la Société Géog.,' Paris 1882, pp. 409–12.

DE LA CROIX, Sieur : *Relation universelle de l'Afrique, ancienne et moderne, où l'on voit ce qu'il y a de remarquable, tant dans la terre ferme que dans les isles, avec ce que le Roi a fait de mémorable contre les corsaires de Barbarie, &c.*, Lyon, 1688. 12mo., 4 vols. Also Lyon, 1698, 12mo., 4 vols. See also 'Journal des Savans,' 1689, p. 131.

DE LA CROIX, Sieur: *Mémoires du sieur De la Croix, contenant l'état présent de l'église grecque et les révolutions du Royaume de Tunis.* M.S. Anciens fonds de Versailles, No. 123.

DELAIRE: *Les Chotts tunisiens et la Mer intérieure en Algérie,* art. in 'Correspondant,' July 25, 1881.

DE LANESSAN. See LANESSAN.

DELATTRE, A. L., Prêtre missionnaire: *Objets archéologiques exposés à Amsterdam,* Tunis, 1883.

—— *Inscriptions de Chemtou:* arts. in 'Revue Archéologique,' April and July, 1881.

—— *Inscriptions chrétiennes trouvées sur différents points de l'ancienne ville de Carthage,* art. in 'Revue de l'Afrique Française,' Paris, July, 1886, iv., 241 to 248.

DELAVILLE LE ROULX, J., Docteur-ès-lettres: *La France en Orient au XIVe Siècle — Expéditions du Maréchal Boucicaut,* Paris, Ernest Thorin, 1886. 8vo., 2 vols. Contains several historical notices of Tunisia, and (vol. i., pp. 166 to 200) *Expédition de Barbarie* (1390).

DE LA WARR, Earl: *French Occupation of Tunis,* art. in 'Nineteenth Century,' x., 448.

DELISLE DE SALES, J. B. C. I., Membre de l'Institut: *Histoire de tous les Peuples du Monde, &c.*, Paris, 1779. 12mo., 53 vols., maps and illustrations. Contains *Histoire de Carthage.*

DELSOL: *Sbitla* (Tunis), art. in 'Bulletin Société Géog. Commer.,' Bordeaux, 1878, No. 22.

DEMANCHE, GEORGES: *D'Alger à Kairouan,* arts. in 'Revue Française,' 1886 and 1887. Also in separate form, Challamel, 1887, 8vo.

DEMAY: *Le Clergé français en Tunisie,* art. in 'Correspondant,' Nov. 25, 1886.

DE PURE, M. See BIRAGO.

DERENBOURG, Membre de l'Académie des Inscriptions: *Inscriptions de Carthage sur les Offrandes de Prémices,* with a plate, art. in 'Journal Asiatique,' February, 1874, p. 204.

—— *Sur une Inscription néo-punique de huit lignes trouvée à M'deina en Tunisie, &c.*, art. in 'Académie des Inscriptions,' Oct. 2, 1874.

DESFONTAINES, R. L., Membre de l'Académie des Sciences: *Flora Atlantica, sive Historia Plantarum quæ in Atlante, agro Tunetano et Algeriensi crescunt,* Parisiis, An vi. (1798). 4to., 2 vols., 263 plates. See also PEYSSONNEL.

—— *Observations sur les Plantes économiques qui croissent dans les Royaumes de Tunis et d'Alger,* in 'Nouvelles Annales des Voyages,' 1830. Tome iii. de l'année, pp. 321 to 359.

—— *Lettre à M. Lemonnier, de l'Académie des Sciences,* Idem, 1830. Tome iii. de l'année, 60 to 77. Contains archæological details, and descriptions of Kairouan, Calsa, Le Gerid, Sfaïtla, Sbiba, and the environs of Tunis.

—— *Premier Fragment d'un Voyage dans les Royaumes de Tunis et d'Alger, et dans les montagnes de l'Atlas,* Idem, 1830. Tome ii. de l'année, pp. 189 to 228.

—— *Voyage le long de la côte depuis Tunis jusqu'à Sfax sur les bords de la Petite Syrthe,* Idem, 1830. Tome iii. de l'année, pp. 137 to 164.

DESFOSSÉS, EDMOND, Avocat: *La Tunisie sous le Protectorat et son Annexion à l'Algérie,* Paris, Challamel, 1886. 8vo., pp. 44. A purely political pamphlet in favour, as its title indicates, of the annexation of Tunisia by France.

—— *La Disgrâce de Mustapha Khaznadar, ancien premier ministre de Tunisie, considérée au point de vue des intérêts européens,* 1875. 4to.

DESFOSSÉS, EDMOND, Avocat: *La Tunisie, histoire, politique, finances*, 1877. 8vo.
—— *La Tunisie, physique et économique*. Published originally in the 'Revue de Géographie,' February, 1879.
—— *Les Kroumirs*, with a map, Idem, August, 1879.
—— *L'Aqueduc de Carthage et sa restauration*, art. in 'Réforme Économique,' Oct. 15, 1880.
—— *La Question tunisienne et l'Afrique septentrionale, Angleterre, France, Italie*, 1881. 8vo., pp. 48.
—— *Le Protectorat français en Tunisie, avec texte et commentaire du traité de Kassar-Saïd du mai* 1881. 8vo.
—— *De la Réorganisation administrative et financière de la Tunisie, avec texte officiel des traités*. 1882. 8vo.
D'ESTOURMETTES DE COURTANT: *Les Sociétés secrètes chez les Arabes et la Conquête de l'Afrique du nord*, art. in 'Revue des Deux-Mondes,' March 1, 1886.
DEVARS, M. G. See BESCHERELLE.
DEVOULX, ALPHONSE: *Voyage à l'Amphithéâtre romain d'El-Djem en Tunisie*, Paris, 1830. 8vo., pp. 22. From the 'Revue Africaine,' Alger, 1874, xviii.
D'HÉRISSON. See HÉRISSON.
DILHAN, ALPHONSE: *Histoire abrégée de la Régence de Tunis*, Paris, 1866. 8vo.
DION CASSIUS: *Histoire romaine, par E. Gros*. 7 tom. Gr. and Fr. Paris, 1845-65. He was Roman Governor of North Africa in the reign of Alexander Severus, A.D. 222-235. In the *Fragmenta*, ccxv. to ccxx., is a history of the second Punic War, and in cclxv. to cclxix. is some account of the Jugurthine War.
DIXON, WILLIAM HEPWORTH: *Robert Blake, general and admiral at sea, based on family and state papers*, London, 1852. 8vo. Contains an account of Blake's action at Porto Farina.
DONALDSON, Prof.: *A notice of the recent travels of H.M. Consul-General, Lieut.-Col. Playfair, in the provinces of Algiers and Tunis, in the footsteps of Bruce the traveller, illustrated by Bruce's drawings.* 'Sess. Papers Roy. Inst. Brit. Architects,' No. 3, pp. 33-43, illustrations, 1876.
DOR, H.: *Souvenir du Congrès d'Alger, Tunis et la Kabylie*, Lyon, 1882. 8vo. pp. 93.
DOUMET-ADANSON, M.: *Sur le régime des Eaux qui alimentent les Oasis du sud de la Tunisie*, in 'Comptes rendus de l'Association Française pour l'Avancement des Sciences, Congrès de Blois,' 1884.
—— *Les Silex taillés de Tunisie*, Idem.
—— *Note sur l'origine des Chotts du sud de la Tunisie*. Montpellier, 1876. 8vo. From 'Rev. des Sc. Natur.'
DRAPEYRON, L.: *La Constitution de Carthage*, Paris, 1882. 8vo., pp. 20.
DROUIN, E. A.: *Les Inscriptions de Tunis*, Louvain, 1882. 8vo.
DRU, LÉON: *Extraits de la Mission de M. le commandant Roudaire (see that name) dans les Chotts tunisiens* (1878-1879), Paris, Chamerot. 8vo.
DUBOIS-FONTANELLE: *Anecdotes africaines depuis l'origine ou la découverte des différents Royaumes qui composent l'Afrique jusqu'à nos jours*, Paris, 1775. 8vo.
DU CASSE, R. See CASSE.
DU CASTEL. See BREVES.
DÜMGE, C. G.: *Ansichten von Tripolis, Tunis und Algier, aus dem Reiseberichten eines französischen Missionairs*, Stuttgart, Metzler, 1816. 8vo.
DUESBERG, F. See MANNERT.
DUGASTE. See DUREAU DE LA MALLE.

DUGAT, GUSTAVE: *Le Poëme en l'honneur du bey de Tunis du cheik Farès*, Paris, 1851. 8vo.

DUGAT, GUSTAVE, et le cheik FARÈS ECCHIDIAK: *Grammaire française à l'usage des Arabes de l'Algérie, de Tunis, &c.*, Paris, Impr. Imp. 1854. 8vo., pp. 125.

—— *A Practical Grammar of the Arabic Language, &c.*, London, 1866. 12mo., pp. 162.

DUMAN, H. See CORTAMBERT.

DUMAS, ALEXANDRE: *Le Véloce, ou Tanger, Alger et Tunis*, Paris, 1848. 8vo. Also Paris, 1851, 8vo., 2 vols. 'Le Véloce' is the name of the vessel on which Dumas made his voyage. The publication of his travels was commenced in 'La Presse,' March 12, 1847.

DUMERQUE, E.: *The Chotts of Tunis, or the Great Inland Sea of North Africa in ancient times*, London, 1883. 8vo. p. 27. Also London, Allen, 1884. 8vo.

DUMONT, M. X.: *Guide de la Lecture des Manuscrits arabes. Arab. et Fr.*, Alger, 1842. 8vo., lithographed.

DUMONT, P. J. See QUESNÉ.

DUMONT D'URVILLE, J.: *Histoire générale des Voyages*, Paris, Fûrne & Cie., 1859. 8vo., 4 vols., portraits, illustrations and maps. In chapt. 99, vol. iv., will be found an account of Tunis and of the Ruins of Carthage.

DUNANT, H. J.: *Notice sur la Régence de Tunis*, Genève, J. G. Fick, 1858. 8vo., privately printed.

The volume contains: Historical *résumé*; the town of Tunis; the court; the army, navy, and taxes; climate and products; industry and commerce; towns and various localities; religion and literature; Musulman year; slavery of Moors; Arabs and Djébélias; customs and superstitions of the Jews of Tunis; society and population. Noticed by M. Th. Pavie in 'Revue des Deux-Mondes,' March 15, 1858; also by M. H. de Charencey (see that name).

DUPRAT, PASCAL: *Essai historique sur les Races anciennes et modernes de l'Afrique septentrionale, leurs origines, leurs mouvements et leurs transformations*, Paris, 1845. 8vo. pp. 318.

DUREAU DE LA MALLE, A. J. C. A., Membre de l'Académie des Inscriptions et Belles-Lettres, Membre de l'Institut: *Recherches sur la Topographie de Carthage, avec des notes de M. Dugaste*, Paris, 1837. 8vo., 4 plates. Noticed by M. Letronne in 'Journal des Savants,' Nov. 1837. See also PEYSSONNEL and TEMPLE.

DUREAU DE LA MALLE and YANOSKI, JEAN: *Carthage*, pp. 170, 6 plates, in 'L'Univers Pittoresque,' Paris, 1844.

DURUY, VICTOR: *Histoire des Romains, &c.*, Paris, Hachette & Cie., 1879-85. 4to., 7 vols., illustrated. Carthage, its commerce, wars, and destruction, together with its bishops, their persecution, &c., are very fully treated in this noble work; there are also a plan of the city and numerous illustrations. Thysdrus, Utica, &c., are also described, the former with a view of the amphitheatre.

DUVERNOIS, CLÉMENT: *Les Réformes en Tunisie*, arts. in 'Revue de l'Orient,' 1858, 3 série, vii., 83, 143, 202.

DUVEYRIER, HENRI: *Lettre sur son Voyage dans le sud de la Tunisie, &c.*, art. in 'Nouvelles Annales des Voyages,' 1868, ii. 356.

—— *Exploration du Sahara — Les Touareg du nord*, Paris, Challamel, 1864. 8vo., pp. xxxiv., 499, and 4 unnumbered pages, with a *Supplément* of pp. 37 and 4 unnumbered pages, a portrait of the author, illustrations, and a folding map. Although but a small part of Tunisia is treated of in this volume, it contains much information indirectly applicable to that country, and relating chiefly to the region south of Tunisia.

DUVEYRIER, HENRI: *La Tunisie*, Paris, Hachette, 1881. 8vo., pp. 143.

DUVIVIER, Général: *Recherches et Notes sur la portion de l'Algérie au sud de Ghelma, depuis la frontière de Tunis jusqu'au mont Auress, indiquant les anciennes routes encore apparentes*, Paris, Imp. Vassal, 1841. 4to., pp. 66, map, privately printed.

DUVIVIER, Général FRANCIA DE FLEURUS *Inscriptions phéniciennes, puniques, numidiques, expliquées par une méthode incontestable*, Paris, 1846. 8vo. pp. 16.

DYER, THOMAS H.: *Utica*, art. of 3 cols. in 'Dictionary of Greek and Roman Geography,' W. Smith, LL.D., London, J. Murray, 1854.

ECCHIDIAK, F. See DUGAT.
EL-ABDERY. See CHERBONNEAU.
EL-AÏACHI-EBN-MOULA-AHMED: *Voyages dans le sud de l'Algérie et des États barbaresques de l'ouest et de l'est, trad. sur deux manuscrits arabes par A. Berbrugger; suivis d'Itinéraires et Renseignements fournis par Sid-Ahmed-Ould-Bou-Mezrag et du Voyage par terre de Taza à Tunis par M. Fabre*, Paris, Imp. Royale, 1846. Large 8vo., pp. 396. See also BERBRUGGER and FABRE.

EL-BEKRI: *Description de l'Afrique septentrionale, traduit par Mac Guckin de Slane*, Paris, Impr. Impér., 1859. 8vo.

—— *Description de Tunis. Extrait de la Description de l'Afrique septentrionale d'El-Bekri, traduite par M. de Slane*, in 'Journal Asiatique,' 1858, 5 série, xii., 505.

EL-EDRISI, ABU-ABD-ALLAH-MOHAMMED-AL-: *Commentatio de Geographia Africæ, curavit J. M. Hartmann*, Gottingæ, 1791. 4to. Second edition, Gott., 1796. 8vo.

EL-EDRISI, ABU-ABD-ALLAH-MOHAMMED-AL: *La Géographie d'Edrisi, traduite de l'arabe en français par Paul Amédée Jaubert*, Paris, Imp. Roy., 1837-1841. 4to., 2 vols. See also HARTMANN, J. M.

EL-EGHOUATHY. See AVEZAC.

EL-FIDJANI. Noticed by M. Cherbonneau as one of the best Arab writers to consult for a description of Tunis. See also ROUSSEAU.

EL-HARAÏRA. See GAY, F
EL-KAIROUANI. See EL-RAÏNI.
EL-LOWLOWI: *Extrait de l'Histoire de la Dynastie des Beni-Hafss, par Abou-Abdallah Mahammed-ben-Jbrahim-El-Lowlowi-El-Zerkeschi. Fragment traduit par M. Alphonse Rousseau*, in 'Journal Asiatique,' 1849, 4 série, xiii., 269.

'Ce travail renferme le texte et la traduction française d'un extrait relatif à l'usurpation du pouvoir hafssite par un aventurier du nom de Ahmed-ben-Merzouk-eben-Abi-Amara, qui, l'an 681 de l'hégire, se fit proclamer à Tunis sous les noms de El-Fedhel-eben-Abi-Iakaria-Jehia-el-Ouatsêq.'—A DEMARSY.

El-Lowlowi is noticed by M. Cherbonneau as one of the best Arab writers to be consulted for a description of Tunis.

EL-NEFZAOUI, Cheik Sidi MOHAMMED: *Ouvrage du Cheik, l'imam, le savant, le très érudit, le très intelligent, le très véridique Sidi Mohammed el Nefzaoui : que Dieu très élevé lui fasse miséricorde par sa puissance ! Amen ! Traduit de l'Arabe par M***, Capitaine d'État-major*, 1850. Édition autographiée. First printed as: *Le Jardin parfumé du Cheikh Nefzaoui Manuel d'Erotologie Arabe (xvie Siècle) Traduction revue et corrigée. Imprimé à deux cent vingt exemplaires pour Isidore Liseux et ses Amis*, Paris, 1886. 4to., pp. xv and 298.

There are two editions of the same work in English, both issued in the same year, both in 8vo., and with the same number of pages, viz., xv. and 256,

The Perfumed Garden of the Cheikh Nefzaoui, &c., Cosmopoli, 1886. There are variations on the title-pages, and the later volume is printed in violet with title-page in red and violet. Nefzaoui lived at Tunis and there wrote his book, which, although not specially devoted to the people of Tunisia, throws much light upon their manners and customs at that time. It is not *virginibus puerisque*. A copy of the original Arab text, probably that from which the French translation was made, exists in the National Library at Algiers.

EL-RAÏNI: *Histoire de l'Afrique par Mohammed-Ben-Abi-el-Raïni-el-Kairouani, traduit de l'arabe par MM. E. Pellissier et Remusat*, Paris, Imp. Roy., 1847. 4to. (vol. vii. of 'L'Exploration scientifique de l'Algérie').

'Cet auteur donne une description de Tunis, suivie de l'histoire des différentes dynasties qui ont régné sur Tunis jusqu'à l'an 1681 de notre ère, et terminée par une description des curiosités de la ville et des usages de ses habitants; . . . on y trouve des renseignements originaux et tirés de la tradition orale, surtout dans la dernière partie qui traite de la conquête de Tunis par les Turcs.'—A. DEMARSY.

ESCAYRAC DE LAUTURE, Le Comte d': *Le Désert et le Soudan*, Paris, Dumaine, 1853. 8vo., pp. 625, 2 maps and 12 plates. Divided into 5 books: i. Climats africains; ii. Considérations sur la Barbarie, Études sur l'Islamisme et les Mœurs des Mussulmans actuels; iii. Les Arabes; iv. Les Noirs colonisés; v. Commerce du Soudan.

ESPÉRANDIEU, E., Lieut. d'infanterie: *Archéologie tunisienne. Epigraphie des Environs du Kef. Inscriptions recueillies en 1882-83*, Paris, 1885. 8vo., 7 fascicules, cart., planches.

ESPINA, A., Vice-Consul de France à Sousse: *Notice historique sur le Caidat de Sfax*, art. in 'Revue de l'Orient,' 2 série, xiii., 142.

—— *Lettres archéologiques relatives à Soussa, l'ancienne Hadrumetum*, art. in 'Revue Africaine,' 1859, iii., 368.

ESTRELLA, C. DE. See CALVETE.
ESTOURMETTES, D'. See D'ESTOURMETTES DE COURTANT.
ESTRUP: *Lineæ Topographicæ Carthaginis Tyriæ*, 1821. Map.

'Estrup was a Danish scholár who made use of the MSS. of Camillo Borgia (see BORGIA), a Neapolitan traveller, who had examined the ground attentively, and who died at Naples without being able to publish his work.'

EUTING: *Punische Steine*, Saint-Pétersbourg, 1871.

EWALD, CHRISTN. FERD.: *Reise von Tunis über Soliman, Nabal, Hammamet, Susa, Sfax, Gabis, Gerba nach Tripolis, und von da wieder zurück nach Tunis, im Jahre 1835. Herausgegeben von Paul Ewald*, Nürnberg, Ebner, 1837-38. Large 8vo., 3 parts, 1 map, 8 black and 5 coloured engravings.

—— *Tunis and Tripoli*, art. in 'Penny Mag.,' vii., 12.

—— *Scenes in Tunis*, Idem, viii., 332.

EWALD, J.: *Manners of Tunis*, art. in 'Penny Mag.,' ix., 129.

EXIGA, dit KAYSER, Interprète militaire: *Description et Histoire de l'Ile de Djerba, traduit du Manuscrit de Cheik Mohammed Abu Rasse Ahmed En-Naceur*, Tunis. Small 4to. Arabic and French.

EVRIÈS: *Carthage*, art. of 10 cols. in 'Encyclopédie Moderne,' Paris, Firmin Didot, 1854.

—— *Détail sur l'Amphithéâtre de Thysdrus*, art. in 'Nouvelles Annales de Voyages.'

FABRE, J.: *Essai sur la Régence de Tunis*, Avignon, 1881. 8vo., pp. 188. See also EL-AÏACHI.

FAIDHERBE, Général: *Epigraphie phénicienne*, Paris, 1873. 8vo.

—— *Inscription libyque, trouvée aux environs de Tunis*, art. in 'Bulletin de l'Académie des Inscriptions,' &c., Jan., 1881.

FAIRMAIRE, L. See LEFÈVRE.
FALBE, C. T., Captain and Danish Consul at Tunis: *Recherches sur l'Emplacement de Carthage, suivies de renseignements sur plusieurs inscriptions puniques inédites, avec le plan topographique des ruines de la ville,* Paris, 1837. 8vo., with atlas and 6 plates in fol. See also TEMPLE.

FALBE ET LINDBERG: *Annoncé d'un ouvrage sur les médailles de l'ancienne Afrique par MM. Falbe et Lindberg, avec un aperçu des découvertes de M. Lindberg dans la numismatique de Carthage, de la Numidie, et de Mauritanie,* Kopenhague, 1843. 8vo., pp. 20.

FALBE, LINDBERG and MÜLLER: *Numismatique de l'Ancienne Afrique. Ouvrage préparé et commencé par C. T. Falbe et J. Chr. Lindberg, refait, achevé et publié par L. Müller,* Copenhague, Imp. de Bianco Luno par F. S. Muhle, 1860-61. 4to., 2 vols., illustrations in the text. In vol. ii. the moneys of Carthage are considered at length; those also of Utica, &c. are noticed.

'This learned work was commenced in this year (1860) and completed in 1862. It contains a scientific classification of all the Greek and Roman money of North Africa from Cyrene to Mauritania. It is one of the most important works ever written on Africa.'—PLAYFAIR.

FALLOT, ERNEST: *Par delà la Méditerranée: Kabylie, Aurès, Kroumirie,* Paris, Plon, 1887. 18mo., woodcuts.

M. Fallot is secretary of the Geographical Society of Marseilles. His book is reviewed in 'Le Livre,' Sept. 1887.

FARÈS ECCHIDIAK. See DUGAT.

FARINE, CHARLES: *Kabyles et Kroumairs,* Paris, Ducrocq, 1882. 8vo. pp. 423.

FAULTRIER, GODARD: *Étude sur un Vase en plomb trouvé dans les ruines de Carthage,* Angers, 1867. 8vo.

The same vase, which was exhibited at the Exposition Universelle of Paris in the Tunisian section, furnished M. EDM. LE BLANT (see that name) with the subject of a communication to the 'Société des Antiquaires de France.'

FAURE, A. LE. See LE FAURE.
FAVÉ. See YVON-VILLARCEAU.
FÉRAUD, L.: *Kitab-el-Adwani, ou le Sahara de Constantine et Tunis,* 'Rec. Not. et Mém. Soc. Arch. Const.,' 1868, vol. xii., pp. 1-208.

'This is an Arabic work of modern date, a curious picture of tribal history and desert life.'—PLAYFAIR.

FERRY, JULES: *Les Affaires de Tunisie, Discours,* Paris, 1882. 12mo., pp. 212.

FEUILLERET: *Les Romains en Afrique,* Limoges, 1869.

FIELDING, Viscount. See KENNEDY.

FINOTTI, GUGLIELMO: *La Regenza di Tunisi considerata nei suoi rapporti geografici, storici, archeologici, idrografici, commerciali, etc.* Malta, 1857. 8vo., pp. 440.

FISCHER, THEOBALD: *Tunesien als französische Colonie,* art. in 'Deutsche Rundschau,' Oct. 1887, pp. 101 to 119.

FLACCUS ILLYRICUS. See ILLYRICUS.

FLAUBERT, GUSTAVE: *Salammbô,* Paris, 1862. 8vo.

In 1857 the author visited Tunis, and on the ruins of Carthage the subject and materials of his romance suggested themselves.

In 1883 a portrait of the author and four etchings to illustrate *Salammbô* were made under the auspices of M. Billard of the Society of the 'Amis des Livres' of Paris.

Reprinted in 1887 by Quantin, Paris, in 1 vol., 8vo., undated, with 'Dix compositions par A. Poirson.'

There are two English versions, both of London and of the same year, 1886: one by Mr. M. F. Sheldon, published by Messrs. Saxon & Co.; the other by Mr. J. S. Chartres, issued by Messrs. Vizetelly & Co.

FLAUX, A. DE: *La Régence de Tunis au XIXᵉ Siècle,* Paris, 1865. 8vo.

The author was sent on a mission to Carthage by the Count Walewski, then Minister of State. He travelled through Tunisia in every direction. To his work he adds: a translation of the Tunisian

Constitution, an analysis of the principal treaties concluded by the Bey with western powers, and a translation of some Arab poems. Notices of M. Flaux's book will be found in 'Journal des Savants,' Sept. 1866, and by M. Privas in 'Annales des Voyages,' 1866, ii., 228. See also NONCE-ROCCA.

FLORIUS, L. See SYLBURGIUS.

FOLARD, Chevalier de. See SÉRAN DE LA TOUR.

FONCIN, PIERRE: *L'Alliance française et l'enseignement de la langue nationale en Algérie et en Tunisie*, arts. in 'Bulletin de la Société Historique et de Saint-Simon,' No. 2, 1884; and No. 2, 1885; art. with same title in 'Revue Scientifique,' Dec. 27, 1884.

—— *Les Écoles françaises en Tunisie*, art. in 'Revue Politique et Littéraire,' 1884.

—— *La Tunisie*, art. in 'Revue Politique et Littéraire,' January 9, 1886.

—— *Tunisie*, art. in 'Revue de l'Afrique Française,' Paris, July, 1886, iv., 267 to 277.

FONTANELLE. See DUBOIS-FONTANELLE.

FONVENT, H. P. DE. See PONTET DE FONVENT.

FONVIELLE, W. DE: *La France à Tunis*, political art. in 'Revue du Monde Colonial,' 1864, 3 série, i., 352.

FORBIGER, ALBERT, Doktor der Philosophie: *Handbuch der alten Geographie, aus den Quellen bearbeitet von Albert Forbiger*, Leipzig, Mayer und Wigand, 1842–1848. 8vo., 3 vols., maps. Carthage and Tunis are comprised in this erudite compilation.

FOSBROKE, T. D., M.A., F.S.A.: *Foreign Topography, &c.* London, J. B. Nichols & Son, 1828. 4to., illustrations. Two pages are devoted to Carthage.

FOURNEL, MARC. JÉR. H., Ingénieur des Mines: *Étude sur la conquête d'Afrique par les Arabes: et recherches sur les tribus berbères qui ont occupé le Magreb central*, Paris, 1857. 4to., pp. 165.

FOURNEL, MARC. JÉR. H., Ingénieur des Mines: *Les Berbers, étude sur la conquête de l'Afrique par les Arabes, d'après les textes imprimés*, Paris, n. d., 4to.

'Both works are of considerable importance.'—PLAYFAIR.

—— *La Tunisie, le Christianisme et l'Islam dans l'Afrique septentrionale*, Paris, Challamel, 1886. 12mo.

FRANCESCO, J. DE: *Considérations sur le Conflit franco-tunisien*, Cagliari, 1879. 8vo., pp. 48.

FRANCOWITZ, M. See ILLYRICUS.

FRANK, Dr. LOUIS, and MARCEL, J. J.: *Tunis, Description de cette Régence, par le Dr. Louis Frank, Ancien Médecin du Bey de Tunis, &c. Revue et accompagnée d'un Précis historique et d'Éclaircissements tirés des Écrivains orientaux, par J. J. Marcel, Ancien Membre de l'Institut d'Égypte, &c.*, art. of pp. 224, with woodcuts in text, and an engraving of the *Ruines du grand aqueduc de l'ancienne Carthage*, in 'Univers Pittoresque,' Paris, Firmin Didot, 1850. 1 map. Reissued in separate form in 1851, as *Histoire de Tunis*, with a map and engravings. 8vo.

FRANKS, A. W.: *Excavations at Carthage*, art. in 'Archæologia,' xxxviii., 203.

FREPPEL, Évêque d'Alger: *Saint-Cyprien et l'Église d'Afrique au IIIe Siècle*, Paris, 1873. 8vo., pp. 474. See also CYPRIEN.

FRIEDRICH, Dr. THOMAS: *Biographie des Barkiden Mago, ein Beitrag zur Kritik des Valerius Antias*, Wien, C. Konegen, 1880. 8vo., pp. 54.

FUCHS, M.: *Les Gîtes de Plomb et de Fer de la Tunisie*, in 'Comptes rendus de l'Association française pour l'Avancement des Sciences, Congrès d'Alger,' 1881.

FURNARI, Dr. SALVATO : *Voyage médical dans l'Afrique septentrionale*, Paris, 1845. 8vo.

GACHET, EMILE: *Documents inédits relatifs à la Conquête de Tunis par l'Empereur Charles-Quint, en* 1535, Bruxelles, 1844. 8vo., pp. 50.

GAFFAREL, P.: *Quelques mots sur les Khroumirs.* 'Bull. Soc. Géogr.' Dijon, 1882, vol. i., No. 1, pp. 4-12.

GAIDOZ: *Un Sacrifice humain à Carthage*, art. in 'Revue Archéologique,' Sept. 1886.

GAILLARDON, B., Négociant en vins, Rédacteur au 'Moniteur Agricole :' *Manuel du Vigneron en Algérie et en Tunisie*, Paris, 1886. 18mo.

GALAND, A. See HERBELOT.

GALEOTTI, LEOPOLDO, and others: *Corte di Cassazione de Firenze, Memoria in Causa Governo di Tunisie e Samama*, Firenze, Tipografia Bonducciana di A. Alessandri, 1881. Large 8vo., pp. vi. and 299.

This report is signed by Leopoldo Galeotti 'Estensore,' Ferdinando Andreucci, Tommaso Corsi, Federigo Spantigati, Augusto Pierantoni, Odoardo Luchini, Ferdinando Santioni de-Sio, Bartolommeo Operti, Eugenio Brunetti, and Angiolo Castelli.

GALLAND, ANT., Professor of Arab, born 1646, died 1715: *Relation de l'esclavage d'un marchand français de la ville de Cassis à Tunis*, Paris, 1810. 8vo. Posthumous work, first published by M. Langlès in 'Magasin Encyclopédique,' 1809, i. and ii.

GALLENGA, A.: *Tunis*, art. in 'Contemporary Review,' xl., 116.

GANNEAU, M. C. CLERMONT. See CLERMONT-GANNEAU.

GASSELIN, ÉDOUARD, Chancelier du Consulat de France à Mogador: *Dictionnaire français-arabe*, Paris, Leroux, 1886.

M. Gasselin travelled also in Tunisia, in order to study the colloquial words and expressions of that country.

GAUTIER, JUDITH: *Les Missions scientifiques de France en Afrique, les Ruines romaines*, art. in 'L'Officiel,' Dec. 13, 1879.

GAY, FERDINAND, Attaché au Consulat de France au Maroc: *Le Progrès en Tunisie*, art. in 'Annuaire de la Société d'Ethnographie de Paris,' 1864, 42 to 49.

GAY, FERDINAND, and SOLIMAN-EL-HARAÏRA: *Les Parfumeurs indigènes de Tunis*, in 'Ouvriers des deux Mondes.'

GAY, OSCAR: *La Tunisie, notice historique*, Paris, 1861. 8vo.

GERVAIS, PAUL: *Énumération de quelques espèces de reptiles provenant de Barbarie.* 'Extrait des Ann. des Sci. Nat.,' 1837, 2ᵉ sér., vi., pp. 303-13.

GERVAISE, NICHOLAS, Missionary: *Mémoires historiques du Royaume de Tunis*, Paris, 1736. 8vo.

GESENIUS, H. F. W.: *Paläographische Studien über phönizische und punische Schrift*, Leipzig, 1835. 4to.

—— *Scripturæ Linguæque Phoeniciæ Monumenta quotquot supersunt edita et inedita*, Leipzig, 1837. 4to., 48 plates.

GIBBON, EDWARD: *The History of the Decline and Fall of the Roman Empire*, London, Longman, 1848. 8vo., 8 vols. Numerous editions. Contains an account of the bishopric of Carthage, of the factions of Cæcilian and Donatus, of the destruction of the city by Hassan, &c.

GIFFARD, PIERRE *Les Français à Tunis*, Paris, Victor Havard, 1881. 8vo.

Impressions, written in a style suitable for the 'Figaro,' to which journal M. Giffard was a contributor Not much instruction is to be obtained from the book, which is largely occupied by tirades against the Italians and English, with a goodly amount of French glorification.

GILBERT: *Rom und Karthago*, Leipzig, 1877.

GIRAULT DE PRANGEY: *Essai sur l'Architecture des Arabes et des Maures, en Espagne, en Sicile et en Barbarie*, Paris, 1842. 8vo.

GODARD FAULTRIER. See FAULTRIER.

GODEFROY: *État des Royaumes de Barbarie, Tripoli, Tunis et Alger: contenant l'histoire politique et naturelle de ces pais; la manière dont les Turcs y traitent les esclaves, comme on les rachète, et diverses aventures curieuses. Avec la tradition de l'Église pour le rachat des captifs*, Rouen, Machuel, 1731. 12mo.

GODINS DE SOUHESMES, G. DES: *Tunis: Histoire, Mœurs, Gouvernement, Administration, etc.*, Paris, 1875. Favourably noticed in 'Le Livre,' June 10, 1881.

GOLBÉRY, P. DE: *Carthage*, art. of 22 cols. in 'Encyclopédie des Gens du Monde,' Paris, Treuttel et Würtz, 1835.

GONZAGA, FERRANDO: *Copia de una Littera del signor Ferrando Gonzaga de la Presa de Tunisi, con tutte la particularita que sono seguite de poi* (1535).

GORRINGE, H. H.: *Tunis in 1878*, art. in 'Nation,' xxvi. 289.

—— *French Occupation of Tunis*, art. in 'Nation,' xxxii. 311.

GRÄBERG DA HEMSÖ, Count J. C., formerly Swedish and Sardinian Consul in Morocco: *Notizia intorno alla famosa opera istorica d'Ibn-u-Khaldùn, filosofo africano del secolo xiv.* Firenze, 1834. See also IBN-KHALDUN.

GRAHAM, ALEXANDER: *Notes on Tunis*, art. of 3 cols., with illustrations, in 'Builder,' January 10, 1885.

—— *Remains of the Roman Occupation of North Africa, with special reference to Tunisia*, London, 1886. 4to., pp. 32, with a map, 17 full-page illustrations and plans of which six are folding, and four illustrations in the text. Extracted from the 'Transactions' (vol. ii., new series) of the 'Royal Institute of British Architects.' Sequel to a similar paper referring to Algeria, 1885.

'Valuable and instructive papers.'—*Playfair.*

GRAMAYE, I. B.: *Africae illustratae libri decem, in quibus Barbaria gentesque ejus ut olim, et nunc describuntur*. Tornaci Nerviorum, 1622. 4to., 2 vols. The part referring to Tunis occurs in vol. ii., pp. 77 to 125.

Sir R. L. Playfair writes: 'This is a mere plagiarism of Marmol and Leo' (see those names). See also 'Purchas his Pilgrimes,' ii., 1561.

GRASSET, D.: *Rapport à M. le Gouverneur-Général de l'Algérie sur l'instruction publique en Tunisie*, Paris, 1878. From the 'Revue Africaine,' xxii., 19.

GRASSET ST-SAUVEUR, J., Vice-consul dans le Levant: *Description des principaux Peuples de l'Afrique, contenant le détail de leurs Mœurs, Coutumes, Usages, Habillements, Fêtes, Mariages, Supplices, Funérailles, etc. Accompagnée d'un tableau représentant les différents Peuples de cette partie du Monde, chacun dans le costume qui lui est propre, etc.*, Paris, an vi. de la Républ. 67 p. in-4, et un tableau.

GREAVES, JOSEPH: *Journal of a Visit to some parts of Tunis*, forms the Appendix (53 pages) to 'Christian Researches in Syria and the Holy Land,' &c., by William Jowett, London, Seeley & Son, 1825. 8vo. Reprinted by same publishers in following year. See also JOWETT.

GREENHOW, R.: *History .. of Tripoli, with some accounts of the other*

Barbary States, Richmond, U.S., 1835.

GROS, E. See DION CASSIUS.

GROSJEAN: *Le Télégraphe en Tunisie*, art. in 'Annales Télégraphiques,' 1860, iii.

GROTE, GEORGE: *A History of Greece.* Fourth Edition, with portrait, maps, and plans, &c. London, 1872. 8vo., 10 vols. Other editions: 1846, 1854, 1862, 1869. Translated into French by A. L. de Sadous as: *Histoire de la Grèce*, Paris, 1864-67. 8vo., 19 vols. Maps and plans. Into German by N. N. W. Meissner, as: *Geschichte Griechenlands*, Leipzig, 1850-55. 8vo., 6 vols. Contains 'some sensible remarks' concerning Carthage.

GUBERNATIS, ENRICO DE: *Lettere sulla Tunisia, &c.*, Firenze, 1867.

—— *Osservazioni sulla Cartografia del Sähel (Tunisia)*, art. in 'Bollettino della Società Geografica Italiana,' Firenze, 1868, Anno i., Fas. i., pp. 243 to 249, map.

GUÉRIN, V.: *Voyage archéologique dans la Régence de Tunis, &c., ouvrage accompagné d'une grande carte de la régence et d'une planche reproduisant la célèbre inscription bilingue de Thugga, &c.*, Paris, H. Plon, 1862. Large 8vo., 2 vols.

One of the most important works on Tunisia, absolutely indispensable for the traveller. It is a plain narrative of the author's journey through the greater part of the Regency in 1860, undertaken at the expense of M. le Duc de Luynes. The discovery and deciphering of inscriptions being the principal object, most of the pages are devoted to this subject. Apart from this, the work contains much general information, which, allowing for changes introduced since the French occupation, is invariably reliable. The alphabetical index, confined to names of places, ancient and modern, might be more exact and comprehensive. Before publishing his book, the author gave a syllabus of the principal results of his journey in 'Nouvelles Annales des Voyages,' Dec. 1860.

M. Guérin's *Voyage* was noticed by M. E. Reclus in 'Revue des Deux-Mondes,' March 1, 1863; by M. de Circourt in 'Nouvelles Annales des Voyages,' 1863, ii.; and by M. Foulain de Bossay in 'Bulletin de la Société de Géographie,' 1864, 5 série, viii.

GUÉRIN, V.: *Établissements catholiques dans la Régence de Tunis*, art. containing information about Tunis, Gouletta, Carthage, Soussa, Mahedia, Sfax, Porto Farina, Bizerta, and Djerba, in 'Bulletin de l'Œuvre des Écoles de l'Orient,' January, 1865.

—— *Utilité d'une Mission archéologique permanente à Carthage*, art. in 'Exploration,' May 12, 1881.

—— *Gabès*, Idem, August 18, 1881.

—— *Kairouan*, art. in 'Bulletin de la Société de Géographie,' 4 série, xx., 425; art. with same title in 'Exploration,' Sept. 1, 1881.

—— *La France catholique en Tunisie, à Malte et en Tripolitaine*, Tours, 1886. 8vo., frontispiece.

GUERNSEY, A. H.: *Explorations at Carthage*, art. in 'Harper's Mag. xxii., 766.

GUEST, MONTAGUE, M.P.: *The Tunisian Question and Bizerta*, London, Chiffenel & Co., 1881.

GUILLERMUS DE NANGIS: *Historiæ Francorum ab Anno Christi DCCCC. ad Ann. M. CC. LXXXV. scriptores veteres xi., &c.*, Francoforti, apud A. Wecheli heredes Claudium, M.D.XCVI. Fol. Contains the history of Saint-Louis' expedition to Tunis. See also JOINVILLE.

GUITER, A., Lieutenant: *Les Ruines de Tiboursek, en Tunisie*, art. in 'Nouvelles Annales des Voyages,' 1862, ii., 115.

—— *Exploration en Tunisie*, art. in 'Revue Africaine,' iv., 422.

—— *De Tunis à Soussa*, arts. in 'Touriste,' Dec. 1871, and following numbers.

GÜNTHER, ALBERT: *On the reptiles and fishes collected by the Rev. B. Tristram in Northern Africa*, 'Proc. Zool. Soc., London,' 1859, p. 469.

GURNEY, H.: *Punic Inscriptions on the Site of Carthage*, art. in. 'Archæologia,' xxx., 111.

GUSTAVINI, G.: *Istoria di Mons. Uberto Foglietta, nobile genovese, della sacra lega contra Selim, e dell' impresa del Gerbi Soccosa d' Oran*, Impresa del Pignon di Tunigi, etc., Genova, 1596. 4to.

GUYON, Dr. J. L.: *Étude sur les Eaux thermales de la Tunisie, &c.*, Paris, 1864. 8vo., pp. 69.

—— *Histoire chronologique des épidémies du nord de l'Afrique*, Alger, 1855. 8vo.

GUYOT, YVES: *Application de l' 'Act-Torrens' en Tunisie*, arts. in 'Revue Géographique Internationale,' Oct. and Dec. 1886.

GUYS, CHARLES: *Lettre*, in 'Bulletin de la Société de Géographie,' 1 série, v., 548.

'Cette lettre rappelle les souvenirs historiques de la Régence et est accompagnée d'une note sur l'Ile de Zerbi' (or Djerba).—A. DEMARSY.

GUYS, HENRY, ancien Consul de France: *Recherches sur la destruction du Christianisme dans l'Afrique septentrionale, &c.*, Paris, 1865. 8vo. pp. 32.

HAKLUYT, RICHARD: *The Principal Navigations, Voyages, Traffiques and Discoveries of the English Nation, &c., within the compasse of these 1600 yeres,&c.*, London, George Bishop, 1599. 4to., 3 vols. The second volume contains: '*The Voyage of Henry, the fourth King of England, to Tunis in Barbarie; and Epitaph of Peter Read, in Saint Peters Church, Norwich, who was knighted by Charles the first at the winning of Tunis in the yeere of our Lord 1538.*' The compilation of R. Hakluyt is in course of republication by Messrs. E. & G. Goldsmid of Edinburgh.

HALY O'HANLY, STANISLAS: *La Chute de Carthage, poëme en 8 chants*, Paris, 1818. 8vo.

HAMAKER, H. A.: *Diatriba philologico-critica monumentorum aliquot punicorum interpretationem exhibens, &c.*, Lugd. Batav., 1822. 4to., pp. 72, 3 plates. To which is generally added:

—— *Periculum animadversionum archæologicarum ad cippos punicos humbertianos musei antiquarii*, Lud. Batav., 1822. 4to.

—— *Miscellanea Phœnicia, sive Commentarii . . . de Punicæ gentis, rebus, lingua, etc., ex inscript. illustr.*, Lud. Batav., 1828. 4to., pp. x. and 368, 3 plates. Analysed by M. SYLV. DE SACY (see that name) in 'Journal des Savants,' 1829, p. 736.

HANNEGGER. See SAKAKINI.

HANNO, the Carthaginian: Περίπλους. *The Periplus of Hanno* has been frequently printed with Greek and Latin text, and translated into the leading languages of Europe, *inter alia*, by CHATEAUBRIAND (see that name) in his *Essai sur les Révolutions*. See also BAYLE, P., BOUGAINVILLE, KANNGIESSER, QUATREMÈRE DE QUINCY, WALCKENAER.

HARRIS, JOHN, A.M.: *Navigantium atque Itinerantium Bibliotheca*, or a *complete collection of voyages and travels, consisting of above four hundred of the most authentic writers; beginning with Hackluit, Purchas, &c., in English; Ramusio in Italian; Thevenot, &c., in French; De Bry and Grynæi 'Novus Orbis' in Latin; the Dutch East India Company in Dutch; and continued with others of note,&c.&c.*, London, 1705. 2 vols., folio, pp. 862 and 928; [App.] 56.

HARTMANN, J. MICH.: *Commentatio de Geographia Africae Edrisiana in cert. liter. civium Acad. Georg. Aug. praem. ornata*, Göttingae, Dieterich, 1792. 4to. See also EL-EDRISI.

HASE, M.: *L'Établissement romain en Afrique*, art. in 'Revue Africaine,' 1871, xv.

HAUSER: *Wer veranlasste die Berufung der Vandalen nach Africa?* Dorpat, 1842. 4to.

HAVET, E.: *Cyprien, Évêque de Carthage*, art. in 'Revue des Deux-Mondes,' Sept. 1885. See also CYPRIEN.

HEBENSTREIT, J. E., Professor of Medicine at the University of Leipzig: *De Antiquitatibus Romanis per Africam repertis*, Leipzig, 1733. 4to.
'Dissertation latine peu développée et peu instructive.'—V. GUÉRIN, *Voyage*, i., p. xii.

—— *Vier Berichte von seiner auf Befehl Friedrich Augusts I. im Jahre 1732 in Begleitung einiger anderer Gelehrten und Künstler auf den Afrikanischen Küsten nach Algier, Tunis und Tripolis angestellten Reise.*

—— *Voyage à Alger, Tunis et Tripoli, entrepris aux frais et par ordre de Frédéric-Auguste, Roi de Pologne, en 1732, par J. E. Hebenstreit*, in 'Nouvelles Annales des Voyages,' 1830, tome ii. de l'année, pp. 5 to 90.
'C'est la traduction de quatre lettres adressées en allemand au roi de Pologne, et publiées après la mort de l'auteur, par Bernoulli, " Sammlung kleiner Reisen," Berlin et Leipzig, 1780. A partir de la p. 60, commence le récit du voyage de Hebenstreit à Tunis. On y trouve des renseignements sur les anciens aqueducs, le port, le gouvernement, les noms et distances des villes et ruines le long de la côte, la population, le commerce, les usages, les productions, etc.'—A. DEMARSY.

HEEREN, A. H. L.: *Ideen über die Politik, den Verkehr und den Handel der vornehmsten Völker der alten Welt*, 3 Theile, Göttingen, 1793-1812. 8vo. Also *Dritte Ausgabe*, Göttingen, 1815. 8vo. Translations:

HEEREN, A. H. L.: *Historical Researches into the Politics . . . of the Carthaginians, &c.*, Oxford, 1838.

—— *Idées sur la Politique et le Commerce des Anciens, traduit par W. Suckau.* 8vo., 6 vols.

—— *Idées sur les Relations politiques et commerciales des anciens Peuples de l'Afrique*, Paris, An viii. (1799). 8vo., 2 vols.

—— *Manuel de l'Histoire ancienne, traduit par Thurot*, 1836. 8vo.

HENDREICH, CHRISTOPHORUS: *Carthago, sive Carthaginensium Respublica, quam ex totius ferè antiquitatis ruderibus primus instaurare conatur C. H.*, Francofurti ad Oderam, 1664. 8vo.

HENIN, Baron ET. F. D': *Mémoire concernant le système de paix et de guerre que les puissances européennes pratiquent à l'égard des Régences barbaresques.* Translated from the Italian, printed at Venice in 1787. 12mo.—PLAYFAIR.

HENNEBERT, E., Capitaine du Génie: *Histoire d'Annibal*, Paris, Impr. Imp., 1870. 8vo., atlas. Carthage, its history, architecture, topography, fortification, coins, &c., are very fully treated.

HENTY, G. A.: *The Young Carthaginian; or, A Struggle for Empire. A Story of the Times of Hannibal.* London, Blackie & Son, 1886. 8vo., 16 full-page illustrations by C. J. Staniland, R.I.

HERBELOT, D', VISDELOU, C., et GALAND, A.: *Bibliothèque orientale, ou Dictionnaire universel, contenant généralement tout ce qui regarde la Connaissance des peuples de l'Orient, leurs Histoires et Traditions véritables ou fabuleuses, leurs Religions,*

Sectes et Politique, leurs Sciences et leurs Arts, les Vies et Actions remarquables de tous leurs Saints, etc., Maestricht, 1776. Fol. Le Supplément de MM. Visdelou et Galand est de 1780.

HERBERT, Lady: *A Search after Sunrise, or Algeria in 1871*, London, Richard Bentley, 1872. 8vo., illustrated. The last chapter is devoted to Tunis and Carthage.

HÉRISSON, Comte d': *Relation d'une Mission archéologique en Tunisie*, Paris, 1881. 4to.

HERODOTUS: *Historiarum libri novem. Nova editio stereotypa.* Curavit F. Palm. Lipside, 1839. 8vo., 3 tom. Vol. i., p. 461. A circumnavigation of the coast of Africa by orders of Neco—a doubtful story. i., 232. Lotophagi, consumers of the lotus. i., 540. Wine made from the lotus. Several notices of the Carthaginians.

HERVILLIERS, E. C. DE L'. See CAILLETTE DE L'HERVILLIERS.

HESSE-WARTEGG, ERNST VON: *Tunis: Land und Leute.* Mit 40 Illustrationen und 4 Karten, Wien, Hartleben, 1882. 8vo. Done into English as:

—— *Tunis: the Land and the People.* With twenty-two illustrations, London, Chatto & Windus, 1882. 8vo., pp. x. and 292.

HJELT, O. I.: *Korsika och Tunis*, Stockholm, 1882. 8vo., pp. 192.

HODGSON, W. B., late U.S. Consul at Tunis: *Notes on Northern Africa, the Sahara and the Soudan*, New York, 1844. 8vo., pp. 107.

HOLUB, E.: *Die Colonisation Africa's. Die Franzosen in Tunis*, Wien, Hölder, 1881. 8vo.

HOUDAS, O., et BASSET, RENÉ, Professeurs à l'École des Lettres d'Alger: *Epigraphie tunisienne avec carte et planches*, Alger, 1882. pp. 40. Noticed in 'Revue Critique,' February 12, 1883.

HOUDOY, J.: *Tapisseries représentant la Conqueste du Royaulme de Thunes par l'Empereur Charles-Quint. Histoire et Documents Inédits par J. Houdoy*, Lille, Imprimerie L. Danel, 1873. 8vo., pp. 30 and 8, issue 210 copies.

The documents refer to the Tapestries executed in 1546 by Guillaume Pannemaker of Brussels from the designs of Jehan Vermay, who accompanied Charles V. on his expedition. They are preserved in the Royal Palace at Madrid, and have been photographed by Laurent.

HUBERSON, G.: *L'Expédition de Tunise*, Paris, 1884. 12mo., pp. 370.

HUGELMANN, G.: *Le Conflit tunisien. Lettre à S. E. M. de Moustiers, ministre de nos affaires étrangères*, Paris (1868). 8vo., pp. 23.

HUGHES, THOS. PATRICK, B. D., M.R.A.S.: *A Dictionary of Islam, being a Cyclopædia of . . . . the Muhammadan Religion, with numerous illustrations*, London, W. H. Allen & Co., 1885. Large 8vo., pp. vii. and 750.

HUGONNET: *La Question africaine et le Prince de Bismarck*, art. in 'Revue Générale,' February 15, 1885.

HUMBERT, Major J. E., Dutch officer: *Notice sur quatre Cippes sépulcraux et de deux fragments découverts en 1817 sur le sol de l'antique Carthage*, La Haye, 1821. Fol. There is also a plan of Carthage by Major Humbert reproduced by DUREAU DE LA MALLE (see that name).

HURD, WILLIAM, D.D.: *A New Universal History of the Religious Rites, Ceremonies, and Customs of the World, &c., including the Ancient and Present State of Religion among the Jews, Egyptians, Carthaginians, &c.*, Newcastle-upon-Tyne, 1812. 4to.

HUTTON, CATHERINE: *The Tour of Africa, containing a concise account of all the Countries ... hitherto visited by Europeans, &c., selected from the best authorities and arranged by Catherine Hutton*, London, Baldwin, &c., 1819 to 1821. 8vo., 3 vols., 3 maps. Chapts. 25 and 26 of vol. iii. are devoted to Tunisia, with an account of the visit of Queen Caroline to Tunis.

IBN-ABI-DINAR. Noted by M. Cherbonneau as among the best Arab writers to be consulted for descriptions of Tunis.

IBN-BATUTA. See LEE, S.

IBN-CHEMMA. Noted by M. Cherbonneau as among the best Arab writers to be consulted for descriptions of Tunis.

IBN-CHESSAT. Noted by M. Cherbonneau as among the best Arab writers to be consulted for descriptions of Tunis.

IBN-EL-DYN. See AVEZAC.

IBN-HAUKAL: *The Oriental Geography of Ibn-Haukal, an Arabian Traveller of the 10th Century, translated by Sir W. Ouseley*, London, 1800. 4to.

—— *Description de l'Afrique par Ibn-Haucal, traduite de l'Arabe par M. le Baron de Slane*, 1842. 8vo.

—— *Note sur Tunis dans une Description de l'Afrique d'Ibn-Haugal, traduite par le baron Slane*, in 'Journal Asiatique,' 1842, 1 série, xiii., 177. Also in separate form 1842. 8vo.

IBN-KHALDOUN: *Histoire de l'Afrique sous la Dynastie des Aghlabites, &c. Texte arabe accompagné d'une Traduction française par Noël des Vergers*, Paris, 1841. 8vo.

—— *Histoire des Berbères et des Dynasties musulmanes de l'Afrique septentrionale. Traduite de l'Arabe par le Baron de Slane*, Alger, 1852-56. 8vo., 4 vols. Also Alger, 1847-51. 4to., 2 vols.

'On trouve dans cet ouvrage l'histoire de plusieurs des dynasties qui ont régné sur Tunis, et notamment de celle des Hafssites.'—A. DEMARSY.

'The original work is a general history of the Mohammedan world, and is unsurpassed in Arabic literature as a masterpiece of historical composition. It was printed at Bulac, in 7 vols. royal 8vo., in A.H. 1284. He was a native of Tunis; taught at Tlemçen; was first the captive and subsequently the friend of Timur, and died at Cairo in A.D. 1406.'—PLAYFAIR.

IBN-KHALDOUN: *Autobiographie d'Ibn-Khaldoun, traduite de l'arabe par Mac Guckin de Slane*, Paris, Imp. Royale, 1844. 8vo. See also GRÄBERG DE HEMSÖ and MERCIER.

IBN-KONFOND. Noted by M. Cherbonneau as one of the best Arab writers to be consulted for description of Tunis.

IBN-MUHAMMED-AL-WAZZAN. See LEO AFRICANUS.

IBN-OMAR-EL-TOUNSY, Cheikh MOHAMMED: *Voyage au Ouaddy, traduit de l'arabe par le Dr. Perron, Directeur de l'École de Médecine du Caire, ouvrage accompagné de Cartes et de Planches, et du Portrait du Cheikh*, Paris, 1851. 8vo., pp. lxxv. and 752. In chapt. v. is an account of his journey from Mourzouk to Tripoli, thence to Djerba, Sfax, El-Djem, and so to Tunis.

IBN-OUDRÂNE. See CHERBONNEAU.

ILLYRICUS, MATTHIAS FRANCOWITZ (or FLACCUS ILLYRICUS): *Historia Certaminum inter Romanos Episcopos et Sextam Carthaginensem Synodum, Africanasque Ecclesias, de Primatu seu Potestate Papæ, bonâ fide ex authenticis Monumentis collecta, &c.*, Bas, 1554. 8vo.

INCOGNITO, Bey: *Trois Mois de Campagne double en Tunisie*, Paris, 1881. 8vo., pp. 72.

JACKSON, J.: *Account of the Ruins of Carthage*, art. in 'Archæologia,' xv., 145.

JAL, A.: *L'Antique Port de Carthage et les navires antiques*, notice on the work of M. BEULÉ (see that name) in 'Dict. critique de Biographie et d'Histoire,' Paris, 1872, p. 321.

JALLOT, le Sieur: *Nouveau Voyage fait au Levant ès années 1731 et 1732. Contenant les descriptions d'Alger, Tunis, Tripoly de Barbarie, &c.*, Paris, 1722. 12mo., pp. 354.

JAMESON, Professor; WILSON, JAMES; and MURRAY, HUGH: *Narrative of Discovery and Adventure in Africa, from the earliest Ages to the present Time, with illustrations of the Geology, Mineralogy, and Zoology. With a Map, Plans of Routes, and Engravings*. Edinburgh, Oliver & Boyd, 1830. 8vo.

JANSON, C. W., of the State of Rhode Island: *A View of the present Condition of the States of Barbary; or an Account of the Climate, Soil, Produce, Population, Manufactures, and Naval and Military Strength of Morocco, Fez, Algiers, Tripoli, and Tunis. Also a Description of their Mode of Warfare; interspersed with Anecdotes of their cruel treatment of Christian Captives.* Illustrated by a Hydro-Geographical Map drawn by J. J. Asheton, 1816. 12mo.

JAUBERT, P. A.: *Ruines de Carthage*, art. in 'Journal Asiatique.' 1 série, i. Jaubert has also translated EL-EDRISI (see that name).

JEZIERSKI, L. See LE FAURE.

JOHNSTON, KEITH: *Africa, by the late Keith Johnson, F.R.G.S.* Third Edit. London, E. Stanford, 1884. 8vo. The Regency of Tunis, with two woodcuts, occupies pp. 59 to 68.

JOINVILLE, JEHAN, Sire de: *Histoire de Saint Louis. Les annales de son règne par Guillaume de Nangis. Sa vie et ses miracles par le confesseur de la reine Marguerite*, Paris, Imp. Roy., 1761. Fol., maps. An account of the expedition against Tunis, with a list of the peers and others who took part in it. See also GUILLERMUS DE NANGIS.

JOUAULT, A.: *Les Ruines de Carthage, et la Chapelle de Saint-Louis*, art. in 'Revue de l'Orient,' 1853, 2 série, xiv., 123.

JOURNAULT, LÉON: *Le Protectorat tunisien*, art. in 'Revue Politique et Littéraire,' 1881.

—— *La Tunisie en 1883*, arts. in 'Revue Politique et Littéraire,' June 23, July 21, 1883.

JOWETT, Rev. WILLIAM: *Christian Researches in the Mediterranean, from MDCCCXV. to MDCCCXX., in furtherance of the objects of the Church Missionary Society, &c.*, London, L. B. Seeley, 1822. 8vo., 1 map. The special reference to Tunis is brief, but much of the vol. refers to the state of religion in that country. Reprinted by same publishers in 1824. See also GREAVES.

JUDAS, DR. A. C.: *Essai sur la Langue phénicienne avec deux inscriptions puniques inédites*, Paris, 1842. 8vo., 8 engravings.

—— *Étude démonstrative de la langue phénicienne et de la langue libyque*, Paris, 1847.

—— *Sur diverses médailles de l'Afrique septentrionale, avec des légendes puniques.* 'Bull. Archéol. de l'Athen. Franc.', 1855, p. 104, and l. c. 1856, pp. 5 and 13.

—— *Lettre à M. Cherbonneau, sur les inscriptions numidico-puniques, libyennes ou berbères et palmyréniennes, insérées dans les deux premiers Annuaires de la Société.* 'Ann. Soc. Arch., Const.', 1858, vol. iii., p. 1.

JUDAS, DR. A. C.: *Sur un Tarif des Taxes pour les Sacrifices, en langue punique, trouvé à Carthage et analogue à celui de Marseille*, Paris, 1861. 8vo.

—— *Sur divers Médaillons d'argent attribués soit à Carthage, soit à Panorme, ou aux armées puniques en Sicile*, Paris, 1869. 8vo.

—— *Nouvelle Analyse de l'Inscription libyco-punique de Thugga*, Paris, 1869. 8vo.

—— *Nouvelle Analyse de l'Inscription phénicienne de Marseille*, Paris, 1857. 4to.

JULIEN, FÉLIX : *Tunis et Carthage, souvenirs d'une station sur la côte de l'Afrique*, art. in 'Revue Contemporaine,' 1864, xlii., 388.

JULIUS CÆSAR. See CÆSAR.

JUSSERAND, JULES : *La Régence de Tunis et le protectorat français*, art. in 'Revue des Deux-Mondes,' Oct. 1, 1882.

> M. Louis Monery remarks: 'L'auteur de ce très remarquable travail, un Forézien, M. Jules Jusserand, de Saint-Haon-le-Châtel (Loire), avait été envoyé en mission spéciale à Tunis. Il est aujourd'hui (1886) sous-directeur au ministère des affaires étrangères et supplée cette année M. Guillaume Guizot dans son cours du Collège de France.'—*L'Intermédiaire*, xix., 273.

KANNGIESSER, PET. FR.: *Hanno's Periplus*, art. of 9 cols. in 'Allgemeine Encyclopädie von Ersch und Gruber,' Leipzig, 1828. See also HANNO.

KAYSER. See EXIGA.

KENNEDY, Capt. J. C.: *Algeria and Tunis in 1845: an Account of a Journey made through the two Regencies by Viscount Fielding and Capt. Kennedy*, London, Colburn, 1846. 8vo., 2 vols. Reviewed in 'Dub. Univ. Mag.', xxviii., 285 to 98.

KERR, ROBERT, F. R. S.: *A General History and Collection of Voyages and Travels*, Edinburgh, W. Blackwood, 1811 to 24. 8vo., 18 vols., maps. In vol. xviii. is a sketch of the rise and fall of Carthage.

KERSANTÉ, Vice-Président de Comice Agricole : *La Tunisie au point de vue politique, agricole et commercial. Impressions de Voyage. L'Afrique au XIXe siècle*. Paris, 1871. 8vo.

KING, S. P.: *Duplicity or Diplomacy, the last phase of the Tunisian Question*, London, 1881. 8vo.

KIVA: *La Mer intérieure et le Commandant Roudaire* (see that name), art. in 'Spectateur Militaire,' Nov. 1, 1884.

KLUGER, F. G. See ARISTOTELES.

KOBELT, W.: *Reiseerinnerungen aus Algerien und Tunis*, Frankfurt am Main, 1885. 8vo., pp. 480, 13 plates and 11 woodcuts in text.

—— *Die Säugethiere Nordafrikas*, 'Zoolog. Garten, J.,' 1886, xxvii., No. 6-8.

KOPP, U. F.: *Bemerkungen über einige punische Steinschriften aus Karthago*, Heidelberg, 1826.

KRAKLI, M. L. See COSSON.

KREMER, ALFR. DE: *Description de l'Afrique par un Géographe arabe anonyme du 6e siècle de l'hégire. Texte arabe publié par la première fois par Alfr. de Kremer*, Vienne, 1852. Lar. 8vo. (Braumüller). Also:

—— *Vortrag über ein vorgelegtes Druckwerk: Description de l'Afrique. &c.* (Aus den Sitzungsberichten 1852 der K. Akad. der Wissensch.) Lex. 8. Wien, 1852 (Braumüller).

LABAT, Le Père: *Mémoires du Chevalier d'Arvieux, contenant ses voyages à Constantinople, dans l'Asie, la Syrie, la Palestine, l'Egypte et la Barbarie, recueillis par le père Labat*, Paris, 1735. 12mo., 6 vols.

LABERGE, ALBERT DE: *En Tunisie. Récit de l'Expédition française,*

Paris, Firmin Didot, 1881. 8vo., pp. 378, map.

    In the first part the French expedition and its causes are described; in the second the author's journey, general aspect of the country, soil, races, agriculture, government, and religion; the third part is devoted to a history of the different denominations—Carthaginian, Roman, Byzantine, Arab, Turkish, &c. See 'Le Livre', Sept. 1881.

LACOMBE, JACQUES: *Scipion à Carthage: opéra en 3 actes*, An iii. (1795). 8vo., pp. 62. The music is by Méreaux.

LA CROIX, FRÉDÉRIC: *Notice sur la carte de l'Afrique*, Paris, 1864. 4to.

    'M. Lacroix, a young and studious officer of Engineers, who died in 1851, commenced the work which M. de Champlouis (see that name) finished.'—PLAYFAIR.

LACROIX, PHÉROTÉE DE, Professeur de Géographie à Lyon: *Relation universelle de l'Afrique ancienne et moderne*, Lyon, 1688. 12mo., 4 vols. Also Paris, 1689, 12mo., 4 vols.; and Lyon, 1713, 2 vols., maps and illustrations.

    Quérard observes: 'Cet ouvrage est tiré en grande partie de celui de DAPPER' (see that name).

LA FAYE, P. J. B. DE, Mathurin: *État des Royaumes de Barbarie, Tripoly, Tunis et Alger, contenant l'histoire naturelle et politique de ce pays, etc., avec la tradition de l'Église pour le rachat et le soulagement des captifs*, Rouen, 1703. Also La Haye, 1704; Rouen, Machoel, 1731; all 12mo.

—— *Voyage pour la Rédemption des Captifs aux Royaumes d'Alger et de Tunis, fait en 1720, par les Pères François Comelin, Philémon de La Motte et Joseph Bernard*, Paris, Sevestre, 1721. 12mo., 1 illustration, edited by P. J. B. de La Faye. Translated by J. Morgan as:

—— *Voyage to Algiers and Tunis, &c.,* London, 1735. 8vo., pp. 10, 146 and 158, folding maps and illustrations.

LA FAYE, P. J. E. DE,: *Relation du Voyage pour Rédemption des Captifs aux Royaumes de Tunis et d'Alger, en 1723, 1725, par J. de la Faye*, Paris, 1726. 12mo.

LAGRANGE, O.: *Souvenirs de voyage — Algérie et Tunisie — Correspondance*, Langres, 1868. 12mo., pp. 409, autograph.

LAMALLE. See DUREAU DE LA MALLE.

LA MOTTE, P. DE. See LA FAYE.

LANDAS, Commandant: *Port et oasis du bassin des chotes tunisiens*, Paris, 1886. 4to., pp. 72, 2 maps.

    'This gives an account of the artesian well at Oued el-Melah, and of the port it is intended to create there.'—PLAYFAIR.

LANESSAN, J. L. DE: *L'Expansion coloniale de la France. Étude économique, politique et géographique sur les établissements français d'outremer*, Paris, F. Alcan, 1886. 8vo., 19 maps. Contains a notice of Tunisia. See 'Le Livre,' Oct., 1886, p. 526.

—— *La Tunisie, avec une carte en couleurs*, Paris, Félix Alcan, 1887. Large 8vo., pp. 268. Noticed in 'Le Livre,' August, 1887, p. 426: 'C'est un rapport après enquête.'

—— *Bizerte, port militaire*, art. in 'Revue Géographique Internationale,' May, 1887.

LANGLÈS. See GALLAND.

LANSING, J. G., D.D.: *An Arabic Manual*, Chicago, 1886. 8vo., pp. 180.

LAPLAICHE, A.: *Algérie, Tunisie, esquisse géographique*, Paris, 1885. 12mo.

LATASTE, F.: *Étude de la fauna des vertébrés de Barbarie*, 'Soc. L. Bord.' 1885. 4ᵉ sér., vol. ix., pp. 129-299.

    'An exhaustive paper on the fauna of N. Africa.'—PLAYFAIR.

—— *Catalogue provisoire des mammifères apélagiques sauvages de Barbarie [Algérie — Tunisie — Maroc]*, Extrait des 'Actes Soc. Linn.,' Bordeaux, 1886, xxxix., 129.

LATOUR, ANTOINE DE: *Voyage de S. A. R. Mgr. le Duc de Montpensier à Tunis, en Égypte, en Turquie et en Grèce, en* 1845, Paris, 1847. 8vo., with a folio atlas of 32 plates in two colours.

LA TOUR, S. DE.   SÉRAN DE LA TOUR.

LATRONNE.   See DUREAU DE LA MALLE.

LAUGEL, A.: *The French Occupation of Tunis*, art. in 'Nation,' xxxiii., 70.

(LAUGIER DE TASSY): *État chrétien et politique des Royaumes de Tunis, d'Alger, de Tripoli et de Maroc, contenant l'histoire naturelle et politique des peuples de ces contrées, la manière dont les Turcs y traitent leurs esclaves, comme on les rachète, et diverses aventures*, Rouen, 1703. 12mo. And La Haye, 1704.

'Cet ouvrage promet par son titre beaucoup plus qu'il ne donne, et ne renferme que des notions très superficielles.'

—— *Histoire des États barbaresques qui exercent la piraterie, contenant l'origine, les révolutions et l'état présent des Royaumes d'Alger, de Tunis, de Tripoli et de Maroc, avec leurs forces, leurs revenus, leur politique et leur commerce, par un auteur qui a résidé plusieurs années avec caractère public, traduit de l'Anglais par Royer de Prebadé*, Paris, Imbert et Hérissant, 1737. 12mo., 2 vols.

'C'est une retraduction augmentée de l'ouvrage de Laugier de Tussy (*sic*), qu'un anglais s'était approprié. Dans cet état, dit Boucher de la Richarderie, il est principalement recommandable sous les rapports de l'économie politique et de l'état militaire et maritime des trois régences. Cet ouvrage fut encore réédité sous le titre :

—— *État général et particulier de Royaume et Ville d'Alger, de son gouvernement, de ses forces de terre et de mer, par Leroi*, La Haye, 1750. Petit in-8º. 'Il est augmenté de notes tirées du dictionnaire de Moreri (see that name) et del' "État chrétien et politique des royaumes de Tunis, d'Alger, de Tripoli et de Maroc, imprimé à Rouen en 1703," et cité plus haut.'—A. DEMARSY.

LAUTURE, E. DE.   See ESCAYRAC.

LAVIGERIE, Cardinal : *Mission de Carthage et de Tunis*, letters in 'Annales de la Propagation de la Foi,' March and May, 1885, 1 portrait and 3 views.

—— *De l'utilité d'une Mission archéologique permanente à Carthage, Lettre à M. le Secrétaire perpétuel de l'Académie des Inscriptions et Belles Lettres*, Alger, 1881. 8vo., 62 pages of letterpress, 64 pages, 3 plates, 1 plan of Carthage, printed for private circulation.   See also CROZALS and DE CAMPON.

—— *Officia propria provinciæ ecclesiastica algerianæ ac carthaginensis et tunetani vicariatus . . . de mandato Ill. et Rev. D.D. Caroli Martialis Allemand-Lavigerie, archiepiscopus, etc.*, Turonibus, 1882. 18mo Pars hiemalis, pp. 148 ; Pars æstiva pp. 90.

LAVIGNE, G. : *Percement de l'Isthme de Gabés*, Paris, 1869. 8vo.

LE BLANT, EDMOND, Membre de l'Institut : *Communication à la Société des Antiquaires sur un Vase de plomb trouvé à Carthage*, Paris, 1867. See also FAULTRIER.

LE BON, Dr. GUSTAVE : *La Civilisation des Arabes. Ouvrage illustré de* 10 *chromolithographies,* 4 *cartes et* 366 *gravures*, Paris, Firmin-Didot et Cie., 1884. 4to.

LEE, SAMUEL, D.D. : *The Travels of Ibn-Batuta, translated from the abridged manuscript copies in the Public Library of Cambridge.* Printed for the Oriental Translation Committee, London, 1829. 4to., pp. xviii. and 242.

    Chap. i. treats of Tangiers, Tilimsān, Milyāna, Algiers, Bijāya, Kosantina, Būna, Tūnis, Susa, Safākus, Kābis, Tripoli, &c.

    'Ibn-Batuta left his native city, Tangier, about 1324, and spent two years in making his journey.'—PLAYFAIR.

LEE CHILDE, Mme.: *En Tunisie*, art. in 'Revue des Deux Mondes,' August 15, 1884.

LE FAURE, A.: *Le Voyage en Tunisie . . . . précédé d'une préface de M. L. Jezierski, avec une vue de Kairouan et le portrait de M. le Faure*, Paris, 1882. 4to., pp. 69.

LEFÈVRE, ED.: *Liste des Coléoptères recueillis en Tunisie en 1883 par M. A. Letourneux, membre de la mission de l'exploration scientifique de la Tunisie, dressée par M. Ed. Lefèvre, ancien président de la société entomologique de France, &c., avec le concours de MM. L. Fairmaire, de Marseul et Dr. Senac*, Paris, Imprimerie Nationale, 1885. 8vo., pp. 16.

LEGRAND, AD., Attaché au Ministère de la Guerre: *La Tunisie, étude historique*, Paris, 1873. 8vo., pp. 63.

LEGUEST, l'Abbé: *Essai sur la formation et la décomposition des racines arabes*, Alger, 1856. 8vo., pp. 31.

LELEWELA, JOACHIMA: *Odkrycia Karthagów i Greków na Oceanie Atlanckim, w Warszawie, w Drubarni XX*. Püarów, 1821. 8vo., pp. 177, 2 maps. Translated into German as:

—— *Die Entdeckungen der Carthager und Griechen auf dem atlantischen Ocean, von Joachim Lelewel, mit einem Vorworte von Professor Ritter*, Berlin, Schlesinger, 1831. 8vo., pp. xiv. and 145, 2 maps.

LEMARCHAND, MAURICE: *Club Alpin Français—Section de Carthage— Renseignements sur Tunis et ses Environs*, Tunis, B. Borrel, 1886.

    This small pamphlet of fourteen pages compiled by M. Lemarchand, Judge at the French tribunals, and Secretary to the Club, contains succinct but most useful notes as to what should be seen at Tunis and other places in the Regency.

LEO AFRICANUS: *Leoni Africani Totius Africæ Discriptionis*, Lib. viii. Leyden, 1682. 8vo.

    'This work was originally written in Arabic, then translated into Italian by the author, and from Italian into Latin, French, Dutch, and English. The Italian translation is the only correct one: to the French, which is expanded into two vols. folio, and was published at Lyons in 1566, there are appended several accounts of voyages and travels in Africa. Leo was a Spanish Moor, who left Spain at the reduction of Grenada, and travelled a long time in Europe, Asia, and Africa; his description of the northern parts of Africa is most full and accurate.'— R. KERR.

    The author's Moorish name is HASAN-IBN-MUHAMMED-AL-WAZZAN-AL-FÁSI, and the title of the Italian version mentioned above: *Il Viaggio di G. Leone, etc. Nuova Edizione, emendata ed arricchiata*, Venezia, 1837. 4to. He was taken by Corsairs, and baptized by Leo X. The English version bears the title: *A Particular Treatise of all the Main lands and Isles described by John Leo, with map*, London, 1600. 4to. See also 'Purchas his Pilgrimes,' ii., 749. A notice of Leo Africanus, from the pen of A. Berbrugger (see that name), will be found in the 'Revue Africaine,' 1857, xii., 353.

LÉOTARD: *Les Guerres puniques*, art. in 'Controverse et Contemporain,' February, 1887.

LEROI. See LAUGIER DE TASSY.

LEROY, A. L.: *Notes et impressions de voyage d'Alger à Tunis*, Alger, 1886. 8vo.

—— *L'Algérie et la Tunisie agricoles. Étude concernant le sol, le climat, les cultures diverses,&c.*, Paris, 1886. 8vo., pp. 235.

—— *De Ghardi-maou à Tunis*, art. in 'Revue Géographique Internationale,' April, 1886.

LEROY, A. L.: *Tunis et Carthage*, Idem, July, 1886.

—— *L'Algérie et la Tunisie agricoles, étude pratique sur le sol, le climat, les cultures diverses, la viticulture, etc. Avec des notices précises et intéressantes pour les émigrants et les touristes*, Paris, Challamel aîné, 1887.

LEROY - BEAULIEU, ANATOLE: *La Tunisie et l'opposition*, art. in 'Revue Politique et Littéraire,' 1881.

LEROY- BEAULIEU, PAUL: *L'Algérie et la Tunisie*, Paris, Guillaumin et Cie. 1887. Large 8vo., pp. viii., 472. Tunisia occupies pp. 305 to 351.

—— *La Colonisation française en Tunisie*, art. in 'Revue des Deux Mondes,' Nov. 15, 1886.

—— *De la Colonisation scientifique chez les Peuples modernes*, 3ᵉ édit. revue et corrigée, Paris, 1886. 8vo.

LESSEPS, FERDINAND DE: *Sur les lacs amers et autres points de l'isthme de Suez ; inondation des Chotts algériens et tunisiens*, art. in 'Rev. Scient.,' 1876. p. 527.

—— *La Mer intérieure de Gabès*, Idem. April 21, 1883.

—— *L'Utilité de la Topographie : Suez, Panama, Gabès*, art. in 'Revue de Géographie,' January, 1886.

LESSEPS, J. DE. See LONGPÉRIER.

LETAILLE. 'M. Letaille gave an account of the archæological mission with which he had been charged (this is the second one) in Tunis. During six months he had thoroughly explored the region of Hamada, the least known part of Tunis. The excavations he had made at Macler had enabled him to find several inscriptions, one of these giving the ancient names of the town. He had been able to dig out the forum, circus, a temple, and to discover an ancient Christian chapel.'—' Proceedings of the Royal Geographical Society,' 1884, vol. vi., p. 477.

LETOURNEUR, M.: *Sur le projet de Mer intérieure*, in 'Comptes rendus de l'Association Française pour l'Avancement des Sciences, Congrès de Blois,' 1884.

LETOURNEUX, A. See LEFÈVRE and SIMON.

LETRONNE, J. A., Professeur d'Archéologie au Collège de France: *Sur les Colonnes militaires de la frontière de Maroc et de Tunis*, art. in 'Revue Archéologique,' i., 183.

—— *Observations historiques et géographiques sur une inscription de borne militaire qui existe à Tunis et sur la voie romaine de Carthage à Theveste*, Paris, 1845. 8vo. See also DUREAU DE LA MALLE.

LÉVÊQUE Mme. (née Cavelier): *Lilia, histoire de Carthage*, Amsterdam (Paris), 1736. 12mo. Also in 'Amusements du Cœur et de l'Esprit,' iv.

LEWAL, Cap. J.: *Recherches sur le champ de bataille de Zama*, art. in 'Revue Africaine,' Alger, 1858, i. See also CREULY.

LINDBERG, J. CHR. See FALBE.

LION: *La Mer intérieure africaine*, art. in 'Nouvelle Revue,' May 1, 1883.

LIVIUS, T.: *The Second Punic War*, Eton, 1881. 8vo., pp. 170.

LLOYD, JULIUS, M.A.: *The North African Church*. Published by the 'Society for the Promotion of Christian Knowledge,' London, 1880. 12mo., pp. 411.

LONDON, FRIEDERIKE, H.: *Die Berberei. Eine Darstellung der religiösen und bürgerlichen Sitten und Gebräuche der Bewohner Nordafrica's. Frei nach englischen Quellen bearbeitet und auf eigene Beobachtung gegründet*, Frankfurt a M., Heyder und Zimmer, 1845. Large 12mo.

LONGPÉRIER, M. DE: *La Régence de Tunis à l'Exposition de 1867. Histoire du travail.*
    Concerning this publication M. A. Demarsy furnishes the following note: 'Dans la deuxième partie du catalogue de l'Histoire du travail, p. 628, se trouve une notice sur la collection d'antiquités exposée, provenant des fouilles pratiquées dans le sol de Carthage par les soins de S. E. Sidi Mohammed ben Moustafa, fils du premier ministre du bey. Le résultat de ces recherches avait été communiqué à M. de Longpérier; et c'est un extrait du catalogue rédigé par M. de Longpérier, pour l'Académie des inscriptions, que M. le baron Jules de Lesseps, commissaire général du gouvernement tunisien a cru devoir insérer. En première ligne, se trouvent vingt-deux inscriptions carthaginoises qui doivent prendre place dans le recueil des inscriptions sémitiques que prépare l'Académie des inscriptions; puis viennent des sculptures antiques, inscriptions latines, mosaïques, monnaies, pierres gravées, vases, lampes et manuscrits.'

LONLAY, DIC DE: *En Tunisie, Souvenirs de sept mois de campagne*, Paris, Dentu, 1882. 8vo., 58 dessins de l'auteur. Relates to the French occupation.

LUBOMIRSKI, Le Prince J.: *La Côte barbaresque et Le Sahara, Excursion dans le Vieux Monde. Illustrations de Ferdinandus*, Paris, E. Dentu, 1880. 8vo., pp. xxii. and 309. The first five chapters relate to Tunis and Carthage.

LUCAS, PAUL: *Voyage du Sieur Paul Lucas, fait par Ordre du Roy, dans la Grèce, l'Asie Mineure, la Macédoine et l'Afrique. Description de l'Anatolie, la Caramanie, la Macédoine, Jérusalem, l'Egypte, le Fioume, et un Mémoire pour servir à l'histoire de Tunis, depuis 1684*, Paris, 1712. 12mo., 2 vols., illustrated.

—— *Mémoire pour servir à l'Histoire de Tunis, &c.*, Paris, 1712.

LUCHINI, O. See GALEOTTI.

LUMBROSO, Dr. ABRAHAM: *Lettres médico-statistiques sur la Régence de Tunis*, Paris, 1841. 8vo.

LUX, JEAN: *Trois Mois en Tunisie, journal d'un volontaire*, Paris, Aug. Ghio, 1882. 18mo., pp. 201.
    Favourably noticed in 'Le Livre,' February 10, 1883, p. 108.

LUYNES, Duc de. See BARGÈS and GUÉRIN.

MAC CARTHY, O.: *Africa Antiqua, Lexique de Géographie comparée de l'Ancienne Afrique*, art. in 'Revue Africaine,' 1886, No. 175, p. 1 et seq.

—— *K'sar H'announ, the Ksar of Hannon, a Carthaginian City*, 1850.

—— *Étude critique sur la géographie comparée et la géographie positive de la guerre d'Afrique de Jules César*, in 'Rev. Afr.,' 1865, ix., 430.

—— *Note sur les marées du Golfe de Gabès (d'après l'Amiral Smyth)*, 'Explorateur,' 1876. No. 81, p. 200.

MACGILL, THOMAS, *An Account of Tunis: of its Government, Manners, Customs, and Antiquities; especially of its Productions, Manufactures, and Commerce*, London, Longman, 1816. 8vo., pp. 187. First published at Glasgow, 1811. 8vo.
    The author, who writes in a straightforward, unpretending manner, visited Tunis for 'commerce, not pleasure.' The book is curious rather than valuable, much of the information given in it being now out of date.

—— *Nouveau Voyage à Tunis, publié en 1811; traduit de l'Anglais avec Notes* (par Louis Ragueneau de La Chesnaye), Paris, Panckouke, 1815. 8vo.
    In vol. vii. of the 'Neue Bibliothek der wichtigsten Reisebeschreibungen, &c., von F. J. Bertuch, Weimar, 1815-35, will be found a translation:

—— *Maggil's neue Reise nach Tunis, nach der im Jahre 1811 herausgegebenen französischen Uebersetzung bearbeitet von M. M. Schilling*, 1816.
    Art. on *Macgill's Account* in 'Eclectic Review,' xiv., 828.

MAC GUCKIN DE SLANE. See EL-BEKRI and IBN-KHALDOUN.

MACHUEL, Directeur de l'Enseignement public en Tunisie: *Rapport adressé à M. le Ministre résident de la République française à Tunis*, Tunis, 1885. 4to.,pp. 44. Gives an interesting account of the state of education since the French protectorate.

MACKENZIE, H.: *The Prince of Tunis, a Tragedy in Five Acts and in Verse*, Edinburgh, 1773. 8vo.

MAGO. See CAHUN and FRIEDRICH.

MAHUDEL, NICOLAS: *Lettres sur une Médaille de la ville de Carthage*, Paris, 1741. 8vo.

MAILHE, ALBERT. See RIVIÈRE.

MAIUS, J. H.: *Specimen linguæ punicæ, in hodierna Melitensium ætate superstites*, Marpurgiæ, 1718. 8vo. Reprinted in 'Thesaurus antiq. italicar.' x.

MALTZAN, HEINRICH, Freiherr von: *Sittenbilder aus Tunis und Algerien*, Leipzig, Dyk'sche Buchhandlung, 1869. 8vo., pp. 452, with a frontispiece representing a male and female figure.

A carefully written volume on the religion, education, manners and customs, costumes, &c., of the two countries, interspersed with characteristic conversations and anecdotes. There being neither chapters nor index, the matter is difficult to get at.

—— *Reise in den Regentschaften Tunis und Tripolis. Nebst einem Anhang: Ueber die neuentdeckten phönicischen Inschriften von Karthago. Mit Titelkupfer, Plan von Tunis und 59 lithographirten Inschriften*, Leipzig, Dyk'sche Buchhandlung, 1870. 8vo., 3 vols. The frontispiece to the third vol. gives a poor representation of the amphitheatre of El-Djem.

—— *Der Völkerkampf zwischen Arabern und Berbern in Nord-Afrika*, art. in 'Das Ausland,' 1873, No. 23, pp. 444 et seq.

MANNERT, KONRAD: *Geographie von Africa, &c.*, Leipzig, 1825. 2 vols. Done into French by L. Marcus and F. Duesberg as:

—— *Géographie ancienne des États barbaresques d'après l'allemand de K. Mannert, enrichie de notes et de plusieurs mémoires,&c.*, Paris, 1842. 8vo.

MARCEL, J. J.: *Vocabulaire français-arabe des dialectes vulgaires d'Alger, de Tunis, de Maroc, et d'Egypte*, Paris, 1837. 8vo.

—— *Dictionnaire française-arabe des dialectes vulgaires d'Alger, d'Egypte, de Tunis et de Maroc*, Paris, 1869. 8vo., pp. 572, double cols.

—— *Numismatique de la Régence de Tunis*. Oblong folio, plates. See also FRANK.

MARCELLINUS, AMMIANUS: *Lives of the Emperors from Constantine to Valens and Gratian*. V. Sylburgius *Historiæ Romanæ Scriptores Latini minores*. 1588, &c. Vol. ii.

MARCHESI, V.: *Tunisi e la Repubblica de Venezia*, Venezia, 1882. 8vo. pp. 88.

MARCHOT, MÉRIADE (de Tombeckem): *Abrégé de l'Histoire de la Régence de Tunis*, Bruxelles (1866). 8vo., pp. 40.

MARCUS, L.: *Histoire des Vandales accompagnée de recherches sur le commerce que les états barbaresques firent avec l'étranger dans les 6 premiers siècles de l'ère chrét.*, Paris, 1838. 8vo. See also MANNERT.

MARÉCHAL, SYLVAIN: *Voyage de Pythagore en Egypte . . . à Carthage, &c., suivi de ses lois politiques et morales*, Paris, An vii. (1799). 8vo., 6 vols., engraved frontispiece and maps.

MARETTI, F. See PETRARCA.

MARGA, A., Commandant du Génie: *Géographie militaire*, Paris, Berger-Levrault et Cie., 1885. Large 8vo. In première partie, tome ii., pp. 277 to 288, will be found a chapter (iv.) on Tunisia.

MARICHARD, J. O. DE. See OLLIER DE MARICHARD.

MARLOW, CHR.: *Dido, Queen of Carthage*. Tragedy, left unfinished by Marlow, and after his death, 1593, completed by his friend Thomas Nash.

MARMOL Y CARVAJAL, LUYS: *Primera Parte de la Descripcion general de Africa con todos los successos de guerras que ha havido entre los infieles y el pueblo christiano, y entre ellos mismos desde que Mahoma invento su secta, hasta el anno del señor mil y quinientos y setenta y uno,* Granada, 1573, and Malaga, 1599. Fol., 3 vols.

—— *L'Afrique de Marmol*, by Nicolas Perrot d'Ablancourt, Paris, 1667, with maps by M. Sanson. 4to.

'This translation of a very scarce Portuguese (Spanish) writer is not made with fidelity. The subsequent discoveries in Africa have detailed several inaccuracies in Marmol; but it is nevertheless a valuable work; the original was published in the middle of the sixteenth century.'—R. KERR.

'Marmol was a native of Granada, served in the expedition of Charles V. against Algiers, was taken prisoner, and travelled during seven years and eight months over a great part of North Africa.'—PLAYFAIR.

MARSEUL. See LEFÈVRE.

MARTYN, JOHN, F.R.S.: *Dissertations &c., upon the Æneids of Virgil; containing . . . a full Vindication of the Poet from the charge of Anachronism with regard to the foundation of Carthage, &c.*, London, 1770. 12mo.

MAS-LATRIE, J. M. J. L. DE, Sous-directeur de l'École des Chartes: *Traités de Paix et de Commerce &c. concernant les Relations des Chrétiens avec les Arabes de l'Afrique septentrionale au Moyen-Age, Supplément et Tables*, Paris, 1865. 4to. Other editions: Paris, 1868, 4to.; Paris, 1873, 4to. Documents collected and published by order of the Emperor, of which many relate to the connexion between the Italian Republics and Tunis, &c. Thirty-five of the documents relate to Tunis.

MAS-LATRIE, J. M. J. L. DE: *Instructions de Foscari, doge de Venise, au consul de la République chargé de complimenter le nouveau Roi de Tunis, en* 1436, art. in 'Bibliothèque de l'École des Chartes,' 3ᵉ livre, 1881.

—— *L'Épiscopus Gummitanus et la Primauté de l'Évêque de Carthage,* art. in 'Bibliothèque de l'École des Chartes,' part i., 1883.

MASQUERAY, É.: *Rapport à l'Académie Royale des Sciences de Berlin sur le voyage d'après ses instructions pendant l'hiver 1882-83 en Algérie et à Tunisie par Johannes Schmidt de Halle*, translation by E. Masqueray in 'Bull. Corresp. Afr.,' 1882, pp. 394-401.

'The author was charged with the preparation of the 8th vol. of Roman Inscriptions.'—PLAYFAIR.

MASSEBIAU: *Les Sacrifices ordonnés à Carthage au commencement de la persécution de Décius*, art. in 'Revue de l'Histoire des Religions,' February, 1884.

MAUREL: *Conquête pacifique de l'Afrique septentrionale par les Français,* in 'Comptes rendus de l'Association Française pour l'Avancement des Sciences, Congrès d'Alger,' 1881.

MAUROY, P.: *Précis de l'histoire et du commerce de l'Afrique septentrionale depuis les temps anciens jusqu'aux temps modernes . . . . Précédé de deux lettres du Duc d'Isly sur la question d'Alger*, Paris, 1852. 8vo., 4ᵢᵐᵉ ed. corrigée et refondue.

MAX, GUS., Cons. Gén. de Belgique: *L'Algérie, la Tunisie et l'Exposition d'Anvers,* 'Rapport commercial,' 1885, lii., p. 470.

MAYER, H. L., and BERGK, J. A.: *Ansichten von der Türkei* . . . .

nebst einer Auswahl merkwürdiger Ansichten von .... den berühmtesten Städten Korinth, Karthago und Tripoli, nach den Originalzeichnungen des Hrn. Ludw. Mayer und mit Erläuterungen von J. Ad. Bergk, Leipzig, Baumgärtner, 1812. Fol., 20 engravings.

MAYET, VALERY, Professeur à l'École d'Agriculture de Montpellier: *Voyage dans le sud de la Tunisie*, Montpellier, Boehm et fils, 1886. 8vo., pp. 207, with a map, issue 100 copies. See also SIMON, E.

MAYEUX, F. J.: *Les Bédouins, ou les Arabes du Désert, ouvrage publié d'après les notes inédites de D. Raphaël*, Paris, 1816. 18mo., 3 vols., illustrated.

MAYSTRE, H.: *Excursion en Algérie et en Tunisie, mai-juin 1883*, arts. in 'Bibliothèque universelle et Revue Suisse,' July, August and Oct. 1884.

MELON, PAUL: *Les Événements de Tunis, du Rôle de l'Italie et de l'Action du Gouvernement français*, Paris, Rouvier, 1881. 12mo., pp. 22.

—— *La Nécropole phénicienne de Mahédia*, art. in 'Revue Archéologique,' Sept. 1884.

—— *De Palerme à Tunis, par Malte, Tripoli et la Côte, Notes et Impressions*, Paris, Plon, 1885. Illustrated. Of little value.

MELTZER, DR. O. *Geschichte der Karthager*, 1879.

MENTELLE, M.: *Carthaginiens*, art. of 9 cols. in 'Encyclopédie Méthodique,' Paris, Panckoucke, 1787.

MENU DE ST.-MESMIN, E.: *Les Ruines de Carthage et d'Utique*, arts. in 'Moniteur Universel,' Oct. 9, 10, 31, 1868.

MERCIER, E.: *Examen des Causes de la Croisade de S. Louis contre Tunis (1270)*, art. in 'Revue Africaine,' 1872, xvi.

—— *Histoire de l'Établissement des Arabes dans l'Afrique septentrionale selon les Documents fournis par les auteurs arabes, et notamment par l'histoire des Berbères d'Ibn-Khaldoun* (see that name), Constantine, 1875, gr. in-8, axec deux cartes.

MERCIER, E.: *Les Arabes d'Afrique jugés par les auteurs musulmans*, art. in 'Rev. Afr.' 1873, xvii., 43.

—— *Historique des connaissances des anciens sur la géographie de l'Afrique septentrionale*, art. in 'Rec. Not. et Mém. Soc. Arch. de Const.,' 1874, xvi., 19.

—— *Comment l'Afrique septentrionale a été arabisée*, Paris, 1875. 8vo.

MERIGON, B. R.: *Mémoire adressé au Roi* (Henri IV. ou Louis XIII.), *par Blaise Reimond Merigon, de Marseille, sur les avantages de conquérir les Royaumes d'Alger, de Tunis et de Tripoli*. MS. Fonds Saint-Germain, n° 778.

MEULEMANS, AUG.: *Études sur la Tunisie au point de vue du Commerce belge*, Bruxelles, 1867. 8vo., pp. 29. Extracted from 'Revue Trimestrielle,' Oct. 1867, 2 série, xvi.

MEYNARD, B. DE. See BARBIER.

MICHEL, LÉON: *Tunis, l'Orient africain, Arabes, Maures, Kabyles, Juifs, Levantins, Scènes de Mœurs, Intérieurs maures et israélites, Noces, Sérail, Harems, Musiciens, Almées, Villégiature orientale, Carthage, Deuxième édition*, Paris, Garnier Frères, 1883. 8vo., pp. vi. and 314.

MIGNARD, M. P. See CLARIN DE LA RIVE.

MOHAMMED ABOU RASSE AHMED EN-NACEUR. See EXIGA.

MOHAMMED EL NEFZAOUI. See EL-NEFZAOUI.

MOMMSEN, THEODOR: *Römische Geschichte, siebente Auflage*, Berlin, 1881. 8vo., 3 vols. Other editions: 1856, 1861, &c. Translated into English with additions by W. P. Dickson, as:

—— *The History of Rome*, new edition, London, 1868-70. 8vo., 4 vols.

First edition 1862; recently reissued by R. Bentley & Sons in demy 8vo., 2 vols., 2 maps. Done into French by C. A. Alexandre, as:

MOMMSEN, THEODOR: *Histoire romaine*, Paris, 1863.
    Contains a brilliant sketch of Carthage.
—— *Inscriptiones Africæ Latinæ*, Berlin, 1863. 2 vols. 4to.
MONTAGU, Lady MARY WORTLEY. See WORTLEY.
MONTPENSIER, Duc de. See LATOUR, A. DE.
MORCELLI, S. A.: *Africa Christiana, &c.*, Brixiæ, 1816-1817. 4to., 3 vols.
MOREAU: *La Mer intérieure africaine*, art. in 'Science et Nature,' March 1, 1884.
MOREL, LOUIS: *Mémoires sur la nécessité de réformer le système des poids et mesures de la Régence de Tunis*, Oran, 1860. 8vo., pp. 16.
MORERI, LOUIS: *Carthage*, art. of 3 cols., containing an account of the Churches, Councils, and Bishops of Carthage, in 'Grand Dictionnaire Historique,' Amsterdam, 1740.
MORGAN, JOSEPH: *A Complete History of Algiers. To which is prefixed, An Epitome of the General History of Barbary, from the earliest Times, &c.*, London, J. Bettenham, 1728. 4to., 2 vols. Section II. is devoted to Carthage and its Empire. Also 1750.

'This was translated into French by Boyer de Prebandier in 1757. The work is of little value; it is a mere translation of Laugier de Tassy, who again copied from Marmol. Morgan was an indefatigable plagiarist.'—PLAYFAIR.

—— *Voyage of the Mathurin Fathers to Algiers and Tunis for the Redemption of Captives in 1720*, London, 1735. 8vo.
MOUCHEZ, M. *Positions géographiques des principaux points de la côte de Tunisie*, art. in 'Revue Scientifique,' 1877.

MOVERS, Dr. F. K.: *Die Phönizier, Religion der Phönizier mit Rücksicht auf die Carthager, &c.*, Bonn, 1841 to 1856. 8vo., 3 vols.

'The standard work on the Phœnicians.'—OSCAR BROWNING.
'A most important work.'—PLAYFAIR.

MÜLLER, L. See FALBE.
MULLER, H. L., Négociant au Havre: *Le Commerce du Globe. Compte de revient des marchandises échangées entre toutes les principales places de commerce du monde. Seconde édition, refondue et augmentée*, Le Havre, A. Lemale, 1865. 4to., 2 vols., vol. ii. issued in 1872. Carthage is comprised in the *Zone de la Méditerranée*, which with other 'zones' is sold separately. The English translation, *The Commerce of the Globe, &c.*, does not include Carthage.
MUNK, S. See ROZOIR, C. DU.
MÜNTER, F.: *Die Religion der Karthager*, Kopenhagen, 1821. 4to., pp. 171, illustrated. To which add:
—— *Beilage zu der Religion der Karthager*, Kopenhagen, 1822.
—— *Linea Topographica Carthaginis Tyriæ*, 1821.
—— *Primordia Ecclesiæ Africanæ*, Hafniæ, 1829. 4to.
MURRAY, HUGH. See JAMESON.

NÆVIUS, GNÆUS *Fragmenta de Bello Punico*, published in *Collectio Pisaurensis Omnium Poematum, Carminum, Fragmentorum Latinorum, &c. Tomus Quartus, &c.*, Pisauri, 1766. 4to. Also: In Bothe's 'Poetarum Latinorum fragmenta,' Bd. 2, Halberstadt, 1824. And: 'De bello Punico,' by Vahlen, Leipzig, 1845.
NANGIS, G. DE. See GUILLERMUS DE NANGIS, also JOINVILLE.
NAPOLÉON, S.: *Discours au vray de tout ce qui s'est passé tant au voiage que le sieur Samson Napoléon, gentilhomme ordinaire de la chambre du Roy et chevalier de l'ordre de Saint-*

Michel, a faict à Constantinople par le commandement de S. M. qu'à Thunis et Arger pour le traité de la paix de Barbarie avec le compte et l'estat de la recepte et dépense sur ce faitte et rachapt des esclaves (1623). MS. in Bibliothèque Impériale, fonds Serilly.

M. A. Demarsy adds : ' Nous publierons prochainement ce document que nous croyons inédit.'

NEIL, O.: *Géographie et itinéraire de l'Algérie et de la Tunisie*, Bône, 1882. 2 vols., map.

NEU, JUSTIN : *La Vérité sur la Tunisie,* Paris, (1870). 8vo., pp. 42.

NEUMANN, C. : *Das Zeitalter der Punischen Kriege*, Breslau, 1883. 8vo., pp. 598.

NEWMAN, Cardinal : *Callista: a Story relating to the Persecutions of the early Christians*, London, 1855. The scene is laid at El-Kef.

NEWTON, THOMAS : *A View of Valyance; descriving the ... Martiall Exploits of ... the Romans and Carthaginians for the Conqueste and Possession of Spayne. Translated out of ... Rutilius Rufus ... a Capitaine ... vnder Scipio, in the same Warres*, London, 1580. 8vo.

NIEBUHR, B. G.: *Lectures on Ancient Ethnography and Geography, &c.,* translated by Dr. Leonhard Schmitz, London, Walton and Maberly, 1853. 8vo., 2 vols., contains (ii., 330) a short account of Carthage and Utica.

NIEL, O.: *Tunisie, Géographie et Guide du Voyageur*, Paris, Challamel, 1883. With map.

NIEULY, GIORGIO: *Documenti sulla Storia di Tunis*, Livorno, 1838. 8vo.

NOAH, MORDECAI M.: *Travels in England, France, Spain, and the Barbary States, in the years 1813-14 and 15*, New York, Kirk and Mercein ; London, John Miller, 1819. 8vo., pp. vi., 431, and xlvii., portrait of the author and illustrations. About 100 pages are devoted to Tunisia—Carthage, Utica, &c.

NOËL DES VERGERS. See IBN-KHALDOUN.

NONCE-ROCCA: *A propos d'un livre récent sur la Tunisie. Observations*. Paris, 1866. 8vo.

The book in question is that by M. A. DE FLAUX (see that name).

OCKLEY, SIMON, Professor of Arabic in the University of Cambridge : *The History of the Saracens, comprising the lives of Mahommed and his successors to the death of Abdalmelik, the eleventh Caliph. With an account of their most remarkable Battles, Sieges, Revolts, &c.,* Londres, 1848. Small 8vo.

—— *Histoire des Sarrasins, contenant leurs premières Conquêtes et ce qu'ils ont fait de plus remarquable sous les onze premiers Califes ou Successeurs de Mahomet. Traduit de l'Anglais*, Paris, 1748. 12mo., 2 vols.

For other edits. consult Lowndes and Brunet, the former notes it as 'a curious and very entertaining work.'

O'HANLY, S. H. See HALY O'HANLY.

O'KELLY, Comte ALPHONSE: *Études politiques sur le Royaume de Tunis,* Bruxelles, 1871. 8vo.

OLLIER DE MARICHARD, JULES, et PRUNER-BEY: *Les Carthaginois en France. La Colonie libyo-phénicienne du Liby, canton de Bourg-Saint-Andéol (Ardèche)*, Paris, 1870. 8vo.

OPERTI, B. See GALEOTTI.

OUSELEY, Sir W. See IBN-HAUKAL.

PALLU DE LESSERT, CLÉMENT: *Les Monuments antiques de la Tunisie, le décret beylical, la loi française,* art. in ' Revue de l'Afrique Française (ancien ' *Bull. des Antiquités Africaines*'), Paris, 1886. iv., 237 to 240.

PANANTI, FILIPPO: *Avventure e osservazioni di Filippo Pananti sopra le Coste di Barberia*, Milano, 1829. 12mo., 2 vols. Also Mendrisio, 1841.

PANSA, GUILL.: *Historia nuova della guerra di Tunigi di Barberia; in cui si contiene la navigatione da Genova in Africa*, Milano, 1585. Small 8vo. Account of the expedition under Charles-Quint.

PAPIRICE-MASSON, JEAN: *Gesta collationis Carthagine habitæ inter Catholicos et Donatistas*, Paris, 1596. 8vo.

PARADIS, VENTURE DE: *Grammaire et Dictionnaire abrégés de la Langue berbère*, published in 'Recueil de Voyages et de Mémoires,' Paris, 1854. vii., 4to.

In his preface the author says that it is the language spoken 'depuis les montagnes de Sous, qui bordent la mer océane, jusqu'à celles de Meletis, qui dominent les plaines de Kairouan.'

PARTASCH, J.: *Die Veränderungen des Küstensaumes der Regentschaft Tunis in historischen Zeiten*, (1883). 4to.

PATON, ÉMILE: *Tunis et son Gouvernement*, Paris, 1868. 8vo., pp. 22.

PAUR, THÉODORE : *Charles-Quint et l'Afrique septentrionale. D'après les documents du XVIe siècle*, 1848.

PAVIE, K. See DUNANT.

PAYSANT, L.: *Le Bey de Tunis devant l'opinion publique*, Alger, 1870. 8vo., pp. 15.

PECHAUD, JEAN: *Excursions malacologiques dans le nord de l'Afrique. De la Calle à Alger—D'Alger à Tunis*, Paris, 1883. 8vo., pp. 112.

PELET, J. J., Général: *Maroc, Alger, Tunis, avec une carte de l'Algérie dressée au dépôt de la guerre*, Magdebourg, 1846.

PELLISSIER DE REYNAUD, E., Membre de la Commission scientifique de l'Algérie, Consul-général de France à Tripoli: *Description de la Régence de Tunis*, Paris, Masson, 1853. 8vo., pp. 455, map. Géographie, Description physique, Nature et produit du sol, Vocabulaire français et arabe des noms propres qui se trouvent dans la partie géographique. Inscriptions. Médailles. Histoire naturelle. Forms part of the *Exploration de l'Algérie*, noticed in 'Revue des Deux Mondes,' May 1, 1856.

PELLISSIER DE REYNAUD, E.: *Trois Lettres à M. Hase*: 1°, *Sur les Antiquités de la Régence;* 2°, *Sur les Antiquités de la partie ouest de la Régence;* 3°, *Sur les Antiquités de Nakter et de l'ancienne Zeugitane*, 1847 *et* 1848. 8vo. Extracted from 'Revue Archéologique.'

—— *La Régence de Tunis, le gouvernement des beys et la société tunisienne*, art. in 'Revue des Deux Mondes,' May 1, 1856.

'M. Pellissier ayant habité plusieurs années la Régence en qualité de vice-consul de Sousa, l'a parcourue à diverses reprises, et les détails qu'il nous donne sont surtout d'un grand intérêt en ce qui concerne l'état actuel de la Tunisie, son administration, ses produits, etc. Au point de vue archéologique, il a ajouté peu de chose aux découvertes des voyageurs qui l'avaient précédé.'—V. GUÉRIN, *Voyage*, i., p. xiii.

PÉRIER, A.: *D'Alger à Kairouan*, 'Bull. 5° de la Sect. Lyon. du Club Alpin,' 1886.

PERPETUA, Prof. G.: *Geografia della Tunisia compilata del Comm. Prof. G. Perpetua*, 1882, G. B. Paravia e Comp., Torino, &c. 8vo.

This useful little hand-book has been translated into French in an abbreviated form, and published in Tunis.

—— *La Tunisie; faune, commerce, navigation*, art. in 'Revue Géographique Internationale,' July 1885.

PERRON, Dr.: *Femmes arabes avant et depuis l'Islamisme*, Paris, 1858. 8vo. See IBN-OMAR.

PERROT, GEORGES: *Le Rôle historique des Phéniciens*, art. in 'Revue Archéologique,' Nov. 1884.

PERRY, AMOS, U.S. Consul at Tunis: *Carthage and Tunis, past and present*, Providence, U.S., 1869. 8vo.

PERUZZI, M.: *Tunis et l'Italie*, followed by *Réponse à M. Peruzzi*, arts. in 'Revue Politique et Littéraire,' 1881.

PESCHEUX, R.: *Kabiles, Maures et Arabes, ou leurs métiers, industries, arts, sciences, etc.*, published in parts, 8vo., beginning 1853.

PETRARCA, FRANCESCO: *L'Africa, in ottava rima, tradotta da Fabio Maretti, col testo latino*, Venet., 1570. 4to. Numerous editions. On the Punic war.

PEYSSONNEL et DESFONTAINES: *Voyages dans les Régences de Tunis et d'Alger*. Publiés par M. Dureau de la Malle (see that name), de l'Institut, Paris, 1838. 8vo., 2 vols., with 1 map and 6 lithographs.

Charles, Comte de Peyssonnel, made his journey from 1724 to 1725; Desfontaines (see also that name), from 1783 to 1786.

PHARAON, FL., et BERTHERAND, E. L.: *Vocabulaire français-arabe à l'usage des médecins-vétérinaires.* 1859. 18mo.

PIERANTONI, A. See GALEOTTI.

PIERRE-CŒUR. See VOISINS.

PIESSE, LOUIS: *Guide de l'Algérie*, Paris, 1873. Contains Tunis and environs, with a map.

—— *Itinéraire de l'Algérie, de Tunis et de Tanger*, 7 cartes, Paris, Hachette et Cie., 1881. 8vo., pp. cxliv. and 548, double cols.

—— *De la Goulette à Tripoli*, art. in 'Bulletin Trimestriel de Géographie,' Oran, 1885, v., 8 to 16, 8 illustrations.

PIGEONNEAU, H.: *L'Annone romaine et les corps de naviculaires particulièrement en Afrique*, art. in 'Revue de l'Afrique Française,' Paris, July 1886, iv., pp. 220 to 236.

PINART, MICHEL, Membre de l'Académie des Inscriptions: *Mémoire sur le nom de Byrsa donné à la citadelle de Carthage bâtie par Didon*, art. in 'Recueil de l'Académie des Inscriptions,' 1 série, i., 150.

PLANCK: *Karthago und seine Heerführer*, Ulm, 1874.

PLAYFAIR, Lieut.-Colonel Sir R. LAMBERT, K.C.M.G.: *Travels in the Footsteps of Bruce in Algeria and Tunis*. Illustrated by Fac-similes of his original drawings, London, Kegan Paul & Co., 1877. 4to.

Besides the drawings of Bruce, the volume contains photographs taken on the spot. As the greater part of the edition was destroyed in the fire which occurred at the publishers' in 1883, the volume is now scarce.

Concerning this work, the author writes: 'Bruce the traveller was Consul-General at Algiers from 1763 to 1765. He subsequently made extensive explorations in Algeria and Tunis, and magnificent architectural drawings of all the Roman remains he visited, but he left no account of his journey. These drawings are in the possession of his descendant, Lady Thurlow. The author has published an account of his journey over the ground traversed by Bruce, illustrated by fac-similes of his drawings.'

See also DONALDSON.

—— *On the Re-discovery of Lost Numidian Marbles in Algeria and Tunis*. Read at the British Association (Geological Section), at Aberdeen, Sept. 1885, pp. 12, with a coloured map.

—— *Report of a Consular Tour in the Regency of Tunis during March and April*, Consular Commercial Reports, 1876, p. 1187.

—— *Report by Consul-General Playfair of a Consular Tour in Tunis*, in 'Commercial Reports,' No. 3 (1886). Part i., pp. 19 to 53, with 3 maps.

—— *Une visite au pays des Kroumirs*, in 'Comptes rendus de l'Association française pour l'avancement des sciences, Congrès d'Alger,' 1881.

PLAYFAIR, Lieut.-Colonel Sir R. LAMBERT, K.C.M.G.: *Report of a Consular Tour to La Calle and the country of the Khomair*, in 'Consular Commercial Reports.' Also 'Journal of Royal Asiatic Society,' 1882, vol. xviii., part 1.

—— *La Calle and the Country of the Khomair, with a note on North African Marbles*, 'Journ. R. Asiat. Soc. of Gt. Brit. and Irel.,' 1886, vol. xviii., p. 28.

—— *Report of a Consular Tour in Tunis*, 'Consular Reports, part I, No. 3, p. 19.
  This contains an account of the proposed inland sea.

—— *Handbook to the Mediterranean, &c., Second Edition*, London, John Murray, 1882. 8vo., 2 parts. Comprises Tunis, Carthage, Zaghouan, Oudena, El-Djem, Djerba, &c.

—— *Handbook for Travellers in Algeria and Tunis, Third Edition*, London, John Murray, 1887. 8vo., with maps and plans.

—— *On the Changes which have taken place in Tunis since the French Protectorate.* 'Proceedings of the Geographical Section of the British Association, Aberdeen Section,' 1885.

PLOETZ, KARL: *Auszug aus der alten, mittleren und neueren Geschichte, siebente Auflage*, Berlin, A. G. Ploetz, 1880. Edition edited by Dr. O. Meltzer. Translated into English by W. H. Tillinghast of Harvard College, Cambridge, U. S. A., as:

—— *An Epitome of History, &c.* Contains useful references on Carthage and Tunis.

POCOCKE, RICHARD, successively Bishop of Ossory and of Meath *A Description of the East and some other countries*, London, 1743-45. Fol. Comprised also in the collections of J. H. Moore and of J. Pinkerton; also in 'The World Displayed.' Translations:

POCOCKE, RICHARD: *Voyage de R. Pococke en Orient, &c.*, Neuchatel, 1772-73. 12mo., 7 vols.

—— *Beschreibung des Morgenlandes, &c.*, Erlangen, 1754-5, 4to., 3 parts, illustrations.

—— *Dissertatio de Geographia Ægypti*, Londini, 1743. Fol. Contains *An Account of the Bey of Tunis; his Court and Government*.

POINSSOT, JULIEN: *Tunisie: Ain Tounga, Guelaa, Maatria, Gotnia, Description des Ruines, Inscriptions inédites recueillies par M. le Dr. Darré, Médecin Aide-Major*, art. in 'Bulletin de la Société de Géographie et d'Archéologie d'Oran,' 1884, pp. 136 to 156, with plan of Ain Tounga and 2 illustrations.

—— *Tunisie: Inscriptions inédites recueillies pendant un voyage exécuté en 1882-83, sur l'ordre de S. E. le Ministre de l'Instruction Publique*, arts. in 'Bulletin de la Société de Géographie et d'Archéologie d'Oran, 1883, i. 288, and ii. 68, 151, 225, 361.'

—— *Voyage archéologique en Tunisie exécuté en* 1882-83. See 'Bulletin des Antiq. Afr. Oran,' 1883, i., 289, 291; ii., 68, 150, 226; iii., 16, 89, 174, 265; iv., 1, many illustrations.

—— *Le Pont romain Siguese-Tuscubis, ou Ucubis*, art. in 'Revue de l'Afrique Française,' Paris, July, 1886, iv., 249 to 251.

POIRET, Abbé: *Voyage en Barbarie, ou Lettres écrites de l'ancienne Numidie pendant les années 1785 et 1786, sur la Religion, les Coutumes et les Mœurs des Maures et des Arabes-Bédouins; avec un essai sur l'histoire naturelle de ce pays*, Paris, 1789. 8vo., 2 vols. Translated as:

—— *Travels through Barbary, etc., in the years 1785 and 1786; containing* an Account of the Customs and Manners of the Moors and Bedouin Arabs, London, 1791. 12mo.

'L'auteur était un botaniste distingué qui herborisa pendant une année dans les environs de Bône, de la Calle, de Constantine, et dans une partie de la Tunisie. Le premier volume contient ses études de mœurs faites dans le pays, études dans lesquelles il se montre sans préjugés contres les Arabes, Maures et Berbères ; il assure même que l'éducation de famille des enfants arabes était supérieure à celle des enfants européens. Il fait aussi cette remarque que la haine des arabes pour les roumis ne date que des Croisades. Le 2º vol. contient ses recherches sur l'histoire naturelle de la Numidie.'

POIRON, M.: *Mémoire concernant l'état présent du Royaume de Tunis et ce qui s'est passé de plus remarquable entre la France et cette Régence, depuis 1701 jusqu'en 1752, par M. Poiron, commissaire des guerres à Toulon.* Manuscript in folio. Bibliothèque Impériale, n° 13084, p. 148 à 276. Analysed by M. A. Demarsy at p. 40 of his excellent 'Essai de Bibliographie.'

POLYBIUS : *Historiarum Libri V. Latine, ex versione Nicolai Perroti,* Roma, 1473. Fol. Various other editions. Translated into English by Edward Grimestone, 1634 ; Henry Shears, 1693 ; Hampton, 1756 ; also by C. Watson and Sir Walter Raleigh, which two latter names see.

Polybius was present at the taking of Carthage.

POMEL, M.: *La Mer intérieure d'Algérie et le seuil de Gabès,* art. in 'Revue Scientifique,' 1877.

—— *Géologie de la province de Gabès et du littoral oriental de la Tunisie,* art. in 'Comptes rendus de l'Association Française pour l'Avancement des Sciences, Congrès du Havre,' 1877.

—— *Le projet de Mer intérieure et le Seuil de Gabès.* 'Rev. Géogr. Internat.,' 1878, Nos. 29, 30, and 31.

'The author denies that the Chotts ever communicated with the Mediterranean.'—PLAYFAIR.

POMPONIUS MÉLA ; *De situ Orbis.* A full geographical description of the coast of North Africa and the principal towns.

The author was a Spanish geographer of the first century.

PONTET DE FONVENT, HENRY: *La Tunisie, son Passé, son Avenir, et la Question financière,* 1872. 8vo., pp. 32.

POOLE, GEORGE AYLIFFE: *The Life and Times of Saint Cyprian,* Oxford, 1840. 8vo. Done into French as :

—— *Histoire, &c., de Saint Cyprien,* Lyon, 1842. See CYPRIEN.

POSTEL, RAOUL, ancien magistrat aux Colonies: *En Tunisie et au Maroc, avec 15 dessins originaux par le Dr. L. M. Reuss,* Paris, Libraire de Vulgarisation (1885). 8vo., pp. 6 and 221.

POULAIN DE BOSSAY. See GUÉRIN.

PRADEL, E. DE COURTRAY DE. See COURTRAY DE PRADEL.

PRANGEY, G. DE. See GIRAULT DE PRANGEY.

PRAX: *Observations sur Tunis et le nord de l'Afrique,* art. in 'Revue de l'Orient,' March, 1850.

—— *Tunis,* arts. on the Population, Customs, Measures and Moneys, Natural History, Industry, Commerce and Agriculture, Ibid., 2 séri vi., 1849 ; and ix. and x., 1851.

'L'auteur s'attache à donner des renseignements précis sur les calendriers musulmans, la division du jour chez les Arabes, la longueur des journées de marche des caravanes, l'évaluation du mille arabe et les monnaies, poids et mesures, de Tunis.'—A. DEMARSY.

PREBADÉ, R. DE. See LAUGIER DE TASSY.

PRÉVOST, F.: *La Tunisie devant l'Europe,* Paris, 1862. 8vo., pp. 31

PRICOT DE SAINTE MARIE, E. See SAINTE MARIE, E. PRICOT DE.

PROCOPIUS: *De la guerre contre les Vandales*, Paris, 1670. 8vo.

This Greek historian, a native of Cæsarea, accompanied Belisarius as his secretary in the expedition to North Africa, A.D. 534. His history is divided into eight books, two of which are devoted to the Vandal war.

Several editions of the original exist, and one English translation by Sir Henry Holcroft.

—— *History of the Warres of the Emperour Justinian*, 8 books, London, 1653. Folio.

'This translation is exceedingly rare. No copy exists in the British Museum or the Advocates' Library in Edinburgh; there is one at the Bodleian. In the second book, *De Bello Vandalico*, is a notice of the celebrated inscription said to have existed near Tangier, "We flee from the robber Joshua, the son of Nun." For the original text see "Corpus Scriptorum Historiæ Byzantinæ," Bonnæ, 1838.'—PLAYFAIR.

PRUNER-BEY. See OLLIER DE MARICHARD.

PTOLEMY, CLAUDIUS: *Géographie*. Edidit C. F. A. Nobbe. Editio stereotypa Gr. 3 tom., Lipsiæ, 1843-45. 16mo.

A celebrated geographer and astronomer in the reigns of Hadrian and Antonine. According to his system the world was in the centre of the universe.

PUECKLER-MUSKAU, Fürst H. L. H. VON: *Semilasso in Afrika. Aus den Papieren des Verstorbenen.* Stuttgart, Hallberger'sche Verlagshandlung, 1836. Large 8vo., 5 parts, 1 coloured lithograph. The accompanying atlas contains: Ansicht von Algier, Bivouac in Khraschna, Der Bey im Audienz-Saal, Ankunft beim Sauwan, Ansicht von Tunis, Villa des englischen Consuls, Halt bei Thugga, 1837. Fol.

—— *Semilasso in Africa, &c.* London, R. Bentley, 1837. 3 vols. Vols. ii. and iii. relate chiefly to Tunisia.

PUECKLER-MUSKAU, Fürst H. L. H. VON: *Chroniques, Lettres et Journal de Voyage, extraits des papiers d'un défunt*, Paris, 1837. 8vo., 3 vols.

PUGET DE LA SERRE, JEAN: *Le Sac de Carthage, tragédie en prose*, Paris, 1643. 4to.

PUGET DE SAINT-PIERRE: *Les Hauts Faits de Scipion l'Africain*, Paris, Laurens ainé, 1814. 12mo.

PUGLIA: *Il Miracolo grande apparuto al Re de Tunici . . . La afferta fatta per el preditto Re de Schiani Christiani, etc. Data in Tunici*, 26 Junio, 1534, (and signed) *S. Ludovico de Marchesi di Puglia*.

PURCHAS, SAMUEL: *Purchas his Pilgrimes, &c.*, London, H. Fetherstone, 1625. Fol., 4 vols.

In vol. ii. is some curious but antiquated and crude information concerning Tunisia and other countries of Barbary.

PURE, M. DE. See BIRAGO.

PYNACKER, Dr. CORNELIS: *Rapport van 't gebesoigneerde tot Tunis en Algiers in de jaren 1622 en 1623. Rapport aan de Hooge Mogende Heeren Staten Generael, gedaen by Doctor Cornelius Pynaker van syne legatie tot Algiers ende Tunis*, Utrecht, 1863. 8vo.

PYNE, J.: *Phœnicians and their Voyages*, art. in 'National Quarterly Review,' xxxii., 123.

PYRKER, JOH. LADISLAW, Bishop of Erlau, Hungary: *Tunisias* (Poem). Vienna, 1820; 3rd ed. 1826. Translated into Italian by Malipiero, Venice, 1827.

QUATREMÈRE, E. M., Membre de l'Institut: *Mémoire sur quelques Inscriptions puniques*, Paris, Imp. Royal, 1828. 8vo., pp. 19. Extracted from 'Journal Asiatique.'

QUATREMÈRE DE QUINCY: *Fondation de Carthage*, art. in 'Journal des Savants,' 1857.

—— *Investigation d'Hannon le long*

des côtes occidentales de l'Afrique, Idem, p. 249. See also HANNO.

QUESNÉ, J.-S.: *Histoire de l'Esclavage en Afrique, de P.-J. Dumont, de Paris*, Paris, 1819. 8vo., 2 portraits, and a facsimile of writing.

QUINCY, Q. DE. See QUATREMÈRE DE QUINCY.

RABUSSON, A.: *Carthage retrouvée*, Paris, J. Corréard, 1856.

The author affirms that the site of Carthage is at Bougie in Algeria.

—— *De la Géographie du nord de l'Afrique pendant les périodes romaines et arabes*, Paris, Corréard, 1856. 8vo., map. Also the same, 2ᵉ mémoire, 1857. 8vo., maps.

—— *Lettre à M. le maréchal de Mac-Mahon au sujet de la seconde Expédition du Roi Saint Louis en Afrique*, Paris, Corréard, 1867. 18mo., engravings.

RAE, EDWARD *Barbary, the Country of the Moors, or Journey from Tripoli to the Holy City of Kairwan*, London, Murray, 1877. 8vo., with maps and 6 etchings.

RALEIGH, Sir WALTER: *The Story of the War between the Carthaginians and their own Mercenaries from Polybius, &c.*, London, 1647. 4to. See also POLYBIUS.

RAMBAUD, ALFRED: *La France coloniale. Histoire, Géographie, Commerce. Ouvr. publié sous la direction de M. Alf. Rambaud, avec la collaboration de MM. le commandant Archinard de l'artillerie de marine, le capitaine Bouinais, etc. etc.* Paris, 1886. 8vo., 12 coloured maps.

RAPHAËL, D. See MAYEUX.

RAYNAL, Abbé G. T.: *Histoire philosophique et politique des Européens dans l'Afrique septentrionale, &c.*, augmenté d'un Aperçu de l'état actuel de ces établissements, &c., Paris, 1826. 8vo., 2 vols., 1 map. Tunis is contained in livre iv.

RAYNAL, Abbé G. T.: *Philosophische und historische Geschichte der Niederlassungen und des Handels der Europäer in Nordafrika. Nach dessen Tode herausgegeben von . . . Peuchet. Aus dem Franz. von F. G. Henning*, Leipzig, Fr. Fleische, 1829. Large 8vo., 2 vols., map.

READE, WINWOOD: *The African Sketch-Book, with maps and illustrations, in two volumes*, London, Smith and Elder, 1873. 8vo. A *Carthaginian Log-Book* occupies the first ten pages of vol. i.

REBATEL et TIRASEL, Docteurs de Lyon: *Voyage dans la Régence de Tunis*, in 'Tour du Monde,' 1874, No. 748, p. 289 et seq.

—— *Viaggio nella Reggenza di Tunisi*, with a map and numerous woodcuts, in 'Biblioteca di Viaggi,' Milano, 1876, xxxvii., 81 to 151.

REBOVA, Capitaine M. L.: *Tabarca (Thabraca). Ruines, mosaïques, inscriptions inédites*, art. in 'Bull. de la Soc. de Géog. et d'Arch. d'Oran,' 1884, No. 20, p. 122.

RECLUS, ELISÉE: *Nouvelle Géographie universelle*, Paris, Hachette, 1875–1886.

In the eleventh vol. of this great work, 130 pages, with numerous maps and illustrations, are devoted to Tunisia. See also GUÉRIN.

REID, T. WEMYSS: *The Land of the Bey. Being Impressions of Tunis under the French*, London, Sampson Low, 1882. 8vo.

A narrative of personal adventure during a few weeks' holiday. The author seeks to amuse his readers rather than to impart serious information. The moment of Mr. Reid's visit was that of the French seizure of the country, altogether an abnormal time.

REINACH, JOSEPH: *Le Traité du Bardo*, art. in 'Revue Politique et Littéraire,' 1881.

REINACH, SALOMON: *Les Fouilles de Carthage*, art. in 'Revue Politique et

Littéraire,' February 13, 1886. See also CAGNAT.

REINAUD. *Mémoire sur les populations de l'Afrique septentrionale,* Paris, 1857. 4to., pp. 17. See also CHAMPOLLION.

RENAN, E.: *Trois Inscriptions phéniciennes trouvées à Oumm-El-Awamid,* Paris, 1864. 8vo.

—— *Mission de Phénicie* (1860-1861), dirigée par Ern. Renan, Paris, 1874. 4to., with atlas.

—— *Inscriptions phéniciennes,* arts. in 'Revue Archéologique,' January, 1881.

—— *Les Mosaïques de Hammam-Lif,* Idem, March, 1883, and May, 1884.

RÉNIER, LÉON: *Note sur quelques Noms puniques,* art. in 'Revue Archéologique,' viii., 702.

RÉVÉRONI DE SAINT-CYR, Comte: *Notes sur le Génie militaire et la Tactique des ... Carthaginois et des Romains; avec la relation raisonnée des principales expéditions militaires de ces guerriers,* Paris, 1783. 4to., 48 plates.

REYNALD: *Carthage et les Carthaginois,* art. in the 'Temps,' July 21, 1880.

REYNAUD, P. DE. See PELLISSIER DE REYNAUD.

REYNIER, J. L. EBNEZER: *De l'Économie publique et rurale des Peuples anciens,* Genève et Paris, 1823. 8vo. Includes the Carthaginians.

General Reynier accompanied Bonaparte in Egypt.

RIALLE, GIRARD DE: *La Mer intérieure du Sahara,* art. in 'Revue Scientifique,' 1876.

—— *Monuments mégalithiques de Tunisie,* art. in 'Bulletin de la Société de Géographie et d'Archéologie d'Oran,' 1884, partie archéologique, pp. 260 to 268, 8 illustrations.

RICHOUFTZ, FRÉD. DE: *Dernière Croisade et mort de Saint Louis,* Paris, 1845. 8vo.

RICQUE, Dr. CAMILLE: *Les Dieux de Carthage,* art. in 'Revue de l'Orient,' 1863, 3 série, xvi., 376. Issued in separate form in 1864.

—— *Recherches ethnologiques sur les populations musulmanes du nord d'Afrique,* art. in 'Rev. de l'Orient; Bull. de la Soc. Orientale de la France,' Dec., 1863, pp. 363-75.

RIPA, GIULIO CESARE: *La Vera Guerra di Tunigi. Commentario da Giulio Cesare Ripa della Guerra de Tunigi,* Milano, Cotardo de Ponte, 1535.

RIPLEY, GEORGE, and DANA, CHARLES A.: *The American Cyclopædia, &c.,* New York, D. Appleton & Co., 1873-6. 8vo., 16 vols., and 1 vol. Index, 1878. Contains arts. on Carthage, 8 cols., with an illustration, &c.

RITTER, CARL: *Geschichte der Erdkunde und der Entdeckungen, &c.,* Berlin, Georg Reimer, 1861. 8vo., pp. vi. and 265, with portrait of the author. 19 pages are devoted to the Carthaginians.

—— *Géographie générale comparée, ou Étude de la Terre, &c.,* traduit de l'Allemand par E. Buret et Edouard Desor, Paris, Paulin, 1835. 8vo., 3 vols. Tunis, Carthage, &c., occupy pp. 197 to 209 of vol. iii.

—— *Die Erdkunde im Verhältniss zur Natur und zur Geschichte des Menschen, &c.,* Berlin, G. Reimer, 1822-1859. 8vo. Tunis and Carthage are described in part i., book i., pp. 914 to 922. See also LELEWELA.

RIVE, A. C. DE LA. See CLARIN DE LA RIVE.

RIVIÈRE, AMÉDÉE: *La Tunisie, Géographie, Evénements de 1881, Organisation politique et administrative, Organisation judiciaire, Instruction publique, Finances, Armée, Commerce, Industrie, Travaux publics, Système monétaire, &c.* Préface par Albert Mailhe, Paris, Challamel, 1887. 8vo., pp. x. and 145.

RIVIÈRE, M. A. et CH.: *Les Bambous, Végétation, Culture, Multiplication en Europe, en Algérie et généralement dans tout le bassin méditerranéen, nord de l'Afrique, Maroc, Tunisie, Egypte,* Paris. 8vo., nombreuses figures.

ROBERTSON, Dr. WILLIAM, D.D.: *The History of the Reign of the Emperor Charles V.*, London, 1817. 2 vols. 8vo.

Pp. 49-58, vol. ii., give an account of the origin of Turkish domination in North Africa, and of the expedition of Charles against Tunis.

ROBIANO, Abbé et Comte L. M. F. DE: *Études sur l'Écriture, &c.*, Paris, 1834. 4to. At the end of the vol. is an *Essai sur la Langue punique.*

ROBINET, J. F. E.: *La Politique positive et la Question tunisienne*, Paris, 1881. 8vo., pp. 32.

ROCHAS, AIMÉ: *Excursion à Carthage et à l'amphithéâtre d'El-Djem*, art. in 'Revue Archéologique,' ix., 87.

ROCHELLE, R. DE. See ROUX DE ROCHELLE.

ROCOLES, J. B., DE. See DAVITY.

ROHLFS, GERHARD: *Neue Beiträge zur Entdeckung und Erforschung Afrika's*, Cassel, T. Fischer, 1881. 8vo.

Contains very little about Tunisia, being chiefly devoted to the Sahara and inland sea. There is a long chapter on Halfa, or Esparto Grass.

—— *Philippeville, Bona und Tunis*, art. in 'Das Ausland,' 1869, No. 1, pp. 6-19; No. 2, pp. 32-5.

—— *Liegt ein Grund vor, die Städtebevölkerung von Marokko, Algerien, Tunisien, und Tripolitanien als eine besondere zu betrachten und zu benennen.* 'Ausland,' 1882, No. 16, pp. 301-7.

ROLAND DE BUSSY, TH.: *Petit dictionnaire français-arabe et arabe-français*, 1870. 18mo.

ROLLAND: *La Mer saharienne*, art. in 'Revue Scientifique,' Dec. 6, 1884.

ROLLIN, CHARLES: *Histoire ancienne des Egyptiens, des Carthaginois, &c.*, Paris, 1730, &c. 12mo., 14 vols., with atlas 4to. Numerous editions.

—— *Ancient History of the Carthaginians*, London, 1881-82. 8vo.

ROSNY, LÉON DE: *La Constitution de Tunis et sa nouvelle promulgation*, art. in 'Revue Orientale et Américaine,' 1860, v., 285 and 321.

The Constitution, of which this is a translation, with an historical preamble, was elaborated in 1858 and promulgated in 1860. Issued also in separate form.

ROSSI, DE: *De Christianis titulis Carthaginiensibus*, Paris, 1858. 4to.

—— *Secchia di piombo trovata nella Reggenza di Tunisia*, art. in 'Bolletino d'Architectura Cristiana,' Roma, 1867, p. 77.

—— *Mémoires sur un vase de plomb trouvé dans la Régence de Tunis*, traduit de l'Italien par A. Campion, Caen, 1869. 8vo., pp. 37, illustrated. Extracted from 'Bulletin Monumental,' published at Caen.

ROUDAIRE, Commandant, E.: *Nivellement en Tunisie. Rapport à la Soc. de Géographie*, arts. in 'Explorateur,' No. 73, p. 655; 'L'Ann. Géogr.,' 2e sér., t. i., p. 55, 1876.

—— *Rapport à M. le Ministre de l'Instruction publique sur la Mission des Chotes*, Paris, 1877. 8vo., with a map.

—— *La Mission des Chotes et le Projet de Mer intérieure en Algérie*, art. in 'Exploration,' July 7, 1881.

—— *Rapport sur la dernière Expédition des Chotes*, Paris, 1881. 8vo., pp. 187.

—— *Extrait de la Mission de M. le Commandant Roudaire dans les Chotes tunisiens*, Paris, 1881. 8vo., pp. 79.

—— *Commission supérieure pour l'examen du projet de Mer intérieure dans le sud de l'Algérie et de la Tunisie*, Paris, Imp. Nationale, 1882. 4to., pp. 548, map.

ROUDAIRE, Commandant, E.: *La Mer intérieure africaine et l'ancienne Baie de Triton*, art. in 'Nouvelle Revue,' May 1, 1884. See also BERNARD GEORGES, DRU LÉON, and KIVA.

ROUIRE, Dr.: *L'Ancienne Mer intérieure d'Afrique*, art. in 'Nouvelle Revue,' July 15, 1883; there is an art. with same title in 'Revue Scientifique,' April 19, 1884.

—— *Le Littoral tunisien*, art. in 'Revue de Géographie,' Sept. 1883.

—— *Le Littoral de la Tunisie centrale; Voies et Communications du Sahel; la Mer intérieure d'Afrique*, Idem, January, 1884.

—— *L'Emplacement de la Mer intérieure d'Afrique*, art. in 'Bulletin de l'Académie des Inscriptions et Belles Lettres,' 1884.

—— *L'ancienne Mer intérieure africaine*, art. in 'Revue Scientifique,' 1884.

—— *La Mer intérieure africaine*, art. with 2 maps in 'Comptes rendus de l'Association Française pour l'Avancement des Sciences, Congrès de Blois,' 1884.

—— *La Découverte du Bassin hydrographique de la Tunisie centrale*, art. in 'Revue Critique d'Histoire et de Littérature,' April 25, 1887.

—— *La Découverte du Bassin hydrographique de la Tunisie centrale et l'Emplacement de l'ancien Lac Triton (ancienne mer intérieure d'Afrique)*. Avec 9 Cartes, Paris, Challamel ainé, 1887. 8vo., pp. xix. and 187.

ROULX, J. D. LE. See DELAVILLE LE ROULX.

ROUSSEAU, Baron ALPHONSE, Consul de France: *Voyage du Scheikh El-Fidjani dans la Régence de Tunis, pendant les années* 706, 707 *et* 708 *de l'hégire* (1306 *à* 1308 *de l'ère chrét.*), *traduit de l'arabe*, arts. in 'Journal Asiatique,' 1852, 1 série, xx.; et 1853, 5 série.

ROUSSEAU, Baron ALPHONSE: *Bibliothèque de Tunis, notice et catalogue*, art. in 'Revue Africaine,' vi., 222.

—— *Lettre sur une mosaïque trouvée à Carthage*, in 'Revue Archéologique,' vii., 260.

—— *Lettre sur la découverte d'une mosaïque à Oudnah*, Idem, 1846, p. 142, with plate.

—— *Excursion à Nebel, l'ancienne Neapolis*, art. in 'Revue Africaine,' 1858, xii., 391.

—— *Annales tunisiennes, ou aperçu historique sur la Régence de Tunis*, Alger, 1864. 8vo.

'Faire un précis historique des événements dont la Régence de Tunis a été le théâtre, puis raconter avec plus de détails les faits écoulés depuis l'expédition de Charles-Quint, en 1535, jusqu'à la prise d'Alger en 1830, tel est le but que s'est proposé M. Rousseau.'—BARON AUCAPITAINE (see that name),' Nouvelles Annales des Voyages,' 1865, ii., 93. M. A. Demarsy adds: 'La collection des textes des traités conclus entre les beys et les différents États de la Chrétienté complète cet ouvrage.'

—— *History of the Conquest of Tunis and of the Goletta by the Ottomans*, A.H. 981 (A.D. 1573). Translated from the French (of the late M. A. Rousseau) by *J. T. Carletti*. With a Portrait (of Selim II.), London, Trübner & Co., 1883. 8vo., pp. 40.

ROUX DE ROCHELLE: *Remarques sur un voyage de M. Brandin à Tunis, et sur les sages réformes commencées par S. A. Ahmet-Bey*, art. in 'Bulletin de la Société de Géographie,' 1847, 3 série, vii., 68. See also BRANDIN.

ROYAUMONT, B. DE: *La Tunisie par un Tunisien*, art. of 5 columns, signed 'B. de Royaumont,' in 'L'Expansion Coloniale,' with rough woodcuts and portrait of the Bey, Mohammed-es-Sadek.

The article is statistical, and unimportant.

ROYER DE PREBADÉ. See LAUGIER DE TASSY.

ROYSTON, PHILIP, Viscount, F.R.S.: *An Account of the Earthquakes which happened in Barbary, &c.*, in 'Phil. Trans.,' 1755. Abr. x., 663.

ROZIER, DU. See SAUVAGNER.

ROZOIR, CHARLES DU, et MUNK, S.: *Carthage*, art. of 19 cols. in ' Dictionnaire de la Conversation,' M. W. Duckett, Paris, Michel Lévy, 1852.

RUFIGNY, H. C. See CHEVALIER-RUFIGNY.

RUFUS, RUTILIUS. See NEWTON.

RUINART, Dom: *Historia Persecutionis Vandalicæ*, Paris, 1694. 8vo.

RUPHY, J. F.: *Dictionnaire abrégé françois-arabe à l'usage de ceux qui se destinent au Commerce du Levant*, Paris, Imp. de la République, An x. [1802, V. St.]. 4to., pp. 227.

RUSSELL, Rev. MICHAEL, LL.D.: *History and Present Condition of the Barbary States, &c., with a map and eleven engravings*, Edinburgh, Oliver & Boyd, 1835. 8vo., pp. 453, of which 52 pages are devoted to *Tunis and its Dependencies*.

—— *Gemälde der Berberie, oder Geschichte und gegenwärtiger Zustand der Staaten Tunis, &c., übersetzt von A. Diezmann*, with 1 map and illustrations, forms parts 5 and 6 of the *Edinburger Cabinets-Bibliothek, &c.*, Hartleben, Pesth, 1836-37. 8vo.

RUTILIUS, RUFUS. See NEWTON, T.

RUYTER, M. A. DE: *Journaal der expeditie naar Tunis*, Amsterdam, 1662. 4to.

—— *Journaal van den manhaften tocht op de Rovers van Barbaryen*, Amsterdam, H. Hendricksen, 1662. 4to.

RYNACKER: *Reis naar Africa, Tunis, Algiers, &c.*, Haarlem, 1650. 4to.

SABATIER: *L'Ethnologie de l'Afrique du nord*, art. in 'Revue d'Anthropologie,' July, 1884.

SABLON DE LA SALLE, M. M. V. G.: *L'Avenir de la Tunisie*, Paris, 1870. 8vo., pp. 39.

SACY, Baron SYLVESTRE DE: *De quelques monnaies arabes et des monnaies de Tunis, d'Alger et du Maroc*, Paris, 1797. 8vo. Extracted from 'Magasin Encyclopédique,' 3 année, iii.

—— *Mémoire sur le traité fait entre Philippe le Hardi et le roi de Tunis en 1270, pour l'évacuation du territoire de Tunis par les Croisés*, Paris, 1825. 8vo., pp. 16. Extracted from 'Journal Asiatique,' and inserted in 'Mémoires de l'Académie des Inscriptions,' 1826, xix., 448.

The original document is preserved in the national archives of Paris.

—— *Mémoires sur quelques monnaies arabes en or des Almohades et des Mérènites*. Extracted from 'Journal des Savants,' 1837. See also HAMAKER.

SAFFAREL, PAUL: *La Mer intérieure du Sahara*, Paris.

SAINT-CYR, R. DE. See RÉVÉRONI DE SAINT-CYR.

ST. GERVAIS, DE, Consul de France à Tunis: *Mémoires historiques qui concernent le Gouvernement de l'ancien et du nouveau Royaume de Tunis, avec des Réflexions sur la Conduite d'un Consul et un détail du Commerce*, Paris, 1736. 12mo., published at Geneva, although the title-page has Paris.

SAINT-LAGER, JUILLET: *La Régence de Tunis, Géographie physique et politique, Gouvernement, Administration, Finance, etc.* 1875. 8vo.

—— *Guide général du voyageur en Algérie et en Tunisie*, 1873. 16mo., pp. 196, maps.

SAINT-MARC GIRARDIN: *De la Domination des Carthaginois et des Romains en Afrique, comparée avec la Domination française*, art. in 'Revue des Deux-Mondes,' May 1, 1841.

SAINT-MARC GIRARDIN: *L'Afrique sous St. Augustin*, 2 arts. in 'Revue des Deux Mondes,' 1842.

SAINT-MARTIN, J. A.: *Notices chronologiques, historiques, et généalogiques des principaux souverains de l'Asie et de l'Afrique septent.*, art. in 'Nouveau Journal Asiatique,' 1828.

SAINT-MARTIN, L. V. DE. See VIVIEN DE SAINT-MARTIN.

SAINT-MESMIN, E. M. DE. See MENU DE ST. MESMIN.

SAINT-PIERRE, P. DE. See PUGET DE SAINT-PIERRE.

SAINT-PRIX, JACQUES. See BERRIAT.

SAINT-SAUVEUR, G. See GRASSET ST.-SAUVEUR.

SAINTE MARIE, E. DE: *Mission à Carthage*, Paris, 1884. 8vo., pp. 234, illustré. Ouvr. publié sous les auspices du Ministère de l'Instruction Publique.

—— *Communications sur deux mille inscriptions puniques trouvées à Carthage*, art. in 'Bulletin de l'Académie des Inscriptions et Belles-Lettres,' 1873 to 1875.

—— *Note sur l'emplacement d'un édifice antique situé à Carthage contre le Forum et contre la Mer*, with a plan of Carthage, and designs of the building in question both ruined and restored, art. in 'Recueil de la Société Archéologique de Constantine,' 1875.

—— *Notice sur l'emplacement d'un édifice ancien à Carthage (Temple de Baal, Curie, Couvent de Salomon, Basilique restituée et divers Thermes) avec deux planches*, Constantine, 1875. 8vo., pp. 11. Extracted from 'Recueil des Notices de la Soc. Archéologique du Dép. de Constantine,' xvii., 131.

—— *Les Ruines de Carthage, emplacement de la Chapelle de Saint Louis, Carthage punique, avec deux planches et une carte de la Tunisie*, art. in 'Explorateur,' Paris, 1876, 4to., iii., 60.

SAINTE MARIE, E. DE: *Notice sur Utique*, art. in 'Bulletin de la Société de Numismatique,' Paris, 1875.

—— *La mission du Capitaine Roudaire* (see that name) *en Tunisie et la mer intérieure*, with maps, art. in 'Explorateur,' 1876, No. 59, p. 273.

—— *Essai sur l'histoire religieuse de la Tunisie*, art. in 'Missions Catholiques,' No. 387, p. 517.

—— *Bibliographie carthaginoise* (see p. 211 *ante*).

In the preface to his bibliography the author gives a sketch of the history of Carthage.

—— *La Tunisie chrétienne*, Lyon, Pitrat, 1878. 8vo., pp. 152, map.

SAINTE-MARIE, EVARISTE PRICOT DE, Chef d'Escadron d'État-major: *Antiquités de la Régence de Tunis*, comprising inscriptions found at El-Djem, art. in 'Bulletin de la Société de Géographie,' 1847, 3 série, viii.

—— *Lettre*, giving an account of an excursion to Cape Bon and to the town of Troglodytes, now called Grar - Mta - Dar - el - Amen, Idem, 3 série, ix.

SAKAKINI: *Extrait d'une Lettre de M. Sakakini sur les travaux de M. Hanegger dans la Régence de Tunis*, art. in 'Bulletin de la Société de Géographie,' 1835, 2 série, iii., 64.

M. A. Demarsy adds: 'M. Hanegger, professeur d'archéologie à Donaueschingen, s'était alors rendu à Tunis depuis deux ans pour y rédiger une statistique générale de la régence, accompagnée de levés topographiques. . . . Les objets provenant de ces fouilles furent envoyés au British Museum.'

SALADIN, HENRI, Architecte diplômé du Gouvernement: *Description des antiquités de la Régence de Tunis, monuments antérieurs à la conquête arabe. Fascicule I. Rapport sur la* mission faite en 1882-83, par M. Henri Saladin, architecte diplômé du Gouvernement. Paris, Imp. Nat., 1886. 8vo., 365 fig. intercalées dans le texte, 6 pl. hors texte, et 2 phototypies. In course of publication. Noticed in 'Revue d'Histoire et de Littérature,' July 26, 1886. See also CAGNAT.

SALADIN, HUBERT: *Lettre sur la colonisation des possessions françaises dans le nord de l'Afrique*, Genève, 1837. 8vo.

SALES, J. B. C. I. DELISLE DE. See DELISLE DE SALES.

SALLE, M. M. V. G. S. DE LA. See SABLON DE LA SALLE.

SANDWICH, JOHN, Earl of: *Voyage round the Mediterranean in the years 1738-9*, London, 1799. 4to., pp. 539, with map and plates.

The only place in Africa at which he touched was the Kerkennah Islands.

SANDWITH, THOMAS BACKHOUSE, C.E., H.B.M. Consul at Tunis: *Report on the Trade and Commerce of Tunis for the year* 1885, in 'Commercial, No. 12 (1886) (Trade Reports),' part v., pp. 715 to 723.

—— *Report on the advantages which would accrue from direct steam communication with Tunis.* 'Foreign Office, Miscellaneous Series,' 1886, No. 25, pp. 3.

—— *Report on the Forests of Tunis.* Idem, 1887, No. 63, pp. 3, map.

—— *Report on the Tunisian Budget for the year* 1886-87. 'Foreign Office, Annual Series,' 1886, No. 64, pp. 3.

—— *Report for the year 1886 on the Trade of Tunis.* Idem, 1887, No. 206, pp. 8.

SANSON, NICOLAS, d'Abbeville: *Partie de la Coste de Barbarie en Afrique, où sont les Royaumes de Tunis et de Tripoli et pays circonvoisins, tirés de Sanuto*, Paris, 1655. See also SANUTO.

SANSON, NICOLAS, d'Abbeville: *L'Afrique en plusieurs Cartes et plusieurs Traités de Géographie et d'Histoire*, Paris, 1856. 4to., 18 coloured maps. Tunis is included.

SANTI, F. L.: *Memento Carthago, pensieri*, Milano, 1881. 8vo., pp. 105.

—— *Italia e Tunisi*, Milan, 1881. 8vo., pp. 105.

SANTIONI DE-SIO, F. See GALEOTTI.

SANUTO, M. LIVIO: *Geographia Distincta in xii. libri*, Vinegia, D. Zenaro, 1528. Fol., 12 maps. Description of Africa. See also SANSON.

SAULCY, L. F. J. C. DE. See CAIGNARD DE SAULCY.

SAUVAGNER, FR. CH., et DU ROZIER: *Abrégé de l'Histoire de Carthage*, Paris, 1843. 12mo.

SAVARY, FRANÇOIS. See BREYES.

SCHELSTRATE, E. A.: *Ecclesia Africana sub primate Carthaginiensi*, Parisiis, 1679. 4to. Also Paris, 1680, 4to.; Anvers, 1680, 4to.

SCHILLING, M. M. See MACGILL.

SCHLOEZER, A. L. VON: *Summarische Geschichte von Nord-Africa, namentlich von Marocko, Algier, Tunis, und Tripoli*, Göttingen, 1773. 8vo.

SCHMIDT, J. See MASQUERAY.

SCHNEIDER, C.: *Von Algier nach Tunis und Constantine*, Dresden, 1872. 8vo., pp. 137.

SCHULZ, F. E.: *Sur le grand ouvrage historique et critique d'Ibn-Khaldoun, appelé Kitab-al-ibr we Diwan-ol-Moubteda wal K'haber*, Paris, 1826. 8vo., pp. 36. From 'Journal Asiatique.' See also IBN-KHALDOUN.

SCHWAB, MOÏSE: *Mémoire sur l'Ethnographie de la Tunisie*, Paris, 1868. 8vo., pp. 72. Extracted from 'Mémoires couronnés par la Société d'Ethnographie,' i.

SEARS, E. I.: *Phœnicians and their Civilisation*, art. in 'National Quarterly Review,' xv., i.

SÉDILLOT. See SIMON, E.

SENAC, Dr. See LEFÈVRE.

SÉRAN DE LA TOUR, Abbé: *Histoire de Scipion l'Africain . . , avec des observations du Chevalier de Folard sur la bataille de Zama*, Paris, Didot, 1738. 12mo.

—— *Histoire de Scipion l'Africain et d'Épaminondas, nouvelle édition*, Paris, 1752. 12mo.

—— *Parallèle de la conduite des Carthaginois à l'égard des Romains dans la seconde guerre punique, avec la conduite de l'Angleterre à l'égard de la France dans la guerre déclarée par les puissances en 1756*, Paris, 1757. 12mo.

SERRE, J. P. DE LA. See PUGET DE LA SERRE.

SEVESTRE, H.: *D'Alger à Tripoli; mission de l'aviso le 'Kléber,' mai et juin 1874*, art. in 'Rev. Mar. et Colon,' Dec., pp. 685-782.

'The *Kléber* had to visit the coral fisheries and to "show the flag" in Tunis and Tripoli.'—PLAYFAIR.

SHAW, THOMAS, D.D., F.R.S.: *Travels, or Observations relating to several parts of Barbary and the Levant*, Oxford, 1738-46. Fol., 2 vols. Other editions: London, 1757, 4to., with illustrations; Edinburgh, 1808, 8vo., 2 vols., with illustrations and life of the author; also in 'Pinkerton's Collection,' xv.; in 'Voyages and Travels,' xvii., xviii.; in 'The World Displayed, 1778,' xviii.; and in 'J. H. Moore's Collection,' ii. Translated into French:

—— *Voyages dans plusieurs provinces de la Barbarie, &c.*, La Haye, 1743, 4to., 2 vols., with map and illustrations; into German:

—— *Reisen in der Barbarey, &c.*, Leipzig, 1765, 4to.

'Dr. Shaw was chaplain to the Consulate at Algiers. This is one of the most valuable works ever written on North Africa.' See 'Quarterly Review,' vol. xcix., p. 331.

'In an Appendix he gives:—'Sylloge excerptorum ex veteribus Geographis Historicis, &c., or a collection of such extracts from the old Geographers, Historians, &c., as chiefly relate to that part of Africa or Barbary known by the name of the Kingdom of Algiers and Tunis, as follows:—Herodoti Histor., Libro iv., Lug. Bat., 1715. Scylacis Caryandensis Periplo, Oxon., 1698. Strabonis Rerum Geographicæ, Libris ii. and xvii., Amst., 1619. Cl. Ptolemæi Geographiæ, Libro iv. and viii., Amst., 1619. Pomponio Mela, De Situ Orbis, Isc Dumnon., 1711. C. Plinii Secundi Hist. Naturalis, Libro v., Par. 1685. J. Solini Polyhistore, Traj. ad Rhen., 1685. Antonio Aug. Itinerario, Lug. Bat., 1738. Æthici Cosmographia, Lug. Bat., 1696. J. Honorii Oratoris excerptis, ibid. Sexti Rufi Breviario Hist. Romanæ, Hanov., 1611. Pauli Orosii adversus Paganos Historia, Col., 1582. Martiani Mincí Felicis Capellæ de Nuptiis Philosophiæ, Lib. vi., Bas., 1577. Isidori Hispalensis Originum, Lib. xiv., ibid. Collatione Carthaginensi, Notitia Episcoporum Africæ sub Hunerico, Concilio Carthaginensi sub Cypriano, &c.; sive Notitia omnium Episcopatuum Ecclesiæ Africanæ; quæ præfigitur S. Optuli de Schism. Donatistarum, Libris septem, opera et studio M. Lud. Ell. Du Pin, Antuer., 1702. Notitia utraque Dignitatum cum Orientis tum Occidentis, ultra Arcadii Honoriique tempora, Lugd. 1608. Ravenate anonymo, Amst., 1696. Tabula Peutingeriana, ex edit. G. Hornii, Amst., 1654. [This table, which is indispensable for students of the Ancient Geography of North Africa, has been reproduced in autograph from the original MS. in the Imperial Library at Vienna by E. Chambrier, "Commis auxiliaire au Secrétariat du Conseil de Gouvernement du Gouvernement Général de l'Algérie."]'—PLAYFAIR.

'D'une érudition très-variée, il (Shaw) a, pendant un séjour de douze années en Afrique, parcouru les Régences de Tunis et d'Alger. Dans son ouvrage, l'un des plus importants, sans contredit, que nous possédions sur ces deux contrées, il traite de la géographie, de l'histoire naturelle, du gouvernement et des mœurs des pays qu'il a visités, et il essaye, par des rapprochements quelquefois erronés, mais souvent aussi fort exacts, d'identifier les noms modernes avec les noms antiques.' —V. GUÉRIN, *Voyage*, i. p. xi.

An art. on Shaw from the pen of

M. Boucher de la Richarderie will be found in 'Bibliothèque de Voyages,' iv., 18 to 37.

SHAW, THOMAS, D.D., F.R.S.: *Geographical Description of the Kingdom of Tunis*, in 'Phil. Trans.,' 1729. Abr. vii., p. 364.

SHIPPEN, E., Med. Director, U.S.A.: *A Forgotten General*, art. in 'United Service Monthly Review,' Philadelphia, 1881. Vol. v., No. 1, pp. 2 to 21.

'Gives an account of the filibustering expedition of William Eaton, the well-known American 'General' in the Cyrenaica. He was named U.S. Consul at Tunis. After a short and troubled residence there he proceeded to Egypt, whence he marched with an ill-assorted and mutinous force to Derna, which he took, though he was speedily obliged to evacuate it.'—PLAYFAIR.

SIBOUR, l'Abbé, afterwards Archbishop of Paris: *Étude sur l'Afrique chrétienne. État de l'Afrique avant les Vandales*, Digne, 1844. 8vo.

—— *Lettres sur la translation à Hippone de la relique de Saint Augustin*, Paris, n. d. 8vo.

SIDI KHALIL: *Précis de jurisprudence musulmane suivant le rite Malekite*, Paris, 1857. 8vo., Arabic text.

'This rite is followed in nearly every part of Africa. The work in question was written by an Egyptian doctor in the fourteenth century.'—PLAYFAIR.

SIGONIUS, C. See SYLBURGIUS.

SILIUS ITALICUS, CAIUS: *Silii Italici Punicorum*, Roma, 1471. Fol. Several reprints.

—— *La Seconde Guerre punique, poëme traduit par Lefebvre de Villebrune, avec le texte latin*, Paris, 1781. 12mo., 3 vols.

—— *Les Puniques, traduction nouvelle par E.-F. Corpet et N.-A. Dubois*, Paris, 1837. 8vo., 2 vols., Latin 'en regard.'

There is a *Dissertation sur Silius Italicus* by Baron Chaudruc de Crazannes, with a translation of some passages of his poem, in 'Mémoires de l'Athénée du Gers.'

SIMON, EUGÈNE: *Étude sur les Crustacés terrestres et fluviatiles recueillis en Tunisie en 1883, 1884 et 1885, par MM. A. Letourneux, M. Sédillot et Valery Mayet, membres de la Mission de l'Exploration scientifique de la Tunisie, par Eugène Simon, ancien Président des Sociétés entomologique et zoologique de France*, Paris, Imprimerie Nationale, 1885. 8vo., pp. 21, with illustrations in the text.

—— *Étude sur les arachnides recueillis en Tunisie en 1883 et 1884* (as above), pp. 55.

SISSON, THIÉBAULT: *M. Emile Bœswillwald, et les Monuments de Tunisie*, art. in 'Revue Alsacienne,' Dec. 1885.

SLANE, Baron de. See EL-BEKRI, IBN-HAUGAL, and IBN-KHALDOUN.

SMITH, PHILIP: *Carthago*, art. of 50 cols. with illustrations in 'Dictionary of Greek and Roman Geography,' W. Smith, LL.D. London, J. Murray, 1854.

Mr. Oscar Browning qualifies this art. as 'admirable.'

SMITH, R. BOSWORTH, M.A.: *Carthage and the Carthaginians*, London, Longmans, Green, & Co., 1879. 2nd edition, small 8vo., with maps and plans.

This is a standard work on the subject, carefully written and containing a mass of information little known to the student of Ancient History. No one should visit the site of Carthage without a previous acquaintance with this admirable book.

SMITH, Admiral Sir SIDNEY: *Mémoire sur la nécessité et les moyens de faire cesser les pirateries des États barbaresques. Reçu, considéré et adopté à Paris en septembre, à Turin le 14 octobre*, 1814; *à Vienne durant le Congrès*. See also 'Quart. Rev.,' xv., 139.

—— *Translation of Documents annexed to the Report of the President*

(*Sir Sidney Smith*) *of the Reunion of the Knights-Liberators of the White Slaves of Africa, assembled at Vienna on the* 29th *December,* 1814, Paris. 8vo., pp. 58.

SOMBRIM: *Notes sur la Tunisie, Souse et le Kef,* art. in 'Bulletin Société Géog.' Constantine, 1878, No. 10, 212-216.

SPANTIGATI, F. See GALEOTTI.

SPRATT, Lieut., R.N.: *Remarks on the Lakes of Benzerta,* in 'Journal of the Geographical Society,' 1846, xvi., p. 251. Analysed in 'Bulletin de la Société de Géographie' of Paris, 1847, 3 série, vii.

STAFFORD, WILLIAM COOKE: *The World as it is, a new and comprehensive system of Modern Geography,* London, P. Jackson, (1853). 4to., double cols., 3 vols., maps, portraits, and views.

A short account of Tunis will be found in vol. iii. chap. 2, with engravings of Tunis and Carthage.

STANLEY, EDWARD: *Observations on the City of Tunis and the adjacent country, with a View of Cape Carthage, Tunis Bay, and the Goletta,* London, 1786. 8vo.

STEIN, H.: *Un Dessein français sur Alger et Tunis sous Louis XIII.,* art. in 'Revue de Géographie,' January, 1883.

STENNING, RALLI: *Tunis,* 3 arts. in 'Good Words,' London, Isbister & Co., vol. for 1881, p. 384 et seq., numerous illustrations.

STRABO: *Strabonis Rerum Geographicarum Libri xvii., cum notis Casauboni et aliorum, &c. Græc. et Lat.,* Amstelod., J. Wolters, 1707. 4to., 2 vols.

—— *Strabonis Rerum Geographicarum Libri xvii. Gr. et Lat. cum variorum Animadversionibus, Codicum MSS. Collationem, Annotationes et Tabulas geographicas adjecit T. Falconer:* *subjiciuntur Chrestomathiæ, Gr. et Lat.,* Oxon, 1807. Fol., 2 vols.

Literally translated into English by H. C. Hamilton and W. Falconer, with notes and index, 3 vols. of 'Bohn's Classical Library,' 1854-56-57. Into French by De La Porte, Du Theil, Coray, and Letronne, with notes and introduction by Grosselin, as :

STRABO: *Géographie de Strabon, traduite du Grec en Français,* Paris, Impé., An xiii.=1805-19. 4to., 5 vols. Carthage is described in vol. v., chapt. ii.

SUBTIL, E.: *Tripoli et Tunis. Considérations sur la possibilité d'une invasion des Turcs dans la Régence de Tunis par les frontières de Tripoli,* art. in 'Revue de l'Orient,' 1845, vii., 281.

SUMNER, CHARLES, LL.D.: *White Slavery in the Barbary States,* 1847. 8vo., published in the U. S. Also a new edition, in 12mo., same title, 1853.

SYLBURGIUS, F.: *Historiæ Romanæ Scriptores Latini,* Francofurti, 1588-1590. 4to., 2 vols.

A chronological history based on the writings of Latin authors. An account of the rise of Carthage and of the first Punic war, by L. Florus. Subjugation of Carthage in the Commentaries of Car. Sigonius, vol. i.

TARDIEU, AMBROISE, Historiographe de l'Auvergne ; *Voyage archéologique en Italie et en Tunisie, &c.* (avec vingt-cinq vues de villes et de monuments, dessins d'antiquités), Chez l'Auteur, A. Herment (Puy-de-Dôme) MDCCCLXXXV. 4to., pp. 27, privately printed.

M. Tardieu was secretary of the expedition sent by Napoleon III. under the direction of the Comte d'Hérisson to explore Utica. Of these explorations he gives a short but interesting account, together with several 'photogravures' in the text of the objects discovered. Noticed in 'Il Bibliofilo,' June, 1885. See also HÉRISSON.

TARMINI, ALMERTÉ: *Voyage de S. M. la Reine d'Angleterre et de Baron Pergami (Bergami), en Allemagne, en Italie, en Grèce, et à Tunis, de 1816 à 1820*, Paris, 1820. 8vo.

The author was attaché to the queen during her journeys.

TASSY, L. DE. See LAUGIER DE TASSY.

TAUXIER, H.: *Ethnographie de l'Afrique septentrionale au temps de Mahomet*, in 'Rev. Afr.,' 1863, vii., 453.

TCHIHATCHEFF, P. DE: *Espagne, Algérie et Tunisie. Lettres à M. Michel Chevalier*, Paris, Challamel, 1880. 8vo., pp. 596, map. There is a German translation, Leipzig, 1880. Noticed by M. R. Radau in 'Revue des Deux Mondes,' Oct. 1, 1880.

TEMPLE, Lieut.-Col. Sir GRENVILLE: *Excursions in the Mediterranean, Algiers and Tunis*, London, 1835. 8vo., 2 vols. Analysed in 'Nouvelles Annales des Voyages,' lxvii.

'An admirable and scholarly account of his journeyings in the two countries during 1832-33. The original drawings made during his expedition are numerous and of great interest. One of them was published in the work above quoted, and thirteen others in "The Shores and Islands of the Mediterranean," Rev. G. N. Wright. London, Fisher & Son, 1839. 4to. The originals are in the possession of Sir Lambert Playfair.'—PLAYFAIR.

V. Guérin remarks: 'Cet ouvrage est, avec celui de Shaw, le plus savant et le plus exact que nous ayons sur cette matière.'—*Voyage*, i., p. xii.

'Renferme des détails utiles à consulter sur l'amphithéâtre de Thysdrus.' —A. DEMARSY.

—— *On Phœnician Inscriptions, in a Letter addressed to the Royal Asiatic Society, with a Translation of the same by Sir William Betham*, London, 1834. 8vo., 2 plates.

TEMPLE, Lieut.-Col. Sir GRENVILLE, et le Chev^{lr}. FALBE: *Relation d'une Excursion de Bône à Guelma et à Constantine, &c. Accompagné d'un recueil d'inscriptions et de quatre planches représentant des monuments antiques, des mosaïques et des peintures à fresque découverts à Carthage*, Paris, 1838. Published by Dureau de la Malle in 'Excursions dans l'Afrique Septentrionale par les Délégués de la Société établie à Paris pour l'Exploration de Carthage.' See also CHAUX, DUREAU DE LA MALLE, and FALBE.

TENANT DE LA TOUR, L. A.: *Voyage de S. A. le duc de Montpensier à Tunis, en Egypte, en Turquie et en Grèce*, Paris, 1847. 8vo., with an Album designed by Sinety.

TESTA. At p. 9 of his 'Essai de Bibliographie' M. A. Demarsy notes:

'M. le baron de Testa a publié dans le *Recueil des traités de la Porte ottomane avec les puissances étrangères* (Bibliothèque diplomatique, Paris, 1864) une collection des traités de la France avec les régences de Tunis et de Tripoli depuis 1604 (appendice du tome 1er, pag. 320). Il doit dans les autres volumes de cette collection donner l'analyse des traités des autres puissances avec ces régences.'

THOU, J. A. DE: *History of his own time. Translated from the Geneva edition of 1620 by Bernard Wilson, A.M.*, London, 1729. Folio, 2 vols., pp. 699 and 568.

Written originally in Latin: *Historia sui temporis, &c*. Books vii. and xx. give an account of the affairs of Africa—Fez, Morocco, Tremezen, and Tunis, and descent of the Turks on Africa, at Tripoli, in the 53rd year of that century (sixteenth).

TIRASEL, Dr. See REBATEL.

TISSOT, CHARLES, ancien Ambassadeur, Membre de l'Institut: *La Tunisie*, art. in 'Revue Africaine,' 1866, No. 58.

—— *Des Routes romaines du sud de la Byzacène*, Idem, i., 184.

—— *Archéologie tunisienne*, Idem, v., 286.

—— *Inscriptions de l'Amphithéâtre d'El-Djem*, Idem, 1856, with plate.

These inscriptions had already been pointed out by Dr. Barth (see that name).

TISSOT, CHARLES : *Notice sur Thuburbo Majus*, Idem, i., 424.
—— *La voie romaine de Carthage à Théveste*, art. in 'Comptes rendus des Séances de l'Académie des Inscriptions et Belles-Lettres,' 1879, vii.
—— *Exploration scientifique de la Tunisie*, Paris, 1884. 4to., pp. viii. and 697, in course of publication, one volume only having as yet appeared. Noticed in 'Le Livre,' February, 1885, p. 74.
—— *Sur une Inscription du VIIe siècle récemment trouvée à Carthage*, art. in 'Revue Archéologique,' July, 1880.
—— *Rapport sur les Missions archéologiques en Afrique*, art. in 'Bulletin de l'Académie des Inscriptions et Belles-Lettres,' 1884.
—— *Géographie comparée de la Province romaine d'Afrique*, art. in 'Revue Critique d'Histoire et de Littérature,' Nov. 10, 1884.
—— *Quatrième Rapport sur les Missions archéologiques en Afrique*, art. in 'Archives des Missions Scientifiques et Littéraires,' 1885, xi., 254 to 269, with plate of Inscription of Makter. See also vol. x.
—— *Le Bassin du Bagrada et la Voie romaine de Carthage à Hippone par Bulla Regia*, Paris, Imp. Nat., 1881. 4to., pp. 116, maps, plans. Extracted from the 'Mémoires présentés par divers savants à l'Académie des Inscriptions et Belles-Lettres.'

'This treatise, like its predecessor, *Mauritanie Tingitaine*, is a combination of historical geography and archæology. It contains the results of the author's rapid exploration of the valley of the Medjerda, along which the line is to run that is to unite Tunis with the Algerian railway system, now in course of construction, and of which the necessary engineering operations are destroying the last vestiges of many Roman cities. M. Tissot has succeeded in fixing certain positions hitherto unknown, and in preserving memorials of various monuments of which all traces would soon have been lost. There are two maps of the Medjerda and plans of the ruins of Bulla Regia (Hamman Darradji) and Utica, with coloured views of Simittu and Trajan's bridge there, Bulla Regia, Tiberius' bridge, and Vespasian's camp between Picus and Vicus Augusti.'—*Extr. from 'Catalogue of Royal Geogr. Soc.'*

TISSOT, JACQUES: *La Tunisie*, art. in 'La France Coloniale,' par A. Rambaud, Paris, A. Colin et Co, 1886. 8vo., 12 maps.

TOLLOT, JEAN BAPTISTE: *Voyage fait au Levant, ès années 1731 et 1732, contenant la description d'Alger, Tunis, Tripoli, Alexandrie, Terre-Sainte, etc.*, Paris, 1742. 12mo., pp. vi. and 354.

TORRES, ANTONIO DE: *Letteratura dei Numidi, Memoria dell' Abb. A. de Torres*, Venezia, 1789. 4to.

The Jesuit, A. de Torres, traces the origin of the Numidians, and gives a genealogy of the principal rulers, notes many indications of culture among those people, their literature up to the first century, their connexion with the Carthaginians, and adds a general biography of the principal literary men and philosophers whom that country produced.

TOUR, A. L. T. DE LA. See TENANT DE LA TOUR.

TOURNAFOND: *La Régence de Tunis*, art. in 'Exploration,' April 21, 1881.
—— *L'Ile Tabarka*, Idem, April 28, 1881.

TRÉMAUX, PIERRE: *Voyage au Soudan oriental, &c., exécuté de 1847 à 1854, comprenant une exploration dans l'Algérie, la Régence de Tunis, &c., avec un atlas de vues pittoresques, scènes de mœurs, types de végétaux, &c.*, Paris, 1852, &c. 8vo., with maps and 61 plates. Also Paris, 1863-64. 8vo., 3 vols., with atlas of 61 plates.
—— *Parallèles des édifices anciens et modernes du continent africain, dessinés et relevés, de 1847 à 1854, dans l'Algérie, les Régences de Tunis et de Tripoli, &c.*, Paris, 1858.

In-f° en livraisons, avec 89 pl. en noir et en couleur.

TRISTRAM, Rev. H. B., subsequently Canon: *The Great Sahara: Wandering south of the Atlas Mountains*, London, 1860. 8vo., pp. 435.

    An interesting record of travel in a region then little known; not without historical errors. The appendices contain physical geography, geological system, history, mammals, birds, reptiles, mollusca.—PLAYFAIR.

—— On the Ornithology of Northern Africa, The Ibis. 1860, pp. 74. See also GÜNTHER.

TULIN, CHARLES, Swedish Consul at Tunis: *Le Royaume tunisien et les représentants des puissances étrangères à Tunis*, 1864.

TURNER, Rev. J. M.: Carthage, art. of 38 cols. in 'David Brewster's Edinburgh Encyclopædia,' Edinburgh, W. Blackwood, 1830.

URVILLE, J. D. D'. See DUMONT D'URVILLE.

VALBERT, G.: *Les Origines du Protectorat en Tunisie*, art. in 'Revue des Deux Mondes,' Nov. 1, 1886.

VARIOT, M.: *L'Hôpital arabe de Tunis*, art. in 'Revue Scientifique,' 1881.

VAUDONCOURT, G. DE: Annibal, art. of 3 cols. in 'Dictionnaire de la Conversation,' M. W. Duckett, Paris, Michel Levy, 1852.

VAYNES VAN BRAKEL, H. J. L. T. DE : *Zestien Zeereizen*, Amsterdam, 1870. 8vo. Hoofst. xi. en xxvi. Tunis, Algiers en Alexandrië.

VÉLAIN, M.: *L'Algérie dans le pays des Kroumirs*, with a view of the island Tabarca and Fort Djedid, art. in 'Revue Scientifique,' 1881.

VENOSTA, F.: *I Francesi a Tunisi*, Milano, 1881. 8vo., pp. 127.

VENTURE DE PARADIS. See PARADIS.

VERCOUTRE, Dr.: *Sur la céramique romaine de Sousse*, pp. 12, art. in 'Revue Archéologique de Constantine,' 1884, 3 série, iii.

VERGERS, NOËL DES. See IBN-KHALDOUN.

VICTOR, Tunnunensis, Saint, Bishop of Vita or Utica: *Chronicon*, in Scaliger's 'Thesaurus Temporum,' and in 'Gallandi Bibl.,' pp. viii., 321, &c.

—— *The Memorable and Tragical History of the persecutions in Africke, under Gensericke and Hunericke, Arrian Kings of the Vandals*, London, 1605. 18mo.

—— *Historia persecutionis Africæ provinciæ, tempore Genserici et Hunerici regum Vandalorum*, 1874. 16mo. See Hurter (H. von), 'Sanctorum patrum opuscula selecta,' vol. xxii. 16mo.

—— *Vies de plusieurs Saints, &c., avec l'Histoire des Martyrs de l'Église d'Afrique, persécutée par les Vandales*, trad. du latin de Saint Victor, Évêque d'Utique, par Robert Arnauld d'Andilly, Paris, 1664.

VIDENS: *Les Français en Tunisie*, Londres, 1881. 8vo., pp. 19.

VIEUSSEUX: *I Barbareschi e i Christiani*, Ginevra, 1822. 8vo., pp. 64, of which 37 pages are notes.

    Relates principally to the conduct of the Bey of Tunis since 1815. There is a 'contrefaçon' under the title of *Cenni Storici sui Barbareschi.*

VIGNON, LOUIS: *La France dans l'Afrique du nord. Algérie et Tunisie*. Paris, Guillaumin & Cie, 1887. 8vo., map. Noticed in 'Le Livre,' Sept., 1887.

VILLAIN, G.: *Étude sur l'Histoire de la Tunisie depuis la Conquête arabe*, art. in 'Bulletin de l'Association Scientifique de France,' 1882.

T

VILLOT, Commandant du 125⁰ de ligne : *Description géographique de Tunis et de la Régence, avec notes historiques, ethnographiques, et archéologiques*, Paris, Challamel, 1881. 8vo., pp. 45, map.

—— *Mœurs, Coutumes et Institutions des Indigènes de l'Algérie*, Constantine, L. Arnolet, 1871. 8vo., pp. 438.

Many of the superstitions and customs described in this carefully compiled volume are also prevalent in Tunisia.

VILLOTTE, le Père JACQUE : *Voyage d'un Missionaire de la Compagnie de Jésus en Turquie, en Perse, en Arménie, en Arabie et en Barbarie*, Paris, 1730. 12mo., pp. 647.

'The writer finished his voyages by proceeding along the coast of Africa from the Syrtes to Bône, whence he proceeded to Marseilles.'—PLAYFAIR.

VINCHON, Baron de : *Histoire de l'Algérie et des autres états barbaresques*, Paris, 1839. 8vo.

VIRGIL : *Æneid*. In Book I. the foundation and building of Carthage are described, as well as the appearance of the city and the occupations of its inhabitants. See also MARTYN.

VISDELOU, C. See HERBELOT.

VIVIEN DE SAINT-MARTIN, LOUIS : *Le Nord de l'Afrique dans l'antiquité grecque et romaine*, Étude historique et géographique, Impr. Impériale, 1863. Large 8vo., pp. xix. and 519, 4 maps.

VOGEL, CH. : *Tunis*, art. of 8 cols. in 'Encyclopédie des Gens du Monde,' Paris, 1844.

VOISINS, Mme. de (PIERRE-CŒUR) : *Excursions d'une Française dans la Régence de Tunis*, Paris, M. Dreyfous, 1884. 8vo., pp. viii. and 273.

VOLTAIRE : *Essai sur les Mœurs*, chap. vi. and vii. Remarque ix.
—— *Fragments sur l'Histoire*, art. xxvi.
—— *Dict. philosophique*, arts. 'Alcoran, Arabes, Mahométans.'

VRIES, S. DE. See DAN.

WAILLE, MARIAL, Rédacteur du 'Petit Algérien :' *La France d'Afrique et ses destinées*, Paris, A. Ghio, 1883. 8vo. Noticed in 'Le Livre,' January 1885, p. 27.

WALCKENAER, Baron : *Hannon*, art. of 4 cols., giving the various editions and translations of the *Periplus* in 'Encyclopédie des Gens du Monde,' Paris, 1840. See also HANNO.

—— *Barbarie*, excellent art. of 15 cols. Idem.

WALLACE, B. J. : *Carthage and Phœnicia*, art. in 'American Presbyterian Review,' x., 291.

WARR, Earl DE LA. See DE LA WARR.

WARTEGG, E. VON H. See HESSE-WARTEGG.

WATSON, C. : *The Hystories of . . : Polybius; discoursing of the Warres betwixt the Romans and Carthaginenses, &c.*, London, 1568. 8vo. See also POLYBIUS.

WESTON, S. : *A Phœnician Coin*, art. in 'Archæologia,' xiv., 132.

WHEDON, D. A. : *Carthage and her Remains*, art. in 'Methodist Quarterly,' xxii., 429.

WILMANNS, GUSTAV : *Inscriptiones Africæ Latinæ*, ed. T. Mommsen, Berlin, 1863. 4to.

—— *Die Römische Lagerstadt Afrikas Commentationes philologæ*, Berlin, 1877. 4to.

WILSON, JAMES. See JAMESON.

WINDHAM, W. G. : *Up among the Arabs in 1860; or, Jottings in Algeria and Tunis, Descriptive and Sporting*, London, 1860. 12mo., pp. 96, with several poor illustrations.

'A work of no merit.'—PLAYFAIR.

WINGFIELD, Hon. LEWIS : *Under the Palms in Algeria and Tunis*. In 2 vols. London, Hurst and Blackett, 1868. 8vo. Two rough woodcut frontispieces and two title-vignettes.

The work is written more for amusement than instruction, and ' contains a good deal of interesting reading.'—*Saturday Review*, Sept. 12, 1868.

WINKLER, Lieut. A.: *Notes sur les ruines de Bulla Regia*, with plan, art. in 'Bulletin des Antiquités Africaines,' 1885, iii., 112.

—— *Description of the Ruins of Bulla Regia*, art. in 'Revue Africaine,' No. 172, pp. 304 to 320.

WOLTERS: *Le lac Triton et la Mer intérieure*, art. in 'Bulletin Soc. Géog.' Constantine, 1883, No. 4, 82–112.

WOODBURY, A.: *Carthage and Tunis*, art. in 'Christian Examiner,' lxxxvi., 279.

WORTLEY MONTAGU, Lady MARY: *Letters descriptive of her Travels, &c.*, Edinburgh, 1865. 8vo.
A letter to the Abbé . . . . dated Tunis, July 31, o.s. 1718, gives a short description of Tunis and a visit to the site of Carthage.

WRIGHT, JOHN, Chairman of the South-Western Railway: *Project for Constructing Railways in Algeria, &c.*, London, 1852. 8vo.

—— *Projet de Chemin de fer à établir entre l'Algérie, l'Égypte et l'Inde*, 1854. 8vo.

YANOSKI, JEAN, Professeur d'Histoire à Paris: *L'Afrique chrétienne et la Domination des Vandales en Afrique*, pp. 102, in 'L'Univers Pittoresque,' Paris, 1844. See also DUREAU DE LA MALLE.

YONGE, C. D.: *The History of the British Navy from the earliest period to the present time*, London, 1863. 8vo., 2 vols., pp. 716 and 809.
'At vol. i. p. 51, is an account of Sir R. Mansel's war on Algiers in 1620–21; at p. 76 a narration of Blake's operations at Tunis and Algiers; at p. 83 Lord Sandwich's bombardment; and in vol. ii. p. 418, an account of Lord Exmouth's battle in 1816.'—PLAYFAIR.

YVON-VILLARCEAU ET FAVÉ: *Rapport sur les travaux géodésiques et topographiques exécutés en Algérie par M. Roudaire et sur un projet de mer intérieure à exécuter au sud de l'Algérie et de la Tunisie, présenté par M. Roudaire* (see that name). 'Comptes rend. Acad. Sc.,' 7th, 12th, and 28th May, 1877.

ZACCONE, C., Capitaine détaché aux affaires arabes: *Notes sur la Régence de Tunis*, Paris, 1875. 8vo., map.

ZANDER, C. LUDWIG ENOCK: *Der Heerzug Hannibals über die Alpen*, Göttingen, 1828. 8vo., map.

ZIELINSKI, T.: *Die letzten Jahre des zweiten Punischen Krieges*, Leipzig, 1880. 8vo., pp. 174.

ZITTEL, C. A.: *Ueber den geologischen Bau der libyschen Wüste*, München, 1880. 4to., pp. 47.

ZOTEMBERG, HERMANN *Inscription phénicienne de Carthage*, art. in 'Revue Archéologique,' 1866.

ANONYMOUS.

CARTHAGE, UTICA, &c.

Corpus Inscriptionum Semiticarum ab Academia Inscriptionum et Litterarum Humaniorum conditum atque digestum, Parisiis, 1881. Fol. In the session of the 'Académie des Inscriptions et Belles-Lettres' of April 17, 1868, it was decided to undertake this publication, under the auspices of MM. Renan, Longpérier, Mohl, de Saulcy, de Rougé, de Slane, &c. Its object is to form a complete collection of Phœnician, Punic, and Neo-Punic inscriptions. It is still in progress.

Bulletin de Correspondance africaine. Antiquités libyques, puniques, grecques et romaines (École Sup. des Lettres d'Alger), Alger, 8vo.

'The first number was published in Jan., 1882, by Emile Masqueray, "Le Directeur de l'Ecole."'—PLAYFAIR.

Exempla Scripturæ Epigraphicæ Latinæ a Cæsaris dictatoris morte ad ætatem Justiniani. Edidit Æmilius Hübner. Auctorium Corporis Inscriptionum Latinarum. Berolini, 1885. 4to.

'This contains many inscriptions from various parts of Algeria and Tunis.'—PLAYFAIR.

L'Afrique septentrionale après le partage du monde romain en empire d'orient et empire d'occident. l. c., p. 81. 1856.

L'Afrique romaine, art. in 'Revue des Questions Historiques.' July, 1881.

Guerres puniques, art. of 4 cols. in 'Encyclopédie des Gens du Monde.' Paris, 1844.

Guerres puniques, art. of 4 cols. in 'Dictionnaire Général de Biographie et d'Histoire,' par Ch. Dezobry et Th. Bachelet, Paris, Delagrave, 1883.

Annibal, art. of 6 cols. in 'Encyclopédie des Gens du Monde,' Paris, 1833.

Autobiographie d'un laboureur tunisien (époque romaine), art. in 'Magasin Pittoresque,' June 15, 1887.

Excursions dans l'Afrique septentrionale, par les délégués de la Société établie à Paris pour l'exploration de Carthage: ouvrage accompagné d'inscriptions et de planches en noir et en couleur. Publié par la Société, Paris, 1838. 8vo., pp. xx.+108+[35].

Histoire ancienne des Egyptiens . . . des Carthaginois, avec Cartes, à l'usage des maisons d'éducation (religieuses), Lyon, 1869. 18mo., pp. 232.

Carthaginians and Phœnicians, art. in 'Foreign Quarterly Review,' xiv., 197.

History of the Carthaginians, London, Religious Tract Society, 1840.

Carthage and Tunis, art. in 'Fraser's Magazine,' lxx., 109.

The Parallel between England and Carthage, and between France and Rome, examined, by a Citizen of Dublin, London, Murray, 1803. 8vo.

Carthage and the Carthaginians, art. in 'National Quarterly Review,' iii., 331.

History of Carthage, art. in 'Christian Remembrancer,' xix., 373.

Recent Discoveries at Carthage, art. in 'Dublin Review,' xlix., 383.

BIBLIOGRAPHY.

Remains of Carthage, art. in 'Blackwood's Magazine,' lxxxix., 149.

Ruins of Carthage (16 pp.), in 'Modern Traveller,' edited by Conder, London, J. Duncan, 1829. 30 vols., maps and illustrations.

Les Ruines de Carthage d'après les écrivains musulmans, art. in 'Magasin Pittoresque,' 1866.

Les Comptoirs carthaginois des Syrtes, art. in 'Instruction Publique,' April 18, 1885.

Carthage, art. of 31 cols. in 'Encyclopædia Perthensis,' **Edinburgh**, J. Brown, 1816.

Carthage, art. of 17 cols. in the '**London Encyclopædia**,' London, Thos. Tegg, 1829.

Carthage and *Carthaginians*, arts. of 6 and 37 cols. in Dr. A. Rees's '**Cyclopædia**,' London, Longman, 1819.

Carthage, art. of 8 cols. in the '**Penny Cyclopædia**,' London, Charles Knight, 1836.

Carthage, art. of 47 cols. in Burrowes's '**Modern Encyclopædia**.'

Carthage, art. of 13 cols. in '**The Oxford Encyclopædia**,' Oxford, 1828.

Carthage, art. of 35 cols., with portrait of Hannibal, in '**Encyclopædia Londinensis**,' by John Wilkes, London, 1810.

Carthage, art. of 2 cols. in '**Dictionnaire Général de Biographie et d'Histoire**,' par Ch. Dezobry et Th. Bachelet, Paris, Delagrave, 1833.

Carthage, art. in '**Edinburgh Review**, cxiv., 65.

Carthago, art. of 18 pages in Pauly's '**Real-Encyclopädie**,' Stuttgart, 1862.

Carthage, art. of 17 cols. in '**Grand Dictionnaire Universel**,' par Pierre Larousse, Paris, 1867.

Karthago, art. of 4 cols. in Pierer's '**Universal-Conversations-Lexikon**,' Oberhausen, 1877.

Karthago, art. of 8 cols. in Meyer's '**Konversations-Lexikon**,' Leipzig, 1876.

Karthago, art. of 3 cols. in Brockhaus' '**Conversations-Lexikon**,' Leipzig, 1885.

The Ruins of Carthage, notice with woodcut in '**Ill. London News**, 1881, lxxviii., 488.

Notice sur la construction et la dédicace de la Chapelle de St.-Louis, érigée par Louis-Philippe Ier, sur les ruines de l'ancienne Carthage, &c., Paris, 1841. 4to., illustrations and maps.

La Chapelle Saint-Louis à Tunis, Paris, 1874. 9 plates.

Les Ruines d'Utique, arts. in '**Dix-neuvième Siècle**,' Oct. 30 and 31, 1881.

Les Fouilles d'Utique, art. in '**Revue Britannique**,' October, 1881.

BARBARY STATES, &c.

Globus. Illustrirte Zeitschrift für Länder- und Völkerkunde, &c., herausgegeben von (originally) Karl Andree, (now) Dr. Richard Kiepert, (published formerly at) Hildburghausen, (now) Braunschweig, F Vieweg & Sohn. Vol. i. bears date 1862. 4to. Scattered through the 49 vols. of this excellent publication, still **in progress**, will be found arts., notices of books, and various notes concerning Tunisia.

L'Afrique explorée et civilisée, journal mensuel, fondé (en 1879) et dirigé par M. G. Maynier, paraît le premier lundi de chaque mois, par livraisons in-8 de 20 à 30 p. chacune, avec cartes.

Revue algérienne et tunisienne de législation et de jurisprudence publiée par l'école de droit d'Alger, 1885.

Grand Annuaire, industriel, administratif, agricole et vinicole de l'Algérie et de la Tunisie, Paris, 1886. 8vo., in progress.

Annuaire algérien - tunisien. Administration, bâtiments, travaux publics, arts industriels, agriculture et commerce, Alger, 1886. 8vo.

Turcici Imperii Status; accedit de Regno Algeriano atque Tunetano Commentarius, Lugduni Batavorum, Elzevir, 1634. 8vo.

Schauplatz barbarischer Sclaverey oder von Algier, Tripoli, Tunis und Sale, Hamburg, 1694. 8vo.

État des Royaumes de Barbarie, Tripoly, Tunis et Alger, contenant l'histoire naturelle et politique de ces pays, La Haye, 1704. Also Rouen, 1703 and 1731. 12mo.

A Complete History of the Pyratical States of Barbary, London, 1750. 8vo. Said to be based upon the works of Laugier de Tassy and Saint-Gervais (see those names). Translated into German: *Die Staaten der Seeräuber*, &c. Rostock, 1753. 8vo., with a map and plan of Algiers. Also into Italian, Venice, 1754.

Histoire des États barbaresques qui exercent la piraterie, contenant l'origine, les révolutions et l'état présent des Royaumes d'Alger, de Tunis, de Tripoli et du Maroc, avec leurs forces, leurs revenus, leur politique et leur commerce, Paris, 1757. 12mo.

Historical Memoirs of Barbary and its Maritime Power, as connected with the Plunder of the Seas; including a Sketch of Algiers, Tripoli, and Tunis, an account of the various attacks made upon them by several States of Europe, considerations of their present means of defence, and the original treaties entered into with them by K. Charles II., London, 1816.

Statistisch-geographische Beschreibung der Afrikanischen Seeräuber-Staaten Algier, Tunis, Tripolis, und der Reiche Fetz und Marocco, mit einer kurzen Geschichte ihrer Entstehung und der bisher von Europäischen Mächten gegen sie unternommenen Kriege, etc., aus besten Quellen, Stuttgart, J. F. Steinkopf, 1816. 8vo., 2 parts, 1 map.

Neue Beschreibung der barbarischen Staaten Ma-okko, Algier, Tunis und Tripolis, mit 1 Karte und Ansichten der 6 grossen Häfen der Seeräuber: Tunis, Tanger, Oran, Tripolis, Anger und Salee, Leipzig, 1817. Fol.

Rapports sur les recherches géographiques, historiques, archéologiques à entreprendre dans l'Afrique septentrionale. Paris, 1838. 4to., pp. 85.

Résumé de l'histoire ancienne de l'Algérie, de la Régence de Tunis et du Maroc avant la conquête musulmane, Paris, Impr. Imp. 1864. 12mo., (en français et en arabe).

Die Wehrkraft des osmanischen Reiches und seiner Vasallen-Staaten, Egypten, Tunis und Tripoli, 1871. 8vo.

Istoria degli stati di Algeri, Tunisi, Tripoli e Marocco. Trasportata fedelmente dalla lingua Inglese nell' Italiana, in Londra, 1754. 12mo., pp. 376.

État des places que les princes mahométans possèdent sur les côtes de la mer Méditerranée. MS., Supplément français, n° 19.

Anzug etlicher Meilendischen und Genuesischen frischen Schreiben der kayserlichen und christlichen Armata Anzug und Kriegsrüstung in Africa betreffend, 1535. 4to.

Das ist der erst Kriegszug und wahrhaftige Geschicht so auf dem Barbareyschen Kayserlichen Zug gehandelt und geschehen ist, Nürnberg, S. Hammer, 1536. 4to.

Rerum a Carolo V. Cæsare Augusto in Africa Gestarum Commentarii

&c., Antverpiæ, apud J. Bellerum, 1555. 8vo.

Relazione del Viaggio e della Presa di Bona en Berberia fatta delle Galere della Religione di S. Stefano il 16 *Settembre,* 1607, *sotto il commando di Salvio Piccolomini,* Firenze, Martelli, 1607. 8vo.

Famosa y admirable Relacion de la gran Victoria que el Señor Marques de Santa-Cruz a tenido contra las Galeras de Viserta y Argel, Sevilla, Cabrera, 1624. Fol.

Relacion Verdadera de la gran Victoria que el Sr. D. Antonio de Zúñiga y de la Cueua Marques de Flores de Avila del Consejo de Guerra de su Majestad, su Governador y Capitan General de Oran, Reinos de Tremecen y Túnez, tuvo con los Moros Venerajes distantes de Oran veinte y quatro leguas, a los 7 de Octobre de 1632. Reprinted in 'Coleccion de Libros Españoles Raros et Curiosos,' Madrid, 1881. tomo 15.

Relacion verdadera de la Presa que las Galeras de Venecia han alcançado de las de Tunez y Argel, Madrid, J. Sanchez, 1638. 4to.

A Relation of the whole proceedings concerning the Redemption of the Captives in Argier and Tunis, London, 1647. 4to.

Instructie van de Staten Generael voor I. B. van Mortaigne, consul op de kust van Barbaryen, en G. de Vianen, fiscaal over's lantsvloot naar Algiers en Tunis, 1664. 4to.

Remarques d'un voyageur sur la Hollande, l'Allemagne, l'Italie, l'Espagne, le Portugal, l'Afrique et quelques isles de la Méditerranée, La Haye, 1728. 12mo. Tripoli, Tunis, Alger, Oran, Ceuta, Tanger, &c., are noticed.

Reis naar Africa. Tunis en Algiers, beschreven door een liefhebber op de vloot derwaarts uit Holland gezonden om de Christen Slaven te verlossen in't Jaar 1625, Hague, 1630. 4to.

A Book of the Continuation of Foreign Passages. That is . . . from General Blake's Fleet. 'The Turks in Algiers do consent to deliver all the English slaves, and desire a firm peace,' London, 1657. 4to., pp. 61.

'This pamphlet contains many interesting documents, amongst others an account of General Blake's "battering Tunnis" and "the submission of the Turks in Algiers."'—PLAYFAIR.

Voyage dans les États barbaresques du Maroc, Alger, Tunis et Tripoly, ou Lettres d'un des Captifs qui viennent d'être rachetés, par MM. les Chanoines réguliers de la Sainte-Trinité, Paris, 1785. 12mo. Translated into German, Lubeck, 1780. 8vo. 'Un tissu d'absurdités,' Jean Gay, 'Bibliographie,' art. 483.

Leaves from a Lady's Diary of her Travels in Barbary. In two vols. London, H. Colburn, 1850. 8vo. The greater part of vol. ii. is occupied by descriptions of Carthage, and of Tunis, and its inhabitants.

Blätter aus dem afrikanischen Reise-Tagebuch einer Dame. Braunschweig, Vieweg und Sohn, 1849. 8vo. Two parts. i. Algerien. ii. Tunis.

Reise eines französischen Offiziers nach Tunis, Tripolis, Algier, &c. Mit 1 Karte. Forms Part ii. of Vol. vii. of Steger's 'Bibliothek älterer Reisen,' Leipzig, 1856.

Tunis and Algeria in 1845, art. in 'Dublin University Magazine,' xxviii., 285.

Tunis, Algeria, and Morocco, art. in 'North British Review,' xlix., 141.

American Diplomacy with the Barbary Powers; their piracies and aggressions, 'American Whig Rev.,' 1851, vol. xiii., pp. 27-33.

Les Colonies nécessaires: Tunisie, Tonkin, Madagascar, par un Marin, Paris, P. Ollendorf, 1885. 12mo. Noticed in 'Le Livre,' October 1885, p. 527.

Le Commerce de la Tunisie et de l'Algérie, art. in 'Revue Géographique Internationale,' March, 1887.

De l'urgence d'assimiler les produits tunisiens aux produits algériens à l'entrée en France, art. in 'Économiste Français,' July 17, 1886.

La Colonisation française et les voies ferrées dans l'Afrique du nord, art. in 'Économiste Français,' March 8, 1884.

La Tunisie et les chemins de fer algériens, avec une carte des chemins de fer algériens et tunisiens, Paris, (1877). 8vo., pp. 31.

Tunis and Egypt in Bankruptcy, art. in 'Bankers' Magazine' (N. Y.), xxxiii, 513.

Histoire des dernières révolutions du Royaume de Tunis et des mouvements du Royaume d'Alger, Paris, 1689. 12mo. Reprinted, Paris, 1713. 12mo.

La Curée de l'Afrique; la Dissémination des Propriétés, l'Alfa et l'Industrie française, art. in 'Économiste Français,' February 28, 1885.

La Curée de l'Afrique, la Responsabilité et la Solidarité, Idem, March 7, 1885.

L'Inondation du Sahara, la Mer algérienne, &c., art. in 'Revue Britannique,' Dec. 25, 1879.

Mer intérieure. Rapport présenté au Président de la République par le Ministre des affaires étrangères sur les travaux de la commission instituée pour l'examen du projet de mer intérieure dans le sud de l'Algérie et de la Tunisie et sur les conclusions de cette commission, 'Journ. Off.,' 4th August, 1882, pp. 4213-4216.

Conseil de Guerre de la Province de Constantine. L'Affaire de l'Oued Mahouine, Paris, 1870. Large 8vo., pp. 94. Massacre of a caravan composed of Hammams, a tribe of Tunisia.

L'Avenir de la France dans l'Afrique du nord, art. in 'Économiste Français,' July 2, 1887.

TUNISIA.

La Revue tunisienne, publication bimensuelle littéraire, artistique, historique et archéologique. Directeur-Administrateur-Gérant: M. Albert Duvau, Rédacteur-en-chef: M. Ferdinand Huard. Bureaux: Rue de Carthage, 3, *à Tunis.* Started in 1886. In course of publication.

Indicateur tunisien pour 1886, *guide de l'administration, du commerce, de l'industrie et de l'agriculture. Annuaire de la Régence,* Tunis, 1886. 8vo.

Società Lessicografica Tunisiana. Statuti. Cagliari, (1871), pp. 8.

Copie de Lettere mandate de Tunisi al molto magnifico messer Sebastiano Gandolfo, con il disegnio del paese di Tunisi, 1536. 4to.

La Régence de Tunis. Géographie physique et politique. Description générale, gouvernement, etc., Alger. 8vo.

Tunis et son historien El-Kairouani, par un sous-lieutenant attaché aux affaires arabes. Marseille, (1871). 8vo. pp. 39. See EL-RAÏNI.

BIBLIOGRAPHY. 281

Tunis, art. of 2 cols. in 'Encyclopédie de Diderot et D'Alembert,' 1765.
Tunis, art. of 4 cols. in 'Encyclopédie Méthodique,' Paris, Panckoucke, 1788.
Tunis, art. of 4 cols. in Dr. A. Rees's 'Cyclopædia,' London, Longman, 1819.
Tunis, pp. 20, *Tunis to Bizerta*, pp. 12, *Tunis to Jerba*, pp. 22, three arts. in 'Modern Traveller,' London, J. Duncan, 1829. 30 vols., maps and illustrations.
Tunis, art. of 19 cols. in 'Penny Cyclopædia,' London, Charles Knight, 1843.
*Une Promenade à Tunis en 1842, par le Capitaine * * *, ancien officier suisse*, Paris, 1844. 8vo., pp. 225.
La Tunisie, art. in 'Revue de l'Orient,' 1847, 1 série, i., 1 to 19.
La Regenza di Tunis nell' 1869, Alger, 1870. 4to., pp. 68.
La Régence de Tunis, art. in 'Nouvelles Annales de Voyages de Malte-Brun,' 1870.
Tunis, and *Tunisie*, arts. of 3 and 6 cols. in 'Grand Dictionnaire par M. Pierre Larousse,' Paris, 1876.
Tunis, art. of 4 cols. in 'Meyer's Konversations-Lexikon,' Leipzig, 1878.
L'Insigne de la Plume dans la Régence de Tunis, art. in 'Magasin Pittoresque,' Oct. 1881.
Tunis, and *Tunisie*, arts. of 2 and 2½ cols. in 'Dictionnaire Général de Biographie et d'Histoire, par Ch. Dezobry et Th. Bachelet,' Paris, Delagrave, 1883.
La Tunisie, ses progrès et son organisation, art. in 'Économiste Français,' Dec. 20, 1884.
Documents diplomatiques relatifs aux affaires de Tunisie, avec une Carte de la Régence, Paris, Imp. Nationale, 1886. 4to., pp. 312.
Tunis, art. of 7 cols., with map, in 'Brockhaus' Conversations-Lexikon,' Leipzig, 1886.
Tunis, art. in 'Blackwood's Magazine,' cxxx., 128. Same art. in 'Living Age,' cl., 308.
Letters from Tunis, art. in 'Good Words,' iv., 699.
Sketches of Tunis, art. in 'Penny Magazine,' viii., 413.
Sketches in Tunis, arts. with woodcuts in 'Ill. London News,' 1882, lxxxi., 473; 1883, lxxxii., 231, 450.
Tale of Tunis, art. in 'Chambers Journal,' lviii., 235.
Il Maraviglioso honore fatto dal vicete e signori Napolitani al re de Tunisi per la sua venuta a Napoli, &c., Venetia, 1534.
Zweyrley newe Zeitung vom Bapst Clements Absterbung . . . und dem Königreych Tunisi, (1534). 4to.
Newe Zeytung von Kayserlicher Majestät Kriegsrüstung wider den Barbarossa gegen der Stadt Thunis, in Africa zu schicken, aus Neapolis und andern Orten geschrieben, 1535. 4to. Without place of publication. Also. Nürnberg, 1535.
Verteutscht Schreiben v. Kayserlicher Majestät wunderbarlicher Eroberung der Königlichen Stadt Tunis, in Africa, den xxiii. July, 1535, Nürnberg, 1535. 4to.
Römischer Keyserlicher Maiestät Christenlichste Kriegs Rüstung wider die Unglaubigen . . . . in Africa und Eroberung des Ports zu Thunisie im Monat Junio, anno 1535, *aus Teutschen, Italianischen und Frantzösichen Schriften*. 4to.
Capitoli del apontamiento fatto tra Ceserea Maesta dello Imperatore e il Re de Tunisi, 1535.
Copia d'una Littera in la quale se contiene la Presa della Goletta, con tutte le sue particolarita, (1535).
S'ensuit la Coppie des Lettres envoiées par l'Impériale Majesté à monseig-

BIBLIOGRAPHY.

neur de Linkerke, ambassadeur en France, touchant la Prinse de la Goulette et la Défaite de l'Exercite de Barberousse, et Prinse de Tunis, Imprimé à Anvers par Guillaume Vostreman et Nicolas de Graue, 1535. 4to.

Kurtze Verzeigniss wie Kayser Karl der V. in Africa, dem König von Tunis so von dem Barbarossen vertrieben mit Kriegsrüstung zu Hülfe kompt und was sich zugetragen, etc., 1535. Fol., illustrations.

Kayserlicher Majestät Eroberung des Königreichs Tunisi, Nürnberg, 1535. 4to.

Wahrhaftige neue Zeitung des Kayserlichen Sigs zu Goletta und Thunis geschehen, 1535. 4to. With a woodcut on the title giving the plan of Tunis.

Vertragsartickel römischer Keis. Ma. und des restituirten Königs von Tunisi. Sampt irer Majestet Ankunfft in Italien und ettlichen andern frischen Zeytungen, (1535). 4to.

Sendtbrief so die R. K. und H. Majestät ihres erlangten Sygs gegen dem Barbarossa im Königreich Thunis, auss Africa zugeschrieben hat, (1535). 8vo.

La copia de la littera venuta da Tunesi cò li ordini a provisione fatte dal Barbarossa, in la prefata citta et la gionta de la Maesta Cesarea con la Preda fatta de la sua potentissima Armata, (1535). 4to.

Newe Zeitung wie die Romisch Kayserlich Mayestät von Tunis, auss Africa, in Messina und Napoles ankommen, etc. 1536.

Diarium Expeditionis Tuniceæ a Carlo V., 1535, susceptæ, Joanne Etrobio interprete, Lovanii, 1547. 4to.

Relation de la Conquête de Tunis par Charles-Quint, art. in 'Archives du Nord de la France,' &c. iv., 54 to 60.

Traslado de la Capitulacion assentada entre el poderoso Rey de Tunez, Muley-Hamet, y el illustre y muy magnifico señor D. Alonzo de la Cueva y de Benavides, capitan general, alcayde y gobernador de la Goleta de Tunez por su Majestad. Baeça, 1551. 4to.

Il vero Aviso della Presa di Tunesi, Roma, 1573. 4to.

Ragguaglio del Acquisto de Tunisi ed altere particolarità, Roma, 1573.

Il vero Ragguaglio della Presa di Biserta con l'ultimo avviso del Successo di Tunisi, 1573.

La Nouvelle Conqueste de Tunis et de Biserte faite sur les Turcqs et Mores, par le Seigneur don Jouan d'Austrie, au mois d'Octobre dernier, Paris, J. Dallier, 1573. 8vo.

Discorso della Goleta e del Forte di Tunisi, Macerata, S. Martellini, 1574. 4to.

La Victoire obtenue par les Galions de Malthe sur les Vaisseaux turcz de Tunis, avec la prise d'un vaisseau turc par les galères du même ordre, Paris, J. Jacquin, 1621. 8vo.

Relazione della presa di due Bertoni di Tunisia, fatta in Corsica, da quattro Galere di Toscana quest' anno, 1617, li 23 di Nos., Florence (?), 1617. 4to.

La Deffaicte de cinq cents hommes et de quatre vaisseaux de guerre (de Tunis) par le sieur de Beaulieu, capitaine d'une des galères du roi, Paris, N. Alexandre, 1621. 8vo.

Relazione del Viaggio e Pressa de due Galere Tunesine, fatte dalle Galere di Malta, al oltimo de 1628, (1628).

Relazione della Presa di due Galere de guerra di Biserta, fatta il di 3 d'Ottobre, 1628, dalle Galere della religione di S. Stephano, Firenze, 1628. 4to.

Relation véritable du Combat et Prise de deux Galères du Roi de Tunis, *par les Gallions de Malthe, commandés par M. de Cremeaux*, Lyon, J. Roussin, 1629. 8vo. The same work, Paris, J. de Bordeaux, 1829.

Voyage et Prise de quatre Gallions de Tunis, Paris, 1629.

Relation du voyage et prinse de quatre galions du Roy de Tunis en Barbarie, faite par les galères de Malte, &c. Traduit de l'Italien, Paris, 1629. 4to.

Traité de Paix entre le Roi, la Ville et le Royaume de Tunis, fait à la baie de la Goulette, le 28 juin, 1672, par le Marquis de Martel, &c. 4to.

Copie des articles conclus au nom de Sa Majesté Impériale et Catholique par les Commissaires impériaux avec la Régence de Tunis, à l'intervention et médiation des Commissaires ottomans sur la libre Navigation, abstractivement de tout Commerce, à Tunis le 23 Septembre, 1725, Bruxelles, 1726.

Relacion de la redempcion de cautivos . . . en la Ciudad de Tunez, (1726). 4to.

Traité de Paix entre Frédéric Roi de Danemark et Ali-pacha du Royaume de Tunis, 8 déc. 1751. Published also in separate form in Danish and in German. Also to be found in the collections of Wenck, iii. 1.

Treaty of Peace and Commerce between Great Britain and the State of Tunis, concluded . . . January 22, 1762.

Tratado de Paz . . . ajustado entre el Rey nuestro Señor y el Bey y la Regencia de Tunez, aceptado y firmado por S. M. el 19 Julio de 1791-1791. 4to.

L'Expédition de Tunisie, art. in 'Revue Scientifique,' 1881.

Conférence sur l'Expédition de Tunisie, arts. in 'Bulletin de la Réunion des Officiers,' July 30, 1881 ; Dec. 22, 1883 ; Feb. 23, 1884.

A propos de la Guerre d'Afrique, art. in 'Bulletin de la Réunion des Officiers,' Sept. 17, 1881.

Caractères de la Guerre d'Afrique, art. in 'Revue Scientifique,' Sept. 24, 1881.

Itinéraires en Tunisie, 1881–82, Paris, Ministère de la Guerre, 1882. 4to., maps.

L'Expédition française en Tunisie, art. in 'Spectateur Militaire,' January, 1883.

The French Expedition to Tunis, illustrated notices in 'Ill. London News,' 1881, lxxviii., 445, 448, 449, 496, 512.

The French in Tunis, Ibid., 1881, lxxix., 92, 305, 352, 614.

The War in Tunis, French Column on the march, Idem, 1882, lxxx., 152.

The French Expedition to Tunis, illustrated notices in 'Graphic,' 1881 xxiii., xxiv.

The French Occupation of Tunis, Idem, 1882, xxv.

Mémoire sur la question des finances tunisiennes, Florence, 1869. 4to.

Mémoire portant plusieurs avertissements présentés au roi par le capitaine Foucques, &c., avec une description des grandes cruautés et prise des chrestiens par les pyrates Turcs de la Ville de Thunes, &c., Paris, Guillaume Marretto, 1609. 8vo. Reprinted by the same publisher in 1612.

Relation véritable de tout ce qui s'est fait et passé dans l'accommodement de Tunis et de plusieurs esclaves catholiques, &c. (le 17 juin-8 juillet, 1728), (Paris). 4to.

Lettre d'un comédien à un de ses amis, touchant sa captivité et celle de vingt-six de ses camarades, chez les corsaires de Tunis, &c., Paris, 1741. 8vo.

Relazione della Conversione alla Santa Fede del primogenito del Re di Tunisi, Mamet Celebi, vagi detto D. Felippe Dai, Roma, 1644. 4to. The same work, Firenze, 1644.

Relazione della venuta alla Cristianita ed in Palermo di Mamet figliulo primogenito di Amat Dey, Re di Tunisi, Palermo, 1646. 8vo.
La Tunisie chrétienne, Lyon, 1878. 8vo. Published by the 'Société des Missions Catholiques.'
Des rapports de la Tunisie avec l'Europe, par un Cosmopolite, Paris, 1865. 8vo.
La Questione Tunisiana, Firenze, 1868. 8vo.
Tunisian Question, Duplicity or Diplomacy: the last phase of the Tunisian question, London, 1881. 8vo., pp. 9.
Le Protectorat de la France en Tunisie, art. in 'Revue Britanique,' June, 1881.
Tunis en France. Questions politiques contemporaines, par un Diplomate, 1882. 8vo.
La France en Tunisie, art. in 'Revue des Deux Mondes,' Feb. 15, 1887.
A Brief Remonstrance of Injuries and Indignities from the Dey of Tunis, London, 1653.
Le Bey de Tunis par D. et H., art. in 'Revue de l'Orient,' 1844, iv., 83
  'Polémique à propos de diverses questions politiques.'—A. DEMARSY.
Un nouveau danger de notre politique coloniale: les Intrigues à Tunis, art. in 'Économiste Français,' July 11, 1885.

Mémoire sur la question des finances tunisiennes, Florence, 1869. 4to.
Grandeur et Décadence de la Dette tunisienne, &c., Paris, (1871). 16mo., pp. 25.
Loi sur la propriété foncière en Tunisie, Tunis, 1885. 8vo. pp. 110. This is a new law, simplifying the termination of real property, based on the Australian 'Torrens Act.'
Tunis and the Enfida Estate, art. in 'All the Year Round,' xlvii., 5, 250.
La Question de l'Eau en Tunisie, Idem, 1882.
Les Oasis tunisiennes, art. in 'Nature,' March 27, 1886.
L'Ile de Djerba, art. in 'Exploration,' August 4, 1881.
Observations on the City of Tunis, London, 1786. 4to.
Le nom punique d'Hadrumète, art. in 'Revue critique d'Histoire et de Littérature,' April 26, 1880.
Kairwan, art. of 21 pp., with 15 illustrations, in 'Harper's Magazine,' May, 1884.
The Holy City of Kairouan, art. in 'All the Year Round,' xlvii., 277.
Mosque of Okhba at Kairouan, art. in 'American Architect,' x., 291.
Découverte d'une nécropole chrétienne à Sfax, art. in 'Bulletin de l'Académie des Inscriptions et Belles-Lettres,' January, 1887.

MAPS.

THE BARBARY STATES.

Carte de Peutinger, made by Konrad Peutinger from an ancient map found at Spire in 1500, now in the library at Vienna. 1500
Partie de la Coste de Barbarie, où sont les Royaumes de Tunis et Tripoli, par Sanson. 1655
Mapa general que comprehende los Reynos de Marruecos, Fez, Alger, y Tunez. 1775
Generalkarte der Königreiche Marokko, Fez, Algier und Tunis, nach den besten Karten und neuesten Nachrichten verfasst von Don Lopez y Vargas. Massstab 1:2,800,000. Imp. Fol., Wien, 1789, F. A. Schraembl. 1789

Karte von Algier, Tunis und Tripoli, von Kr. Mannert. Kupferstich und color. Roy. Fol., Nürnberg, 1799, Schneider und Weigel. 1799

Karte der Nordküste Afrikas, oder der Staaten Morokko, Fez, Algier, Tunis, Tripoli, und Aegypten, von J. C. M. Reinecke. Kpfrst. und color. Imp. Fol., Weimar, 1802 (Landes-Industrie - Comptoir); also 1804. Massstab 1·6,000,000. 1802-4

Karte von Algier und Tunis mit der südlichen Küste von Frankreich und einem Plan von der Bay Algiers. Lithogr. von E. Zinck. Gr. Fol., Offenbach, 1830, (Frankfurt, Schaefer). 1830

Carte de la Colonie française d'Alger, de la Régence de Tunisie, &c. 1836

Carte comparée des Régences d'Alger et de Tunisie. 1838

Carte des Régences d'Alger, de Tunis, et de Tripoli. 1840

Carte des Côtes de Sicile et de la Régence de Tunis. 1840-56

Karte der Regentschafften Algier, Tunis, und Tripolis. 1844

Karte von Marocco, Algier, und Tunis, nach der Carte de l'Algérie, dressée au dépôt général de la guerre sous la direction de M. le Lieut.-Général Pelet und nach J. Arrowsmith von Albr. Platt. Lith. und color. Imp. Fol., Magdeburg, 1846, Kaeglemann. 1846

Carte des Régences d'Alger, de Tunis, et de Tripoli, avec l'Empire du Maroc par Hérisson, Paris, 1847, one sheet. 1847

Côtes de Sicile et de la Régence de Tunis. 1874

Algerien und Tunisien . . . Von H. Kiepert. Maasstäbe in 1·2,000,000. 1881

TUNISIA, including CARTHAGE.

Terra di Tunizi. [By] A[gostino] V[eneziano, Florence (?)]. 1535

Carte de la Régence de Tunis, dressée au dépôt général de la guerre, sous la direction de M. le Lieut.-Gén. Baron Pelet. Echelle, 1·400,000, 2 sheets, Paris. 1842

Carte de la Régence de Tunis, gravée sur pierre, au 400,000^e, 1857. 2 feuilles. 1857

Carte de la Régence de Tunis, du dépôt de la guerre, publiée en 1843, d'après les matériaux fournis par MM. Falbe, capitaine de vaisseau danois, et Pricot de Sainte-Marie, capitaine français. 1843

Carte de la Régence de Tunis, dressée au Dépôt de la Guerre, d'après les Observations . . . de M. Falbe, capitaine de vaisseau danois, de M. Pricot Ste Marie. Echelle, 1·400,000, 2 sheets, Paris. 1857-82

Carte de la Tunisie ancienne, dressée d'après les recherches de M. E. de Sainte Marie, par Ph. Caillat. Missions Catholiques, Lyon. 1876

Carte de la Régence de Tunis, par Pellissier, membre de la Commission scientifique de l'Algérie, au 800,000^e.

Carte de la Tunisie, par M. Périer, à l'échelle de 1·200,000.

Carte de la Régence de Tunis, dressée . . . par H. Kiepert. Echelle de 1·800,000, Berlin. 1881

Il vero disegno della città di Tunisi e Biserta, [Venice, 1571 (?)] 1571

The Coast of Tunis from Africa City to the Fratelli Rocks. By Captain W. H. Smyth, assisted by Messrs. Elson and Slater (Admiralty Chart), London. 1827

Côte de Tunis, Paris. 1864

Tunis: Soussa to Mehediah, with the Kuriat Islands. Surveyed . . . under the direction of Commander G. R. Wilkinson, 1864 (Admiralty Chart), London. 1866

Tunis: Fratelli Rocks to Mehediah; Cape Carthage to Mehediah. By Commander Wilkinson and the Officers of H.M.S. *Firefly*, London. 1867

Tunis: Mehediah to Ras Makhabez; Mehediah to Tafalmah. By Commander Wilkinson and the Officers of H.M.S. *Firefly* (Admiralty Chart), London. 1867

View of Cape Carthage, Tunis Bay, and the Goletta. By E. Stanley (with Observations). 1786

Plan des environs de Tunis et du mouillage de la Goulette. Levé et dressé en 1849, par M. C. B-Rivière, Paris. 1850

Piano del Golfo di Tunisi, Genoa (?). 1855 (?)

Carte générale de la mer Méditerranée, 1re Feuille. Baie de Tunis. 1860

Bay of Tunis surveyed .... under the direction of Commander G. R. Wilkinson (Admiralty Chart), London. 1865

Baie de Tunis. Partie comprise entre le Cap Carthage et la Côte Sud, levée en 1876, Paris. 1878

Environs de Tunis et de Carthage. Levés exécutés par MM. les Capitaines Derrien, Koszutski ... en 1878. Dépôt de la Guerre. Echelle de 1·40,000, Paris. 1883

N.W. of the City and Lake of Tunis. By C. Tulin, 1777; engraved by Green and Jukes. W. A. Barron. 1783

Tunis Harbour. By Captain W. H. Smyth, 1882 (Admiralty Chart), London. 1838

Land- und Seekarte des Mittelländischen Meeres ... Hafen von Tunis. Nach W. H. Smith (sic), 1871

Karte des Kriegsschauplatzes in Tunesien, nach den Franz. Generalstabskarten bearbeitet. Maasstab 1·800,000. J. Wurster and Co., Zurich, Winterthur (printed). 1881.

Carte des Itinéraires de la Régence de Tunis, au 1·400,000°, gravure sur pierre. 1882, 2 feuilles. 1882

Carte de la Tunisie, photozincographié et imprimé au Dépôt de la Guerre. Echelle 1·200000. Tirage Janvier, 1885. Édition provisoire. 18 feuilles. Paris.

Carte des Itinéraires de la Tunisie, au 800,000°, Paris, Challamel aîné, 1887, in 3 colours. 1887

Carte de la Tunisie centrale, par Dr. Rouire.

Carte de la Région des Chotts, par M. Roudaire.

Carte de la Mer intérieure africaine, par M. Roudaire.

L'ultimo disegno dove si dimostra il vero sito di Tunisi et la Goletta, con il novo forte hora dal esercito del Turco assediate dove si vede il modo che tengono nell' assedio quest' anno 1574, alli 14 d'Agosto, [Venice (?)]. 1574

La vera descrittione del sito della Città de Tunisi et della Goletta, sua fortezza, con il novo forte fatto dalli Turchi nell' assedie di essa mese d'Agosto, 1754, [Rome (?), 1600 (?)]. 1754

Statt und Schloss von Tunis, G. Bodenehr excudit. Aug[ustæ] Vind[elicorum, 1740 (?)]. 1740

Thunes en Affricque, [Venice, (?) 1536 (?)]. 1536

Città di Tunisi. ... Ex æneis fortis B. Zaltezij, Venetiis. 1566

Vue gravée de la ville de Tunis, prise de la mer, 0·55 sur 0·40 c., vers 1572

Vue gravée de la ville de Tunis, prise de l'intérieur, 0·55 sur 0·40 c., vers 1572

Thunis inn Africa. Warhaffte unnd aigentliche Contrafactur der gewaltigen unnd Königlichenn Statt Thunÿss. [By] B. Jenichen, [Nuremberg]. 1573

The City of Tunis. [By J. Seller (?), London, 1680 (?)]. 1680

P. *Schenkii Hecatompolis. Tunis, &c.*
1702
Karte der Umgegend von Tunis. Lithogr. Fol., Leipzig, 1832, W. Vogel. 1832
Pianta del nuovo forte di Tunesi. [By G. F. Camotti, Venice. 1571 (?)]
A Plan of the Citadel of Tunis. 1574
Vue gravée de la ville d'Africa (olim Aphrodisium), prise de l'intérieur, 0'55 sur 0'40 c., vers 1572
Plan restauré de Carthage, par Dedreux, architecte, Paris. 1839
See also p. 4, *ante.*

VIEWS.

Prise du Port, par Charles-Quint, en 1535, G. Bruin. 1535
Reprise de Tunis aux Espagnols, par Occhiali, 1574. Fol., engraved by Georges Bruin. 1574
Tunis, par Merian.

PICTURES.

The Foundation of Carthage. By Turner.
The Fall of Carthage. By Turner.
The Sack of Carthage. By Giulio Romano, engraved by Penez.

INDEX.

ACCOMMODATION, 2, 89, 96
Agbia, 168, 170
Ahmed Bey, 37
Ain-Draham, 182, 184, 186
Ain-el-Caïd, 176
Ain-Hedjah, 168, 169, 170
Amphitheatre of El-Djem. See El-Djem.
Amusements, 3, 65, 110
Animals, cruelty to, 6, 131
Aphrodisium, 57, 59
Aqueducts, 37
Arabs, their character, 5
 „ courteous and hospitable, 6, 68, 80, 158
 „ cruel, 6, 131
 „ results of their occupation of Tunisia, 7
 „ their jealousy, 63, 196
 „ dress of the women, 64
 „ music, 65, 110
 „ treatment of women, 77
 „ mode of living, 100
 „ equipment of animals, 6, 151
 „ a tent described, 154
 „ a house visited, 198
Archæology, Tunisia a good field for, 1
Artesian well, 97
Ass stolen, 41
Assuras, 163
Attar of roses, 23

Bagla, river, 110
Bagradas, river, 11
Bagradas river and Regulus, 45
Bahira, lake, 14, 34
Barbers' shops, 24
Bardo, palace, 29
Bazaars. See Souks.
Bedouin women, 199

Bedouins, 42, 77, 200
Beggars, absence of, ii.
Béja, 11 (note)
Beni-Mazeu, 188
'**Bernous** of the Prophet,' 14
Bernous, garments, 23
Birds, 137, 149 (note), 158
Bir-el-Arbain, 54
Bir-el-Bouïta, 54, 55
Bir-el-Bey, 53
Bled-es-Sers, plain, 164, 165
Bône, a pleasant town, 9
 „ described, 10
Bordj-Messaoudi, 166, 169
Borghaz, lake, 14
Bou-Chater, ruins of, described, 48
Bou-Kohil, mountain, 166
Bouquets, 69
Bridges, 2, 7
British influence, decline of, 103
British Museum, inscription removed to, 172, 174
Bruce, J., on Temple at Dougga, 172 (note)
 „ quoted on Tabarca, 183 (note)
Bulla Regia, 188

Cæsar, Julius, quoted on Utica, 48
 „ mentioned, 48 (note)
Cairwan. See Kairouan.
Calle, La, 181
Cambon, V., on population of Kairouan, 128 (note)
Carbonaro, MM., 41, 205
Caroline, Queen, her visit to Tunis, 31
Carthage, site of, 14, 33
 „ modes of conveyance, 33
 „ chapel of St. Louis, 33
 „ the cisterns, 34
 „ literature, 34, 35

U

INDEX.

Catada, river, 38
Cato, 48 (note)
Cats, 169
Chachia caps, 23, 40
Chambi, mountains, 146
Charles V., 90, 183
Chemtou, 193, 194
Chenneni, 98
Chotts, 97
Cisterns, 114
Coffee-houses, 24, 65, 80
Col de Babouch, 186
Collin, M., 39 (note)
Colonia Scillitana, 146
    ,, Simittu, 194
    ,, Sufetanæ, 157
Compagnie Transatlantique, ii., 2
Coral fishing, 181 (note)
Cork oak, gigantic, 187
Couscousou, national dish described, 90, 159, 201 (note)
Cret, Captain, 113
Crosha, river, 57
Cuscusu. See Couscousu.

Dancing, 111
Dar-el-Bey, town, 57, 59
    ,, palace, 30
Date-gathering, 99
Decauville road, 107, 108
Defla, river, 54
Desfontaine on Tabarca, 183 (note)
Diligence, journey in a, 11
Djard, 98
Djedeida, 11 (note)
Djerba coats, 23
Djiljie, mountain, 158
Djilma. See Oued-Gilma.
Djiriba, marsh, 57, 59
Doctoring the natives, 150
Dogs, 81, 100, 165
    ,, flesh of, eaten, 201 (note)
Domestic life, 196
Donkey. See Ass.
Dougga, situation, 171
    ,, ruins, 172
    ,, the sheik, 174
Dress of women, 64

Duruy, V., quoted on amphitheatre at El-Djem, 85 (note)

El-Bahira, lake, 14, 34, 202
El-Bekri, quoted on the marble of Carthage, 35 (note)
    ,, ,, the aqueduct of Carthage, 38
    ,, ,, Kairouan, 119, 120, 121
El-Darb, river, 146
El-Djem, first view of the amphitheatre, 78
    ,, surrounding plain described, 78, 85, 86
    ,, the fondouk, 79
    ,, the café, 80
    ,, the amphitheatre, its present filthy condition, 82
    ,, ,, its size, 82, 83
    ,, ,, by whom built, 83
    ,, ,, described, 83
    ,, ,, never finished, 84
    ,, inscription found at, 91
El-Edrisi, quoted on Sufetula, 140 (note)
    ,, ,, coral fishing, 181 (note)
El-Hout, lake, 182
El-Kebir, river, 184
El-Kef, 189, 190
El-Kerib, plain, 167
El-Mahdi, 90
El-Nefzaoui, Sheik, 205
Embroidery of Tunis esteemed, 23
    ,, done by men, 23
Enfida estate, 52
Englishmen, rare, 16, 104
Esparto grass, 93, 97, 145
Es-Sahel, 87

Falhar, river, 176
Fatima, hand of, 24, 26
Female dress, 64, 197
Fernana, 187
Fez caps, 23, 40
Flavius Secundus, mausoleum erected by, 147
Fleas, 81

INDEX.

Flies, 63
Fondouks, 3, 55, 79, 81, 110, 164, 168
Forests, destruction of, 7
Fortresses, 170
François, our servant, 104

Gabès, the town, 96
  „ the river, 97
  „ the inland sea, 97
  „ an artesian well, 97
  „ the gardens, 99
  „ the scenery, 101
Galea, Mr., 93, 96, 102, 103
Game, 149 (note)
Gatte, Mr., 104
Gayangos, P. de, iv.
Gerges, 140 (note)
Ghardimaou, 11, 13
Gilma. See Oued-Gilma.
Gnats, 60 (note)
Gorat-el-Kerib, plain, 167
Gordian, the elder, 83
  „ the younger, 84
Gouletta, 14, 202
Gourbi, one described, 154
Government, good, ii.
Greeting, mode of, 156, 159
Gregory, 140 (note)
Groumbelia, 53
Guerra-el-Hout, 182
Guide-books, 4
Guérin, V., quoted on Utica, 47 (note)
  „   „ Bir-el-Bouïta, 54 „
  „   „ Sebkha-Djiriba, 60 „
  „   „ population of Kairouan, 128 (note)
  „   „ El-Djem, 85 (note)
  „   „ Sufes, 157
  „   „ Teboursouk, 175 (note)
  „   „ Sicca Veneria, 190 „

Hadjeb-el-Aïoun, 131, 133, 149, 152
Hadrian, Emperor, 37
Hadrumetum, 61
Halfa. See Esparto.
Halk-el-Menzel, lake, 58
Hammam-el-Lif, 51, 52
Hand of Fatima, 24, 26

Harbours, 2
Harem life, 196, 198
Harness, 6, 23
Hassan, mosque rebuilt by, 119, 121
Hatob, river, 152, 153
Herglah, 58
Hélouis, Captain, 61, 107
Herrech, mountain, 194
Hesse-Wartegg, quoted on Bedouins, 43 (note)
  „   „ quoted on population of Kairouan, 128 (note)
  „   „ quoted on fattening of women, 201 (note)
'Home, sweet home,' 205
Horrea Cœlia, 58
Horse-livers, eaten, 201 (note)
Horses, mode of picketing, 155
Hotels, 2, 96, 110
  „ See also Fondouks.
Houses, an Arab one described, 94

Information, difficult to obtain, 3, 153
Inland sea, 97
Inscription, an, 167 (note)
  „ removed to British Museum, 172, 174

Jasmine, oil of, 23
Jews, not jealous, 65 (note), 201
  „ hospitable, 201
  „ at Kairouan, 110, 128
Jewesses, dress of, 64
  „ immorality, 65 (note)
  „ artificial obesity, 200
  „ their dress, 200
  „ their beauty, 201
  „ of Gabès, 101
Jouaouda, mountain, 167

Kabika, mountain, 176
Kairouan, the hotel, 110
  „ music and dancing, 110
  „ various spellings of name, 112 (note)
  „ its holiness, 112, 127
  „ its influence lost, 113

Kairouan, the kasba, 113
" the reservoirs, 114
" its foundation, 115, 117
" walls and gates, 116
" houses, 117
" mosques, 117, 118
" streets, 118
" bazaars, 118
" industries, 23, 118
" surrounding country, 128
" devoid of wells, 128
" population, 128
" inhabitants corrupt, 129
" their courtesy, 129
Kairwân. See Kairouan.
Kasr-el-Menara, 56
Kasserine, the river, 146
" the ruins, 146
Kazezin, spring, 110
Kelbia, lake, 108
Kenatir, river, 56, 58
Kerkenah, islands, 92, 93
Kerma, river, 184
Kerouan. See Kairouan.
Kerwan. See Kairouan.
Keys of their Spanish homes kept by the Moors of Tunis, 24
Khallad, river, 176
Kheir-ed-din, 52
Khoumair, country described, 180
" people " 184
Ksiba, 71, 76
Ksour, 158, 161, 162
Ksour-es-Sef, 86, 88
Kusskussu. See Couscousou.

La Calle, 181
La Goulette, 14, 202
Languages, ancient, 172 (note)
Lapine, M., 149, 150
Largeau, M., quoted on destruction of forests, 7 (note)
Law-courts, 203
Lemarchand, M., 203
Literature, iii.
" neglect of, 204
Logerot, General, 99
Louis, Saint, chapel of, 33

Lubomirski, Prince J., on domestic life, 198 (note)
Lumbroso, A., 90, 91

Macgill, Thos., quoted on character of the Arabs, 5 (note)
" " quoted on fattening of women, 200 (note)
Magaran, 39
Mahedia, difficulty of obtaining food, 89
" a couscousou, 90
" its position, 90
" its history, 90
" the roadstead, 91
Mahia, mountain, 176
Maltzan, Freiher von, at Kairouan, 113 (note)
Manouba, 11 (note), 15
Marble, 172 (note), 193
Marcius, brothers, 172
Marsa, palace, 30
Marseillaise, 68
Mascula, 52
Medjerda, river, described, 11, 12, 13, 45, 177, 193
Medjez-el-Bab, 11 (note)
Melian river, 51
Mellegue, river, 189, 193
Menzel, 77, 98
Merilah, mountain, 152
Merkey, mountain, 15
Mirage, 60 (note)
Mohammedia, palace, 29, 37
Monastir, 106
Montagu, Lady Mary Wortley, her visit to the harem, 199 (note)
Moors, their character described, 5 (note)
" keep the keys of their Spanish homes, 24
" women, 197
Moureddine, 108
Msaken, 70
Music, 65, 110
Mustafa-ben-Azooz, 141
Musti, 167

Nebour, 189

INDEX.

Noah's ark, 204
Nostrils of asses, slit, 6
Novaïri, on Kairouan, 117
Novak, N., 91, 105
Nouba, mountains, 146

Oasis of Gabès, 99
Obeid-Allah, 90
Okbah founds Kairouan, 115, 117, 118
Olive-crushing, 77
Ornaments, female, 199
Oudena, ruins of, described, 43
Oued-Gilma, 134, 135, 149
Oued-Meliz, 11 (note), 193, 195
Outfit, 179, 181

Palaces, ruined, 29
 „ abandoned, 37
Pariente, S. R., 202, 205
Payne, John Howard, 205
Pellissier, E., quoted on population of Kairouan, 128 (note)
 „ „ Kasserine, 147 (note)
Perfumers of Tunis, 23
Perronell, Capt., 133, 149
Phœnician tombs, 105
Playfair, Sir R. L., iv., 44
 „ quoted on archæology in Tunisia, 1 (note)
 „ „ aqueduct of Carthage, 39 (note)
 „ „ esparto grass, 93 (note)
 „ „ artesian wells, 98
 „ „ population of Kairouan, 128 (note)
 „ „ river Sbeitla, 139 (note)
 „ „ couscousou, 160 (note)
 „ „ temple at Dougga, 172 (note)
 „ „ Tabarca, 183 (note)
 „ „ Fernana, 187 (note)
Ploughing, 87
Poiret, Abbé, quoted on wheat, 161 (note)
Polygamy, 196, 200
Population, sparse, 161
Presents, 161

Prison, one described, 42
Prostitution, 201

Qaïrouân. See Kairouan
Qirwan. See Kairouan

Radès, 14
Railways, 2
Ras-el-Wad, 99
Ras-er-Rajel, 185
Rats, 81
Reade, Sir Thos., 172, 173
Reclus, E., quoted on character of the Tunisians, 5 (note)
 „ „ Msaken, 70 (note)
 „ „ the people of Sfax, 95 (note)
 „ „ inhabitants of Kairouan, 129 (note)
Regulus and the Serpent, 45
Renan, M., on Phœnician tombs, 106
Reservoirs, 114
Retrospect, 178, 206
Reukaha, mountain, 158
Rivers, neglect of, 7, 57, 137, 177, 178, 193
Roads, 2, 7
Romans, their power, 85 (note), 86
Roses, attar of, 23
Roudaire, Commandant, 97

Sahab, companion of the Prophet, 124
 „ his tomb, 127
Sallecta, 85
Salutation, mode of, 156, 159
Sandwith, T. B., 205
Sardine-salting, 181 (note)
Sbeitla, first glimpse of the ruins, 137
 „ no accommodation, 137
 „ the river, 139, 143
 „ ruins described, 141
 „ our "Grand Hotel," 148
 „ our mode of living, 148
Sbiba, 151, 152, 153, 158
 „ the caïd, 156
 „ the river, 157
 „ the ruins, 157

Scenery, 3
Scillitana Colonia, 146
Scillium, 146
Scipio, 47 (note), 48
Sea, inland. See Inland Sea
Sebbala, 45
Sedjoumi, marsh, 14
Selloum, mountain, 146
Septimius Severus, 37
Serpent-worship, 27
Servant engaged, 104
Sewing done by men, 23
Sfåkès. See Sfax
Sfåksîka. See Sfax
Sfax, soap made at, 23
  „ the roadstead, 92
  „ built upon the sand, 92
  „ its commerce, 93
  „ the sponge market, 93
  „ the gates, 93
  „ characteristic doorways, 94
  „ character of the inhabitants, 95
Sgiff, river, 158
Shaksperian reading, 205
Shaw, Rev. Dr. Thos., quoted on the amphitheatre at El-Djem, 83
Shops. See Souks
Sicca Veneria, 190 (note), 191, 194
Sidi-Abdallah-ech-Cheid, mountain, 167
Sidi-Abd-er-Reubbou, 167
Sidi-Ahmed-Zei, koubba, 158
Sidi-bou-Rouis, 166
Sidi-bou-Said, 14
Sidi-el-Hani, lake, 77, 108
Sidi-Hani, river, 165
Sidi-Khalifa, town, 57, 59
Sidi-Mehrani, koubba, 158
Sidi-Monella, koubba, 158
Simittu Colonia, 194
Slippers, 23
Soap, 23
Sobeitala. See Sufetula
Soliman, 53
Souk-Arras, 11
Souk-el-Arbäa, 11 (note), 189, 193
Souk-el-Tleta, 164, 169
Souks, 20, 63, 94, 118

Soussa, 50, 61, 71, 76, 106, 107
Sponges, 93
Stays, a punishment, 199
Steamers, 2
Story-telling, 69
Street-naming, 104
Sufes, 157
Sufetanæ Colonia, 157
Sufetula, its situation, &c., 139
  „ its destruction, 140 (note)
Sunset, magnificent, 164
Superstitions, 26, 27
Syllectum, 85, 86

Tabarca, island, 182
Tacape, 96
Talismans, 26, 27
Taphrura, 92
Tarboosh, caps, 23, 40
Tarja, 11 (note)
Tebourba, 11 (note)
Tebournok, river, 53
Teboursouk, 175, 176
Temperature, 178
Thabarca, 183
Thacia, 166
Theatres, 3
Thibursicum, 175
Threshing, 158
Thugga, 171
Thysdrus, 75, 85, 86
Tissot, Charles, 97
Tombs, Phœnician, 105
Tourki, 53
Towns, sameness of, 4
  „ one described, 5
Tramway, 107, 108
Tressa, river, 166
Trisha, mountain, 165
Trozza, mountain, 132
Tunis, rapidity of journey to, 9
  „ stations between Tunis and Bône, 11 (note)
  „ the 'Burnous of the Prophet,' 14
  „ description of, 15, 26
  „ its population, 16, 17
  „ the streets, 17

INDEX.

Tunis, the kasba, 17
" the mosques, 18
" Moorish work, 18
" the souks, 20
" commercial rather than manufacturing, 23
" its manufactures, 23
" perfumery shops, 23
" barbers' shops, 24
" coffee-houses, 24
" gateways, 25
" the hand of Fatima, 26
" windowless houses, 28
" a house described, 28
" ruined palaces, 29
" the Dar-el-Bey, 30
" lake El-Bahira, 34
" fine view of, 36
" women of, 197
" a house visited, 198
" women artificially fattened, 200
" French court of law, 203
" court of the cadi, 203
Tunisia, a good field for the study of archæology, &c., 1
" difficulties of travelling in, 1
" reliable information impossible, 3
" sameness of the towns, 4
" description of one, 5
" results of Arab occupation, 7
" women classified, 197
" neglect of literature, 204
Tunisians, their character described, 5 (note)

Tunisians, life in the south, 21
" the perfumers, 23

Uthina, 43
Utica, 47

Vandalism, modern, 38, 173
Voisins, Mme. de, on mirage, 60 (note)
" " quoted on dress of women, 64 (note)
" " " Msaken, 70 (note)

Washing, 108
Wedding ceremony, 41
Wheat, 161 (note)
Whitewash, 15
Women, in the harem, 196
" different classes, 197, 199
" their dress, 64, 197
" stays, a punishment, 199
" artificially fattened, 200
Wortley Montague, Lady Mary, her visit to the harem, 199 (note)

Zaghouan, mountain, 15, 76, 106, 176
" to Tunis, 36
" town of, 39
" skull caps dyed there, 23, 40
" the spring and temple, 41
Zanfour, 162, 163, 169
Zaouias. See Mosques
Zaouiet, 76
Zeroud, river, 109
Zouida, 88
Zramedine, 77

LONDON:
Printed by STRANGEWAYS & SONS, Tower Street, Cambridge Circus.

www.ingramcontent.com/pod-product-compliance
Lightning Source LLC
Chambersburg PA
CBHW020221240426
43672CB00006B/374